STUDY GUIDE

A PEOPLE AND A NATION

VOLUME II: SINCE 1865

STUDY GUIDE

A PEOPLE AND A NATION
VOLUME II: SINCE 1865

Sixth Edition

George C. Warren
Central Piedmont Community College

Mary Beth Norton
Cornell University

David M. Katzman
University of Kansas

David W. Blight
Amherst College

Howard P. Chudacoff
Brown University

Thomas G. Paterson
University of Connecticut

William M. Tuttle, Jr.
University of Kansas

Paul D. Escott
Wake Forest University

HOUGHTON MIFFLIN COMPANY   BOSTON   NEW YORK

Sponsoring Editor: Colleen Shanley Kyle
Senior Manufacturing Coordinator: Sally Culler
Senior Marketing Manager: Sandra McGuire
Editorial Associate: Michael Kerns

Printed in the U.S.A.

ISBN: 0-618-00554-4
123456789-B+B-04 03 02 01 00

CONTENTS

TO THE STUDENT

This study guide will help you master the themes and information in *A People and a Nation*. It won't give you a shortcut—there are no shortcuts—but it will give you direction and strategy, and if you use it conscientiously, you will do well in your history course.

To get the most benefit from your study guide, you should read the introduction entitled "Taking the Mystery Out of Becoming 'Good' at History" before you do anything else. The introduction explains some of the ways of thinking about people and events that are particularly useful to history students, and it reviews the basics of good study habits applicable to a reading and writing course like history. Of course, it also tells you about how the book is arranged and what the standard chapter sections are for. You should read it carefully even before the course gets under way and you begin reading the first chapter of the textbook.

Once you get into an individual chapter in the study guide, you should do all the exercises and do them in order. It may be tempting to skip to the multiple-choice questions before you do the more time-consuming exercises or to omit the vocabulary exercise altogether. Don't yield to temptations. The less time-consuming exercises like the multiple-choice questions test the effectiveness of the work you have done on the more time-consuming exercises, such as the "Identification and Significance" and "Interpreting Information" sections.

Remember as you use this book that it is working with the material that will make you understand and remember ideas and evidence. To do well requires a lot of hard work, but the right kind of hard work will make you do well. This study guide directs you toward the right kind of hard work.

TO THE INSTRUCTOR

Looking over other study guides with all their fill-in-the-blanks, true-falses, and multiple-choices may have made you feel as though you were rifling through the files of some sorority or fraternity house on campus. But that's not how you are going to feel if you look closely at this one.

This study guide puts the objective question in its place. It does offer plenty of multiple-choice practice questions, but it places them near the ends of chapters where students can use them as culminating quizzes to find out how much they have learned. The multiple-choice section follows a series of exercises that have led students through the kind of active, mind-stretching studying you know they have to do to master the material. The answers to the multiple-choice questions in this book (at the back) are instructive, too—they explain why the right answers are right and the wrong answers are wrong. This same kind of approach to the answers section is seen in the instructive answer to the "Interpreting Information" exercises for Chapters 1 (Volume I) and 18 (Volume II). Students are given partial answers that help them see whether they are on the right track without simply providing a whole essay written out for them to memorize.

And there's more.

Instead of the skeletal outline of each chapter that you see elsewhere, in this study guide you will see "Thematic Guides"—overviews in essay form presenting the major themes of the chapter in the textbook. The key word is *work*. Look at some of the "Identification and Significance," "Organizing Information," and "Interpreting Information" exercises, for example. These call upon the student to collect and synthesize information, to organize it, and to write out answers to potential essay questions using the information they have collected.

The "Interpreting Information" exercises tackle the problem of getting students, especially freshmen, to understand what's expected of them on essay tests, what your injunction to "be concrete and specific" means. In the first several chapters, these exercises lead students through the process of creating working drafts of answers to very broad essay questions and give them advice on organizing the material for specific, commonly seen kinds of essay questions: comparison or contrast, definition, identification and significance, classification, and so forth. In later chapters, the "Interpreting Information" exercises still require students to write working drafts of essay-question responses covering a lot of ground and still offer help in organizing information. However, in these later exercises, students have to shoulder more of the responsibility for determining the kind of information they need and the best way to collect it.

This study guide should help both you and your students. The exercises should awaken a lot of your students to the depth of information mastery that you expect. For many students those expectations come as a shock, and perhaps the study guide will help them to see that you are not alone in holding out such lofty expectations. In addition, if you are involved in a writing-across-the-curriculum movement, in developing a writing-intensive course on your campus, or in the renewed interest across the nation in helping students develop their critical thinking skills, you may get some ideas or even assignments from these pages.

INTRODUCTION—TAKING THE MYSTERY OUT OF BECOMING "GOOD" AT HISTORY

In a short story set hundreds of years after nuclear war has wiped out all mankind, archeologists from another galaxy excitedly explain highly polished ceramic and metallic relics they have discovered in what they think must have been a religious shrine. As the archeologists describe vessels they think must have once held holy water and surprisingly advanced mechanical devices they have decided must have been for collecting coin offerings to the gods, it dawns on the story's readers that what these archeologists have found is actually a late twentieth-century pay toilet.

For history students, the moral of this story is that it is not just the collecting of facts that is important. What you do with the facts counts, too. History uses clues or facts to explain, or interpret, a society's events, personalities, and places; to explain why a society is as it is, why its events happened as they happened, and why its people decided as they decided and acted as they acted. But, to come up with valid or at least very likely interpretations, history students have to make sure not only to collect enough useful information but also to avoid letting their own or others' blind spots keep them from seeing what's important.

Factors "Good" History Students Consider

Among the most common causes of the kinds of blind spots that can get people off track are people's frames of reference and socialization as well as inappropriate or insufficient data.

Frames of Reference

A real understanding of history will enable us to appreciate the past and apply what we learn to the problems we face today. But it will come only to those of us who can take people's *frames of reference* and *socialization* into account when judging their attitudes and behavior. Frames of reference and socialization are the emotional software that virtually forces people to think, feel, act, and react in particular, sometimes irrational, ways until they are somehow reprogrammed. Frames of reference and socialization are the input; the historical events are the output.

You can think of frames of reference as constantly growing encyclopedias that people carry around in their heads, encyclopedias in which all their personal impressions and experiences have been and are being recorded. People refer constantly to these encyclopedias to make sense of what happens around them.

If you have ever smelled a particular aroma and almost immediately experienced a flood of memories, you have felt the power of your own frame of reference. Cooking aromas or the smells of the street can release a nostalgic flood that represents your own unique way of relating to or making meaning out of—interpreting—the particular smell. Your nostalgia derives from your frame of reference, your unique experiences associated with the smell. Thus, the way you perceive yourself and your surroundings comes from your frame of reference. Occupation, socio-economic status, sex, race, environment, political beliefs, religious beliefs, age, nationality—these all go into people's frames of reference, which determine how they interpret what goes on in their world. The people we study in history are subjected to the force of frames of reference and socialization just as we are, and their behavior must be interpreted in light of the influence of those powerful forces. Their frames of reference must be taken into account.

Socialization

A major part of people's frames of reference comes to them through *socialization,* the sum total of all the teaching done by the members of a society, in whatever way, to make sure its culture survives. In any culture youngsters are taught to believe that some ideas are right and others wrong, some proper and others improper. That is socialization.

You can see the kinds of consequences that can result when people socialized quite differently come into contact in the confrontations between seventeenth-century English colonists and Native Americans (discussed in Chapter 2 of *A People and a Nation)* and between twentieth-century Iranians and Americans (discussed in Chapter 31). In the earlier case, the English had been taught to believe that people have a right to own land individually, but the North American natives had learned to believe that land was meant to be held communally. The differences in their socialization gave these two groups of people different frames of reference and often brought them into conflict. Likewise, the socialization of Iranians and Americans made them value separation of church and state and modern technology quite differently. The two peoples' failure to understand and appreciate each other's value systems contributed to and fed the tension that boiled over during Jimmy Carter's presidency in what is now known as the Iran Hostage Crisis.

Just as the attitudes and behaviors of the individuals who people the pages of history books like *A People and A Nation* result from input in the form of frames of reference and socialization, history books themselves result from input. What you see in your history textbook is the output produced by analysis of millions of bits of raw data or *primary sources* collected over many years by thousands of people. Often writers of a history textbook study the data and analyses of earlier historians and accept their interpretations, but when they think the earlier interpretations are erroneous or when primary sources become available to them that were not available to earlier historians, they provide their own original interpretations or modifications of earlier interpretations. Always, though, primary sources are the raw material of history.

The Kind and Nature of Sources

Primary sources may be contradictory or incomplete or vague. Many primary sources are mere traces of the past, mere clues or hints that historians have to analyze to make sense of them. People in the past left the same kinds of clues that you leave as you go through your daily activities. If you carried around some carbon paper between the pages of a notepad for a few days, traces of your handling the paper in the notepad would remain, even on the sheets of paper you did not use. People from the past have left similar traces, sometimes consciously and sometimes unconsciously, whether in the form of DNA—which, as Chapter 8 in your textbook points out, has been used to confirm suspicions about Thomas Jefferson's relationship with his female slave Sally Hemings—or written documents or farm implements or musical compositions. To the historian, these are like eyewitness accounts, but just as the eyewitnesses of this morning's accident do, historic eyewitnesses give conflicting accounts of what took place. Contradictory and conflicting facts make interpreting events difficult, and once historians start straightening out and interpreting the jumble of facts they have before them, they inevitably give one fact more weight than another. That is when their own socialization and frames of reference begin influencing the output. Clearly, then, if we are to understand historical events and derive meaning from them, we must recognize the importance of the kind and amount of information with which we are working, and we must attempt to be as objective as possible. We must try to prevent the biases and prejudices that emanate from our own frames of reference and socialization from blinding us to the limitations imposed upon people of earlier times and other places by their own frames of reference and socialization.

Making Interpretations Acceptable to Others

As long as you are a student rather than a professional historian, it is on tests that you will be presenting most of your own interpretations of historical information. For your interpretations to be accepted as valid, you will have to show that they are based on solid information that you have studied and understood. Your indications of how you came up with or derived your interpretations must have two qualities of effective composition: concreteness and specificity.

The Need for Concreteness

The real building blocks of the kind of interpretation that lies at the heart of history as an academic discipline are *facts.* Historians and history students must have something to interpret, and that something is a body of historical facts. So, as a history student who is expected to develop an ability to analyze and interpret data, your starting point is to master the facts themselves, facts that can be used to make an interpretation concrete and specific. Facts are the foundation of effective answers to an essay question; they are what makes answers concrete and specific.

A *fact* is a bit of information perceptible by one or more of the five senses. Facts are seen, heard, felt, tasted, or smelled. The kinds of facts history students use the most are actions and sounds, especially human speech and sights, including measurable characteristics—such as dimensions, weights, distances, costs, counts—and the results of experimentation, including the raw data from polling.

A fact is verifiable, confirmable either by qualified witnesses or, in the case of scientific experimentation or polling, by repetition ending in the same results. The information that the *Mayflower* landed at Plymouth could have been verified by any Native American who was around to meet the Pilgrims at the shore or any Pilgrim who scrambled off the ship. The truth or falsehood of the information could have been established by the visual perception of those present. A fact is not really arguable; it either is or it is not.

Once perceivable, a bit of information is a fact; once perceived, it is a known fact that can be reported as fact over and over again, handed down, for example, from an eyewitness to a historian and then handed on to other historians. And that brings up the problem of reliability.

To decide whether a bit of information that you have gotten second- or third-hand is a fact, you have to consider its source. If the witnesses are incapable of the kind of perceiving called for or if they are dishonest, the information they call fact may not be fact, and you will need other witnesses or other forms of corroboration. Witnesses or reporters can color facts, too, through their interpretations and wording. Like lying, coloring does not really change facts, but it can certainly blur them. For example, if you and your classmates are present when your history teacher comes into the classroom and crosses from the door to the lectern, everyone in the room can perceive the movement, but some will call it *striding*, some *ambling*, some *sidling*, and some *walking*. The only thing you all will agree on is that movement has occurred. The movement is measurable. Your phrasing will affect how the fact is interpreted, but it does not affect the fact itself. The fact is the movement, not the style of movement.

The Need for Specificity

Facts are important to you as a student of history for at least two reasons. First, they are the material that you analyze to arrive at an interpretation. Second, they are essential ingredients in the presentation of the interpretation to others. The validity of an interpretation is going to be convincing only to the degree that it is perceived as having been derived logically from facts. That means that you, the interpreter, must cite the facts on which the interpretation is based (unless you are a widely known and established authority in the field). If you cite enough facts to make your interpretation clear and convincing, you will have made your interpretation "concrete." However, concreteness is not enough. To be convincing, you must also be specific. The difference between "Columbus set sail in the fifteenth century" and "Columbus set sail in 1492" is the degree of specificity. The difference between "The Tainos told Columbus about nearby islanders with strange eating habits" and "The Tainos told Columbus about the Caribs, who ate their captives" also is the degree of specificity. Usually, the more specific the evidence, the more convincing it is.

The Need to Show the Foundation for Interpretations

When professors give fewer points for responses to essay questions than their students think they should, many students complain, "He just doesn't like my opinions." In a way, those students are right—but they are also wrong.

Often what professors object to is not so much the "opinions" students offer but the failure to show any solid foundation for the "opinions." Professors expect their students to show that their conclusions—what they refer to loosely as "opinions"—are well founded by citing the facts and authoritative inferences on which they are based. The conclusions are supposed to be interpretations of evidence. The professor wants to know what evidence there is.

The kind of evidence students should cite to convince the professors that their interpretations are well founded is a mixture of specific, relevant facts and authoritative inferences. Inferences are arguable assertions or interpretative conclusions based on facts and other inferences. When you look at a series of photographs of someone in a magazine and conclude that in the first picture the individual is angry, in the second sad, and in the third embarrassed, you are making inferences. Using clues or facts in the pictures—facts such as the contortions of facial muscles, for example—you infer what the individual's emotional state is. *Inferences*, then, are ideas *created* from facts, and to be logical, an inference must account for all the available facts on the topic. As far as history students are concerned, "all the available facts" are all the facts and relevant inferences presented to the student by his professor and the authors of his textbook. (The "How Do Historians Know" feature appearing in each chapter of *A People and a Nation* gives some idea of the types of facts the authors and your professors use to come up with the inferences they present you with.)

A historian's total or final interpretation of an event may be based on several narrower inferences. Facts are the building blocks of narrow inferences, and narrow inferences are the building blocks of a total interpretation, which is simply a broad inference.

An inference is not the same thing as an opinion. An inference can be thought of as a kind of educated guess—educated because it is clearly based on and derived from facts. An *opinion*, which is just as likely to be an uneducated guess as it is to be an educated guess, is a strong belief or conviction that may or may not be based on the facts. The person who offers a "mere" opinion simply does not cite the evidence that makes the basis of the opinion clear. On the other hand, the person who presents an inference is not expressing a "mere opinion."

Speculation is still another matter. Historians do occasionally speculate. A speculation is a cross between an opinion and an inference. It is a guess about the future or about a matter we can explain only with guesses either because we have inherited a shortage of facts or because the issue is such that facts alone cannot provide a clear-cut answer. Suggestions in films and television dramas about the private relationship between President Richard Nixon and his wife Pat and about the nature of Thomas Jefferson's feelings for Sally Hemings are pure speculations. Exactly why Alexander Hamilton did not fire his pistol or why he missed his target in the famous Hamilton-Burr duel discussed in Chapter 9 of your textbook remains speculative. Beyond the fact that witnesses' accounts of what happened do not totally agree, it is simply impossible to get inside the mind of Hamilton himself.

Key to your success as a history student is your willingness to interpret, along with your willingness to master the facts on which to base your interpretations. It will be important not only in the way you read your history book and listen in class, but also in the way you share your thoughts with others and evaluate the thinking that others share with you. As you develop your interpretative approach to history, you will become more critical of your own ideas and learn to anticipate other people's objections to them or to the way you support them. Your anticipation of possible objections will force you into refining your thinking—and your interpretations.

How to Study Systematically

To master the facts, you will need to develop convincing interpretations of historical data and you must study effectively. To study effectively, you have to interact deeply with the important components of the course—the textbook, the lectures, the students, and the professor. Merely attending class is not enough. Passively reading just to get to the end of each chapter is not enough. Answering questions only when you are directly asked to is not enough.

Previewing the Text

The component of your history course with which you will have to deal most independently is your textbook. Before you do anything else, you should get a feel for the course by previewing your text. To familiarize yourself with the textbook, you need to open it and do the following.

1. Read the title and ask what it says about the material inside. Doesn't the title *A People and a Nation* tell you that the book presents a social and cultural history as well as a political history of the United States?
2. Read the preface to find out what the authors' purpose and approach are.
3. Read the biographical data about the authors to see how much authority they have and what their special interests and areas of expertise are.
4. Read the table of contents to see where the course is going to take you; compare the dates given in the titles of chapters in your book with those listed in the title of your course to determine which chapters your class will be covering.

Studying Individual Chapters

Once you have previewed the text, you are ready to study your first chapter systematically, using both your textbook and your Study Guide.

To use your textbook effectively, it is a good idea to adopt the "Survey Q3R" system of studying developed some fifty years ago by F. P. Robinson, and the learning aids and exercises in this study guide Research confirms the effectiveness of the system's five processes: (1) Surveying, (2) Questioning, (3) Reading, (4) Reciting, and (5) Reviewing—SQ3R.

Surveying and Questioning. The first two steps in the system, surveying and questioning, are intimately linked. As you survey each chapter, jot down questions about the material in it. For that purpose, you need a reading notebook. Then, when you begin your close reading of the chapter, you will find that your reading is purposeful. You are looking for answers to your questions.

The surveying process itself begins with your actively reading the chapter title, making sure you understand the meaning of each word. Consider how this suggestion applies to your survey of Chapter 1. The words "old worlds" in the title "Three Old Worlds Create a New, 1492–1600" may take you by surprise—traditionally, American history textbooks have referred to Europe as the "old world" and the Americas as the "new world." Is there an implication here that both Europe and the Americas had flourishing civilizations of long standing? What is the third world referred to in the title? Maybe you need to scan the chapter itself to find out: Does it refer to Europe, North America, and South America? Or, are the "three worlds" Europe, Africa, and the Americas?

The surveying and questioning process also includes going back to the textbook and studying the chapter's headings, introductory vignette, illustrations, and other special features and then framing questions that they suggest to you. The introductory vignette, which personalizes and illustrates themes covered in the chapter, the headings, which provide a road map of the chapter, and the illustrations (pictures, maps, diagrams, tables) all suggest questions, questions that you should ask yourself and record in your reading notebook.

Your survey of the first chapter—and later chapters as well—will reveal other helpful, regular features of your textbook, such as explanations providing insight into how historians work and how they know what they know and "legacy" sections focusing on how people and events from the period covered relate to issues and attitudes that remain important today. In Chapter 1, for example, your survey will lead you to a discussion of how the work of archeologists and the artifacts they have uncovered contribute to the knowledge the authors are sharing with you and a reminder that in some American communities Christopher Columbus is no hero and Columbus Day is no day for celebration.

As you move from chapter to chapter, you will find that special learning aids in this study guide will help you complete the surveying and questioning process. You can derive questions from them just as you derive questions from the title, headings, vignette, "legacy," and illustrations in the chapter in the textbook. The questions you come up with will help you tell what's most important when you come across it.

In the Study Guide, the Learning Objectives and Thematic Guides are going to be a big help later on if you get bogged down in the details and lose your way, so to speak. The Learning Objectives and Thematic Guide help you separate the trees from the forest. Chapter themes and the factual details are like a long row of coat hooks and the coats hanging from them. The themes give you "hooks" on which to hang the facts. Without those hooks, you might be buried under a pile of "coats." You can refer to both the Thematic Guide and the Learning Objectives for help in ordering the facts in an understandable and meaningful way. They can help you anticipate what is important and see the relevance of the material you are reading to your goals in studying the chapter and to one or several of the major themes of the chapter. To what particular themes does it relate? Is it a minor or a major contributor to those themes?

The Building Vocabulary section for each chapter is still another feature of this study guide that is particularly useful in the surveying and questioning steps of the SQ3R system. Each Building Vocabulary section lists words and terms that you really have to grasp in order to understand the chapter in your textbook. Look up any words on the list that are unfamiliar to you in a dictionary and jot down their definitions in the space provided in your Study Guide, so you will have some of the definitions you'll need when you study the chapter.

Of course, you may run across additional words or terms in the chapter that are unfamiliar to you. When that occurs, if not being familiar with the word or term absolutely prevents you from understanding the passage, then look up the word in a good dictionary, add it and its definition to the Building Vocabulary section in your study guide, and then go back and re-read the sentence in the passage in which it occurs. Paying a little extra attention to how the term is used in the passage and every time you run across it in the near future will soon give you a feel for the term and make it a useable part of your own vocabulary. On the other hand, if being unfamiliar with some term in a passage does not prevent you from understanding the passage you are reading—perhaps because its context gives you a pretty good idea of what it must mean—simply underline the term and put a question mark in the margin. Then, pay special attention to how the term is used the next few times you come across it. You can look it up after you have finished the chapter if you want to, but even if you don't look it up, paying special attention to how other people use it will soon enable you to grasp its precise meaning and how to use it yourself.

One learning aid in the Study Guide, the Finding the Main Idea exercise, appears only in its first chapter and offers you a special kind of help related to the surveying process. It is a helpful bridge between surveying the chapter and actually beginning to read the material in the chapter. If you have ever had trouble figuring out what information is really important for you to get from your textbooks, doing the Finding the Main Idea exercise in the study guide's first chapter should give you a good start on solving the problem.

The exercise is closely related to the explanations of how to find main ideas and mark up your textbook that you will come across later in this introduction. It's also related to a simple but important technique you might want to make a part of your preliminary chapter survey. This technique is simply to identify each of the chapter's segments, groups of usually between two and five consecutive paragraphs (occasionally a single paragraph is a segment, though) devoted to a single topic or idea. Just take a pencil and draw a line between the last paragraph of one segment and the first paragraph of the next segment. Then, when you begin "looking for the main ideas," you will be looking for the main ideas of these segments or series of paragraphs.

The number of activities involved in surveying the chapter should tell you just how important surveying is. Only after you have done all of them, which sounds more time consuming than it really is, are you ready to dive into the chapter itself.

Reading. The next step is to begin reading the body of the chapter, looking for answers to your questions—and coming up with more questions Two features of the Study Guide will help you with the reading part of the SQ3R system: the Learning Objectives and Identification and Significance sections. However, three other features are also helpful: the Thematic Guide, Essay Questions, and, in some chapters, the Organizing Information exercises.

As you begin this step in the SQ3R system, keep in mind that the verb study is an active verb. Staring at a textbook an arm's length away, counting pages as you mentally trudge to the last page of the chapter, flipping pages with the end of a pencil—none of that is studying. Studying is successful and rewarding only when you actively, physically involve yourself in the material you are studying. That's why it is so important for you to read with a pen or pencil in your hand and use it to mark your textbook, record questions and notes in a reading notebook, and write definitions and answers to exercises in the pages of your Study Guide. The act of doing these things, the physical act of writing, is what makes studying effective.

When you actually begin your close reading of a chapter, you should read manageable blocks of material rather than straight through the entire chapter. If in your surveying of the chapter you have drawn lines dividing the chapter into its segments, then each segment is what constitutes a manageable block.

Once you have read a block of material, you can stop and analyze the material you have read in that block to figure out what its main idea and important sub-ideas are.

In this reading step you should be on the lookout for information you need to compose your responses to items in the Identification and Significance exercise in the Study Guide. Once you find the information you need to identify and indicate the significance of an item on the list, write out your response to the item in your own words. (Merely copying from the textbook won't do. Copying is a rote, no-thinking-required activity, as any skilled typist who routinely types long documents without having any idea what they say will tell you.) As you read the material, pay close attention to the questions you should answer to identify the item and those you need to answer to explain the item's significance. For some items, the significance section will be longer than it will be for others because some items have more consequences (significance) than others.

Reciting. The reciting part of studying should be both mental and physical. As you go over material you just read, rephrase some of the points as questions. Then look away from your textbook and recite both the question and the answer to yourself. It is best to keep working on formulating the answer until you can do it without looking at the text. You can do the same thing physically by putting your answer in writing, of course. After you can recite a pretty good answer mentally, then put your answer in writing without looking at the text. Some students create flashcards this way; they write the question on one side of an index card and their answer on the other. Those cards come in handy just before a test. At any rate, for this kind of reciting, limit yourself to relatively small questions—definitions, identifications, and so forth.

There will be time enough later to combine your answers to several of these little questions scattered throughout the chapter to produce the answers to broader, more complex questions. Many of the Organizing Information and Interpreting Information exercises in this study guide will help you with the reciting process as it applies to those longer, more complex questions. Once you have completed such exercises, you can use the charts or notes you produced in much the same way you would use flash cards. Some of these exercises lead you through the whole process of gathering information from scattered parts of chapters and using the information to compose working drafts for responses to essay questions. Others simply call upon you to go through the information-gathering and answer-planning process. They all give you practice in using textbook information to make your own interpretations of historical events, personalities, and concepts.

Reviewing. In the last stage of the SQ3R method, you review. Each day, before you begin the process of studying and learning new material, review the material you have studied and learned up to that point. Go back and recite answers to the questions listed in your reading notebook; go over your underlining and reading notes, and go over all of the Study Guide exercises for the chapter that you have already completed.

Improving Your Reading and Recall

No matter how systematically you work, for your studying to pay off in a history course, you have to read effectively and develop techniques that will help you remember what you read. For reading to be effective, it has to be active. In studying a textbook, both the brain and the hand have to be engaged. With the brain and hand engaged, you can do a good job of picking out main ideas and inserting simple and clear reminders in your textbook as you read. That will be quite helpful when you do your note taking and complete your Study Guide exercises no matter whether you record your notes in outline form or leave them in some less structured form.

Finding Main Ideas

As you begin your first history course, you probably want to know how you are supposed to recognize what's important in each chapter and what you should be underlining and including in your reading notes. Well, as is surely clear by now, the key to recognition is anticipation.

Using Textbook Features as Clues. In studying *A People and a Nation,* two sets of clues will help you: (1) features of the textbook and Study Guide and (2) knowledge about essay and paragraph structure that you have gained from your previous training in English composition.

As you now know, each chapter in this Study Guide begins with a feature called the "Thematic Guide," and each chapter in your textbook has an introduction (opening with a vignette) and a conclusion. Reading the Thematic Guide and the chapter's vignette and scanning the introduction and the conclusion of the chapter before you really dig into the rest of the chapter will prepare you to recognize main ideas. The stories about individuals or events recounted in the vignettes highlight one or more key ideas in the chapter for you to be on the lookout for as you continue your reading. The remainder of the chapter's introduction brings up other topics that are going to be significant and states or implies the overall point of the chapter as a whole, a very broad point that serves as a kind of umbrella for all the other important points in the chapter. Reinforcing the hints in the introduction, the chapter's conclusion re-directs your attention back into the depths of the chapter and interprets all the evidence and sub-points found there. It indicates what, above all else, the author wants you to get out of the chapter. A conclusion says, basically, "In case you have missed the point, here it is."

Using Structural Features as Clues. A second aid in recognizing the main ideas you are going to be expected to know and explain at test time comes from a clear understanding of how the writing in your textbook is likely to be structured. In that regard, your training in English composition class about paragraph and essay structure and about topic sentences and thesis statements should help you a lot in recognizing where one division or subdivision ends and the next begins as well as in appreciating the relative importance of the ideas presented.

In a way, each chapter in your textbook is like one big essay that includes several sub-essays strung together one after another. Some of those sub-essays are themselves made up of two or three even shorter essays. Each of the sub-essays focuses on one of the chapter's major subtopics and has an introduction, a body, and, often—but not always—a conclusion. What would normally go into a sub-essay's conclusion may instead be reserved for and incorporated into the conclusion of the entire chapter. Likewise, the conclusion of any of the little essays in a sub-essay may be reserved for and incorporated into the sub-essay's conclusion.

Identifying Chapter Sub-Divisions. How can you tell where one sub-essay ends and another begins or where one of the little essays within a particular sub-essay ends and another begins?

Remember those one-paragraph introductions, one-paragraph conclusions, and the little transitional paragraphs you were taught to use in your beginning English composition class? Those paragraphs are all what can be called *functional paragraphs*. They are connectors. Functional paragraphs announce ideas and shifts in focus, but they do not include any evidence to support the ideas they announce. If you want to find where one sub-essay ends and another begins, look for those connectors—the introductions and conclusions. But be careful. Because even the sub-essays within a chapter in your textbook are likely to be longer than an essay written in a beginning English composition class, their introductions and conclusions likewise are likely to be longer. They may be several paragraphs long.

Most of the time, if you locate an essay's thesis you have located its introduction. Obviously, in each of the essays within a chapter, you will be looking for the thesis anyway—either an explicit thesis statement or the implied thesis. It makes no difference whether you are looking at one of the chapter's sub-essays or at one of the little essays within a sub-essay. The thesis is likely to appear at the end of the essay's introduction. If, however, the author chooses to give the essay a conclusion, he or she may state the thesis for the first time somewhere in that conclusion That's why you should resist the temptation to decide what the thesis is until you have finished reading all of the essay.

Consider a few additional hints that should help you decide what the thesis is. The thesis is the whole point—not just the first point—of a whole essay. It does not matter whether the essay in question is a little one made up of a simple introduction, body, and conclusion, or whether it is a long one made up of several little essays each of which has an introduction, body, and conclusion. If the thesis is implicit rather than explicit, you are going to have to be able to state it yourself. To do that, simply answer the question, "What does all this add up to?" or, even better, "What does all this mean?" Of course, if the thesis is explicit, the author of the chapter has provided the answer for you.

In an introduction that includes an explicit thesis statement, the thesis statement is likely to come at the end of the introduction, which of course, helps you to see where the introduction ends and the body begins. In an essay whose thesis is implicit, things are not so clearcut. You have to read the entire essay and state the thesis for yourself. Then, when you go back and start reading from the beginning, you will find that as soon as you come across an idea that is only a part of or a contributor to the thesis you have formulated and that idea is followed immediately by evidence and clarifying information, you know you have gotten into the essay's body. The preceding information is the introduction.

Recognizing where the conclusion begins is a matter of remembering what you've read. A conclusion interprets evidence already presented. Thus, if you move into a discussion of the significance of points that have already been presented and "proved," you have moved into a conclusion.

The other kind of functional paragraph you are going to run across is the *transitional paragraph*. In fact, you are going to run across transitional passages made up of a series of paragraphs. None of a chapter's main ideas is going to be stated solely in a transitional passage. Any main idea that happens to be stated in a transitional passage also will be stated somewhere else. A transitional passage merely connects one passage to another. It typically announces that the focus is shifting and sometimes provides a bit of context, maybe even an illustration. In one sense, the vignette at the beginning of each chapter in *A People and a Nation* is a transitional passage designed to help you shift focus as you move from one chapter to the next. In fact, the openings of the introductions to sub-essays within any chapter also serve as transitional devices. However, you are going to come across some paragraphs within even the shortest of a chapter's essays that serve merely as connectors and focus shifters. As helpful as such paragraphs are, they have no topic sentences and no real evidence. They simply make the road you are navigating through the chapter smoother by keeping the curves from getting too sharp for you to handle.

That takes us back to the bodies of all those essays inside the covers of *A People and a Nation*. In analyzing the bodies of even the shortest essays in a chapter, you have to know where one body paragraph ends and the next body paragraph begins. After all, the base ingredient of an essay is the paragraph.

Understanding Textbook Paragraphing

Think for a moment about those little essays of ten or fewer paragraphs assigned in English composition classes. In such assignments, aside from the one-paragraph introduction, the one-paragraph conclusion, and perhaps one or two transitional paragraphs used in the body, all the other paragraphs (referred to loosely as "body paragraphs") are what are properly called *developmental paragraphs*. Each of these developmental paragraphs begins with a paragraph indention. That's the signal that a new paragraph is about to begin.

But if you translate each paragraph indention in your history textbook as the signal that a new paragraph has begun and you think a paragraph is exactly what your English teacher says it is, you are going to be led astray. When the pages in books and other publications are divided into columns, as is the case in *A People and a Nation*, the elements of what your English composition teacher would recognize as "real" developmental paragraphs usually get spread out a bit. As a result, a developmental paragraph's topic sentence may be separated from the rest of its paragraph and look as though it were a whole paragraph all by itself. Similarly, one of the paragraph's sub-points—with or without its supporting details—may begin with a paragraph indention and merely look like a whole paragraph.

As you read chapters in *A People and a Nation*, then, you will nearly always have to mentally re-join all of the segments of a developmental paragraph to the paragraph's topic sentence. You will know the "real" paragraph is complete when you've added enough segments to fully support the topic sentence and when the next indention introduces a new idea that neither support nor clarifies it. Fortunately, with practice, this reconstituting of paragraphs becomes habitual and quite subconscious.

So what does all this theorizing about recognizing main ideas boil down to? Well, it should tell you that the main ideas in any chapter should be those statements or implied ideas that correspond to thesis statements and topic sentences. If a writer uses thesis statements and topic sentences to express the points he considers most important—just as his English composition teacher taught him to do—it only makes sense for the reader of a chapter in *A People and a Nation* to consider each of the chapter's thesis statements and topic sentences the expressions of the chapter's main ideas.

Reading Passages Analytically

Because it is not safe to assume that every passage or little essay in a chapter starts off with its main idea or even that the first idea in a passage that sounds important is the main idea, you need to resist the temptation to start underlining or entering marginal notes too soon. As you do your preliminary reading of a passage, go ahead and let your highlighter or pen twitch if it must. Only when you have read the whole passage and analyzed it will you be ready to decide what the most important ideas are and how you should mark up the passage.

To see why this preliminary, analytical reading is so important, take a look at the sample passage reprinted from Chapter 1 of *A People and a Nation.* Short as it is, the passage shows what can happen if you try to mark it up before you really know what it says.

Sample Marked Passage

Americans' religious beliefs varied even more than did their political systems, but all the peoples were polytheistic, worshipping a multitude of gods. Each group's most important beliefs and rituals were closely tied to its means of subsistence. The major deities of agricultural peoples like Pueblos and Muskogeans were associated with cultivation, and their chief festivals centered on planting and harvest. The most important gods of hunters were associated with animals, and their major festivals were related to hunting. A band's economy and women's roles in it helped to determine women's potential as religious leaders. Women held the most prominent positions in those agricultural societies (like the Iroquois) in which they were also the chief food producers, whereas in hunting societies men took the lead in religious as well as political affairs.

> Kind of econ. determined relig. beliefs & whether women could be relig. leaders
>
> Agricult. tribes cultivation-centered religion
>
> Hunting tribes Animal-centered religion
>
> women possibly relig. leaders—if major food producers

If you pick out the first sentence that "looks important" in this passage before you have read the whole thing, you will be tempted to say that the main point is that there was a lot of variety in the mainly polytheistic Native American religions, right?

On the other hand, if you wait until after you have read the whole passage, you are going to dismiss the variety idea in the first clause as a transitional device and the polytheism idea in the second clause as simply one of the paragraph's details. After all, the only support for the claim about how varied Native American religious systems were is the suggestion that there were two broad categories. As for the polytheism idea, it goes nowhere in the body of the paragraph. The author provides no lists of gods or of tribes and their gods and no information about the average number of gods per tribe.

What a preliminary reading of the whole passage uncovers is these pretty much equally emphasized points in the body of the paragraph:

1. The kind of religious beliefs and practices a tribe had depended on the tribe's economic system, and
2. Whether women could be religious leaders depended on the tribe's economic system.

The equal emphasis suggests that neither is the main point. But clearly both points are important. Perhaps the two points add up to some larger point.

Studying the two points makes the function of the word *religious* in the paragraph's opening sentence clear. Religion is part of both of these points. If these two points are the most important points stated in the paragraph, then religion must be the topic of the paragraph. If religion is the topic of the paragraph, then the paragraph's main point has to be about religion.

A closer look shows that both points link religion to economic systems. To figure out the main point of the paragraph, then, all we have to do is add those two points together. Once we do, it turns out that the main point is that both the particular form of religion a Native American tribe adopted and a woman's chances of being a religious leader depended on the tribe's means of subsistence, its economy, in other words.

Of course, there can be other points besides the main idea in even one short paragraph. It's just that other ideas and pieces of clarifying information are subordinate. You may want to mark them in some way, but you don't want to treat any of them as the main idea.

Marking Up Passages

As our earlier discussion of the reading step in the SQ3R system suggests, marking the text can be a very useful technique that makes it easier to remember what you have read and find information later. Not only does it help you concentrate on what you are reading but it will help you take notes on your reading. Exactly how you mark a passage will depend on the passage and on the style of marking that you find comfortable. Unless you have very legible handwriting, putting a lot of notes in the margin is not likely to do much good. Remember, moderation is what's called for. If you do too much marking, nothing will stand out. If you cram the margins with notes, the notes aren't going to be legible.

With experience, you will develop the style of marking that most suits your needs. You may discover that whenever the author provides a succinct statement of the main idea of a passage, it's useful to emphasize it by drawing a box around it. Or, if the author takes more than one sentence to express the main idea or merely implies it, you may want to put the idea in your own words in the margin. You probably won't want to underline or highlight whole sentences that provide what are merely supporting details, but you may want to underline key words or phrases in them. When the author lists a number of like items, you might want to write what the list consists of—causes, effects, parts, contributors, features, or whatever—and put numbers beside each one in the margin.

The sample marked passage on page xxi illustrates one reader's style of marking a passage as applied to the paragraph we discussed in the previous section. Notice that the student has written the main idea in the margin and underlined key words in the passage. He has freely used abbreviations, which is fine as long as he can translate them without difficulty later on.

Outlining Chapters

With your reading done and passages marked to your satisfaction, you can outline the chapter to help yourself separate the important from the unimportant and produce a guide for your final, practice recitations before examinations. Whether you choose to outline the whole chapter probably should depend on how effectively you can outline. You may prefer to outline key subsections of the chapter instead of outlining the whole chapter or, if you really just cannot outline very well, to replace outlining with other forms of note taking.

The actual outlining process is one of dividing and re-dividing. You start with a "whole," and you divide it. The "whole" is the overall point of the piece of writing you are outlining, what all the evidence supports and adds up to. Once you have read and marked this whole piece of writing—and, as the logic of outlining makes clear, you absolutely must do that first—you see that what you start out with is a whole idea. You have to think of that idea as a whole "thing" just as you would think of a pie as a whole thing. You then find the largest parts into which you can cut your pie, usually between two and five parts. No matter how many of these largest sub-topics you recognize, each is now to be considered an absolutely new, whole subject. You divide the first into what you recognize as its largest components and then do the same with the second and the others until you have subdivided all of your largest sub-topics into their largest sub-topics. You then go back and treat each of the sub-sub-topics as a divisible whole subject.

How long you keep up the dividing and subdividing process depends on what you're using the outline for. If you are merely trying to identify the main themes to help you in both in-class and out-of-class note taking, then the process does not go much past three levels of division. If you are reducing all of your out-of-class notes to outline form and plugging in information from your class notes, then you need a very thorough outline, one whose lowest-rank headings either cannot be subdivided or are enough to trigger your memory of the unnamed subdivisions. Outlines whose headings are too broad are not very helpful, but forcing unnecessary specificity into an outline wastes precious time.

It's a good idea to follow conventional outlining style in most particulars. Good headings are specific and substantive headings. They reflect the subject matter clearly and trigger recall of details. That rules out useless status headings (*Introduction*, *Body*, and *Conclusion*), which indicate the locations of information rather than the information itself. Good outline design includes a number-letter heading designator system and an indention system that suggest the rank and relative importance of the headings. The conventional system that you can find illustrated in almost any freshman English composition handbook is helpful, but when an outline is being created merely as a study aid, its format should never take on more importance than its content.

Preparing for Tests

Ideally, of course, you go to all this trouble because you want to learn about the history of the United States to become a more cultured person and a better citizen or observer of American society and politics. But you probably are interested in doing well in your American history course also because how well you are deemed to have succeeded in it will become a part of your academic record. This second interest explains your desire to do well on history tests this term. How well you do on your tests will depend on how well you anticipate questions and how well you prepare yourself to answer the questions you anticipate.

Preparing for Essay Questions

The first step in preparing for essay questions is guessing what's likely to be asked. Obviously, you can figure out some of the questions you will have to be able to answer simply by doing the exercises in this study guide. But you will want to enlarge that list of possibilities with some suggestions of your own growing out of your class notes, your supplementary reading assignments, and your familiarity with your instructor's emphases. One important way you can come up with potential essay questions that may not have occurred to you is to find subject matter in your class and textbook notes that suits some of the writing styles most commonly called for on essay tests.

Anticipating the Questions

Questions calling for answers written in several particular writing styles crop up on almost all essay tests. Therefore, thinking up questions that call for answers written in these styles pays off most of the time. As you are going to see, the process of developing questions to suit the particular styles is illustrated in several of the Interpreting Information exercises in this Study Guide. Among the most commonly used types of questions are ones calling for exemplification, comparison, contrast, definition, causal analysis, and classification. We can add to this list a type almost peculiar to history courses, the analytical narration (or "trace the development of") question. In the exemplification type, you are to show that you can back up one of your opinions by citing examples; in the comparison type, that you can show how two or more persons, events, or concepts resemble each other; in the contrast type, that you can show how two or more persons, events, or concepts differ from each other; in the definition type, that you can explain what something is or means or who someone is; in the causal analysis type, that you can explain the causes or the effects of something; in the classification type, that you can identify the types or kinds of something; and, in the analytical narration type, that you can trace the development of something by citing and explaining the key changes it has gone through.

To anticipate questions, you simply go through all of your notes and find subject matter that suits any of the particular writing styles. You might find as many as twenty or twenty-five potential matches. Once you find a match, you state the question that arises out of it. From the list of questions that results, you cull the most likely candidates, trying to create a set of questions that covers all of the material the test is to cover and providing the best style-to-subject matter matches you can produce.

Composing Mock Answers

Once you have your list of potential essay questions, it is time to plan your answers to those questions. That's right: actual answers to the questions you have produced. Some of the Interpreting Information exercises in this study guide lead you step-by-step through the whole process.

Think of it as taking an open-book, take-home test. You pore through your notes, your textbook, and your study guide to find all the relevant examples and other evidence you have been exposed to. For each of your questions, you frame your basic one-sentence response based on the sum of the evidence you collect. You then outline the material that supports your one-sentence answer (perhaps in the form of a chart like those in many of the Organizing Information and Interpreting Information exercises) or actually write out your whole answer in the form of the working draft of an essay. The one-sentence answer is the thesis of your response, whose body is the written-out evidence that you have gathered from throughout the chapter and from your class notes and that you have now organized. Such gathering, synthesizing, and organizing is, of course, exactly what you are asked to do in many of the Organizing Information and Interpreting Information exercises in this study guide. Be warned, though: You cannot expect to be able to write out such a full answer under the time and psychological pressure of the testing situation. What you can only hope will happen at test time is in fact what usually does happen. The pressure of the situation ends up forcing you to concentrate on the truly significant points and then select the best evidence from all that which you collected.

Preparing for Multiple-Choice Questions

If you have done a really good job of studying for an essay examination, you have automatically done virtually all the studying necessary for you to do well on a multiple-choice test. That's because good answers to essay questions rely for their support on the kinds of examples and specific details that are the mainstay of multiple-choice questions. However, you may want to supplement the effort you put into preparing for essay questions just in case.

One of the best ways is to make your own flash cards as you go back through the chapter—once you have finished marking it up—to find details in each passage that you thought significant enough to underline or highlight. Any such detail that your instructor has emphasized in any way is likely to show up on a test as a multiple-choice question. You might want to make a flash card for each question, writing the question on one side of the card and the answer on the other. You can use those cards to keep testing yourself until you are confident that every time you see one of the questions you can come up with its answer without turning the card over.

You might find other possibilities in the identification questions in your Study Guide. Any question that can be phrased to call for just a few words or for a single clause or sentence in response would make a good multiple-choice question.

Of course, once you have determined what topics *you* think should be covered in multiple-choice style questions, you might want to see what another reader thinks. The multiple-choice questions in this study guide should give you a pretty good idea of what a history teacher might think would make good material for multiple-choice questions.

A Final Bit of Encouragement

When all is said and done, becoming good at history isn't such a mysterious process after all. Yes, it takes hard work, but hard work does pay off. All the techniques we've been looking at—from adopting an interpretative approach to history to marking passages in the textbook, from outlining, to anticipating test questions, to writing out mock answers to the questions anticipated—have helped generations of young people become more interested in and knowledgeable about America's history and, yes, better history students. But, if you think that will never happen to you, here's one more suggestion for you: Find your own reason for being interested, not some reason your Study Guide authors give you or your parents give you or your history teacher gives you but a reason of your own. That's when you'll discover the kind of joy in learning that propels you to real success as a history student.

CHAPTER 16

Reconstruction: An Unfinished Revolution, 1865–1877

Learning Objectives

After you have studied Chapter 16 in your textbook and worked through this study guide chapter, you should be able to:

1. Examine the clash between the executive and legislative branches of government over the issue of Reconstruction, and discuss the events and forces that affected the development of the congressional Reconstruction plans.

2. Examine and evaluate the Reconstruction experience for blacks.

3. Explain the divergence between the provisions of President Johnson's Reconstruction plan and its actual operation.

4. Cite the major provisions of the Fourteenth and Fifteenth Amendments; indicate the reasons for their passage by Congress; and explain the compromises embodied in each.

5. Cite the major provisions of the First Reconstruction Act of 1867; indicate the reasons for its enactment by Congress; and explain why it diverged from the proposals of the Radical Republicans.

6. Discuss the political, social, and economic impact of the Reconstruction governments on southern society.

7. Examine and evaluate the means by which white southern Conservatives attempted to regain control in the South, and indicate the outcome of their efforts.

8. Examine the events and forces that brought a weakening of the northern commitment to Reconstruction and an end to the Reconstruction era.

Thematic Guide

Reconstruction refers to the process by which the nation was rebuilt after the destruction caused by the Civil War. This rebuilding was social, political, and economic. Since there were no guidelines as to how it would be accomplished, questions and disagreements arose. Given such disagreements, as well as the emotional aftermath of four years of war and the force of individual personalities, Reconstruction proceeded by trial and error.

As early as 1863, some two years before the end of the war, a debate began between the President and Congress over key questions relating to Reconstruction. In this debate, and in the Reconstruction proposals put forward by President Lincoln and Congress, it was apparent that the two disagreed over the scope and objectives of the Reconstruction process. Despite these disagreements, in early 1865 Congress and the President were able to work together to secure passage of the Thirteenth Amendment and to create the Freedmen's Bureau.

At war's end and as the power struggle between the executive and legislative branches over control of the Reconstruction process became more pronounced, blacks renewed their determination to struggle for survival and true equality within American society. On one level they placed faith in education and participation in the political process as means of attaining equality, but they also turned to family and religion for strength and support. Denied the possibility of owning land, they sought economic independence through new economic arrangements such as sharecropping. However, sharecropping ultimately "proved to be a disaster" for all concerned.

When Congress reconvened in December 1865, it was faced with a Reconstruction policy advanced by President Johnson that not only allowed former Confederate leaders to regain power at the state and national levels but obviously abandoned the freedmen to hostile southern whites. Northern congressmen and the constituents they represented were unwilling to accept this outcome of the long, bitter struggle against a rebellious South. Believing that it had a constitutional right to play a role in the Reconstruction process, Congress acted. This action led to clashes with an intransigent President Johnson and to the passage of two congressional Reconstruction plans.

The first of these plans, the Fourteenth Amendment, evolved when the wrangling between President Johnson and Congress produced compromises among the conservative, moderate, and radical factions of the Republican party. Although Congress passed the Freedmen's Bureau bill and the Civil Rights Act of 1866 over the president's veto, there was concern that the Supreme Court would declare the basic provisions of the Civil Rights Act unconstitutional. Therefore, those provisions were incorporated into a constitutional amendment that was presented to the states for ratification in April 1866. The Fourteenth Amendment demonstrated that Congress wanted to guarantee equality under the law to the freedmen, but its provisions make it clear that the moderate and conservative Republicans who controlled Congress were not willing to accept the more progressive concept of equality advanced by the Radical Republicans.

When, at the urging of the president, every former Confederate state except Tennessee refused to ratify the Fourteenth Amendment, Congress passed its second Reconstruction plan—the Reconstruction Acts of 1867–1868. Although these acts demonstrated some movement in the Radical direction by extending to blacks the right to vote in state elections, congressmen were still limited by the prejudices of the age. They labeled as extremist the suggestion that southern land be redistributed and so rejected the idea of giving blacks economic independence. They naively assumed that blacks would need only the ballot in their fight for a better life.

The same kinds of limitations worked within Reconstruction governments, preventing fundamental reform of southern society. Concurrently, southern Republicans adopted a policy that returned voting rights to former Confederates. These former Confederates, or Conservatives, ultimately led a campaign designed to return political and economic power to their hands by discrediting the Reconstruction governments. Adopting tactics ranging from racist charges and intimidation to organized violence, the Conservatives were able to achieve their objectives, as events in Alamance and Caswell counties in North Carolina demonstrated.

These setbacks indicated that northern commitment to equality had never been total. The federal government even began to retreat from partial commitment—a retreat made obvious by the policies of President Grant, the gradual erosion of congressional resolve on Reconstruction issues, the conservative decisions of the Supreme Court, and the emergence of other issues that captured the minds of white Americans. Finally, with the resolution of the disputed Hayes-Tilden election in 1876, Reconstruction ended. The promise of equality for black Americans remained unfulfilled.

Building Vocabulary

Listed below are important words and terms that you need to know to get the most out of Chapter 16. They are listed in the order in which they occur in the chapter. After carefully looking through the list, refer to a dictionary and jot down the definition of words that you do not know or of which you are unsure.

suffrage

paramilitary

enfranchise

revert

adroit

usurpation

circumspection

exultant

odyssey

compensation

philanthropy

autonomous

salable

staunch

ardent

vehemently

blatant

haughty

resilient

succumb

grudgingly

repudiate

curfew

sabotage

intransigence

reimburse

humane

ambivalence

irony

infuse

magnanimity

mandate

impasse

confiscation

belligerent

conscientious

repudiate

vacillate

curry

demobilization

apprentice

adamant

exhort

contingent

enmity

reconciliation

vindictive

futile

proportionate

ostracism

subjection

spontaneous

entrench

fiscal

ominous

disparate

elitist

harbinger

purport

deference

chasm

emasculate

acquiesce

Identification and Significance

After studying Chapter 16 of *A People and a Nation,* you should be able to identify fully *and* explain the historical significance of each item listed below.

1. Identify each item in the space provided. Give an explanation or description of the item. Answer the questions *who, what, where,* and *when.*

2. Explain the historical significance of each item in the space provided. Establish the historical context in which the item exists. Establish the item as the result of or as the cause of other factors existing in the society under study. Answer this question: *What were the political, social, economic, and/or cultural consequences of this item?*

Robert Smalls

Identification

Significance

Wade Hampton

Identification

Significance

special Field Order number 15

Identification

Significance

Lincoln's "10 percent" plan

Identification

Significance

the Wade-Davis Bill

Identification

Significance

the Wade-Davis Manifesto

    Identification

    Significance

the Thirteenth Amendment

    Identification

    Significance

the Freedmen's Bureau

    Identification

    Significance

reunification of African American families

    Identification

    Significance

Freedmen's Bureau schools

    Identification

    Significance

the founding of African American colleges

    Identification

    Significance

Francis Cardozo, P. B. S. Pinchback, Blanche K. Bruce, and Hiram Revels

    Identification

    Significance

the founding of African American churches

    Identification

    Significance

the sharecropping system

    Identification

    Significance

cotton and the southern economy

    Identification

    Significance

Johnson's Reconstruction plan

    Identification

    Significance

the black codes

    Identification

    Significance

Radical Republicans

    Identification

    Significance

the civil rights bill of 1866

    Identification

    Significance

the Memphis and New Orleans riots

    Identification

    Significance

the Fourteenth Amendment

    Identification

    Significance

Johnson's "swing around the circle"

    Identification

    Significance

the congressional elections of 1866

    Identification

    Significance

the First Reconstruction Act

    Identification

    Significance

Thaddeus Stevens

    Identification

    Significance

the Tenure of Office Act

    Identification

    Significance

Johnson's impeachment trial

    Identification

    Significance

the presidential election of 1868

    Identification

    Significance

Ulysses S. Grant

    Identification

    Significance

the Fifteenth Amendment

    Identification

    Significance

the southern Republican party

> Identification

> Significance

the constitutional conventions in the former Confederate states

> Identification

> Significance

Republican governments in the former Confederate states

> Identification

> Significance

industrialization in the former Confederate states

> Identification

> Significance

public schools in the former Confederate states

> Identification

> Significance

the southern Conservatives

    Identification

    Significance

the charge of "Negro rule"

    Identification

    Significance

carpetbagger

    Identification

    Significance

scalawag

    Identification

    Significance

Republican tax policies in the former Confederate states

    Identification

    Significance

the Ku Klux Klan

    Identification

    Significance

Klan violence in Alamance and Caswell counties North Carolina

    Identification

    Significance

the Enforcement Acts and the anti-Klan law

    Identification

    Significance

the Liberal Republican revolt

    Identification

    Significance

the Amnesty Act of 1872

    Identification

    Significance

the Civil Rights Act of 1875

    Identification

    Significance

the Panic of 1873

    Identification

    Significance

greenbacks vs. sound money

    Identification

    Significance

William H. Seward

    Identification

    Significance

Ex parte Milligan

    Identification

    Significance

the *Slaughter-House* cases

      Identification

      Significance

Bradwell v. *Illinois*

      Identification

      Significance

United States v. *Cruikshank*

      Identification

      Significance

the presidential election of 1876

      Identification

      Significance

the Exodusters

      Identification

      Significance

Organizing Information

Much of Chapter 16 is devoted to changes in civil rights during the Reconstruction period, much of the change triggered by the immediate situation of the defeat of the Confederacy. To sharpen your understanding of the evolution of civil rights during the period, complete the chart "Evolution of Civil Rights and Legal Empowerment, 1865-1878."

Moving across each row, indicate what legislative, constitutional, or court action listed in Column One had to say about the rights or power/authority of each group or entity named in the headings for Columns Two through Five. In the last column, indicate what happened to the legislative action, amendment or court decision named in Column One. (Was it voted down, enacted, repealed, or what? What kind of effect has it had?)

Your entries should be mere reminders, labels that will stir your recollection of details needed for a full explanation and that can serve as prompts when you review Chapter 16 or plan mock essays to answer essay questions that you anticipate seeing on a test on Chapter 16.

Evolution of Civil Rights and Legal Empowerment, 1865-1878					
Legislative, Constitutional, or Court Action	Former Confederate Leaders	Black Males	Females	States', Federal Government's role in Guaranteeing Civil Rights	Fate and/or Impact
Civil Rights Bill of 1866					
Reconstruction Act of 1867					
Anti-Klan law (1870)					
Enforcement Acts (1870–1871)					
Amnesty Act of 1872					
Civil Rights Act of 1878					
Constitutional Amendments: 13th					
14th					
15th					

Evolution of Civil Rights and Legal Empowerment, 1865-1878 (continued)					
Legislative, Constitutional, or Court Action	**Former Confederate Leaders**	**Black Males**	**Females**	**States', Federal Government's role in Guaranteeing Civil Rights**	**Fate and/or Impact**
Supreme court Decisions: *Slaughter-House Cases*					
U.S. v. Cruikshank					
Bradwell v. Illinois					

Interpreting Information

Analyze the chart you completed as part of the preceding Organizing Information exercise and, based on your chart entries, invent two or three questions that you think would make good essay questions for a test on Chapter 16. Consider the significance of the material that the respondent would be required to provide, how well the question reflects one or more themes of the chapter, the amount of relevant, specific, concrete information on the topic that the chapter and your class notes provide, and what your professor has emphasized in class. Choose the best of your questions, and compose a mock essay that responds directly to it.

Ideas and Details

Objectives 1 and 3

_____   1. Many northerners questioned President Johnson's Reconstruction plan because
            a. it promised federal aid to help the South rebuild.
            b. in actual operation, it returned power to the prewar southern elite.
            c. the plan required repudiation of the Confederate war debt.
            d. it did not extend the vote to the yeoman class.

Objectives 1 and 2

_____   2. Which of the following is true of the black codes?
            a. They required the freedmen to pay "freedom dues" to their former masters.
            b. They extended the right to vote to property-owning blacks.
            c. They were an attempt to relegate blacks to a position of servitude.
            d. They extended to the freedmen equal protection under the law.

Objective 1

_____   3. Congress believed that it had a right to a voice in the Reconstruction process because
            the Constitution
            a. grants treaty-making powers to Congress.
            b. grants Congress the power to declare war.
            c. assigns Congress the duty of guaranteeing republican governments in the states.
            d. assigns Congress the responsibility of "providing for the general welfare."

Objective 1

_____   4. In order to develop a new Reconstruction program, conservative and moderate
            Republicans began to work with the Radical Republicans because
            a. events in the South convinced them that blacks should be given full political rights.
            b. the Radicals convinced them that black freedom depended on a redistribution of
                land in the South.
            c. President Johnson and the congressional Democrats refused to cooperate with them.
            d. the northern electorate clearly favored the goals of the Radical Republicans.

Objectives 1, 3, 4, and 5

_____   5. The northern public became convinced that Johnson's reconstruction policies were too
            lenient due to
            a. the election of Jefferson Davis to the Senate.
            b. the President's appointment of Alexander Stephens to his cabinet.
            c. the President's insistence that the federal government assume the Confederate debt
                in full.
            d. accounts of antiblack violence in the South.

Objective 4

_____   6. The Fourteenth Amendment
   a. guaranteed blacks the right to vote.
   b. was strongly supported by President Johnson.
   c. extended civil and political rights to women.
   d. was the product of a compromise among the Republican factions in Congress.

Objective 5

_____   7. The First Reconstruction Act
   a. required the southern states to ratify the Fourteenth Amendment.
   b. called for a redistribution of land in the South.
   c. guaranteed blacks the right to vote in federal elections.
   d. stipulated that the southern states would be "adjusted" back into the Union over a ten-year period.

Objective 1

_____   8. The Senate's failure to convict President Johnson of the charges brought against him
   a. enhanced Johnson's prestige and power.
   b. established that impeachment was not a political tool.
   c. is evidence that northern opinion toward Johnson and the South was softening.
   d. caused a serious rift between the House and Senate.

Objective 6

_____   9. The new state constitutions of the former Confederate states
   a. eliminated property qualifications for voting.
   b. extended the right to vote to women.
   c. made public school attendance compulsory.
   d. made yearly reapportionment of legislative districts mandatory.

Objective 6

_____   10. The decision of southern Republicans to restore the voting rights of former Confederates
   a. meant that southern Republicans had to gain white support or face defeat.
   b. led to the formation of a broad-based Republican party in the South.
   c. caused the freedmen to support the more liberal southern Democrats.
   d. was politically embarrassing to congressional Republicans.

Objectives 2 and 8

_____ 11. Blacks participating in Reconstruction governments
   a. had little interest in the political process.
   b. were subjected to a racist propaganda campaign against them undertaken by the white Conservatives.
   c. insisted on social equality for blacks.
   d. displayed a vindictive attitude toward their former masters.

Objective 7

_____ 12. Activities of the Ku Klux Klan in Alamance and Caswell counties in North Carolina
   a. were disorganized and sporadic.
   b. were organized by the impoverished classes in North Carolina society.
   c. were undertaken by the former elite for the purpose of regaining political power.
   d. had little success in areas where blacks and yeoman farmers allied.

Objectives 2 and 6

_____ 13. In the final analysis, the Reconstruction governments of the South
   a. were able to alter the social structure of the South.
   b. effected a lasting alliance between blacks and whites of the yeoman class.
   c. gave blacks the means to achieve equality by giving them the right to vote.
   d. left blacks economically dependent on hostile whites.

Objective 8

_____ 14. In the *Slaughter-House* cases, the Supreme Court
   a. ruled that the Fourteenth Amendment did not protect the civil rights of individuals from state interference.
   b. protected a citizen of the United States against discrimination by an individual or a group.
   c. ruled that corporations were legal persons and were protected under the Fourteenth Amendment.
   d. ruled that national citizenship was more important than state citizenship.

Objective 8

_____ 15. From the outcome of the 1876 presidential election, it is evident that the electorate
   a. supported an inflationary monetary policy.
   b. feared that the expansionist policies of Secretary of State Seward would lead to war.
   c. had lost interest in Reconstruction.
   d. rejected government aid to business interests.

Essay Questions

Objective 3

1. Discuss Johnson's Reconstruction plan, and explain its actual operation. How did Congress respond to the plan? Why?

Objectives 1, 4, and 5

2. Discuss the political, social, and economic views of the Radical Republicans, and examine the role they played in the development of Congress's plans for Reconstruction.

Objective 1

3. Examine the attitudes and events that led to the impeachment of President Andrew Johnson, and assess the outcome of his trial by the Senate.

Objective 6

4. Discuss the successes and failures of the Reconstruction governments in the South.

Objective 7

5. Discuss the goals of the Conservatives and the means they used to achieve those goals.

Map Exercise

1. Refer to the map on page 443 in the textbook. In the table below, list the eleven Confederate states, the date each was readmitted to the Union, the date Conservative rule was re-established in each, and the length of time the Reconstruction governments were in power in each.

Former Confederate State	Date Readmitted to Union	Date Conservative Rule Re-established	No. of Years Reconstruction Governments in Power

2. Why was Tennessee readmitted to the Union before passage of the Reconstruction Act of 1867?

3. What states were still under Reconstruction governments in 1876? What bearing did this have on the election of 1876? How was the problem resolved?

CHAPTER 17

The Development of the West, 1877–1900

Learning Objectives

After you have studied Chapter 17 in your textbook and worked through this study guide chapter, you should be able to:

1. Examine the factors that affected the life, culture, and economies of western Indian tribes in the late nineteenth century, and discuss the varying responses of the Indians to the pressures they experienced.

2. Discuss the characteristics of each of the frontier societies listed below, and explain the contributions of each to the economic, social, and cultural transformation of the West.
   a. The mineral, timber, and oil frontiers
   b. The farming frontier
   c. The ranching frontier

3. Discuss the role of women and nonwhites in frontier society, and examine the prejudices these groups experienced.

4. Discuss the early conservation movement in the United States, and indicate its successes and failures.

5. Discuss efforts in the West at land reclamation through irrigation; assess the role played by state and federal governments in these efforts; and explain the debate over water rights that accompanied reclamation efforts.

6. Examine the impact of the expansion of the railroad industry on the American economy, perceptions of time and space, standardization of time, technology, and business organization.

7. Examine and assess the role played by federal, state, and local governments in the expansion of the railroad industry.

8. Explain the responses of Plains' settlers to the living conditions and challenges they encountered, and discuss the impact of their experience on their lives.

9. Discuss the forces responsible for the transformation of American agriculture in the late nineteenth century, and explain the consequences of this agricultural revolution.

Thematic Guide

Chapter 17 begins a series of four chapters that analyze the transition of American society from an agrarian society to an urban, industrialized society. The expansion westward in the late nineteenth century closed the physical frontier that had been part of American society since its beginnings. As in the past, American expansion was carried out at the expense of Indians. Americans were and are an ethnocentric people. They see their civilization, their society, and their value and belief systems as being better than those of other peoples. This ethnocentrism led Americans to believe that they had a right to expand and to impose their values and beliefs on the peoples and societies they encountered. It is this attitude that formed the basis of the failed Dawes Severalty Act.

As Americans sought opportunity in this vast western region, they discovered and developed the riches of the land, thus conquering the natural-resource frontier—a prerequisite for the subsequent development of an industrialized economy. Exploitation of the land and its resources for profit raised questions in several areas: (1) who owns the resources, private developers or the American people; (2) which takes precedence—the desire for progress and profit or the desire to protect the natural landscape; and (3) who has rights to the precious streams, rivers, and basins of the West, only those along their banks or all those who intend a beneficial use of river water.

The natural-resources frontier, especially the mining and lumbering frontiers, produced personalities who enriched American folklore; but reality was far different from folk tales. Most westerners worked long hours as they attempted to eke out an existence for themselves and their families. Women and nonwhites suffered discrimination, especially with the development of racial categories by the dominant Anglo-Americans and European immigrants. Furthermore, although individual initiative was important in the development of the West, individuals usually gave way to corporate interests, which had the capital necessary to undertake the expensive extraction of minerals, timber, and oil. In addition, the federal government, as owner of the western lands, encouraged the development of the area by actively aiding individuals and corporations through measures such as the Timber and Stone Act and the Newlands Reclamation Act.

As frontiers of opportunity were conquered in the West, the expansion of regional and transcontinental railroad lines—made possible by generous government subsidies—helped create a vast national marketplace. Besides providing nationwide economic opportunities to farmers and industrialists, the railroad altered concepts of time and space, gave rise to new communities, and brought technological reforms as well as organizational reforms that affected modern business practices.

Railroad expansion and Indian removal made possible the successful settlement and development of the farming and ranching frontiers. These frontiers shared the characteristics of the natural-resource frontier: use of public land for private enrichment; the importance of technological innovations to successful development; government promotion of settlement and development; the bowing of the individual to corporate interests; the emergence of a frontier folk culture, especially in relation to the ranching frontier; and contributions to urbanization and to national economic growth and expansion.

Building Vocabulary

Listed below are important words and terms that you need to know to get the most out of Chapter 17. They are listed in the order in which they occur in the chapter. After carefully looking through the list, refer to a dictionary and jot down the definition of words that you do not know or of which you are unsure.

expound

egalitarian

persevere

relegate

rogue

exploit

arid

infinity

nomad

sinew

reciprocity

lethal

decimate

convergence

impede

preponderance

qualms

preempt

embellish

interloper

categorize

impute

commandeer

degrade

succumb

recalcitrance

infamous

relentless

utilize

acculturate

assimilation

.diligence

servile

dissolution

messianic

forswear

induce

dupe

demoralize

eradicate

lode

extractive

benevolent

crescent

mestizo

ascribe

demeaning

tier

miscegenation

hedonism

notoriety

exploits (noun)

posterity

eccentricity

reclamation

subsidy

salutary

rhapsodize

exemplify

formidable

burgeoning

harrow

drover

pilgrimage

Finding the Main Idea

When you begin to read material assigned to you in the textbook, it is important for you to look for (and mark) the main idea and supporting details in each paragraph or paragraph series. To see how to do so, reread "Finding Main Ideas" in the Introduction to this study guide. Then work the following two exercises, and check your answers.

Exercise A

Read the paragraph on page 470 of the textbook that begins with this sentence:

> Cutting fir and spruce trees for lumber to be used in construction, another large-scale extractive industry, needed vast tracks of forest land to be profitable.

1. What is the topic of this paragraph?

2.   What is its main idea?

3.   What details support the main idea?

Exercise B

Read the two successive paragraphs on pages 471–472 of the textbook that begin with this sentence:

> To control labor and social relations within this complex population, white settlers made race an important distinguishing social characteristic in the West.

1.   What is the topic of this paragraph series?

2.   What is its main idea?

3.   What details support the main idea?

Identification and Significance

After studying Chapter 17 of *A People and a Nation,* you should be able to identify fully *and* explain the historical significance of each item listed below.

1.   Identify each item in the space provided. Give an explanation or description of the item. Answer the questions *who, what, where,* and *when.*

2.   Explain the historical significance of each item in the space provided. Establish the historical context in which the item exists. Establish the item as the result of or as the cause of other factors existing in the society under study. Answer this question: *What were the political, social, economic, and/or cultural consequences of this item?*

Frederick Jackson Turner's frontier thesis

    Identification

    Significance

Buffalo Bill Cody

    Identification

    Significance

Indian subsistence cultures

    Identification

    Significance

slaughter of the buffalo

    Identification

    Significance

decline of salmon

    Identification

    Significance

United States government's reservation policy

    Identification

    Significance

the Battle of Little Big Horn

    Identification

    Significance

George Manypenny and Helen Hunt Jackson

    Identification

    Significance

Canada's Indian policy

    Identification

    Significance

the Women's National Indian Association and the Indian Rights Association

    Identification

    Significance

the Dawes Severalty Act

Identification

Significance

the government's Indian school system

Identification

Significance

the Ghost Dance movement

Identification

Significance

Wovoka

Identification

Significance

the Massacre at Wounded Knee

Identification

Significance

the Clapp rider to the Indian appropriations bill

      Identification

      Significance

the mining frontier

      Identification

      Significance

the Timber and Stone Act

      Identification

      Significance

mining and lumber communities

      Identification

      Significance

the home mission movement

      Identification

      Significance

women and nonwhites in frontier society

> Identification

> Significance

the conservation movement

> Identification

> Significance

the omnibus bill of 1889

> Identification

> Significance

the Clanton family and Johnny Ringo

> Identification

> Significance

the Earp brothers, "Bat" Masterson, and "Doc" Holliday

> Identification

> Significance

the shoot-out at the OK Corral

    Identification

    Significance

riparian rights versus prior appropriation

    Identification

    Significance

California irrigation legislation of 1887

    Identification

    Significance

the Newlands Reclamation Act

    Identification

    Significance

standard time zones

    Identification

    Significance

westward migration, 1870–1890

    Identification

    Significance

life on the Plains

    Identification

    Significance

the Great Blizzard of 1888

    Identification

    Significance

grasshopper plagues

    Identification

    Significance

the Homestead Act of 1862

    Identification

    Significance

mail-order houses and Rural Free Delivery

      Identification

      Significance

mechanization of agriculture

      Identification

      Significance

the Morrill Land Grant Acts of 1862 and 1890

      Identification

      Significance

the Hatch Act of 1887

      Identification

      Significance

dry farming

      Identification

      Significance

Luther Burbank and George Washington Carver

Identification

Significance

the ranching frontier

Identification

Significance

the long drive

Identification

Significance

open range ranching

Identification

Significance

barbed wire

Identification

Significance

Organizing Information

Fill in the chart "The West: Perspectives in Conflict, 1877-1920" by entering topics brought up in Chapter 17. Reflect, first, on how Native Americans and then on how key Euro-American groups viewed the subjects listed in the first column. The headings in the chart are meant to guide your search for information needed for the writing called for in the Interpreting Information exercise that follows this exercise. The arrangement of the topics in the chart is meant to help you organize that information. You are not expected to be able to make entries in every block.

The West: Perspectives in Conflict, 1877-1920

	Native Americans	Euro-Americans (Whites)		
		Settlers and others migrating to the West	Makers and interpreters of policies and laws	Promoters of religious and cultural values
Wealth and Economic System				
Resources and Resource Management				
Settlement by Whites				

The West: Perspectives in Conflict, 1877-1920

			Euro-Americans (Whites)		
	Native Americans	Settlers and others migrating to the West	Makers and interpreters of policies and laws	Promoters of religious and cultural values
Promotion of Religious or Spiritual, Cultural, and Class Values				
Gov't Policies and Positions Reservations Indian Citizenship Railroad Expansion				
Treaty-Making and Treaties				

Interpreting Information

Compose a good rough draft of an essay on the following question:

> Identify and discuss the key differences between the way Native Americans saw the great migration of whites to the West with all its ramifications and the way Euro-Americans saw it.

Use the chart you completed in the Organizing Information exercise and the following hints about how to go about planning the kind of compound-subject essay such a question calls for to guide you both in selecting the information you should include and in organizing that information to produce a concise but concrete and specific essay.

Hints for Planning A "Compound-Subject" Essay

"Compound-subject" questions like the one above often show up as comparison questions or as contrast questions, but they can show up as any kind of question that links two subjects or two aspects of the same subject ("before" and "after" subjects, for instance). A good starting point in composing essays of this type is to create a chart much like the one in the preceding Organizing Information exercise.

    To answer a compound-subject question, begin by identifying the two "items" you are to discuss, the members of the compound subject—Item One and Item Two. In this case, Items One and Two are "the perspective of the Native Americans" and "the perspective of the Euro-Americans."

    For each of the items involved in a compound-subject question, you also need to identify points of comparison or contrast. In this instance, you should identify points of contrast, which is what you did when you filled out the chart "The West: Perspectives in Conflict, 1877-1920." These points of contrast are features that link the two items.

    Whether the essay you are writing is a comparison of two items or a contrast of two items, the linking features we are referring to here are general characteristics they share and in terms of which they can be compared or contrasted. Notice, though, that even when it seems logical to compare (show similarities) between two items rather than to contrast (show differences), the two items are not exactly alike in terms of their shared characteristics. To understand that, think about the faces of mammals. Two mammals both have noses (a common feature on which they can be compared)

    Once you have identified the items and the features you need to deal with in answering compound-subject questions, organizing the body of your essay (or the major part of it) is simple.

    What follows are your two basic options in simplified, graphic form.

    In this graphic representation, the Roman numeral headings represent the finished essay's major sub-points. And the thesis statement represents the sum of those points, the whole point of the whole essay; that is, the significance of those points and all the details that support them. In composing your mock essay for this exercise, simply follow either of the two plans.

The Item-by-Item Plan	The Feature-by-Feature Plan

Thesis _____
 	
I. Item 1
  A. Feature 1
  B. Feature 2
  C. Feature 3
 	
II. Item 2
  A. Feature 1
  B. Feature 2
  C. Feature 3
 	
Conclusion _____
	Thesis _____
	
	I. Feature I
	  A. Item 1
	  B. Item 2
	
	II. Feature 2
	  A. Item 1
	  B. Item 2
	
	III. Feature 3
	  A. Item 1
	  B. Item 2
	
	Conclusion _____

As you can see, your first option would be to create an essay with a two-part body. In the first part you say everything you have to say about one of the two items, moving from one specific feature to the next until you have covered them all. In the second part, you say everything you have to say about the other item, again moving from feature to feature. Your second option is to begin the body by saying everything you have to say about the first feature and then moving on to the second feature. You then say everything you have to say about the second feature. You continue until you have discussed every feature in terms of both items until you have covered all the features or "areas "of comparison or contrast.

Once you have worked out what you are going to say in the body of your essay, you can formulate a suitable thesis statement with which to begin. That thesis statement should include three elements: (1) the naming of the members of the compound subject—in other words, the two items; (2) an indication of the logical link you are establishing—in this particular case, the fact that they differ; and (3) an indication of the area or basis of comparison or contrast—in other words, what the "features" add up to."

If all that is too theoretical for you, consider this sample of a contrast sentence: "The twins Bill and Phil differ in terms of their attitude toward psychic phenomena." That's a kind of sentence-by-formula, of course, but it does include and illustrate the basic elements that should be in a thesis statement for a contrast essay. The order of the elements does not matter. All that matters is that all three elements are present.

Ideas and Details

Objective 1

_____   1. To achieve subsistence, most western Indian tribes
           a. relied solely on the buffalo.
           b. combined capitalistic trading practices with crop raising.
           c. sold clothing, shoes, and blankets to get the money necessary to buy food in the
               marketplace.
           d. relied on a balance among crop raising, livestock raising, hunting, and raiding.

Objective 1

_____   2. The slaughter of the buffalo by whites
           a. was encouraged by Indians of the Great Plains.
           b. was undertaken to prevent the spread of lethal animal diseases to sheep and goat
               herds.
           c. was only one of a combination of circumstances that doomed the buffalo.
           d. began the process that led to the bison's virtual extinction.

Objective 1

_____   3. Which of the following undermined the subsistence culture of Northwestern Indians?
           a. Salmon reduction
           b. Slaughter of the buffalo
           c. The lack of irrigation facilities during prolonged periods of drought
           d. Animal diseases

Objective 1

_____   4. Which of the following assumptions was generally made by whites settling the Great
               Plains?
           a. Fearing competition from African American workers, white settlers assumed that
               the federal government would bar blacks from the territories.
           b. Well-schooled in egalitarian principles, white settlers assumed that equality of
               opportunity would be extended to all ethnic groups in the territories.
           c. Disregarding the rights of Plains Indians, white settlers assumed that they could
               settle wherever they wished.
           d. Out of concern for Indian cultures, white settlers assumed that the land rights of
               Native Americans would have to be respected.

Objective 1

_____ 5. Which of the following was a feature of the federal government's reservation policy?
   a. It did not allow Indians any say over their own affairs.
   b. It helped foster mutually beneficial trade relationships between Indians and whites.
   c. It forced Indians to concentrate on crop production.
   d. It protected Indians against white encroachment.

Objective 1

_____ 6. As a result of the Dawes Severalty Act,
   a. thousands of Indian children educated in white boarding schools rejected Indian culture.
   b. most western Indians were Christianized.
   c. the community-owned tribal lands of the western Indians were dissolved.
   d. the western Indians were encouraged to actively participate in decisions that would affect their lives and their culture.

Objective 2

_____ 7. The mining, timber, and ranching frontiers had which of the following characteristics in common?
   a. In the earliest stages of development, these frontiers required large capital outlays.
   b. Those associated with the development of these frontiers found ways of using the Timber and Stone Act to their advantage.
   c. Individuals were ultimately replaced by corporations in the development of these frontiers.
   d. Those involved in the development of these frontiers understood the need for careful and planned use of natural resources.

Objectives 2 and 3

_____ 8. In the frontier communities, ethnic minorities
   a. were welcomed because of the skills they brought with them.
   b. usually had to endure white prejudice.
   c. found that opportunities abounded.
   d. were usually able to gain economic and political power.

Objective 6

_____ 9. To help solve scheduling problems, the railroads in 1883
   a. began to coordinate all their schedules through a central clearing-house.
   b. requested that the government establish daylight-saving time.
   c. asked that the government create the Interstate Commerce Commission.
   d. established four standard time zones.

Objectives 2 and 7

_____ 10. Both the cattle-ranching industry and the railroad industry
a. profited from free use of public lands.
b. developed a mutually beneficial relationship with farmers.
c. were respectful of Indian rights and culture.
d. welcomed government regulation of industry.

Objective 8

_____ 11. Which of the following is associated with the Great Plains?
a. A temperate climate
b. An abundance of timber for housing and fuel
c. Grasshopper plagues
d. Vast stretches of desert

Objective 8

_____ 12. Social isolation was a characteristic of life on the Plains because
a. the competitive frontier spirit did not create an atmosphere conducive to social interaction.
b. the rugged terrain made traveling difficult.
c. the absence of farm machinery resulted in no time for socializing.
d. farmhouses on the 160-acre tracts received by settlers under the Homestead Act were widely separated.

Objective 8

_____ 13. Which of the following helped lessen the sense of isolation experienced by farm families in the Plains in the late nineteenth century?
a. Railroad expansion
b. The radio
c. The telegraph
d. Rural Free Delivery

Objectives 2 and 9

_____ 14. The extension of the farming frontier, including the conquering of the Plains, would not have been possible without
a. the expanded use of farm machinery.
b. new pesticides.
c. better fertilizers.
d. extensive use of migrant labor.

Objectives 2 and 9

_____   15. The federal government encouraged the advancement of farming technology by
            a. subsidizing the research of George Washington Carver.
            b. passing the Hatch Act of 1887.
            c. appointing Luther Burbank to head the research division of the Department of
                Agriculture.
            d. funding a vast irrigation network in the Plains.

Essay Questions

Objective 1

1. Discuss the federal government's reservation policy, and explain its impact on western Indian tribes.

Objective 2

2. Discuss the characteristics of the natural-resource frontier and the methods by which developers gained land and extraction rights. What role did the federal government play in the development of this frontier?

Objective 5

3. Discuss the controversy over water rights in the West and assess the importance of this debate and its outcome.

Objective 6

4. Discuss the impact of the expansion of the railroad industry on the American economy.

Objective 7

5. Explain the role of federal, state, and local governments in the expansion of the railroad industry, and discuss the effects of that role.

Objective 8

6. Describe the life of a farm family of the Plains.

CHAPTER 18

The Machine Age, 1877–1920

Learning Objectives

After you have studied Chapter 18 in your textbook and worked through this study guide chapter, you should be able to:

1. Cite the factors related to and resulting from industrialization in the United States.

2. Identify the contributions of Thomas Alva Edison, Henry Ford, and the du Ponts to industrial development in the United States.

3. Discuss the impact of technology on the development of southern industry.

4. Explain and assess the late-nineteenth-century obsession with time studies and scientific management.

5. Discuss late-nineteenth-century changes in the nature of work, in working conditions, and in the workplace itself, and explain the impact of these changes on American workers.

6. Examine the rise of unionism and the emergence of worker activism in the late nineteenth century, and discuss the reaction of employers, government, and the public to these manifestations of worker discontent.

7. Examine the position of women, children, immigrants, and blacks in the work force and in the union movement in the late nineteenth century.

8. Explain the emergence of the consumer society, and discuss the factors that determined the extent to which working-class Americans were able to participate in this society.

9. Discuss the impact of scientific developments and education on living standards between 1900 and 1920.

10. Discuss the impact of each of the following on American attitudes and lifestyles:
    a. The indoor toilet
    b. Processed and preserved foods
    c. The sewing machine
    d. Department stores and chain stores

11. Explain the characteristics of modern advertising and examine its role in industrial America.

12. Examine the corporate consolidation movement of the late nineteenth century, and discuss the consequences of this movement.

13. Explain and evaluate the ideologies of Social Darwinism, laissez-faire capitalism, and the Gospel of Wealth. Explain the impact of these ideas on workers and on the role of government in society.

14. Discuss and evaluate the ideas and suggested reforms of those who dissented from the ideologies of the Gospel of Wealth, Social Darwinism, and laissez-faire capitalism.

15. Discuss the response of all branches of government at the state and national levels to the corporate consolidation movement on the one hand and to the grievances of workers on the other hand.

Thematic Guide

The theme of Chapter 18 is industrialization as a major component of American expansion in the late nineteenth century. Three technological developments that fostered the "second" industrial revolution of the late nineteenth and early twentieth centuries are mentioned in the chapter's introduction (the rise of electric-powered machines; new applications in the use of chemicals; and expansion of engines powered by internal combustion). The relationship between these three developments and industrialization is obvious in the discussion of Thomas A. Edison and the electric industry, Henry Ford and the automobile industry, the du Ponts and the chemical industry, and the factors that furthered industrialization in certain industries in the South. Keep these developments in mind as you study the chapter, and try to determine which developments apply to the various topics discussed in the chapter.

Industrialism changed the nature of work and in many respects caused an uneven distribution of power among interest groups in American society. Industrial workers were employees rather than producers, and repeating specialized tasks made them feel like appendages to machines. The emphasis on quantity rather than quality further dehumanized the workplace. These factors, in addition to the increased power of the employer, reduced the independence and self-respect of workers, but worker resistance only led employers to tighten restrictions.

Industrialism also brought more women and children into the labor force. Although job opportunities opened for women, most women went into low-paying clerical jobs, and sex discrimination continued in the workplace. Employers also attempted to cut wage costs by hiring more children. Although a few states passed child-labor laws, such laws were difficult to enforce and employers generally opposed state interference in their hiring practices. Effective child-labor legislation would not come until the twentieth century.

As the nature of work changed, workers began to protest low wages, the attitude of employers, the hazards of the workplace, and the absence of disability insurance and pensions. The effectiveness of legislation designed to redress these grievances was usually limited by conservative Supreme Court rulings. Out of frustration, some workers began to participate in unions and in organized resistance. Unionization efforts took various directions. The Knights of Labor tried to ally all workers by creating producer and consumer cooperatives; the American Federation of Labor strove to organize skilled workers to achieve pragmatic objectives; and the Industrial Workers of the World attempted to overthrow capitalist society. The railroad strikes of 1877, the Haymarket riot, and the Homestead and Pullman strikes were all marked by violence, and they exemplify labor's frustration as well as its active and organized resistance. Government intervention against the strikers convinced many workers of the imbalance of interest groups in American society, whereas the middle class began to connect organized working-class resistance with radicalism. Although this perception was by and large mistaken, middle-class fear of social upheaval became an additional force against organized labor.

Not only did industrialization affect the nature of work, it also produced a myriad of products that affected the everyday lives of Americans. As America became a consumer-oriented society, most of its citizens faced living costs that rose faster than wages. Consequently, many people could not take advantage of the new goods and services being offered. But, as has been seen, more women and children became part of the paid labor force. Although many did so out of necessity, others hoped that the additional income would allow the family to participate in the consumer society.

Increased availability of goods and services to a greater number of people was not the only reason for a general improvement in living standards. The era also witnessed advances in medical care, better diets, and improved living conditions. Furthermore, education, more than ever a means to upward mobility, became more readily available through the spread of public education.

American habits and attitudes were further affected by the democratization of convenience that resulted from the indoor toilet and private bathtub. At the same time, the tin can and the icebox altered lifestyles and diet, the sewing machine created a clothing revolution, and department stores and chain stores emerged that both created and served the new consumerism.

As American society became more consumer oriented, brand names for products were created. Used by advertisers to sell products, these brand names in turn created "consumption communities" made up of individuals loyal to those brands. As producers tried to convince consumers of their need for particular products, advertising became more important than ever. And since the major vehicle for advertising in the late nineteenth century was the newspaper, advertising was transformed into news.

Although the American standard of living generally improved during the late nineteenth century, there were unsettling economic forces at work. Although rapid economic growth is a characteristic of the period, the period is also characterized by the economic instability and uncertainty produced by cycles of boom and bust. In an effort to create a sense of order and stability out of the competitive chaos, industrialists turned to economic concentration in the form of pools, trusts, and holding companies. Therefore, the search for order led to the merger movement and to larger and larger combinations that sought domination of their markets through vertical integration.

Defenders of business justified the merger movement and their pursuit of wealth and profits by advancing the "Gospel of Wealth," based on Social Darwinism and on the precepts of laissez-faire capitalism. The business elite also used this philosophy to justify both its paternalistic attitude toward the less fortunate in society and its advocacy of government aid to business. The paradoxes and inconsistencies associated with the Gospel of Wealth gave rise to dissent from sociologists, economists, and reformers. The general public also began to speak against economic concentration in the form of monopolies and trusts. The inability of state governments to resolve the problem led to passage of the Sherman Anti-Trust Act by Congress in 1890, but this legislation represented a vaguely worded political compromise, the interpretation of which was left to the courts. Narrow interpretation by a conservative Supreme Court and failure by government officials to fully support the act meant that it was used more successfully against organized labor than against business combinations, again illustrating the uneven distribution of power among interest groups in late-nineteenth-century American society.

Building Vocabulary

Listed below are important words and terms that you need to know to get the most out of Chapter 18. They are listed in the order in which they occur in the chapter. After carefully looking through the list, refer to a dictionary and jot down the definition of words that you do not know or of which you are unsure.

ply

homage

din

relentless

daunting

innovation

tedious

incandescent

oxidation

filament

publicist

entrepreneur

entice

squelch

facilitate

integral

docile

temperance

debauchery

menial

pervade

burgeoning

induce

catalyst

remonstrate

maim

notorious

acute

liability

rationale

carnage

portend

spontaneous

anarchist

malicious

pragmatic

rhetoric

autonomy

dictum

rout

paternalistic

catechize

charismatic

arbitration

ostensibly

espouse

myriad

scourge

amenity

inequity

vanguard

diversify

relegate

compensate

tentative

exemplify

entity

mammoth

wield

extol

inception

emanate

ardent

eclipse (verb)

profiteering

consign

consumerism

Identification and Significance

After studying Chapter 18 of *A People and a Nation*, you should be able to identify fully *and* explain the historical significance of each item listed below.

1. Identify each item in the space provided. Give an explanation or description of the item. Answer the questions *who, what, where,* and *when.*

2. Explain the historical significance of each item in the space provided. Establish the historical context in which the item exists. Establish the item as the result of or as the cause of other factors existing in the society under study. Answer this question: *What were the political, social, economic, and/or cultural consequences of this item?*

Thomas A. Edison

    Identification

    Significance

Menlo Park

    Identification

    Significance

the patent system

    Identification

    Significance

the Edison Electric Light Company

    Identification

    Significance

George Westinghouse

    Identification

    Significance

Samuel Insull

    Identification

    Significance

the General Electric Company

    Identification

    Significance

Granville T. Woods

    Identification

    Significance

Henry Ford

    Identification

    Significance

mass production and the assembly line

    Identification

    Significance

the Five-Dollar-Day Plan

    Identification

    Significance

the du Pont family

    Identification

    Significance

James B. Duke

    Identification

    Significance

southern textile mills

    Identification

    Significance

economies of scale

    Identification

    Significance

Frederick W. Taylor

    Identification

    Significance

producer versus employee

    Identification

    Significance

the occupational patterns of employed women

    Identification

    Significance

child labor

    Identification

    Significance

the "iron law of wages"

    Identification

    Significance

industrial accidents

Identification

Significance

New York City's Triangle Shirtwaist Company fire

Identification

Significance

Holden v. *Hardy*

Identification

Significance

Lockner v. *New York*

Identification

Significance

Muller v. *Oregon*

Identification

Significance

the general railway strike of 1877

       Identification

       Significance

the National Labor Union

       Identification

       Significance

the Knights of Labor

       Identification

       Significance

Terence V. Powderly

       Identification

       Significance

the Southwestern Railroad System strike of 1886

       Identification

       Significance

the Haymarket riot

Identification

Significance

John P. Altgeld

Identification

Significance

the American Federation of Labor

Identification

Significance

Samuel Gompers

Identification

Significance

the Homestead strike

Identification

Significance

the Pullman strike

    Identification

    Significance

Eugene V. Debs

    Identification

    Significance

the Industrial Workers of the World

    Identification

    Significance

"Mother" Jones, Elizabeth Gurley Flynn, and William D. (Big Bill) Haywood

    Identification

    Significance

the "Uprising of the 20,000"

    Identification

    Significance

the Telephone Operators' Department of the International Brotherhood of Electrical Workers

Identification

Significance

the Women's Trade Union League

Identification

Significance

fraternal societies

Identification

Significance

consumer communities

Identification

Significance

public high school enrollment

Identification

Significance

the indoor toilet

    Identification

    Significance

the tin can

    Identification

    Significance

railroad refrigerator cars

    Identification

    Significance

the home icebox

    Identification

    Significance

John H. Kellogg, William K. Kellogg, and Charles W. Post

    Identification

    Significance

the sewing machine

>Identification

>Significance

department stores and chain stores

>Identification

>Significance

the Great Atlantic and Pacific Tea Company

>Identification

>Significance

modern advertising

>Identification

>Significance

consumption communities

>Identification

>Significance

brand names

     Identification

     Significance

boom and bust business cycles

     Identification

     Significance

pools

     Identification

     Significance

John D. Rockefeller

     Identification

     Significance

the trust

     Identification

     Significance

the holding company

      Identification

      Significance

vertical integration

      Identification

      Significance

the merger movement

      Identification

      Significance

the U.S. Steel Corporation

      Identification

      Significance

Social Darwinism

      Identification

      Significance

the principles of laissez faire

       Identification

       Significance

the Gospel of Wealth

       Identification

       Significance

protective tariffs

       Identification

       Significance

Lester Ward

       Identification

       Significance

Richard Ely, John R. Commons, and Edward Bemis

       Identification

       Significance

Henry George

    Identification

    Significance

Edward Bellamy

    Identification

    Significance

the Sherman Anti-Trust Act

    Identification

    Significance

U. S. v. *E. C. Knight Co.*

    Identification

    Significance

Organizing Information

Chapter 18 deals in part with worker unrest in the late nineteenth century and the reasons for that unrest. Learning Objectives 4 and 5 indicate that, upon completion of this chapter, you should be able to explain the changes in the nature of work and examine the unrest and activism that emerged among workers during the late nineteenth century.

Use this exercise to organize information about the nature of work and worker activism. First indicate the underlying causes of worker unrest—changes in the nature of work, the attitude of employers, and the like. Then answer the questions about specific instances of worker unrest; widespread railroad strikes in 1877, the strike of railroads in the Southwest in 1886, the Haymarket riot, the Homestead strike, and the Pullman strike. The questions are intended to help you hone in on the relevant issues concerning worker activism.

Your professor may want to add additional items to this exercise or ask you to do more extensive research on these events. If you want to do additional research, look at the bibliography at the end of Chapter 18, especially the section entitled "Work and Labor Organization," to find a listing of excellent secondary sources that give detailed analyses of worker activism in the late nineteenth century. In any event, use this section as a guide and modify it to serve your study purposes.

Worker Activism in the Late Nineteenth Century

What were the underlying causes of worker unrest in the late nineteenth century?

Widespread Railroad Strikes in 1877

What were the immediate causes of the strikes?

What demands did the striking workers make?

What tactics did the striking workers use to seek redress of their grievances?

How did employers respond to the workers' demands? How did employers try to end the strikes?

Was there any government (state or federal) involvement in the strikes? Explain.

How did the public respond to the strikes?

What was the outcome of the strikes?

What were the political, social, and economic consequences of the strikes?

Strike of Railroads in the Southwest in 1886

What were the immediate causes of the strike?

What demands did the striking workers make?

What tactics did the striking workers use to seek redress of their grievances?

How did the employers respond to the workers' demands?

How did the employers try to end the strike?

Was there any government (state or federal) involvement in the strike? Explain.

How did the public respond to the strike?

What was the strike's outcome?

What were the political, social, and economic consequences of the strike?

The Haymarket Riot

Why was there a labor demonstration in Chicago on May 1,1886?

What happened at the McCormick plant in Chicago on May 3,1886?

Why was there a labor rally at Haymarket Square on May 4,1886?

What happened at the labor rally on May 4,1886?

What were the consequences (immediate and long-term) of this incident?

The Homestead Strike

What were the immediate causes of the strike?

What demands did the striking workers make?

What tactics did the striking workers use to seek redress of their grievances?

How did the employer respond to the workers' demands? How did the employer try to end the strike?

Was there any government (state or federal) involvement in the strike? Explain.

How did the public respond to the strike?

What was the strike's outcome?

What were the political, social, and economic consequences of the strike?

The Pullman Strike

What were the immediate causes of the strike?

What were the political, social, and economic consequences of the strike?

What demands did the striking workers make?

What tactics did the striking workers use to seek redress of their grievances?

How did the employer respond to the workers' demands?

How did the employer try to end the strike?

Was there any government (state or federal) involvement in the strike? Explain.

How did the public respond to the strike?

What was the strike's outcome?

Interpreting Information

How were economic developments between 1877 and 1920 redefining the status of American factory workers and changing their view of themselves? Does the evidence in Chapter 18 suggest that American workers of 1920 would see themselves as better off than workers of 1877, as worse off, or simply as about the same? Follow the four steps outlined below to both collect the information for and write the working draft of an essay answering those questions.

STEP 1. Referring to your textbook and class notes, answer the following four sets of questions.

Set 1

What innovation in industrial production did Henry Ford introduce in 1903? How did this innovation affect the kind of tasks performed by American industrial workers during the Machine Age?

_____

_____

How specialized and skilled and mentally challenging was the labor performed by the industrial worker? How much variety of activity did the work involve?

_____

_____

Who was Frederick W. Taylor? How did changes in the organization of industrial work, influenced by people such as Taylor, affect the role of individual workers on the factory floor in deciding how and when to work and affect the quality of work as a measure of a worker's value?

_____

_____

How did time-motion research like Taylor's affect the number of people employed in a factory? Their wages? Their on-the-job stress?

_____

_____

How long was the workday? Did early unions reflect worker concern over the length of the workday?

_____

_____

What changed industrial workers into "employees"? What had American workers been before? How do the two roles differ?

_____

_____

How did employers influence what workers did off the job? How did workers react? What did Ford workers have to do to qualify for the profit-sharing part of the Five-Dollar-Day Plan?

_____

_____

How safe was the workplace? What effect did mechanization and automation have on worker safety? What happened to workers injured on the job? What happened to the families of workers who were killed on the job?

_____

_____

How effectively did legislation safeguard workers from harsh or dangerous working conditions? How strong was judicial support for such legislation, especially that of the Supreme Court?

_____

_____

Set 2

What was the "Iron law of wages" and what did it mean to the American industrial worker between 1877 and 1920? What stance did the courts take toward the application of this "law"? What effect did this "law" have on the growth of unions and the loyalty of their members?

_____

_____

How significant was the issue of wages in protests by workers, unions, or otherwise?

_____

_____

How much were workers paid? How much did skilled laborers get? Unskilled laborers? Female factory workers? Did factory workers' incomes rise? Did working class families have other sources of income besides the head-of-household's wages? Did the share of the national wealth in the hands of the working class reflect the proportion of the population in the working class?

_____

_____

What alternative to hourly wages did some employers of factory workers offer? What effect did this alternative basis for establishing workers' pay have on their income? Hours? Pressure on the job?

_____

_____

How secure were jobs? Could workers count on holding their jobs year-round? Were workers hurt by any significant "busts" in the boom-and-bust cycle of American business? When?

_____

_____

Set 3

Did the cost of living increase or decrease during the Machine Age? How much? Did incomes change in the same direction? Did incomes change as fast and as much as the cost of living?

_____

_____

How did economic conditions affect the number and ages of persons in a working-class family who worked outside the home for pay?

_____

_____

_____

How did the nature of working-class families' expenditures change during the Machine Age? What items formerly considered luxuries, if any, were becoming necessities; and what items formerly considered necessities, if any, were becoming luxuries?

_____

_____

What important technological innovations and scientific discoveries affected the healthfulness of and variety in the diet of American factory workers from 1877–1920? Did the diet of American workers and their families improve or decline? Were perishable foods and foods produced in other parts of the country more or less readily available to working class families? Why?

_____

_____

How did death rates and life expectancy change during the Machine Age? How did disease-caused deaths change? How did suicide, homicide, and vehicular death rates change?

_____

_____

What changes in technology affected sanitation in the American home and the privacy of individuals in the home during the Machine Age? Did sanitation and privacy increase or decrease?

_____

_____

_____

What innovations affected the amount and kinds of clothing working class families had and who produced it? What was the effect of these innovations?

_____

_____

What, if any, opportunities opened up during the Machine Age that would make it reasonable for factory workers to think they or their children could move upward into the middle or upper economic classes? Were there any signs that people trapped on the lowest rungs of the economic ladder were taking advantage of whatever opportunities were available for their own or their children's advancement?

_____

_____

Set 4

How much help or sympathy would it have been reasonable for factory workers to expect from employers? What did employers say should determine wages and working conditions? How did such big employers as George Pullman and Jay Gould respond to workers' attempts to negotiate for better wages and working conditions? What did the outcome of Terence V. Powderly's efforts to work with employers to improve working conditions suggest about the willingness of big business to compromise with workers on matters of working conditions and wages?

_____

_____

Which, if any, Machine Age people, government agencies, or organizations did anything about providing pensions, insurance, workmen's compensation, job training, and aid for families of striking workers? Did these people, agencies, or organizations represent employers, government or the public, or the workers themselves?

_____

_____

What did legislation passed by Congress indicate about the legislative branch of government's sympathies regarding domestic consumer prices? Was Congress concerned with protecting factory workers from having to pay high prices for consumer goods?

_____

_____

How did the public view factory workers who participated in protests of working conditions? Would public attitudes toward them and their efforts to get better wages and working conditions suggest that the public trusted, respected, and valued them? What responses from the public suggested the public sympathized or did not sympathize with worker complaints and protests?

_____

_____

_____

What did the responses of Presidents Hayes and Cleveland suggest about government sympathies or tolerance of worker protests?

_____

_____

What court decisions indicated whether the courts were sympathetic or not sympathetic to worker complaints about working conditions? Was the court sympathetic to workers? Which segment of society did the Supreme Court's interpretation of the Fourteenth Amendment benefit? Which did it harm? What did the Supreme Court's decisions arising out of antitrust cases suggest about the Court's view of workers' attempts to influence working conditions and wages through strikes and protests and big business's attempts to control competition and consumer prices through creation of monopolies, trusts, and pools?

_____

_____

STEP 2. State your conclusion about each set of questions based on your answers for that set.

Conclusion 1 (Your answer to this question: What impact did the advent of the Machine Age have on American industrial workers and the conditions under which they worked?)

_____

_____

Conclusion 2 (Your answer to this question: What impact did changes in the workplace during the Machine Age have on American industrial workers' income and their ability to increase it?)

_____

_____

Conclusion 3 (Your answer to this question: How did the overall quality of life change for the factory worker during the Machine Age [1877–1920]? Would it be reasonable for large numbers of such workers to look to the future with hope and optimism?)

_____

_____

Conclusion 4 (Your answer to this question: On what or whom could factory workers depend for sympathy or, more importantly, for help in improving their working and living conditions and, indeed, their general economic outlook?)

_____

_____

STEP 3. Basing your response on the *sum* of your four conclusions, state your overall conclusion. (Your one-sentence response to this question: Would developments and features of the American economy between 1877 and 1920 lead realistic American workers of 1920 to portray themselves as better off than workers of 1877, or worse off, or simply as about the same?)

_____

_____

STEP 4. In your Reading Notebook, write the working draft of an essay, using the answer you wrote to complete Step 3 as its thesis, the conclusions you wrote to complete Step 2 as its major subpoints, and information in your four sets of answers as your specific supporting concrete details/evidence.

Ideas and Details

Objective 2

_____   1.   Which of the following innovations by Henry Ford reduced the cost of his automobiles
                 and made them more affordable?
                 a.   Interchangeable parts
                 b.   The machine-tool industry
                 c.   The assembly line
                 d.   Team production

Objective 4

_____   2.   The emphasis on efficient production had the effect of
                 a.   making skilled labor more valuable.
                 b.   lowering the wage scale for most workers.
                 c.   increasing the size of the work force.
                 d.   making time as important as quality in the measure of acceptable work.

Objectives 5 and 6

_____   3.   In relation to the wage system, most wage earners
                 a.   appreciated the freedom it gave them to negotiate with the employer for higher
                      wages.
                 b.   recognized that job competition among workers caused the base pay of all workers
                      to rise steadily.
                 c.   advocated that Congress establish a minimum wage for all workers.
                 d.   felt trapped and exploited in a system controlled by employers.

Objectives 6 and 15

_____   4. In cases involving legislation that limited working hours, the Supreme Court
           a. declared that Congress, not the states, had the power to enact such legislation.
           b. declared that the Fourteenth Amendment did not apply to state actions.
           c. reduced the impact of such legislation by narrowly interpreting which jobs were
               dangerous and which workers needed protection.
           d. consistently upheld the regulatory powers of the states.

Objective 6

_____   5. The Knights of Labor, unlike the American Federation of Labor,
           a. advocated the use of violence against corporate power.
           b. pressed for pragmatic objectives that would bring immediate benefits to workers.
           c. believed in using strikes as the primary weapon against employers.
           d. welcomed all workers, including women, blacks, and immigrants.

Objective 6

_____   6. Which of the following was a consequence of the Haymarket riot?
           a. National legislation was passed mandating an eight-hour workday for industry in
               the United States.
           b. The military forces of the United States were put on alert because of fear of
               revolution.
           c. Revival of the middle-class fear of radicalism led to the strengthening of police
               forces and armories in many cities.
           d. The Knights of Labor was strengthened.

Objectives 6 and 7

_____   7. Which of the following is true of the Women's Trade Union League?
           a. Although initially dominated by middle-class women, working-class leaders gained
               control in the 1910s.
           b. Although its members opposed the idea, its leaders actively worked for a
               constitutional amendment guaranteeing equal rights to women.
           c. Both its leaders and its members worked tirelessly against extension of the vote to
               women.
           d. As an anarchist organization, it advocated working-class unity and the waging of
               war against capitalist society.

Objective 8

_____   8. Data on wages and living costs in the late nineteenth and early twentieth centuries indicate which of the following?
  a. Most working-class wage earners suffered because of declining wages and increasing living costs.
  b. While wages rose for farmers and factory workers, they declined for most members of the middle class.
  c. While incomes rose for most workers, the cost of living usually rose at a higher rate.
  d. Professional workers suffered more from the rising cost of living than did industrial workers.

Objective 10

_____   9. As a result of the indoor bathroom, Americans of the later nineteenth and early twentieth centuries
  a. became conscious of personal appearance for the first time.
  b. viewed bodily functions in a more unpleasant light.
  c. insisted on private facilities in hotels.
  d. were unconcerned about human pollution.

Objectives 8 and 11

_____   10. The main task of advertisers in a society of abundance is to
  a. respond to an individual's particular need by offering a product that uniquely fills that need.
  b. persuade groups of consumers that they have a need for a particular product.
  c. display products in an attractive way.
  d. convince the consumer that a particular product is a quality product offered at a fair price.

Objective 12

_____   11. Businessmen turned to devices like trusts and holding companies because
  a. they were a means by which to combat the uncertainty of the business cycle.
  b. such cooperative business arrangements were responsive to consumer needs.
  c. they allowed business owners to concentrate on quality production while financial specialists handled monetary matters.
  d. they encouraged an open market in which many people had economic opportunity.

Objective 13

_____   12. Social Darwinists believed that in a free society run in accordance with natural law
  a. there would be no poverty.
  b. power would flow into the hands of the most capable people.
  c. wealth would be distributed equally.
  d. people would become less aggressive.

Objective 13

_____ 13. The philosophy accepted by most businessmen in the late nineteenth century included the idea that
   a. government could intervene if it were doing so to protect the disadvantaged.
   b. government power could rightly be used to protect consumers from unfair prices.
   c. government should extend a helping hand to workers by encouraging the development of labor organizations.
   d. government should extend a helping hand to business interests through tariff protection.

Objective 14

_____ 14. Lester Ward expressed the belief that
   a. cooperative action and government intervention could be useful in creating a better society.
   b. business forms, like life forms, evolved from the simple to the complex as part of the natural order of things.
   c. tampering with natural economic laws would lead to economic disaster.
   d. the government had no responsibility in society other than national defense.

Objective 15

_____ 15. In the case of _U.S._ v. _E. C. Knight Co._, the Supreme Court
   a. held all trusts to be illegal.
   b. strengthened the powers of the Interstate Commerce Commission.
   c. reduced the government's power under the Sherman Anti-Trust Act to combat combinations in restraint of trade.
   d. held that workers had the right to organize and strike.

Essay Questions

Objectives 4 and 5

1. Discuss the grievances of workers in the late nineteenth century, the means by which they sought redress and the effectiveness of those means.

Objectives 5, 6, and 15

2. Discuss the Haymarket riot, the Homestead strike, and the Pullman strike. Explain the reaction of the government and the public to these instances of labor unrest.

Objective 7

3. Examine the changing position of women in the labor market in the late nineteenth century.

Objectives 9 and 10

4. Indicate the developments that made the indoor bathroom possible, and discuss its impact on American attitudes and life styles.

Objective 11

5. Explain changes that took place in advertising in American society in the late nineteenth and early twentieth centuries, and discuss the impact of these changes on American society.

Objective 13

6. Explain the concept of Social Darwinism and its use by business leaders to justify their position and wealth in society.

Objectives 13 and 15

7. Analyze the relationship between the three branches of the federal government and the business community in the period between 1877 and 1920.

CHAPTER 19

The Vitality and Turmoil of Urban Life, 1877–1920

Learning Objectives

After you have studied Chapter 19 in your textbook and worked through this study guide chapter, you should be able to:

1. Examine the factors responsible for the birth of the modern city in late nineteenth- early twentieth-century America, and discuss the characteristics associated with the modern city.

2. Examine the factors responsible for urban growth during the late nineteenth century.

3. Discuss the similarities and differences between the immigrants of the period from 1880 to 1920 and previous immigrants.

4. Examine the interaction between immigrants of the late nineteenth century and American society, and discuss the changes brought about by this interaction.

5. Discuss the impact of prejudice and discrimination on nonwhite Americans of the late nineteenth century.

6. Examine the problems associated with American cities of the late nineteenth century, and evaluate the responses to those problems.

7. Examine the means by which upward socioeconomic mobility could be achieved in the late nineteenth century, and discuss the extent to which such mobility was possible.

8. Examine and evaluate the urban political machines and political bosses of the late nineteenth century.

9. Discuss the ideological basis of the urban reform movement, and explain the successes and failures of the reformers associated with this movement.

10. Examine the impact of engineers on urban America and on home life in the United States from 1877 to 1920.

11. Examine household, family, and individual life patterns in American society between 1877 and 1920.

12. Explain the emergence and characteristics of each of the following, and discuss their impact on American society:
    a.   Sports
    b.   Show business
    c.   Moving pictures
    d.   Still pictures and the phonograph
    e.   Popular journalism

13. Define *cultural pluralism*, and discuss its impact on American society.

Thematic Guide

In Chapter 19, we examine urban growth, the third major theme (along with natural resource development and industrialization) associated with American expansion in the late nineteenth century. Urban industrial development combined with mass transportation and urban growth destroyed the old pedestrian city of the past. The physical expansion of the city attracted industry, capital, and people. By the early 1900s, the modern American city, with its urban sprawl and distinct districts, was clearly taking shape.

Cities grow in three ways: through physical expansion, by natural increase, and through migration and immigration. In the late nineteenth century, in-migration from domestic and foreign sources was the most important cause of urban growth. The section "Peopling the Cities: Migrants and Immigrants" shows that native whites, foreigners, and African Americans were the three major migrant groups of the period. We consider why these groups moved to the cities, how they differed from and resembled each other, and, in the case of immigrants, how they differed from and resembled earlier immigrants. In discussing the cultural interaction between foreign immigrants and American society, we find that the city of the late nineteenth century nurtured the cultural diversity that so strongly characterizes modern America.

Rapid urban growth created and then intensified such urban problems as inadequate housing, overcrowding, and intolerable living conditions. This situation led to reforms that strengthened the hand of local government in regulating the construction of housing, but American attitudes toward the profit motive and toward private enterprise placed limits on the reforms enacted.

Although scientific and technological breakthroughs improved urban life, the burden of urban poverty remained. While some reformers began to look to environmental factors to explain poverty, traditional attitudes toward poverty—attitudes that blamed the victim—restricted what most Americans were willing to do to alleviate poverty. Even private agencies insisted on extending aid only to the "worthy poor" and on teaching the moral virtues of thrift and sobriety.

Urban areas also had to contend with crime and violence. Whether crime actually increased or was merely more conspicuous can be debated, but in many cases native whites blamed crime on those they considered to be "outsiders" in American society—foreigners and blacks. The ethnic diversity of the cities, combined with urban overcrowding and uncertain economic conditions, hardened antiforeign and white-racist attitudes and increased the incidence of violence in urban areas. Uneven, sometimes prejudicial, application of laws by law enforcement officials raised questions about the nature of justice, equality, and individual freedom in American society.

In the section "Promises of Mobility," we discuss the two basic ways by which upward socioeconomic mobility was made possible within American society. Certain myths concerning the availability and extent of upward mobility are dispelled, and the limiting impact of sexism and racism is discussed.

As America became a culturally pluralistic society, interest groups often competed for influence and opportunity in the political arena. This competition and the rapidity of change in the urban environment caused confusion. In the midst of this confusion, political machines and political bosses emerged to bring some order out of chaos. Eventually, however, a civic reform movement developed. Most reformers strove for efficiency and focused on structural reform in city government. Some concerned themselves with social reform and with city planning and city design. Whatever the goal, American attitudes limited and undermined these reforms. As noted in the textbook, "urban reform merged idealism with naiveté and insensitivity."

Despite these limiting attitudes, there were technical accomplishments in solving problems such as sanitation, garbage disposal, streetlighting, and bridge and street building. In this respect city engineers, who applied their technical expertise to urban problems, became very important to city governments. Furthermore, engineers also had a tremendous impact on the home life of Americans.

In "Family Life" the focus of the chapter shifts to a discussion of the family in American society and American life. Once distinctions are made between the household and the family, we identify the factors responsible for the high percentage of nuclear families. We also note the varying ways in which households expanded and contracted to meet changing circumstances. Changes in society changed family, as well as individual, lifestyles. Reduction in family size freed adults at an earlier age from the responsibilities of parenthood. Longer life expectancy increased the number of older adults. Childhood and adolescence became more distinct stages of life. As the authors state: "Americans became more conscious of age and peer influence. People's roles in school, in the family, on the job, and in the community came to be determined by age more than by any other characteristic."

The leisure-time revolution brought about by labor-saving devices and by a shortened workweek changed the American way of life. As the average workweek decreased to forty-seven hours by 1910, individuals turned to croquet, bicycling, tennis, and golf as favorite leisure activities. Entertaining the public through spectator sports, the circus, show business, and moving pictures became a profitable business endeavor. Moreover, the mass production of sound and images made possible by the phonograph and the still camera dissolved the uniqueness of experience. Even news was transformed into big business and a mass commodity by the "yellow journalism" tactics of Joseph Pulitzer and William Randolph Hearst.

Mass entertainment and mass culture had a nationalizing effect; however, even though show business provided new opportunities for women, blacks, and immigrants, too often it reinforced prejudicial stereotypes—especially concerning black Americans. Furthermore, in an America that was becoming more culturally diverse, different groups pursued their own form of leisure. This often caused concern on the part of some reformers who tended to label individuals as un-American if their activities did not conform to the Puritan traditions of the nation's past. These reformers wanted to use government to impose their values and lifestyles on immigrant groups. These attempts to create a homogeneous society led to questions concerning the role of government in society and in the life of the individual, questions that are as relevant today as they were in the late nineteenth century.

The cultural pluralism that resulted from the late nineteenth-century influx of immigrants, African Americans, and native white Americans into expanding cities is one of the dominant characteristics of modern America. This heterogeneity is one of America's greatest strengths and has created the richness and the variety that is modern America. In large measure, this diversity is also a reason for the failure of attempts to enforce homogeneity, because the very presence of a number of competing cultural groups prevented any one group from becoming dominant. This has meant, overall, the continued protection of individual rights and the gradual inclusion of more and more groups under the protective umbrella of the Bill of Rights.

Building Vocabulary

Listed below are important words and terms that you need to know to get the most out of Chapter 19.
They are listed in the order in which they occur in the chapter. After carefully looking through the list,
refer to a dictionary and jot down the definition of words that you do not know or of which you are
unsure.

travail

inebriated

nativist

inception

disquieting

mercantile

myriad

centrifugal

centripetal

facilitate

prima donna

burgeon

induce

pogrom

transiency

cosmopolitan

enclave

volition

transitory

intersperse

covenant

amulet

repertoire

accede

minimal

foment

epitomize

erratic

indigence

rationalize

disparate

notoriety

desperado

conspicuous

modicum

demeaning

temper (verb)

adept

freelance

unsavory

savvy

median

resilient

enmesh

pneumatic

scruple

demure

titillate

pander

foible

whet

potentate

sordid

muckraking

homogenizing

apolitical

Identification and Significance

After studying Chapter 19 of *A People and a Nation,* you should be able to identify fully *and* explain the historical significance of each item listed below.

1. Identify each item in the space provided. Give an explanation or description of the item. Answer the questions *who, what, where,* and *when.*

2. Explain the historical significance of each item in the space provided. Establish the historical context in which the item exists. Establish the item as the result of or as the cause of other factors existing in the society under study. Answer this question: *What were the political, social, economic, and/or cultural consequences of this item?*

product specialization

    Identification

    Significance

the electric trolley

    Identification

    Significance

the electric interurban railway

    Identification

    Significance

urban growth

    Identification

    Significance

African American migration

    Identification

    Significance

the "new" immigration

    Identification

    Significance

residential mobility

    Identification

    Significance

urban borderlands

    Identification

    Significance

ghettos

    Identification

    Significance

barrios

    Identification

    Significance

Conservative Judaism

    Identification

    Significance

New York State tenement legislation

    Identification

    Significance

"model tenements"

    Identification

    Significance

public health regulations

    Identification

    Significance

steel-frame construction

    Identification

    Significance

urban poverty

    Identification

    Significance

Charity Organization Societies

    Identification

    Significance

Rufus Minor

    Identification

    Significance

urban crime and violence

    Identification

    Significance

the East St. Louis riot of 1917

    Identification

    Significance

occupational mobility

    Identification

    Significance

acquisition of property

    Identification

    Significance

professional law enforcement

    Identification

    Significance

political machines

>   Identification

>   Significance

the political boss

>   Identification

>   Significance

the urban reform movement

>   Identification

>   Significance

Mayors Hazen Pingree, Samuel Jones, and Tom Johnson

>   Identification

>   Significance

social reformers

>   Identification

>   Significance

the settlement house

>   Identification

>   Significance

Jane Hunter and Modjeska Simkins

>   Identification

>   Significance

the City Beautiful movement

>   Identification

>   Significance

city engineers

>   Identification

>   Significance

family and household structures in late nineteenth- and early twentieth-century America

>   Identification

>   Significance

the birthrate decline

    Identification

    Significance

the practice of boarding

    Identification

    Significance

the importance of kinship

    Identification

    Significance

the gay subculture

    Identification

    Significance

the stages of life

    Identification

    Significance

board games

       Identification

       Significance

baseball, croquet, bicycling, tennis, golf, college football, and basketball

       Identification

       Significance

Intercollegiate Athletic Association

       Identification

       Significance

the circus

       Identification

       Significance

popular drama

       Identification

       Significance

musical comedies

    Identification

    Significance

George M. Cohan and Jerome Kern

    Identification

    Significance

vaudeville

    Identification

    Significance

Eva Tanguay

    Identification

    Significance

the minstrel show

    Identification

    Significance

Burt Williams

     Identification

     Significance

moving pictures

     Identification

     Significance

The Birth of a Nation

     Identification

     Significance

the still camera

     Identification

     Significance

the phonograph

     Identification

     Significance

Joseph Pulitzer and William Randolph Hearst

Identification

Significance

yellow journalism

Identification

Significance

mass-circulation magazines

Identification

Significance

the telephone

Identification

Significance

cultural pluralism

Identification

Significance

Organizing Information

Much of Chapter 19 is devoted to problems faced by city dwellers, especially the urban poor, and how they, with or without much help from others, coped with those problems. As the chapter points out, most of the help that was available came with disadvantages.

To get a clearer understanding of what help was available to the urban poor and the advantages and disadvantages of that help, complete the chart "Sources of Help for the Urban Poor, 1877-1920."

The chart's first column identifies likely sources of support or aid for the problem areas listed in the five columns ranged to the right. Indicate in the appropriate blocks the kind of help offered and advantages and disadvantages of that help.

(If a source in Column 1 rarely if ever made help available, you will have to leave the succeeding blocks to the right blank. That of course will serve as a reminder of which groups or agencies one might expect to offer help that in fact provided little or no help.)

Wherever you see word "Examples" in the first column, list one or two examples of the particular category of support or aid if any specific examples are mentioned in the chapter.

Sources of Help for the Urban Poor, 1877-1920						
Sources of aid, Support		Problem Areas				
		Working Conditions	Prejudice, Discrimin-ation	Crime and Violence	Employment, Job-Prepared-ness Training	Health and Safety
Government Welfare Agencies and Programs Examples:	A D V A N					
	D I S A D V					
Family—Bonds of Kinship Examples:	A D V A N					
	D I S A D V					
Neighborhood Examples:	A D V A N					
	D I S A D V					

Sources of Help for the Urban Poor, 1877-1920 (continued)						
Sources of aid, Support		**Problem Areas**				
		Working Conditions	Prejudice, Discrimination	Crime and Violence	Employment, Job-Preparedness Training	Health and Safety
Private Charity and Charity Organizations Examples:	A D V A N					
	D I S A D V					
Political machines Examples:	A D V A N					
	D I S A D V					
Social reformers, settlement houses Examples:	A D V A N					
	D I S A D V					

Sources of Help for the Urban Poor, 1877-1920 (concluded)

Sources of aid, Support		Problem Areas				
		Working Conditions	Prejudice, Discrimin-ation	Crime and Violence	Employment, Job-Prepared-ness Training	Health and Safety
Political reformers, reform mayors Examples:	A D V A N					
	D I S A D V					
Technology, engineers Examples:	A D V A N					
	D I S A D V					
Other Examples:	A D V A N					
	D I S A D V					

Interpreting Information

Referring to your entries in the Organizing Information chart, focus now on two groups among the urban poor and their special problems and means of coping: poor immigrants and poor African Americans. Based on the information you have provided in the chart plus any other information from Chapter 19 and your class notes, write a mock essay that responds directly to this question:

> Discuss the problems that commonly assailed immigrants and African Americans who found themselves among America's urban poor between 1877 and 1920 and the kind of help in coping with those problems that they found. What price did the urban poor have to pay to take advantage of the kinds of help available?

To help you organize what you have to say, you may want to create now a new, simpler chart centered on the immigrants and African Americans among the urban poor of 1877-1920. Could you compare or contrast the coping strategies of these two groups?

Ideas and Details

Objective 1

_____   1.   Which of the following was the primary agent in making suburban life practical and possible?
a.   Long-term mortgage financing
b.   The automobile
c.   Neighborhood shopping centers
d.   Mechanized mass transit

Objective 2

_____   2.   Which of the following was the major contributor to urban population growth in late-nineteenth- and early-twentieth-century America?
a.   Natural increase
b.   Mergers
c.   Migration and immigration
d.   Annexation of outlying areas

Objective 5

_____   3. Black migrants to urban areas differed from other migrants in which of the following
               ways?
               a. Black migrants were more likely to be males.
               b. Blacks did not have the rural background of most other migrants.
               c. Blacks found it more difficult to get factory employment.
               d. Black migrants did not usually move for economic reasons.

Objective 3

_____   4. "New" immigrants differed from "old" immigrants in that new immigrants were
               a. more likely to be non-Protestants.
               b. less family oriented.
               c. attracted to rural as opposed to urban areas.
               d. escaping from persecution rather than seeking opportunity.

Objective 4

_____   5. Information about immigrant cultures in the United States supports the statement that
               most immigrants
               a. quickly shed Old World attitudes and behaviors.
               b. retained their native languages.
               c. found that religion was the one area not affected by American society.
               d. found that their habits and attitudes had to be modified as they interacted with
                   American society.

Objective 6

_____   6. As a result of concern about urban housing conditions in the late nineteenth and early
               twentieth centuries,
               a. private investors pooled their resources to build low-income housing.
               b. some states enacted legislation that imposed light, ventilation, and safety codes on
                   new tenement buildings.
               c. federal legislation was enacted that established a standard housing code throughout
                   the United States.
               d. state governments established subsidized housing for the disadvantaged.

Objective 6

_____   7. In the face of urban poverty, most Americans accepted which of the following beliefs?
               a. One's socioeconomic position within society is based largely on luck.
               b. Poverty can be cured by improving the conditions in which people live and work.
               c. Poverty is a sign that a person is unfit, weak, and lazy.
               d. The government can be a force for good in alleviating the ills of poverty.

Objective 7

_____ 8. Studies of occupational mobility in the late nineteenth and early twentieth centuries indicate that
- a. American society had become a static society in which there was little chance for occupational advancement.
- b. at least 10 percent of the population could expect to travel the rags-to-riches path.
- c. major urban areas had approximately equal upward and downward occupational movement.
- d. advancement resulting from movement to a higher status job was relatively common among white males.

Objective 8

_____ 9. Urban political machines successfully gained and retained their power because they
- a. were successful in winning and retaining popular support.
- b. brought honesty to city government.
- c. lowered taxes by making city government more efficient.
- d. distributed favors evenly to all groups and classes.

Objective 9

_____ 10. Most civic reform leaders
- a. were among the biggest supporters of the accomplishments of political bosses.
- b. concentrated on structural changes rather than on dealing with social problems.
- c. were interested in making government responsive to the social ills of urban society.
- d. supported district representation in city government.

Objective 9

_____ 11. Which of the following statements best describes the goals of settlement-house founders?
- a. They wanted to establish an agency through which immigrants could find housing and employment.
- b. They wanted to provide for the needs of street people.
- c. They wanted to establish city-run, tax-supported social welfare agencies.
- d. They wanted to offer a variety of activities through which the lives of working-class people could be improved.

Objective 11

_____ 12. The practice of boarding was important in which of the following ways?
- a. It provided a means through which people could find employment.
- b. It provided a transitional stage for many young people between living with their parents and setting up their own households.
- c. It provided childcare facilities to working mothers.
- d. It contributed significantly to overcrowding.

Objective 12

_____ 13. As a result of the popularity of bicycling,
   a. the activities of men and women became more separated.
   b. groups began to demand lighted suburban streets.
   c. women's fashions began to change toward freer styles.
   d. stop and go lights were installed in most cities.

Objectives 5 and 12

_____ 14. Information concerning Burt Williams's career and *The Birth of a Nation* supports which of the following?
   a. Blacks were subjected to prejudicial stereotyping in popular entertainment in the United States.
   b. The ethnic humor in popular entertainment was gentle and sympathetic.
   c. Show business provided economic opportunities to immigrants.
   d. Vaudeville was the most popular form of entertainment in early-twentieth-century America.

Objective 13

_____ 15. The "new" American society created by the urbanization of the late nineteenth century was
   a. a pluralistic society in which different groups competed for power, wealth, and status.
   b. a society in which various ethnic groups had blended into one, unified people.
   c. a smoothly functioning society.
   d. a society in which most people accepted government as an agent for moral reform.

Essay Questions

Objective 1

1. Examine the impact of mass transportation on late-nineteenth-century American cities.

Objective 3

2. Discuss the similarities and differences between "old" immigrants and "new" immigrants, and examine the response of Americans to the latter.

Objective 4

3. Discuss the interaction between Old World culture and New World reality as experienced by immigrants to the United States in the late nineteenth and early twentieth centuries. What changes in immigrant culture resulted from these interactions?

Objective 6

4. Discuss the problem of urban poverty in the United States and the responses of Americans to this problem in the late nineteenth century.

Objective 6

5. Discuss the problem of urban crime and the responses of Americans to this problem in the late nineteenth century.

Objective 7

6. Discuss occupational mobility as a means to get ahead and improve one's status in American society between 1870 and 1920.

Objective 8

7. Analyze the emergence and evaluate the effectiveness of the urban political machines.

Objective 11

8. Explain the usefulness of the practice of boarding in American society during the late nineteenth and early twentieth centuries.

Objective 12

9. Discuss the emergence of mass entertainment as a commodity in American society.

Objective 12

10. Discuss the characteristics of popular journalism in late-nineteenth-century America.

CHAPTER 20
Gilded Age Politics, 1877–1900

Learning Objectives

After you have studied Chapter 20 in your textbook and worked through this study guide chapter, you should be able to:

1. Discuss the characteristics of American politics at the national and state levels during the Gilded Age.

2. Discuss the major political and economic issues of the Gilded Age, and examine governmental action on these issues.

3. Explain the characteristics of American presidents during the Gilded Age, and discuss how each carried out the duties of his office.

4. Explain the social, economic, and political oppression of southern blacks during the late nineteenth century, and discuss the response of the Supreme Court to this oppression.

5. Examine the progress of the women's suffrage movement during the Gilded Age.

6. Discuss the various forces affecting the lives of southern, midwestern, and western farmers during the late nineteenth century, and explain the social, economic, and political impact of these forces.

7. Explain the organizational and ideological development of rural activism from the Grange through the formation of the Populist party and the 1896 presidential election, and discuss the roadblocks encountered by the Populists.

8. Explain the causes and consequences of the depression of the 1890s, and evaluate Grover Cleveland's response to the depression.

9. Discuss the nature and extent of working-class activism during the era of protest, and explain the reaction of government officials and the public to this activism.

10. Analyze the presidential campaign and election of 1896, and explain the political and economic significance of the outcome.

Thematic Guide

In Chapter 20, we focus on the interaction of the political, economic, and social forces within American society during the Gilded Age. This period is characterized by high public interest in local, state, and national elections, political balance between Democrats and Republicans at the national level, and factional and personal feuds within the two parties. Democrats and Republicans in Congress were split on the major national issues: sectional controversies, civil service reform, railroad regulation, tariff policy, and monetary policy. Though Congress debated these issues, factionalism, interest-group politics, and political equilibrium resulted in the passage of vaguely worded, ineffective legislation such as the Pendleton Civil Service Act, the Interstate Commerce Act, and the Sherman Anti-Trust Act. Combined with a conservative Supreme Court, weak presidential leadership, and political campaigns that focused on issues of personality rather than issues of substance, these factors caused the postponement of decisions on major issues affecting the nation and its citizens.

The political impasse built up frustration within aggrieved groups in the nation. Southern blacks, who lived under the constant threat of violence and who remained economically dependent on whites, had to endure new forms of social oppression in the form of disfranchisement and "Jim Crow" laws. This oppression was, in turn, upheld by the Supreme Court, which interpreted the Fourteenth Amendment narrowly. Women were frustrated in their attempts to gain the right to vote by the sexist attitudes prevalent in the male-dominated power structures of the era. Aggrieved workers turned to organized labor, to strikes, and, at times, to violence (discussed in Chapter 18). Aggrieved farmers also began to organize. In "Agrarian Unrest and Populism," we examine the reasons for agrarian discontent and trace the manifestation of that discontent from the Grange, through the Farmers' Alliances, to the formation of the Populist party and the drafting of the Omaha platform in 1892.

The depression of the 1890s added to the woes of the United States. President Grover Cleveland failed to deal with the crisis effectively, and an air of crisis settled over the nation. Workers' protests multiplied; the Socialist Party of America, under the leadership of Eugene V. Debs, reorganized; Coxey's Army, demanding a federal jobs program, marched on the nation's capital; and fear of social revolution led business owners and government officials to use brute force to control what they perceived to be radical protest.

As the crisis persisted, the Populist party gained ground but was hampered both by the reluctance of voters to abandon their loyalties to the two major parties and by issues of race. At the national level, Populists, convinced that the "money power" and its imposition of the gold standard on the nation was the root cause of farm distress and the nationwide depression, continued to call for a return of government to the people and crusaded for the "free and unlimited coinage of silver."

The frustrations that had built up in the Gilded Age—an age of transition from rural to urban, from agrarian to industrial society—came to a head in the emotionally charged presidential contest of 1896. An analysis of the issues, outcome, and legacy of this election, which ended the political equilibrium of the age, is offered in the last section of the chapter.

Building Vocabulary

Listed below are important words and terms that you need to know to get the most out of Chapter 20. They are listed in the order in which they occur in the chapter. After carefully looking through the list, refer to a dictionary and jot down the definition of words that you do not know or of which you are unsure.

venality

partisan

exacerbate

avid

coalition

contentious

crassness

flamboyant

aspirant

mesmerize

pompous

roguish

taint

parlay

harangue

cajole

revelation

demented

impetus

potency

gingerly

conciliator

temperate

retort

enfranchise

subjugation

mandate

strident

nostalgic

egalitarianism

collateral

communal

formidable

reprisal

amalgamation

canny

fervor

garner

ominous

vehemence

rebut

injunction

commandeer

dregs

permeate

vestige

corral

quip

repudiate

inequity

succinct

retrograde

personable

Identification and Significance

After studying Chapter 20 of *A People and a Nation,* you should be able to identify fully *and* explain the historical significance of each item listed below.

1. Identify each item in the space provided. Give an explanation or description of the item. Answer the questions *who, what, where,* and *when.*

2. Explain the historical significance of each item in the space provided. Establish the historical context in which the item exists. Establish the item as the result of or as the cause of other factors existing in the society under study. Answer this question: *What were the political, social, economic, and/or cultural consequences of this item?*

"Pitchfork" Ben Tillman

    Identification

    Significance

James G. Blaine

    Identification

    Significance

the Stalwarts, the Half Breeds, and the Mugwumps

    Identification

    Significance

"waving the bloody shirt"

    Identification

    Significance

the Grand Army of the Republic

    Identification

    Significance

the Pendleton Civil Service Act

    Identification

    Significance

Munn v. *Illinois*

    Identification

    Significance

the *Wabash* case

    Identification

    Significance

the Interstate Commerce Act

    Identification

    Significance

the *Maximum Freight Rate* case

    Identification

    Significance

the *Alabama Midlands* case

    Identification

    Significance

the tariff controversy

    Identification

    Significance

the McKinley Tariff of 1890

    Identification

    Significance

the Wilson-Gorman Tariff of 1894

    Identification

    Significance

the Dingley Tariff of 1897

    Identification

    Significance

the currency controversy

     Identification

     Significance

"the Crime of '73"

     Identification

     Significance

the Bland-Allison Act of 1878

     Identification

     Significance

the Sherman Silver Purchase Act of 1890

     Identification

     Significance

Rutherford B. Hayes

     Identification

     Significance

James A. Garfield

    Identification

    Significance

Chester A. Arthur

    Identification

    Significance

the presidential campaign and election of 1884

    Identification

    Significance

Grover Cleveland

    Identification

    Significance

"rum, Romanism, and rebellion"

    Identification

    Significance

the presidential election and campaign of 1888

       Identification

       Significance

Benjamin Harrison

       Identification

       Significance

the Dependents' Pension Act

       Identification

       Significance

the "Billion Dollar Congress"

       Identification

       Significance

the poll tax

       Identification

       Significance

U. S. v. *Reese*

    Identification

    Significance

the Mississippi Plan

    Identification

    Significance

the "grandfather clause"

    Identification

    Significance

the *Civil Rights cases*

    Identification

    Significance

Plessy v. *Ferguson* and *Cummins* v. *County Board of Education*

    Identification

    Significance

Jim Crow laws

    Identification

    Significance

the National Woman Suffrage Association

    Identification

    Significance

the American Woman Suffrage Association

    Identification

    Significance

Susan B. Anthony

    Identification

    Significance

the crop-lien system

    Identification

    Significance

the Grange movement

    Identification

    Significance

the White Hats

    Identification

    Significance

the Farmers' Alliances

    Identification

    Significance

the subtreasury plan

    Identification

    Significance

the Alliance loan plan

    Identification

    Significance

the Populist (People's) party

      Identification

      Significance

the Omaha platform

      Identification

      Significance

James B. Weaver

      Identification

      Significance

the depression of the 1890s

      Identification

      Significance

the Cleveland-Morgan deal

      Identification

      Significance

the Coeur d'Alene strike

Identification

Significance

Karl Marx

Identification

Significance

Daniel DeLeon

Identification

Significance

Eugene V. Debs

Identification

Significance

Jacob S. Coxey

Identification

Significance

free coinage of silver

      Identification

      Significance

the presidential campaign and election of 1896

      Identification

      Significance

William McKinley

      Identification

      Significance

William Jennings Bryan

      Identification

      Significance

the Gold Standard Act

      Identification

      Significance

Organizing Information

To clarify what led to the agrarian revolt and the rise of populism that followed it, complete the chart "The Climate that Nurtured the Agrarian Revolt and the Rise of Populism, 1877-1896." The chart is divided somewhat arbitrarily into two periods, 1877 to 1887 and 1888 to 1896 simply to suggest that conditions did not remain exactly the same throughout the whole twenty years. You are to indicate the racial climate, the stage of the business cycle the nation was experiencing, trends in governmental policies and ways of responding to public unrest and protests, and the kind of protesting that was being engaged in that would make the populist movement predictable. What conditions created the kind of dissatisfaction among first the farmers and then other groups that might explain the rise of populism?

   After you have done that, complete the other two charts related to the agrarian revolt and populism to bring together information that might explain the fate of the populist movement. Why couldn't or wouldn't the groups within the movement unify enough to have greater success than they did? In this phase of the exercise list—in chronological order as far as possible—the specifics called for, whether they are actions, attitudes, decisions, groups or regions. Be concise; all you are doing in this step is providing reminders that you can use for review purposes and for guidance in composing mock essays in preparation for essay questions you might see on your next history test.

The Climate that Nurtured the Agrarian Revolt and the Rise of Populism, 1877-1896					
Racial and Inter-Regional Relations	**Phases of Business Cycle**	**Governmental Policies and Reactions**			**Social and Political Unrest**
		Tariffs	**Currency**	**Public Protest**	
1877 to 1887					
1888 to 1896					

From the Agrarian Revolt to the Populists (1877-1900), Part I				
Difficulties on the Road to Forming a Coalition with Clout				
Natural Constituencies of the Grange, Farmers' Alliances, Populists	**Which Definable Groups or Regions Had the Potential To Create an Alliance?**	**What Aims, Attitudes, or Economic Factors Made These Groups Natural Allies?**	**What Aims, Attitudes, or Economic Factors Divided These Groups?**	**Outcome (In the Campaign and Election of 1895-1896)**
Sections of the Country				
Economic Have-Nots in the Work Force				
Political Power Have-Nots				
Organized Politically Disaffected Groups				
Other—Race, Gender, National Origin, etc.				
Comment, Outcome, or Summary				

From the Agrarian Revolt to the Populists (1877-1900), Part II _Difficulties on the Road to Finding Support in Government_				
Where in the Government the Populists and Their Predecessors Might Have Found Support	**Actions and Attitudes on Tariff Issues of Concern to the Populists and Their Predecessors**	**Actions and Attitudes on Currency Questions of Concern to the Populists and Their Predecessors**	**Actions and Attitudes on Price/Rate and Regulation Issues of Concern to the Populists and Their Predecessors**	**Actions and Attitudes on the Distribution of Political Power (Voting Rights) Affecting the Success of Populists and their Predecessors**
Congress				
President				
Supreme Court				
State Governments				
Comment, Outcome, or Summary				

Interpreting Information

Use the information you supplied in the three Organizing Information charts to help you arrive at a reasonable explanation of why Populism did not enjoy more success than it did.

Begin by expanding your entries in the charts into full notes and then into the working drafts of three separate little discussions, one of the climate that gave rise to the movement, one of the internal problems that served as barriers to unity in and among the key groups within the movement, and a third on external forces that reduced the movement's chances of success.

Be sure to state your one-sentence conclusion (your essay's thesis) in your essay's introductory paragraph and to indicate what the crowning blow marking the movement's ultimate failure was. The entire working draft should explain the failure of Populism.

Ideas and Details

Objective 1

_____   1.   Which of the following characterized politics during the Gilded Age?
          a. Party allegiance among the voters was so evenly distributed that no one party predominated for very long.
          b. Americans insisted that the government actively pursue solutions to social problems.
          c. There was little public interest in national elections.
          d. Political contests were very impersonal.

Objective 2

_____   2.   In cases arising from the Interstate Commerce Act, the Supreme Court
          a. broadly interpreted the regulatory powers of Congress.
          b. established that government aid to private industry was unconstitutional.
          c. reduced the regulatory powers of the Interstate Commerce Commission.
          d. completely rejected the principle of government regulation of industry.

Objectives 2 and 6

_____   3.   The "Crime of '73" refers to passage of
          a. the Dingley Act.
          b. the decision by Congress to stop coining silver dollars.
          c. passage of the Sherman Silver Purchase Act.
          d. passage of the Pendleton Act.

Objective 3

_____ 4. Which of the following words best describes the presidents of the Gilded Age?
a. Inspiring
b. Lazy
c. Honorable
d. Forceful

Objective 1

_____ 5. Which of the following was an important factor in Grover Cleveland's defeat in the presidential election of 1888?
a. The Republicans successfully engaged in vote fraud in Indiana and New York.
b. The British minister in Washington publicly supported Benjamin Harrison.
c. Cleveland's ethnic jokes offended Irish Catholics.
d. Cleveland offended consumers by suddenly calling for higher tariffs.

Objectives 1 and 2

_____ 6. The action taken by Congress on the issue of veterans' pensions demonstrates that
a. Congress was determined to give equal treatment to Union and Confederate veterans.
b. memories of the Civil War no longer had an impact on national politics.
c. Congress was opposed to all forms of welfare legislation.
d. Congress responded to interest-group pressure.

Objective 5

_____ 7. Which of the following was the most common argument used by senators voting against the Women's Suffrage amendment?
a. If women are given the right to vote, they will demand that the nation disarm.
b. Giving women the right to vote will interfere with their family responsibilities.
c. Women are not well enough educated to vote.
d. Women are too emotional to be given the privilege of voting.

Objective 6

_____ 8. As a result of the crop-lien system, many southern farmers
a. were able to increase the prices they received for their goods.
b. sank deeper and deeper into debt.
c. were given the opportunity to become landowners.
d. began to diversify their crops.

Objectives 6 and 7

_____   9. Farmers hoped that implementation of the subtreasury plan would
    a. lower the cost of farm machinery.
    b. make second mortgages available to farmers facing bankruptcy.
    c. provide higher prices for farm products and low-interest loans to farmers.
    d. lower transportation costs for farm goods.

Objectives 6 and 7

_____   10. The Omaha platform called for
    a. the establishment of national agricultural colleges in all states.
    b. a comprehensive welfare program for destitute farmers.
    c. a two-year moratorium on all debts.
    d. government ownership of railroad lines.

Objective 8

_____   11. The broad-based nature of the 1890s depression was the result of
    a. an interdependent economy.
    b. overspeculation in the stock market.
    c. the Sherman Silver Purchase Act.
    d. the withdrawal of foreign investments.

Objective 9

_____   12. Which of the following became the leading spokesperson for American socialism in the late 1890s?
    a. Jacob Riis
    b. Eugene V. Debs
    c. Ignatius Donnelly
    d. Leonidas Polk

Objective 9

_____   13. To end the depression, Jacob Coxey advocated
    a. government aid to business.
    b. a return to the gold standard.
    c. tax cuts to encourage spending.
    d. the infusion of money into the economy through a federal jobs program.

Objectives 4, 7, and 10

_____ 14. The Populists were hampered in their quest for political power by which of the following factors?
  a. The Socialist Party's endorsement of Populist candidates caused confusion in the minds of voters.
  b. Southern Populists called for equality under the law for African Americans throughout the United States.
  c. The disfranchisement of southern African Americans prevented the emergence of a biracial coalition.
  d. Their endorsement of Jacob Coxey's demands caused voters to associate the Populists with extremist causes.

Objectives 7 and 10

_____ 15. Which of the following best explains Bryan's defeat in the 1896 election?
  a. The silver issue prevented Bryan from building an urban-rural coalition.
  b. Bryan could not match McKinley's spirited campaign style.
  c. The Populists refused to endorse Bryan.
  d. Endorsement of Bryan by the Socialist party caused people to believe that he was a radical.

Essay Questions

Objective 1

1. Discuss the nature of politics, political parties, and political campaigns during the Gilded Age.

Objective 2

2. Discuss the problems that led to passage of the Interstate Commerce Act, and assess the act's effectiveness.

Objective 2

3. Explain the tariff issue, and trace tariff legislation from passage of the McKinley Tariff in 1890 through passage of the Dingley Tariff of 1897. What were the consequences of the tariff policies of the United States during this period?

Objective 4

4. Explain the process that led to the disfranchisement of southern blacks and to the segregation of southern society by law. How did the Supreme Court respond to this process?

Objectives 2, 6, and 7

5. Explain the emergence of the farm protest movement, and examine its development through the 1896 election.

Objective 8

6. Discuss the causes and consequences of the depression of the 1890s.

Objectives 2 and 10

7. Examine the personalities and issues of the 1896 presidential campaign, and explain the election's outcome.

CHAPTER 21
The Progressive Era, 1895–1920

Learning Objectives

After you have studied Chapter 21 in your textbook and worked through this study guide chapter, you should be able to:

1. Explain the emergence of progressivism and discuss the movement's basic themes.

2. Discuss the similarities and differences among the ideologies, goals, and tactics of the various groups that constituted the Progressive movement, and analyze the successes and failures of these groups in achieving political, social, and moral reform.

3. Explain the emergence of the Socialist movement, and indicate how it differed from progressivism in ideology, goals, and tactics.

4. Discuss and evaluate the impact of progressive ideas in education, law, and the social sciences.

5. Explain and evaluate the approaches of African Americans, American Indians, and women to the problems they faced during the Progressive era, and discuss the extent to which they were successful in achieving their goals.

6. Explain the relationship between Theodore Roosevelt's political, social, and economic beliefs and his approach toward the major issues of the day.

7. Indicate the reasons for the break between William Howard Taft and Theodore Roosevelt, and explain the impact of this break on the 1912 election.

8. Examine the similarities and differences between Roosevelt and Woodrow Wilson.

9. Explain and evaluate the reform legislation of the Wilson presidency.

10. Assess the political, social, and economic impact of the Progressive era on American society.

Thematic Guide

In Chapter 21, we focus on the Progressive era and progressivism: a series of movements that brought together reform-minded individuals and groups with differing solutions to the nation's problems in the years 1895 to 1920. The progressives were members of nationwide organizations that attempted to affect government policy. They were people interested in urban issues and urban political and social reform. Although progressives came from all levels of society, new middle-class professionals formed the vanguard of the movement and found expression for their ideas in muckraking journalism.

Revolted by corruption and injustice, the new urban middle class called for political reform to make government more efficient, less corrupt, and more accountable. Such government, they believed, could be a force for good in American society. Some business executives argued for a society organized along the lines of the corporate model; women of the elite classes formed the YWCA and the Woman's Christian Temperance Union. Working-class reformers pressed for government legislation to aid labor and improve social welfare. Although some reformers turned to the Socialist party, they were a decided minority and cannot be considered progressives. Progressives generally had far too great a stake in the capitalist system to advocate its destruction and, as a result, were political moderates rather than radicals.

The many facets of progressivism can be seen in the section "Governmental and Legislative Reform." Progressives generally agreed that government power should be used to check the abuses associated with the industrial age, but they did not always agree on the nature of the problem. At the city and state levels, progressives were initially interested in attacking the party system and in effecting political reform designed to make government more honest, more professional, and more responsive to the people. These aims can be seen through the accomplishments of Robert M. La Follette, one of the most effective progressive governors, and in the Seventeenth Amendment, one of the major political reforms achieved by progressives at the national level. Some progressives also worked for social reform at the state level, to protect the well-being of citizens from exploitative corporate power. Still other progressives believed in using the power of government to purify society by effecting moral reform. Such efforts were behind the Eighteenth Amendment and the Mann Act (White Slave Traffic Act).

The Progressive era also witnessed an assault on traditional ideas in education, law, and the social sciences. In the section "New Ideas in Education, Law, Religion, and the Social Sciences," we examine the new ideas, resistance to them, and the changes they brought, and we evaluate those changes. This section also outlines progressive reforms in public health, the religious foundations of much Progressive reform, and the movement based on the pseudoscience of eugenics. The following section, "Challenges to Racial and Sexual Discrimination," describes the dilemma faced by African Americans, American Indians, and women seeking equality in American society. After contrasting the approaches of Booker T. Washington and W. E. B. Du Bois toward white racism, we look at attempts by American Indians to advance their interests through the formation of the Society of American Indians. We then turn to the various aspects of "the woman movement," contrasting the aims and goals of women involved in the women's club movement with those involved in the feminist movement and discussing the contrasting viewpoints of elite women and feminists involved in the suffrage movement.

The Progressive era reached the national level of government when Theodore Roosevelt became president in 1901. We examine Roosevelt's political, economic, and social frame of reference and evaluate the progressive legislation passed during his administration. The contrast between the Taft administration that followed and the Roosevelt years spurred progressives to found the Progressive party under Roosevelt's leadership. We also discuss the similarities and differences between Roosevelt's New Nationalism and Woodrow Wilson's New Freedom, and we examine the reasons for Wilson's election in 1912.

In "Woodrow Wilson and the Extension of Reform," we analyze Wilson's frame of reference and evaluate the legislation passed during his two administrations. The chapter ends with a summary and evaluation of the Progressive era.

Building Vocabulary

Listed below are important words and terms that you need to know to get the most out of Chapter 21. They are listed in the order in which they occur in the chapter. After carefully looking through the list, refer to a dictionary and jot down the definition of words that you do not know or of which you are unsure.

guerrilla

odyssey

ardent

cornucopia

amenity

entrench

aura

spearhead

vexing

alleviate

indignation

adulterate

bourgeois

pinnacle

rebuke

ideological

unobtrusive

expertise

guise

brothel

ostensibly

vista

grapple

supersede

amenable

inviolable

fruition

invidious

perpetuate

assimilation

accommodation

subtle

redress

poignant

bedevil

promulgate

condescension

exhortation

indispensable

inherent

persevere

pariah

suffice

unscrupulous

rebuff

cajole

exposé

malefactors

insurgent

Armageddon

resolute

jurisprudence

exude

repudiate

bellicose

deprivation

Identification and Significance

After studying Chapter 21 of *A People and a Nation,* you should be able to identify fully *and* explain the historical significance of each item listed below.

1. Identify each item in the space provided. Give an explanation or description of the item. Answer the questions *who, what, where,* and *when.*

2. Explain the historical significance of each item in the space provided. Establish the historical context in which the item exists. Establish the item as the result of or as the cause of other factors existing in the society under study. Answer this question: *What were the political, social, economic, and/or cultural consequences of this item?*

Florence Kelley

   Identification

   Significance

interest-group politics

   Identification

   Significance

muckrakers

    Identification

    Significance

direct primaries and nonpartisan elections

    Identification

    Significance

the initiative, the referendum, and the recall

    Identification

    Significance

the Municipal Voters League and the U.S. Chamber of Commerce

    Identification

    Significance

the YWCA and the Woman's Christian Temperance Union

    Identification

    Significance

Alfred E. Smith, Robert F. Wagner, David I. Walsh, and Edward F. Dunne

   Identification

   Significance

Eugene V. Debs

   Identification

   Significance

"old guard" Republicans

   Identification

   Significance

Robert M. La Follette

   Identification

   Significance

southern progressivism

   Identification

   Significance

the Seventeenth Amendment

    Identification

    Significance

the National Child Labor Committee

    Identification

    Significance

the American Association for Old Age Security

    Identification

    Significance

the war on alcohol

    Identification

    Significance

the Eighteenth Amendment

    Identification

    Significance

white slavery

      Identification

      Significance

The Social Evil in Chicago

      Identification

      Significance

the Mann Act

      Identification

      Significance

G. Stanley Hall and John Dewey

      Identification

      Significance

the expansion of colleges and universities

      Identification

      Significance

Oliver Wendell Holmes, Jr.

    Identification

    Significance

Louis D. Brandeis

    Identification

    Significance

Mueller v. *Oregon*, *Lochner* v. *New York*, and *Holden* v. *Hardy*

    Identification

    Significance

Richard T. Ely

    Identification

    Significance

Lester Ward, Albion Small, and Edward Ross

    Identification

    Significance

Charles A. Beard

    Identification

    Significance

the National Consumers League

    Identification

    Significance

the Social Gospel

    Identification

    Significance

eugenics

    Identification

    Significance

Booker T. Washington

    Identification

    Significance

the Atlanta Compromise

    Identification

    Significance

W. E. B. Du Bois

    Identification

    Significance

the Niagara movement

    Identification

    Significance

the National Association for the Advancement of Colored People

    Identification

    Significance

the Society of American Indians

    Identification

    Significance

"the woman movement"

    Identification

    Significance

the women's club movement

    Identification

    Significance

the National Association of Colored Women

    Identification

    Significance

the feminist movement

    Identification

    Significance

Charlotte Perkins Gilman

    Identification

    Significance

Margaret Sanger

    Identification

    Significance

the suffrage movement

    Identification

    Significance

Harriott Stanton Blatch

    Identification

    Significance

Carrie Chapman Catt and Alice Paul

    Identification

    Significance

the Nineteenth Amendment

    Identification

    Significance

Theodore Roosevelt

Identification

Significance

the Northern Securities Company

Identification

Significance

the Hepburn Act

Identification

Significance

The Jungle

Identification

Significance

the Meat Inspection Act

Identification

Significance

the Pure Food and Drug Act

      Identification

      Significance

the coal strike of 1902

      Identification

      Significance

the Newlands Reclamation Act

      Identification

      Significance

Gifford Pinchot

      Identification

      Significance

the Panic of 1907

      Identification

      Significance

William Howard Taft

    Identification

    Significance

the Payne-Aldrich Tariff

    Identification

    Significance

the revolt against "Cannonism"

    Identification

    Significance

the Mann-Elkins Act of 1910

    Identification

    Significance

the Sixteenth Amendment

    Identification

    Significance

the National Progressive Republican League

    Identification

    Significance

the Progressive party

    Identification

    Significance

Woodrow Wilson

    Identification

    Significance

the presidential election of 1912

    Identification

    Significance

New Nationalism

    Identification

    Significance

New Freedom

  Identification

  Significance

the Clayton Anti-Trust Act

  Identification

  Significance

the Federal Trade Commission

  Identification

  Significance

the Federal Reserve Act of 1913

  Identification

  Significance

the discount rate

  Identification

  Significance

the Underwood Tariff

    Identification

    Significance

the income tax

    Identification

    Significance

the Federal Farm Loan Act of 1916

    Identification

    Significance

the Adamson Act of 1916

    Identification

    Significance

the presidential election of 1916

    Identification

    Significance

the War Industries Board

Identification

Significance

Organizing Information

Much of Chapter 21 outlines the goals, strategies, and, by implication at least, the successes and failures of groups in American society struggling to get out from under limitations on their rights and powers. To sharpen your grasp of how the various groups resembled one another and contrasted to one another in terms of their goals, strategies, and achievements, complete the chart "The Progressive Era, 1895–1920.

Start by identifying the goals and strategies of each group. In the second column, identify the goals and achievements of the specific group named in the first column. And, in the fourth column, identify strategies members of the group established or proposed to accomplish each of the goals.

Then complete the third column by identifying specific individuals in each group who promoted the particular strategies you have named in the fourth column.

Finally, in the last column, indicate some of the barriers to achieving its goals that the group faced.

Remember, you do not need to put in each block much more than names and labels. You can provide fuller identifications and explanations of the names and labels in your notes on the chapter and in any related mock essays you compose. (Some students do like to put text page numbers and/or notes page numbers in the blocks to help them re-find relevant passages in the textbook and in their reading and lecture notes.)

THE PROGRESSIVE ERA, 1895-1920

*Approaches To Achieving Human and Civil Rights and Protection
for Those with Limited Economic and Political Power*

Groups Denied Key Human or Civil Rights or Protection from Health Hazards and Other Abuses	GOALS Successes? Failures? Progress?	The Group's Prominent Figures or Leaders or Outside Advocates Favoring Special Strategies	Strategies for Gaining Rights, Recognition, or Protection These Figures, Leaders, or Advocates Recommended	Actions of the Group's non-Leaders Affecting the Future of the Group or Attitudes Toward It	Specific Factors, Policies, and Attitudes that Helped or Hindered the Group in Achieving Its Human and Civil-Rights Goals
Women					
African Americans					
Indians					
Workers					
Consumers					

Interpreting Information

Review the discussions in Chapter 21 of particular groups that recognized and wanted to overcome limitations on their economic, political, and social power and sometimes struggled over the issue of just how far they wanted to be assimilated into American culture. Then plan and compose a mock essay in direct response to this question:

> Discuss the basic goals and strategies of the various groups of Americans who, during the Progressive Era, saw themselves as facing social, economic, political and legal limitations simply or largely because of the racial, cultural, gender groups to which they belonged. Explain the degree to which the strategies were employed and were successful.

Use your entries in the Organizing Information chart entitled "The Progressive Era, 1895-1920" as indicators of which specific individuals and groups established goals and strategies to overcome limitations. You should include specific examples in your essay to illustrate and clarify what you have to say about all the groups' various goals and strategies.

Ideas and Details

Objective 1

_____ 1. Organizations such as the American Bar Association, the National Consumers League, and the National Municipal League
   a. increased the loyalty of the electorate to political parties.
   b. introduced charismatic personalities to political campaigns.
   c. stifled debate on major urban issues.
   d. made politics more issue oriented than in previous eras.

Objective 2

_____ 2. In calling for direct primaries, middle-class progressives demonstrated which of the following beliefs?
   a. Government should be placed in the hands of professional politicians.
   b. All citizens should be allowed to participate in the decision-making process.
   c. Politics can be improved by reducing the power of political parties.
   d. Government should respect the rights of the individual.

Objectives 1 and 2

_____ 3. With regard to governmental reform, progressives wanted to
- a. bargain with different interest groups to accomplish needed reforms.
- b. use the principles of scientific management to achieve political efficiency.
- c. require literacy tests for voting to ensure that the electorate was educated and responsible.
- d. require full financial disclosure by all political candidates to ensure their independence from special-interest groups.

Objective 2

_____ 4. Unlike middle-class progressives, working-class progressives
- a. were interested more in political reform than in social reform.
- b. rejected the idea that the government should regulate the workplace.
- c. usually supported moral reform movements such as prohibition.
- d. often realized that urban political bosses could aid their reform efforts.

Objectives 1, 2, and 3

_____ 5. Most progressives did not ally with the socialists because
- a. progressives were offended by the abrasive personality of Eugene Debs.
- b. progressives had a stake in the capitalist system and did not want to overthrow it.
- c. progressives rejected the nationalist appeals of the socialists.
- d. progressives accepted the basic tenets of the laissez-faire philosophy.

Objective 2

_____ 6. Governor Robert M. La Follette believed that
- a. corporations should be driven out of politics.
- b. the working classes could never gain social justice in a capitalist society.
- c. regulatory commissions represented a threat to the free enterprise system.
- d. the federal government should nationalize the railroads.

Objective 4

_____ 7. John Dewey believed that
- a. public education should concentrate on the teaching of basic moral principles.
- b. public school teachers should be accredited by a national accreditation agency.
- c. mastery by students of a given body of knowledge should be the primary aim of public education.
- d. public school curricula should be relevant to the lives of students.

Objective 5

_____ 8. Which of the following best expresses the beliefs of Booker T. Washington?
 a. Blacks should passively accept their inferior position in a white-dominated society.
 b. Blacks should prove themselves worthy of equal rights by working hard and acquiring property.
 c. Blacks should demand political and social equality in American society.
 d. Blacks should challenge discriminatory legislation in the courts.

Objective 5

_____ 9. The most decisive factor in the decision to extend the right to vote to women was
 a. acceptance of the argument that all Americans are equal and deserve the same rights.
 b. acceptance of the idea that women would humanize politics.
 c. the contributions made by women on the home front during the First World War.
 d. the militant tactics of women like Carrie Chapman Catt.

Objective 6

_____ 10. President Roosevelt's handling of trusts suggests that he accepted which of the following beliefs?
 a. Businesses must be allowed to operate and organize without government interference.
 b. Antitrust laws should be used to prosecute unscrupulous corporations that exploit the public and refuse to regulate themselves.
 c. Bigness is bad in and of itself.
 d. The tax power of the government should be used to punish irresponsible corporations.

Objective 7

_____ 11. Theodore Roosevelt and William Howard Taft differed in which of the following ways?
 a. Roosevelt acted assertively to expand presidential power; Taft was cautious in his use of power.
 b. Roosevelt took care not to offend business leaders; Taft was tactless and abrasive.
 c. Roosevelt insisted on operating within the letter of the law; Taft was willing to bend the law to his purposes.
 d. Roosevelt was sympathetic to reform; Taft found reform dangerous and unnecessary.

Objective 8

_____ 12. Roosevelt's New Nationalism, unlike Wilson's New Freedom, called for
  a. the destruction of big business.
  b. a restoration of laissez faire.
  c. cooperation between big business and big government through the establishment of regulatory commissions.
  d. equality of economic opportunity.

Objectives 8 and 9

_____ 13. By advocating passage of the Clayton Anti-Trust Act and the creation of the Federal Trade Commission, President Wilson
  a. demonstrated his belief that restoration of free competition was possible.
  b. indicated his determination to challenge rulings of the Supreme Court.
  c. stubbornly challenged the probusiness Democratic leadership in Congress.
  d. acknowledged that government regulatory powers had to be expanded to deal with the reality of economic concentration.

Objective 9

_____ 14. The Underwood Tariff
  a. fostered competition by lowering tariff rates.
  b. was rejected by President Wilson because it levied a tax on personal income.
  c. established a 50 percent tax on incomes over $100,000.
  d. led to a trade war among the major trading nations.

Objective 10

_____ 15. In the final analysis, the progressives were able to
  a. bring about a redistribution of power in the United States.
  b. remove state and national government from the influence of business and industrial interests.
  c. establish the principle that government should intervene in social and political affairs to ensure fairness, health, and safety.
  d. unite behind a comprehensive reform program for American society.

Essay Questions

Objectives 1 and 2

1. Explain the social, political, and economic ideas of middle-class progressives, and evaluate their accomplishments at the local level of American society.

Objective 5

2. Discuss the similarities and differences between the approaches of Booker T. Washington and W. E. B. Du Bois to the problems faced by black Americans.

Objective 5

3. Discuss and evaluate the varying approaches of women to the problems they faced in early twentieth-century America.

Objective 6

4. Explain Theodore Roosevelt's approach to big business and the philosophy behind that approach.

Objectives 8 and 9

5. Defend the following statement: "As president, Wilson had to blend his New Freedom ideals with New Nationalism precepts, and in so doing he set the direction of federal economic policy for much of the twentieth century."

CHAPTER 22

The Quest for Empire, 1865–1914

Learning Objectives

After you have studied Chapter 22 in your textbook and worked through this study guide chapter, you should be able to:

1. Examine the late-nineteenth-century sources of American expansionism and imperialism.

2. Discuss the role of ideology and culture in American expansionism and imperialism during the late nineteenth and early twentieth centuries.

3. Describe the expansionist vision of William H. Seward, and indicate the extent to which this vision was realized by the late 1880s.

4. Examine and evaluate relations between the United States and the following nations in the late nineteenth and early twentieth centuries:
   a. Great Britain
   b. Canada

5. Discuss the modernization of the United States Navy in the late nineteenth century.

6. Discuss the causes and consequences of the Hawaiian and Venezuelan crises.

7. Examine the causes (both underlying and immediate) and discuss the conduct of the Spanish-American-Cuban-Filipino War, and indicate the provisions of the Treaty of Paris.

8. Outline the arguments presented by both the anti-imperialists and the imperialists in the debate over acquisition of an empire, and explain why the imperialists prevailed.

9. Examine and evaluate late-nineteenth- and early-twentieth-century American policy toward Asia in general and toward China, the Philippines, and Japan, specifically.

10. Examine and evaluate United States policy toward the countries of Latin America in the late nineteenth and early twentieth century.

Thematic Guide

The expansionist and eventually imperialistic orientation of United States foreign policy after 1865 stemmed from the country's domestic situation. Those who led the internal expansion of the United States after the Civil War were also the architects of the nation's foreign policy. These national leaders, known collectively as the foreign policy elite, believed that extending American influence abroad would foster American prosperity, and they sought to use American foreign policy to open and safeguard foreign markets.

Many Americans harbored fears of the wider world, but the foreign policy elite realized that those fears could be alleviated if the world could be remade in the American image. Therefore, after the Civil War, these leaders advocated a nationalism based on the idea that Americans were a special people favored by God. Race-based arguments, gender-based arguments, and Social Darwinism were used to support the idea of American superiority and further the idea of expansion, and American missionaries went forth to convert the "heathen." Furthermore, a combination of political, economic, and cultural factors in the 1890s prompted the foreign policy elite to move beyond support of mere economic expansion toward advocacy of an imperialistic course for the United States—an imperialism characterized by a belief in the rightness of American society and American solutions.

The analysis of American expansionism serves as a backdrop for scrutiny of the American empire from the end of the Civil War to 1914. William H. Seward, as secretary of state from 1861 to 1869 and as a member of the foreign policy elite, was one of the chief architects of this empire. In examining Seward's expansionist vision and the extent to which it was realized by the late 1880s, we again see the relationship between domestic and foreign policy.

Acquisition of territories and markets abroad led the United States to heed the urgings of Captain Alfred T. Mahan and to embark on the building of the New Navy. The fleet gave the nation the means to protect America's international interests and to become more assertive, as in the Hawaiian, Venezuelan, and Cuban crises of the 1890s. The varied motives that led the United States into the Spanish-American-Cuban-Filipino War offer another striking example of the complex links between domestic and foreign policy. In these crises of the 1890s, the American frame of reference toward peoples of other nations became more noticeable in the shaping of foreign policy. In the Cuban crisis, as in the Venezuelan crisis, Americans insisted that the United States would establish the rules for nations in the Western Hemisphere.

The Treaty of Paris, which ended the Spanish-American-Cuban-Filipino War, sparked a debate between imperialists and anti-imperialists over the course of American foreign policy. We examine the arguments of the two groups and the reasons for the defeat of the anti-imperialists.

In the last two sections of the chapter, we turn to the American empire in Asia and Latin America. The American frame of reference with regard to other ethnic groups, along with American political, economic, and social interests, shaped the Open Door policy as well as relations with Japan and led to U.S. oppression of the Filipinos. The same factors determined American relations with Latin America. But in Latin America the United States used its power to impose its will and, through the Roosevelt Corollary to the Monroe Doctrine, assumed the role of "an international police power."

Building Vocabulary

Listed below are important words and terms that you need to know to get the most out of Chapter 22. They are listed in the order in which they occur in the chapter. After carefully looking through the list, refer to a dictionary and jot down the definition of words that you do not know or of which you are unsure.

proselytize

ardent

derogatory

gape

indigenous

unabashed

lucrative

disparage

tumultuous

subjugation

espouse

cosmopolitan

luminary

derogatory

infuse

debase

inscrutable

ethnocentric

obviate

mollycoddle

cohort

hegemony

piety

critique

undergird

hypocritical

aggrandizement

fruition

waft

persevere

rapprochement

protectorate

reciprocity

indemnity

postulate

archipelago

oligarchy

rectitude

collusion

fiat

sensibility

insurgent

jettison

inveterate

motley

retort

abate

consortium

rescind

eradicate

chafe

condescending

futile

embroilment

augment

Identification and Significance

After studying Chapter 22 of *A People and a Nation,* you should be able to identify fully *and* explain the historical significance of each item listed below.

1. Identify each item in the space provided. Give an explanation or description of the item. Answer the questions *who, what, where,* and *when.*

2. Explain the historical significance of each item in the space provided. Establish the historical context in which the item exists. Establish the item as the result of or as the cause of other factors existing in the society under study. Answer this question: *What were the political, social, economic, and/or cultural consequences of this item?*

Lottie Moon

    Identification

    Significance

expansionism versus imperialism

    Identification

    Significance

the foreign policy elite

    Identification

    Significance

the idea of a racial hierarchy

    Identification

    Significance

Our Country

    Identification

    Significance

male ethos and imperialism

    Identification

    Significance

Student Volunteers for Foreign Missions

    Identification

    Significance

William H. Seward

    Identification

    Significance

the purchase of Alaska

    Identification

    Significance

the transatlantic cable

    Identification

    Significance

Hamilton Fish

    Identification

    Significance

the Washington Treaty

    Identification

    Significance

the Samoan Islands

    Identification

    Significance

the Burlingame Treaty

    Identification

    Significance

the massacre at Rock Springs, Wyoming

    Identification

    Significance

the Pan-American Conference of 1889

    Identification

    Significance

the *Baltimore* incident

    Identification

    Significance

navalism

    Identification

    Significance

Captain Alfred T. Mahan

    Identification

    Significance

the New Navy

    Identification

    Significance

Turner's frontier thesis

    Identification

    Significance

the Hawaiian-annexation question

    Identification

    Significance

Hawaii's 1887 constitution

    Identification

    Significance

the McKinley Tariff of 1890

    Identification

    Significance

the 1893 overthrow of the Hawaiian government

    Identification

    Significance

the Venezuelan crisis of 1895

    Identification

    Significance

the Cuban revolution

    Identification

    Significance

José Martí

    Identification

    Significance

the Wilson-Gorman Tariff

    Identification

    Significance

General Valeriano Weyler

    Identification

    Significance

the *Maine*

    Identification

    Significance

the de Lôme letter

    Identification

    Significance

McKinley's war message

    Identification

    Significance

the Teller Amendment

    Identification

    Significance

the Spanish-American-Cuban-Filipino War

    Identification

    Significance

Commodore George Dewey

    Identification

    Significance

the Treaty of Paris

    Identification

    Significance

anti-imperialist arguments

    Identification

    Significance

imperialist arguments

    Identification

    Significance

the Boxer Rebellion

    Identification

    Significance

the Open Door policy

    Identification

    Significance

Emilio Aguinaldo

    Identification

    Significance

the Philippine Insurrection

    Identification

    Significance

the Moros

    Identification

    Significance

the Jones Act

     Identification

     Significance

the Portsmouth Conference

     Identification

     Significance

the Taft-Katsura Agreement

     Identification

     Significance

the Root-Takahira Agreement

     Identification

     Significance

the Great White Fleet

     Identification

     Significance

"dollar diplomacy"

      Identification

      Significance

the San Francisco School Board's segregation order

      Identification

      Significance

the United Fruit Company

      Identification

      Significance

the Platt Amendment

      Identification

      Significance

Walter Reed

      Identification

      Significance

Puerto Rican–United States relations

Identification

Significance

the Hay-Pauncefote Treaty of 1901

Identification

Significance

the Panamanian revolution

Identification

Significance

the Panama Canal

Identification

Significance

the Roosevelt Corollary to the Monroe Doctrine

Identification

Significance

American investments in Mexico

    Identification

    Significance

Anglo-American rapprochement

    Identification

    Significance

Organizing Information

Scores of the events involving Americans and their attitudes about peoples of other regions of the world discussed in Chapter 22 can be seen both as promise and warning of the explosion in American power and influence in the twentieth century. These events and attitudes introduced in Chapter 22 are going to turn out to be patterns for behaviors and attitudes dominating American relations with other countries and peoples throughout the twentieth century.

For that reason, it makes sense to begin tracing the development of American foreign relations throughout the twentieth century, adding more information, more examples with each new chapter in the textbook.

The two-fold goal of this exercise is to get started on the job of tracing the complex relationships between the United States and her Latin American neighbors and to begin looking at American-style imperialism, beginning with the real flurry of imperialistic adventures described in Chapter 22. Plan to return to the chart on American-Latin American relations as you proceed through the rest of the chapters in your textbook.

THE UNITED STATES AND LATIN AMERICA

Cuba		Guatemala		Honduras	
Year	Nature of U.S. Involvement	Year	Nature of U.S. Involvement	Year	Nature of U.S. Involvement
1898	Spanish-American War. U.S. troops remain until 1902.	1899			
1903					

Panama		El Salvador		Nicaragua	
Year	Nature of U.S. Involvement	Year	Nature of U.S. Involvement	Year	Nature of U.S. Involvement

AMERICAN-STYLE IMPERIALISM

The first column of the chart "American Use of Its Power Abroad, 1865-1914" lists some basic goals of American foreign policy and the imperialist elite from 1865 to 1914. In the remaining columns you are to list instances of the use of specific imperialistic methods to accomplish these goals and their effects. (In some cases the same example may illustrate more than one method.) Make each entry specific, but enter only enough information to serve as reminders that can be expanded when you write out the working draft of your essay and that can be used in reviewing the material.

American Use of Its Power Abroad, 1865-1914						
Methods of Influencing Asian and American Countries						
Purpose or Consequence of the Use of Power or of Influence Derived from Power	**Diplomatic Pressure**	**Military Actions or Threats**	**Economc Action or Pressure**	**Covert Action, Conspiracies**	**Other (altruism, etc.)**	**Effect On or Response of Other Countries**
To protect the property of citizens living in other countries or of companies doing business in other countries						
To take over territory of or to change the boundaries of countries for the purpose of controlling assets or facilities of military or economic value						
To install leaders who would support American interests or to remove leaders who would oppose American interests						

American Use of Its Power Abroad, 1865-1914 (continued)						
Methods of Influencing Asian and American Countries						
Purpose or Consequence of the Use of Power or of Influence Derived from Power	**Diplomatic Pressure**	**Military Actions or Threats**	**Economc Action or Pressure**	**Covert Action, Conspiracies**	**Other (altruism, etc.)**	**Effect On or Response of Other Countries**
To establish trade and tariff policies designed to protect domestic business interests without regard to the consequences in other nations or to influence the policies of other nations						
To control the forms of government, constitutions or legal institutions, or the trade agreements or treaties of other countries or territories						
To control the outcome of civil wars or insurrections in other countries or the attempts of provinces within other countries to secede						

American Use of Its Power Abroad, 1865-1914 (concluded)						
Purpose or Consequence of the Use of Power or of Influence Derived from Power	**Methods of Influencing Asian and American Countries**					**Effect On or Response of Other Countries**
	Diplomatic Pressure	**Military Actions or Threats**	**Economc Action or Pressure**	**Covert Action, Conspiracies**	**Other (altruism, etc.)**	
To affect the class structure, relative power of social and economic classes, or the racial and religious divisions within another country						
To influence the cultural development (language, dress, education, etc.) or to alter the religious makeup or the value system of another country						

Interpreting Information

Using information about American imperialism you collected from Chapter 22 and your class notes and and entered in the Organizing Information chart "American Use of Its Power Abroad, 1865-1914" as your guide, plan and compose the working draft of an essay answering this question:

> What in Americans' attempts to extend the country's influence and control overseas between 1865 and 1914 explains why many people overseas call the United States imperialistic and fear what it might do next?

Ideas and Details

Objective 1

_____ 1. Foreign policy decisions in the late nineteenth century were shaped largely by
   a. the opinions of the American people.
   b. the business community.
   c. the foreign policy elite.
   d. generals and admirals.

Objective 1

_____ 2. One of the sources of the expansionist sentiment of the late nineteenth century was the
   a. desire of American farmers to learn new agricultural techniques from foreign agricultural specialists.
   b. belief that foreign economic expansion would relieve the problem of overproduction at home.
   c. belief that more immigrants would solve domestic labor problems.
   d. desire of Latin American countries for the United States to exert political control over them.

Objectives 1 and 2

_____ 3. _Our Country_ by Josiah Strong provides evidence that
   a. most American religious leaders in the late nineteenth century were critical of American foreign policy in general and of American imperialism in particular.
   b. belief in the superiority of Anglo-Saxons was used in the late nineteenth century to justify American expansion.
   c. late nineteenth-century American foreign policy was based on the principle that all nations in the world should be allowed to determine their own form of government and economic system.
   d. the unprofessional nature of the American diplomatic corps in the late nineteenth century was a constant embarrassment to the United States.

Objective 3

_____ 4. William H. Seward's vision of an American empire
   a. was confined to the Americas.
   b. included the building of a Central American canal.
   c. involved acquisition of territory by military conquest.
   d. took a giant step forward with the purchase of the Danish West Indies in 1867.

Objective 5

_____   5. The person largely responsible for popularizing the New Navy was
   a. Andrew Carnegie.
   b. Ulysses Grant.
   c. Hamilton Fish.
   d. Alfred T. Mahan.

Objective 6

_____   6. President Grover Cleveland opposed the annexation of Hawaii because he
   a. saw no economic advantages to it.
   b. wanted no close ties with people of another race.
   c. learned that a majority of Hawaiians opposed annexation.
   d. was afraid it would lead to war.

Objective 6

_____   7. In the settlement of the Venezuelan crisis of 1895,
   a. the United States showed a disregard for the rights of Venezuela.
   b. the United States insisted that Venezuela adopt a democratic form of government.
   c. Great Britain was able to bully the United States into submission.
   d. the United States Navy showed its inability to operate in a crisis.

Objectives 7 and 10

_____   8. The Teller Amendment
   a. announced that the United States would annex Cuba.
   b. led to the declaration of war against Spain.
   c. expanded the theater of war to the South Pacific.
   d. renounced any American intentions to annex Cuba.

Objective 7

_____   9. In the final analysis, the United States went to war with Spain because
   a. of a humanitarian desire to help the Cuban people.
   b. of a desire to carry the Christian message to other people.
   c. of the multifaceted spirit of expansionism, which had been building for some time.
   d. war offered an opportunity to fulfill the "large policy."

Objective 7

_____   10. Most American casualties in the Spanish-American-Cuban-Filipino War were incurred
   a. through diseases contracted during the war.
   b. in the Santiago campaign.
   c. in Admiral Dewey's battle with the Spanish fleet in Manila Bay.
   d. by the Rough Riders in the charge up San Juan Hill.

Objective 8

_____ 11. The anti-imperialist campaign against the Treaty of Paris was
   a. based on purely constitutional arguments.
   b. hindered by the inconsistency of the anti-imperialist arguments.
   c. successful because of the influence of people like Mark Twain and Andrew Carnegie.
   d. successful because of Bryan's decision to support the treaty.

Objective 9

_____ 12. Which of the following best expresses the ideology behind the Open Door policy?
   a. The self-determination of other nations must be preserved.
   b. The closing of any area to American trade is a threat to the survival of the United States.
   c. Freedom of the seas will lead to the economic expansion of the world community of nations.
   d. All nations of the world should be considered equals.

Objective 9

_____ 13. In the Philippines, the United States
   a. fought to suppress an insurrection against American rule.
   b. quickly lived up to its promise to give the country its independence.
   c. held a referendum to determine the wishes of the Filipino people.
   d. established a democratic government that guaranteed the same basic rights enjoyed by Americans.

Objective 9

_____ 14. Relations between the United States and Japan were negatively affected by
   a. the extension of American aid to French colonies in Indochina.
   b. American refusal to recognize Japanese hegemony in Korea.
   c. President Roosevelt's extension of military aid to Russia during the Russo-Japanese war.
   d. the involvement of American bankers in an international consortium to build a Chinese railway.

Objective 10

_____ 15. Which of the following best explains the rationale behind the Roosevelt Corollary to the Monroe Doctrine and the imperialistic behavior of the United States in Latin America?
   a. The United States believed it had the duty to help Latin Americans find the political system best suited to their culture.
   b. The United States believed prevention of outside intervention in Latin America, and thus the preservation of its own security, required stability in the region.
   c. The United States believed it should share its wealth and resources with the people of Latin America.
   d. The United States believed that it had the right to colonize Latin America to exploit the resources of the region.

Essay Questions

Objectives 1, 2, 6, 7, 8 and 10

1. Defend or refute the following statement in the context of American policy toward Central America and the Caribbean in the late nineteenth and early twentieth centuries: "The persistent American belief that other people cannot solve their own problems and that only the American model of government will work produced what historian William Appleman Williams has called 'the tragedy of American diplomacy.'"

Objective 1

2. Explain the relationship between domestic affairs and foreign affairs. How did domestic affairs during the late nineteenth century lead to an expansionist foreign policy?

Objective 8

3. Discuss the debate between the imperialists and the anti-imperialists, and explain why the former prevailed.

Objective 9

4. Explain American foreign policy toward China in the late nineteenth and early twentieth centuries.

Map Exercise

1. Label the southernmost states of the United States shown on the outline map on page 203.

2. Locate and mark the following Latin American countries on the outline map (use the map in the textbook, on page 628, as a guide when necessary):

    Countries   *Cities*

    Mexico   Miami
    Guatemala   New Orleans
    British Honduras (now Belize)   Columbus, New Mexico
    Honduras   Mexico City
    El Salvador   Tampico
    Nicaragua   Veracruz
    Costa Rica
    Panama
    Colombia
    Venezuela
    Cuba
    Jamaica
    Haiti
    Dominican Republic
    Puerto Rico

3. Using an atlas, mark the locations of the capitals of the Latin American countries that are shown on the outline map.

4. The United States has long been interested in and involved in Latin American affairs. Why?

CHAPTER 23
Americans in the Great War, 1914–1920

Learning Objectives

After you have studied Chapter 23 in your textbook and worked through this study guide chapter, you should be able to:

1. Discuss Europe's descent into the First World War.

2. Discuss both President Woodrow Wilson's attempts and the attempts of antiwar activists to keep the United States out of the First World War, and explain the ultimate failure of those efforts.

3. Discuss the response of Americans to the First World War and to American entry into the war, and indicate the extent to which United States participation influenced the outcome of the conflict.

4. Describe the characteristics of draftees and volunteers in the American armed forces during the First World War and discuss their lives as soldiers.

5. Examine the impact of the First World War on the American home front, including its impact on the federal government, business, labor, women, and African Americans.

6. Explain and evaluate the record of government at the local, state, and national levels on civil-liberties questions during and after the war.

7. Explain the differences and similarities between Wilsonianism and the provisions of the Treaty of Versailles.

8. Examine the debate over ratification of the Treaty of Versailles and American entry into the League of Nations, and explain the Senate's rejection of the treaty.

9. Examine the impact of the First World War on America's role in world affairs

---

Thematic Guide

In Chapter 23, we deal with the causes of the First World War, American entry into the war, and the political, social, and economic impact of the war on the United States and its people. The nation's entry into the war is discussed in "Precarious Neutrality" and "Submarine Warfare and Wilson's Decision for War." Although President Wilson proclaimed the United States to be a neutral in the European conflict, three realities made neutrality practically impossible. Those realities confirm the interrelation of domestic and foreign policy (a dominant theme in Chapter 22). Furthermore, the discussion of the tenets of Wilsonianism and Wilson's strict interpretation of international law reinforces the concept that a nation's foreign policy is based on its perception of the world community of nations and of its relationship to those nations.

Besides the underlying reasons for American entry into the war, there were obvious and immediate reasons for that decision: the naval warfare between Great Britain and Germany, the use of the submarine by the Germans, and Wilson's interpretation of international law as he attempted to protect the rights of the United States as a neutral nation. The authors' inference that Americans got caught in the crossfire between the Allies and the Central Powers is supported through the tracing of United States policy from the sinking of the *Lusitania* to the adoption of unrestricted submarine warfare by the Germans. Therefore, the Zimmermann telegram, perceived as a direct threat to American security by American officials, the arming of American commercial ships, and additional sinkings of American ships by German submarines brought a declaration of war by Congress. Finally, America went to war because of a special sense of mission. The country went to war to reform world politics, war being the only means that guaranteed Wilson a seat and an insider's voice at the peace table.

In spite of antiwar sentiment in the United States, the country began to prepare for war before the actual declaration, as can be seen in the passage of the National Defense Act, the Navy Act, and the Revenue Act. Once war was declared, the country turned to the draft (the Selective Service Act) to raise the necessary army. Even though American military and political leaders believed that American virtue could reshape the world, they feared that the world would reshape the virtue of American soldiers. To protect that virtue, the government created the Commission on Training Camp Activities. In spite of this, venereal disease became a serious problem within the army. Furthermore, American soldiers could not be shielded from the graver threat of influenza and pneumonia, and more soldiers died from disease than on the battlefield. Another serious problem in the American army—one that government and army officials did little to combat—was racism. Not only were African Americans segregated within the army, but they were also subjected to various forms of racial discrimination.

Mobilization of the nation for the war effort altered American life. Government power increased, especially in the economic sphere. Government-business cooperation became part of official government policy. Centralized governmental control and planning of the nation's economy were largely successful, but there were mistakes and problems. Government policy caused inflation; government tax policies meant that only one-third of the war was financed through taxes; and, although organized labor made some gains, it usually took a back seat to the needs of corporations.

The war intensified the divisions within the pluralistic American society. Entry of more women into previously "male" jobs brought negative reactions by male workers. Increased northward migration of African Americans intensified racist fears and animosities in factories and neighborhoods. The government's fear of dissent and of foreigners led to the trampling of civil liberties at the national, state, and local levels. In the immediate aftermath of the war, events both within and outside the country heightened these fears, culminating in the Red Scare and the Palmer Raids. The American effort to "make the world safe for democracy" brought actions on the home front that seemed to indicate a basic distrust of democracy.

Divisions also intensified on the political front, as the debate over the Treaty of Versailles indicates. In "The Peace Conference, League Fight, and Postwar World" Wilson's Fourteen Points are contrasted with the actual terms of the treaty. The divergence was an issue used in the arguments of those opposed to the treaty and to American entry into the League of Nations. But the core of the problem lay in Article 10 of the League covenant. Critics charged that the collective-security provisions of this article would allow League members to call out the United States Army without congressional approval. The *belief* of many that this was true was at the heart of the debate against the League. Fear that the United States would be forced to forgo its traditional unilateralism in foreign affairs led the Senate to reject the treaty and American entry into the League of Nations.

The American experience in the First World War influenced every aspect of American life, producing consequences for the future. The war changed America's place in world affairs to one of world prominence, and it continued to shape America's institutions and decisions both at home and abroad long after 1920.

Building Vocabulary

Listed below are important words and terms that you need to know to get the most out of Chapter 23. They are listed in the order in which they occur in the chapter. After carefully looking through the list, refer to a dictionary and jot down the definition of words that you do not know or of which you are unsure.

neurosis

psychosis

listless

carnage

regimen

cataclysm

dreadnought

heterogeneous

fractious

pacifist

compulsory

tout

unilateral

collusion

engorge

goad

conflagration

fervently

archetype

prophesy

confiscation

exceptionalism

tenet

emphatically

waive

flout

deftly

reiterate

besmirch

marauding

decadent

acquisitive

impede

avenge

sabotage

filibuster

foment

menial

irreparable

stymie

abdicate

pandemic

conciliate

forage

abate

sleuth

throttle

extol

despotic

clandestine

scapegoat

ominous

stalwart

belfry

vengeful

scoff

reparations

indemnity

punitive

euphoric

rectify

peevish

placate

Identification and Significance

After studying Chapter 23 of *A People and a Nation,* you should be able to identify fully *and* explain the historical significance of each item listed below.

1. Identify each item in the space provided. Give an explanation or description of the item. Answer the questions *who, what, where,* and *when.*

2. Explain the historical significance of each item in the space provided. Establish the historical context in which the item exists. Establish the item as the result of or as the cause of other factors existing in the society under study. Answer this question: *What were the political, social, economic, and/or cultural consequences of this item?*

June 1914 assassination at Sarajevo

   Identification

   Significance

President Wilson's Proclamation of Neutrality

   Identification

   Significance

Wilsonianism

   Identification

   Significance

British naval policy

   Identification

   Significance

neutral rights

    Identification

    Significance

the submarine and international law

    Identification

    Significance

the *Lusitania*

    Identification

    Significance

Secretary of State Bryan's resignation

    Identification

    Significance

the *Arabic*

    Identification

    Significance

the Gore-McLemore resolution

    Identification

    Significance

the *Sussex*

    Identification

    Significance

the peace movement

    Identification

    Significance

unrestricted submarine warfare

    Identification

    Significance

the Zimmermann telegram

    Identification

    Significance

the armed-ship bill

>   Identification

>   Significance

Wilson's war message

>   Identification

>   Significance

Jeannette Rankin

>   Identification

>   Significance

the National Defense Act of 1916 and the Navy Act of 1916

>   Identification

>   Significance

the Selective Service Act

>   Identification

>   Significance

African American enlistees in the military

    Identification

    Significance

Indian enlistees in the military

    Identification

    Significance

"evaders," "deserters," and COs

    Identification

    Significance

the Commission on Training Camp Activities

    Identification

    Significance

"sin-free" zones

    Identification

    Significance

General John J. Pershing

    Identification

    Significance

trench warfare

    Identification

    Significance

venereal disease among American soldiers

    Identification

    Significance

the Food Administration, the Railroad Administration, and the Fuel Administration

    Identification

    Significance

the War Industries Board

    Identification

    Significance

wartime inflation

    Identification

    Significance

the Revenue Act of 1916

    Identification

    Significance

the War Revenue Act of 1917

    Identification

    Significance

the National War Labor Board

    Identification

    Significance

women in the work force

    Identification

    Significance

the Women's Committee of the Council of National Defense

    Identification

    Significance

African American migration

    Identification

    Significance

the East St. Louis riot of 1917

    Identification

    Significance

the "Red Summer" of 1919

    Identification

    Significance

the influenza pandemic

    Identification

    Significance

the civil-liberties issue

    Identification

    Significance

the Committee on Public Information

    Identification

    Significance

the Espionage and Sedition Acts

    Identification

    Significance

Eugene Debs

    Identification

    Significance

the Civil Liberties Bureau

    Identification

    Significance

Schenck v. *U.S.* and *Abrams* v. *U.S.*

     Identification

     Significance

Victor Berger

     Identification

     Significance

Wilson's anti-Bolshevik actions

     Identification

     Significance

the Red Scare

     Identification

     Significance

mail bombs of May 1919

     Identification

     Significance

the Boston police strike

    Identification

    Significance

the steel strike of 1919

    Identification

    Significance

William Z. Foster

    Identification

    Significance

the American left

    Identification

    Significance

the American Legion

    Identification

    Significance

A. Mitchell Palmer

    Identification

    Significance

the Palmer Raids

    Identification

    Significance

Wilson's Fourteen Points

    Identification

    Significance

the Paris Peace Conference

    Identification

    Significance

the principle of self-determination

    Identification

    Significance

the mandate system

    Identification

    Significance

the League of Nations

    Identification

    Significance

Article 10 of the League Covenant

    Identification

    Significance

the Treaty of Versailles

    Identification

    Significance

the Lodge reservations

    Identification

    Significance

the "Irreconcilables"

    Identification

    Significance

collective security vs. unilateralism

    Identification

    Significance

Organizing Information

In the appropriate blocks in the chart "Character and Attitudes of Woodrow Wilson," record evidence about the attitudes and personal style of Woodrow Wilson that affected his handling of people, issues, and events. Your goal in compiling this evidence is to organize specifics needed to compose an analytical portrait of Wilson linking his personal attitudes and style to his effectiveness as a leader.

Character and Attitudes of Woodrow Wilson

Area in Which the Behavior or Comment Arose	Type of Evidence				
	Wilson's Own Statements	Wilson's Own Actions, Behaviors	Others' Comments About Wilson	Others' Behavior in Reaction to Wilson's Behavior	Impact of the Attitude or Character Traits Revealed on Wilson's Achievements
America's Historical and Moral Role in the World					
Racial and Ethnic Groups and Issues					
Britain and Germany Before America's Entry into World War I					
Radicalism and Criticism of His Administration from Among the Private Citizenry					
Imperialism, Colonialism, Interventionism, Sovereignty of Nations, etc.					

Interpreting Information

How would you rate Woodrow Wilson as a leader? How much do his personal style and attitudes influence your rating of him? Which aspects of his personal style and attitudes have a bearing on his effectiveness?

Using the information you recorded in the Organizing Information chart "Character and Attitudes of Woodrow Wilson," compose an analytical portrait of Wilson in which you support your own answer to this question:

To what degree did Woodrow Wilson's personal style and attitudes contribute to or undermine his effectiveness as a leader in the World War I period?

Ideas and Details

Objective 1

_____ 1. Great Britain entered the First World War in response to
   a. the Austro-Hungarian invasion of Russia.
   b. acts of Russian terrorism in the Balkans.
   c. the Serbian invasion of Austria-Hungary.
   d. the German invasion of Belgium.

Objective 2

_____ 2. American neutrality in response to the First World War was never a real possibility because
   a. Wilson wanted to enter the war and force Germany into submission.
   b. the American press had built broad-based sympathy for Serbian nationalism.
   c. the United States had stronger economic ties to the Allies than to the Central Powers.
   d. Secretary of State Bryan worked secretly to bring the United States into the war.

Objective 7

_____ 3. The body of ideas known as Wilsonianism and summarized in the Fourteen Points included the belief that
   a. secret military alliances were the best means by which to maintain world peace.
   b. democratic nations should enter into a collective security agreement to contain and eliminate the communist threat.
   c. democratic nations should build more arms to demonstrate their resolve against autocracy.
   d. empires should be dismantled so that nations could be free to determine and control their own destiny.

Objective 2

_____ 4. William Jennings Bryan resigned his post as secretary of state because
   a. he disagreed with President Wilson's refusal to ban American travelers from sailing on belligerent ships.
   b. the American public responded negatively to his protests concerning Britain's illegal blockade of Germany.
   c. his pro-German sympathies became a liability to the Wilson administration.
   d. President Wilson publicly reprimanded him for advocating American entry into the First World War.

Objective 2

_____ 5. As a result of the Zimmermann telegram, Wilson
   a. broke diplomatic relations with Germany.
   b. decided to rethink his position on international law in relation to the submarine.
   c. became more convinced that Germany was conspiring against the United States.
   d. decided that supporting the Mexican Revolution was in the best interest of the United States.

Objective 2

_____ 6. President Wilson responded to the defeat of his armed-ship bill by
   a. demanding that the antiwar senators responsible for its defeat be censured by the Senate.
   b. ordering naval escorts for American commercial ships in the Atlantic.
   c. arming American commercial vessels anyway.
   d. immediately drafting a declaration of war to present to Congress.

Objective 4

_____ 7. During the First World War, the Commission on Training Camp Activities
   a. was responsible for coordinating the military training of recruits in all of the services.
   b. coordinated the activities of groups that would help protect the virtue of American soldiers.
   c. recommended that military units be racially integrated.
   d. created a network of spies in order to find and prosecute army personnel who questioned the war effort.

Objective 4

_____ 8. General Pershing refused to allow American soldiers to become part of Allied units because he
   a. would have to relinquish control over them.
   b. was afraid they would be corrupted by European ways.
   c. did not want to submit them to the horrors of trench warfare.
   d. did not believe they were as well trained as their Allied counterparts.

Objective 5

_____ 9. In mobilizing the economy for the war effort, the government
   a. rigidly enforced antitrust laws.
   b. protected consumers by instituting a wage and price freeze.
   c. established a partnership between government and business.
   d. insisted on annual cost of living wage increases for workers in war-related industries.

Objective 5

_____ 10. Some men reacted negatively to the movement of women into jobs previously reserved for males because women
   a. were more valued and received higher wages than men.
   b. had a higher productivity rate than men.
   c. began to receive more promotions.
   d. refused to join unions.

Objective 5

_____ 11. Which of the following statements accurately describes the experiences of blacks during the First World War?
   a. Military leaders attempted to combat racism by integrating their units.
   b. Southern whites welcomed the northward migration of blacks.
   c. The ideology used to justify the war was used to dismantle racial barriers within the United States.
   d. Some northern whites reacted with anger and violence to the northward migration of blacks.

Objective 6

_____ 12. In order to achieve its objective, the Committee on Public Information
   a. encouraged Americans to spy on each other and report evidence of suspicious behavior.
   b. encouraged a free and open debate of the American war effort.
   c. held daily briefings with reporters to ensure the dissemination of accurate war news.
   d. sponsored public question-and-answer forums to dispel rumors.

Objective 6

_____ 13. In the case of _Schenck_ v. _U.S._, the Supreme Court ruled that
   a. members of the Socialist party could be required to register with the government.
   b. freedom of speech could be restricted in time of war.
   c. the Sedition Act was unconstitutional.
   d. the teaching of foreign languages could be banned from public schools.

Objective 6

_____ 14. Which of the following statements is accurate in relation to the Palmer Raids?
   a. A well-organized Bolshevik conspiracy against the United States government was crushed.
   b. The attorney general, in dealing with supposed radicals, showed disregard for civil liberties.
   c. Wilson instructed several state legislatures to remove suspected Socialists from their ranks.
   d. Documents confiscated during the raids led the Wilson administration to declare labor unions illegal.

Objectives 7 and 8

_____ 15. Opponents of the Treaty of Versailles objected primarily to
   a. the collective-security provision of Article 10.
   b. Wilson's acceptance of the "mandate" system.
   c. the clause that blamed the war on Germany.
   d. Wilson's inability to secure reparations payments from Germany.

Essay Questions

Objective 2

1. Explain Wilson's attempts to keep the United States out of the Great War in Europe. Why was the country eventually drawn into the conflict?

Objective 5

2. Discuss the impact of the First World War on women and African Americans.

Objective 6

3. Discuss the Wilson administration's record in the area of civil liberties during the First World War.

Objective 6

4. Discuss the fear of communism in American society in the early twentieth century, and explain how that fear manifested itself between 1917 and 1921.

Objective 8

5. Explain the foreign policy debate over ratification of the Treaty of Versailles and entry into the League of Nations. Why did those opposed to ratification and to League membership carry the day?

CHAPTER 24
The New Era of the 1920s

Learning Objectives

After you have studied Chapter 24 in your textbook and worked through this study guide chapter, you should be able to:

1. Discuss the economic characteristics of the 1920s, and explain the reasons for the economic expansion and recovery that began in 1922.

2. Discuss the relationship between government and business during the 1920s, and indicate the factors responsible for the decline of organized labor.

3. Examine the political, social, and economic characteristics of the Harding and Coolidge administrations.

4. Discuss the nature and extent of reform legislation during the decade of the 1920s.

5. Discuss the federal government's Indian policy during the 1920s, and explain its impact on Native Americans.

6. Examine the social, economic, and political changes in the position and attitudes of women and African Americans in American society during the 1920s.

7. Discuss the expansion of the consumer society in America during the 1920s.

8. Examine the impact of the automobile and modern advertising on American society.

9. Explain both the trend toward urbanization and the growth of the suburbs during the 1920s, and discuss the consequences of both of these factors on American society.

10. Indicate the factors that caused an increase in immigration by Mexicans and Puerto Ricans during the 1920s, and discuss the characteristics of their lives in the United States.

11. Discuss the changes that took place in the way Americans used their time during the 1920s.

12. Discuss the causes and consequences of the 1920s trend toward longer life expectancy, and explain the responses of Americans to the needs of the elderly.

13. Examine the impact of social change during the 1920s on the following:
    a. Americans' values
    b. the American family
    c. women in the American work force
    d. images of femininity
    e. views of human sexuality

14. Examine the emergence of the Ku Klux Klan, nativists, and religious fundamentalists, and discuss their impact on American society in the 1920s.

15. Explain the characteristics of each of the following, and discuss the impact of each on American society during the 1920s:
    a. Games
    b. Movies
    c. Sports
    d. Prohibition

16. Examine and evaluate the movements in American literature, art, and music during the 1920s.

17. Discuss the issues and personalities in the 1928 presidential campaign, and explain the election's outcome.

18. Discuss the events that led to the 1929 stock market crash, and examine the causes of the crash and the Great Depression that followed.

Thematic Guide

The decade of the 1920s began with troubling economic signs but soon became an era of economic prosperity for many Americans. Prosperity was accompanied by probusiness attitudes and unparalleled consumerism. The federal government remained active in its support of business interests but became more passive in its regulation of those interests. While the Supreme Court handed down antiregulatory decisions and organized labor suffered setbacks, probusiness attitudes reminiscent of the Gilded Age marked the Harding, Coolidge, and Hoover administrations. Most reforms took place at the state and local levels. Interest in reform concerning Indian affairs led to the reorganization of the Bureau of Indian Affairs, but Indian policy matters continued to be characterized by paternalism. Furthermore, while newly enfranchised women lobbied and gained passage of some legislation helpful to them, women generally struggled to find their political voice.

The consumerism of the age was fueled by the growing purchasing power of many American families and the accompanying ability to acquire the goods associated with a consumer society. Both the automobile and the sophisticated techniques of modern advertising transformed the American life style.

The urbanization of American society continued in the 1920s. Although movement to cities offered opportunities to many, black migrants found that white racism was as prevalent in urban areas as it had been in the rural South. However, blacks' urban ghetto experience aroused their class and ethnic consciousness, as seen both in Marcus Garvey's black nationalist movement and in the cultural outpouring known as the Harlem Renaissance. Racism also shaped the lives of Mexicans, Puerto Ricans, and other newcomers to American cities and contributed to "white flight" from the inner city and to suburban growth.

The way in which Americans spent their time changed. For instance, labor-saving devices lightened the tasks of women working in the home. But since women were still expected to clothe and feed the family and since few women produced clothes and preserved food at home, they spent their time shopping for these goods and became the primary consumers in society.

Altered attitudes and values brought about by societal changes found expression in new clothing and hair styles and in a new openness about human sexuality. Increased longevity resulting from improved diets and improved healthcare led to an increase in the number of older Americans and to limited attempts to respond to their needs. At the same time, compulsory-school-attendance laws increased the influence of the peer group in the socialization of children. Furthermore, a combination of consumerism and economic necessity caused more women, including married women, to work outside the home. The work they performed and the wages they earned were largely determined by the sex-segregated characteristics of the labor market and, for nonwhites, by racial bias. In spite of sexism and racism, however, many women placed family needs above individual needs.

Many people felt threatened by change, and some, attempting to protect traditional attitudes and values, reacted defensively, sometimes with attempts to blame change on scapegoats. The emergence of the "new" Klan and the increase in nativism and fear of radicalism (evidenced in the Sacco and Vanzetti case) can be seen in this light. Religious fundamentalism also gained strength, as the Scopes trial revealed.

More leisure time and a search for entertainment meant that spectator sports and the movies became big business. As the conformist aspects of mass culture caused individuality to fade, Americans found heroes in sports figures, movie idols, and media-created personalities. Caught between two value systems, many Americans gave lip service to the old, as evidenced in their professed support of the Prohibition experiment, but chose the new, as the breakdown of Prohibition in the cities shows.

In literature, the 1920s saw the work of the Lost Generation and of the Harlem Renaissance. In music, it was the age of jazz, America's most distinctive art form, and of such talented composers as Aaron Copland and George Gershwin. In architecture, Frank Lloyd Wright predominated. Overall, the period stands as one of the most creative in American history.

In politics, the presidency remained in Republican hands in 1928 as most Americans affirmed their confidence in the building of a New Era of prosperity for all. But with the stock market crash of 1929, the optimism of 1928 gave way to concern and ultimately, with the onset of the Great Depression, to despair. The Jazz Age ended. The American economic system would have to be rebuilt.

Building Vocabulary

Listed below are important words and terms that you need to know to get the most out of Chapter 24. They are listed in the order in which they occur in the chapter. After carefully looking through the list, refer to a dictionary and jot down the definition of words that you do not know or of which you are unsure.

revered

beset

entice

quash

languish

predatory

crony

dour

cynicism

manipulate

covenant

dilapidated

reminisce

agility

chaste

torrid

reactionary

mete

wane

flout

fundamentalist

irreverence

hedonistic

quip

Pentecostal

poignant

satire

prodigious

prowess

pomade

exuberance

aesthetic

urbane

gregarious

precarious

edifice

collateral

lucrative

mores

emulate

Identification and Significance

After studying Chapter 24 of *A People and a Nation,* you should be able to identify fully *and* explain the historical significance of each item listed below.

1. Identify each item in the space provided. Give an explanation or description of the item. Answer the questions *who, what, where,* and *when.*

2. Explain the historical significance of each item in the space provided. Establish the historical context in which the item exists. Establish the item as the result of or as the cause of other factors existing in the society under study. Answer this question: *What were the political, social, economic, and/or cultural consequences of this item?*

Charles A. Lindbergh

 Identification

 Significance

the installment plan

    Identification

    Significance

oligopolies

    Identification

    Significance

the "new lobbying"

    Identification

    Significance

Chief Justice William Howard Taft

    Identification

    Significance

Coronado Coal Company v. *United Mine Workers* and *Maple Floor Association* v. *U.S.*

    Identification

    Significance

Bailey v. *Drexel Furniture Company* and *Adkins* v. *Children's Hospital*

      Identification

      Significance

welfare capitalism

      Identification

      Significance

Warren G. Harding

      Identification

      Significance

Charles Forbes and Harry Daugherty

      Identification

      Significance

the Teapot Dome scandal

      Identification

      Significance

Calvin Coolidge

Identification

Significance

the McNary-Haugen bills

Identification

Significance

the 1924 presidential election

Identification

Significance

the Indian Rights Association, the Indian Defense Association, and the General Federation of Women's Clubs

Identification

Significance

Native Americans' citizenship status

    Identification

    Significance

the Bureau of Indian Affairs

    Identification

    Significance

the Sheppard-Towner Act

    Identification

    Significance

the Cable Act

    Identification

    Significance

the National Woman Party

    Identification

    Significance

the League of Women Voters

    Identification

    Significance

the automobile

    Identification

    Significance

the Federal Highway Act

    Identification

    Significance

The Man Nobody Knows and *Moses, Persuader of Men*

    Identification

    Significance

the radio

    Identification

    Significance

urbanization

    Identification

    Significance

Marcus Garvey

    Identification

    Significance

Mexican immigrants

    Identification

    Significance

Puerto Rican immigrants

    Identification

    Significance

the growth of the suburbs

    Identification

    Significance

the American family of the 1920s

Identification

Significance

home appliances and household management in the 1920s

Identification

Significance

Isaac Max Rubinow and Abraham Epstein

Identification

Significance

the peer group and the socialization of children

Identification

Significance

women in the 1920s labor force

Identification

Significance

the flapper

    Identification

    Significance

homosexual culture

    Identification

    Significance

Ku Klux Klan

    Identification

    Significance

the Quota (Johnson) Act of 1921

    Identification

    Significance

the Immigration Act of 1924

    Identification

    Significance

the National Origins Act

    Identification

    Significance

Nicola Sacco and Bartolomeo Vanzetti

    Identification

    Significance

the Scopes trial

    Identification

    Significance

Pentecostal religion

    Identification

    Significance

mahjongg, crossword puzzles, miniature golf, and the Charleston

    Identification

    Significance

motion pictures

    Identification

    Significance

baseball

    Identification

    Significance

Jack Dempsey, Harold "Red" Grange, and George Herman "Babe" Ruth

    Identification

    Significance

Rudolph Valentino

    Identification

    Significance

Prohibition

    Identification

    Significance

Al Capone

   Identification

   Significance

the Lost Generation

   Identification

   Significance

the Harlem Renaissance

   Identification

   Significance

the Jazz Age

   Identification

   Significance

the 1928 presidential election

   Identification

   Significance

Herbert Hoover

Identification

Significance

Al Smith

Identification

Significance

Black Thursday

Identification

Significance

J. P. Morgan and Company

Identification

Significance

Black Tuesday

Identification

Significance

the stock market crash

      Identification

      Significance

Organizing Information

The 1920s are often characterized as a pro-business era. To help yourself analyze the validity of that characterization, collect information from Chapter 24 concerning the support business, and especially Big Business, was given during the 1920s that enhanced businesses' potential to make lots of money and have an easier time doing it—including the treatment of labor and encouragement of the availability of plenty of suitable workers. Enter reminders of the information you find in the appropriate blocks in the chart "Business Climate in the 1920s." The chart includes two extra rows in case you find other factors you think should be covered.

Business Climate in the 1920s				
Contributors to the Business Climate	Supreme Court Decisions	Legislation Enacted by Congress	Actions of the President and Others in the Executive Branch	Behavior and Attitudes of the Public
Taxes				
Tariffs				
Regulation				
Labor (Unions, Strikes, Wages)				
Labor Supply and Quality				

Business Climate in the 1920s (concluded)				
Contributors to the Business Climate	**Supreme Court Decisions**	**Legislation Enacted by Congress**	**Actions of the President and Others in the Executive Branch**	**Behavior and Attitudes of the Public**
Public Works Facilitating Business				
Financing: Investors, Borrowing				
Corruption: Bribery, Graft, Scandal; Illicit Enterprises				
Other:				
Other:				

Interpreting Information

Much of the information you found and recorded in the Organizing Information chart "Business Climate in the 1920s" should clarify and support the contention that the 1920s was a very pro-business period in American history, perhaps what could be called an excessively and dangerously pro-business period. Using the information you gathered and organized, plan and compose a working draft of an essay on the following question:

> How did the federal government, financiers, and the public fan the kind of unreasonable optimism about the future of American business and the kind of wild investing in it that contributed in a major way to the stock market crash of 1929?

Ideas and Details

Objective 2

_____   1. In Bailey v. Drexel Furniture Company, the Supreme Court
   a. demonstrated a probusiness stance by striking down restrictions on child labor.
   b. demonstrated that it was moving in a liberal direction in the field of consumer protection.
   c. declared federal aid to a particular industry unconstitutional.
   d. upheld the right to strike by union members.

Objective 2

_____   2. During the 1920s, organized labor
   a. received support from many large corporations.
   b. was encouraged by the rulings of a sympathetic Supreme Court.
   c. continued to attract members in spite of the hostility of the federal government.
   d. was hurt by the policy of welfare capitalism adopted by some large corporations.

Objective 3

_____   3. One area of disagreement between President Coolidge and Congress was
   a. federally funded internal improvements.
   b. farm policy.
   c. foreign policy.
   d. military spending.

Objective 5

_____ 4. Reformers were critical of Indian women for which of the following reasons?
   a. They refused to seek gainful employment.
   b. They refused to send their children to boarding schools.
   c. They encouraged their children to abandon their tribes and land and move to urban areas.
   d. They abandoned their cultural traditions by adopting lifestyles and homemaking methods associated with white middle-class women.

Objective 6

_____ 5. Urban blacks were drawn to Marcus Garvey because he
   a. emphasized racial pride.
   b. promoted education as the route to assimilation.
   c. preached against the evils of the free enterprise system.
   d. was willing to use military means to achieve his objectives.

Objectives 6, 7, and 11

_____ 6. New technology changed the role of housewives in which of the following ways?
   a. Management of the household became a shared family responsibility.
   b. The housewife became the family's chief consumer rather than its chief producer.
   c. Fewer child-raising responsibilities were placed on the housewife.
   d. Housewives began to be seen as specialists in certain tasks.

Objective 13

_____ 7. As a consequence of child-labor laws and compulsory-school-attendance laws,
   a. daily newspaper circulation increased dramatically in the 1920s.
   b. consumption of consumer products began to decline in the 1920s.
   c. the role of the family in socializing children declined while that of the peer group increased.
   d. many industries faced a severe labor shortage.

Objectives 6 and 13

_____ 8. Which of the following statements concerning women in the work force during the 1920s is correct?
   a. The number of women in factories increased dramatically.
   b. Sex segregation in the workplace became less noticeable.
   c. The number of women in the work force declined.
   d. Married women joined the work force in increasing numbers.

Objective 14

_____   9. During the early 1920s, the Ku Klux Klan
              a. had little power outside the South.
              b. lost most of its power in the South because of the new mood of militancy among blacks.
              c. gained power nationally as an antiblack, anti-immigrant, anti-Catholic movement.
              d. was outlawed by Congress as a terrorist organization.

Objective 14

_____   10. Which of the following conclusions may be drawn from the Sacco and Vanzetti case?
              a. The fear of radicalism, which caused the Red Scare, had disappeared.
              b. In the future, immigration laws would be applied equally to all ethnic groups.
              c. Blacks could not be guaranteed a fair trial in the South.
              d. Justice was not necessarily blind to a person's political beliefs or ethnic background.

Objective 15

_____   11. Jack Dempsey, "Babe" Ruth, and Rudolph Valentino demonstrate that the decade of the 1920s was an
              a. age of heroes.
              b. era of great actors.
              c. era of great baseball players.
              d. age of lawlessness.

Objective 15

_____   12. Prohibition failed because
              a. Americans completely rejected the value system out of which it was born.
              b. illegal liquor was foisted on the public by organized crime.
              c. it hurt the nation economically.
              d. many people were willing to break the law in their quest for pleasure and their desire for personal freedom.

Objective 16

_____   13. Many writers of the Harlem Renaissance
              a. rejected the African past of black Americans.
              b. advocated that black Americans return to Africa.
              c. rejected white culture.
              d. were mainly interested in economic issues.

Objective 17

_____ 14. The election of 1928 indicated that
    a. the Democrats were gaining strength in urban areas.
    b. the Democrats were losing their stronghold in the South.
    c. the Republicans were making gains in all sections of the country.
    d. the Republicans had become the minority party.

Objective 18

_____ 15. The government contributed to the stock market crash of 1929 and to the depression that followed in which of the following ways?
    a. Government regulations imposed on businesses reduced profits and investments.
    b. Tax policies before the crash took large sums of money out of circulation.
    c. The Federal Reserve Board followed an easy credit policy in the years prior to the crash.
    d. Government policies toward organized labor encouraged large wage increases and inflation.

Essay Questions

Objective 1

1. Discuss the factors responsible for the economic recovery that began in 1922. How long did this economic recovery last? Why is it said that this recovery was "uneven"?

Objective 2

2. Examine the relationship between government and business during the Republican era of the 1920s. What was the philosophy behind this relationship?

Objective 4

3. Examine the attitude toward reform during the 1920s, and discuss and assess the reforms that were achieved during the decade.

Objective 8

4. Discuss the impact of the automobile on American society, American values, and the American family.

Objective 6

5. Explain the emergence and the rise to power of Marcus Garvey.

Objectives 13 and 14

6. Defend the following statement, and explain how it applies not only to the 1920s but to the twenty-first century as well: "The emotional responses that Americans made to events during the 1920s were part of a larger attempt to sustain old-fashioned values in a fast-moving, materialistic world."

Objective 18

7. Explain why the 1929 stock market crash led to the Great Depression.

CHAPTER 25

The Great Depression and the New Deal, 1929–1941

Learning Objectives

After you have studied Chapter 25 in your textbook and worked through this study guide chapter, you should be able to:

1. Discuss the impact of the Great Depression on the American economic system and on city dwellers, farmers, marriage patterns, and family life.

2. Examine how and why Americans responded to the Great Depression as they did.

3. Explain and evaluate the Hoover administration's attempts to deal with the economic and human crises posed by the Great Depression.

4. Examine the issues and personalities and explain the outcome of the 1932 presidential and congressional elections.

5. Discuss the impact of Franklin D. Roosevelt's personal and professional experiences prior to 1932 on his political, social, and economic views, and examine the relationship between his political, social, and economic views and his handling of the Great Depression.

6. Explain the practical and theoretical basis for the legislative enactments of the First New Deal (1933–1934), and evaluate the effectiveness of the First New Deal in solving the problems of the depression.

7. Examine the variety of criticisms leveled against the New Deal, and discuss the alternatives proposed.

8. Contrast the Supreme Court's reaction to New Deal legislation before and after 1937, and explain the reasons for the shift.

9. Explain the practical and theoretical basis for the legislative enactments of the Second New Deal (1935–1939), and evaluate the effectiveness of the Second New Deal in solving the problems of the depression.

10. Identify the components of the New Deal coalition, and examine the impact of this coalition on the 1936 presidential election.

11. Examine the problems encountered by President Roosevelt during his second term.

12. Examine the power struggle between craft unions and industrial unions during the New Deal era; discuss the victories and defeats of organized labor during this period; and assess the overall impact of the New Deal era on organized labor in the United States.

13.   Examine the impact of the Great Depression and the New Deal era on African Americans, American Indians, Mexican Americans, and women, and explain the responses of these groups to the obstacles they faced.

14.   Discuss the issues and personalities and explain the outcome of the 1940 presidential election.

15.   Discuss the legacy of the New Deal.

Thematic Guide

Chapter 25 opens with a discussion of the Great Depression's impact on people's lives. The human story includes the increase in malnutrition and disease, the sufferings of drought- and debt-ridden farmers, descriptions of hobo towns, altered marital patterns, and changes to family life.

In the midst of the depression, few Americans thought in radical, revolutionary terms. Many accepted the traditional American belief in the self-made man and blamed themselves for the depression. The protests that emerged were relatively mild, the most spectacular being the Bonus March. Furthermore, in the case of the Bonus March, it was the government, not the people, that overreacted.

Hoover's response to appeals from the people that the government extend aid was at first defensive. Hoover was convinced that self-help was the solution, not government aid. As the depression deepened, Hoover reluctantly began to energize the government. But at the same time he pursued policies that caused further deterioration of the economic situation.

An understanding of Franklin Roosevelt's background, his perception of himself, his society, and American government is important to an understanding of his approach to the Great Depression. That background and Roosevelt's frame of reference are outlined as part of the discussion of the presidential election of 1932. Moreover, the authors explain the reasons for Roosevelt's victory and reveal that in spite of a deepening crisis Americans did not adopt radical solutions. Instead, they continued to follow tradition by peacefully exchanging one government for another.

With the aid of the "Brain Trust," Roosevelt adopted a theoretical basis for the New Deal he promised to the American people. Roosevelt believed that government could act as a positive force in American society; in deciding how it should act, he was a pragmatist and thus willing to experiment. At first he accepted the idea that government could and should effectively regulate big business. He accepted the idea that centralized planning by the federal government could solve some of the problems associated with the depression, and he was willing to have government engage in direct relief to alleviate the distress of the nation's citizens. Furthermore, the first New Deal was based on the assumption that overproduction was the underlying problem.

Roosevelt's initial actions, outlined in "Launching the New Deal and Restoring Confidence," demonstrate both the conservative nature of his approach and his realization that the psychology of pessimism within the country was as great an enemy as the depression itself. The legislation that was passed, as well as the fireside chats, provided a sense of movement that helped break the mood of pessimism.

An attempt to solve the problem of overproduction through centralized planning provided the theoretical framework for passage of the AAA, the NIRA, and the TVA. Belief in giving direct relief to states and to individuals may be seen in acts such as the Federal Emergency Relief Act and the CCC. The authors consider these and other measures passed during the Hundred Days, and they also discuss the concept of interest-group democracy, which is important for understanding the politics of the New Deal and the Democratic coalition that emerged.

The statistics provided show that the New Deal was not a cure-all and help explain the emergence of opposition to it. The range of criticism indicates that Roosevelt was a political moderate in the route that he chose. Furthermore, the kind of opposition from popular critics like Huey Long, as well as Supreme Court decisions against the AAA and the NIRA, help explain the launching of the Second New Deal.

The Second New Deal stemmed from the view that underconsumption was the nation's basic problem, that business and banking interests had to be regulated more closely, and that the government had a responsibility to the aged and the needy in American society. These assumptions were behind the Emergency Relief Appropriation Act and five other major pieces of legislation passed during the Second Hundred Days.

The Second New Deal and the forging of the New Deal coalition carried Roosevelt to victory in the 1936 election. Mistakes and political reality meant that Roosevelt did not enjoy successes during his second term like those experienced in his first. He made a political and tactical mistake in his request for a restructuring of the Supreme Court. His dislike of deficit spending and desire for a balanced budget led to drastic cuts in federal spending, which in turn led to a new recession in 1937 and to a renewal of deficit spending. Such mistakes undercut some of Roosevelt's charisma, and with the passage of a new Agricultural Adjustment Act and the Fair Labor Standards Act, the last reforms of the New Deal were enacted.

Having discussed the reforms of the New Deal, the authors consider the impact of the New Deal era on organized labor, nonwhites, and women. Organized labor benefited from both Section 7(a) of the NIRA and the Wagner Act. Therefore, despite determined resistance by management and a division within the labor movement that led to the creation of the Congress of Industrial Organizations (CIO), the union movement made impressive gains during the 1930s.

Although passage of the Indian Reorganization Act indicates a more enlightened governmental approach to American Indians, the experience of African Americans and Mexican Americans demonstrates that racism continued as a force detrimental to the lives of nonwhites. The Scottsboro case serves as a symbol of the "ugliness of race relations in the depression era." Furthermore, despite the presence of the Black Cabinet, President Roosevelt was never fully committed to civil rights for blacks, and some New Deal measures functioned in a discriminatory way. However, there were some indications that change was on the horizon.

First, in relation to cases arising out of the Scottsboro trial, the Supreme Court ruled that the due process clause of the Fourteenth Amendment made the criminal protection procedures (the right to adequate defense counsel and the right to an impartial jury) of the Sixth Amendment applicable to the states. Second, Roosevelt created the Black Cabinet and had within his administration people committed to racial equality. Furthermore, African Americans continued, as they had throughout their history, to work in their own behalf to overcome the injustices and abuses associated with white racism. The March on Washington Movement and Roosevelt's subsequent issuance of Executive Order No. 8802 can be seen in this light.

Like blacks, women continued to suffer discrimination during the depression era. Although their contributions to the family increased, their status within the family remained unchanged. As more women entered the work force, they continued to face hostility, wage discrimination, and limited employment choices because of sex-typed occupations. Women participated in the shaping and execution of the New Deal through the "women's network" and through formal appointment to governmental posts, but the fact remained that much New Deal legislation either discriminated against or excluded women.

The chapter ends with a discussion of the presidential election of 1940 and the way in which historians view the legacy of the New Deal.

Building Vocabulary

Listed below are important words and terms that you need to know to get the most out of Chapter 25. They are listed in the order in which they occur in the chapter. After carefully looking through the list, refer to a dictionary and jot down the definition of words that you do not know or of which you are unsure.

severance

destitution

specter

moratorium

redemptive

ingratiating

analogue

solvent

queue

deflation

vehement

auspices

scrutinize

demagogue

fiscally

innocuous

assail

regressive

disparate

ironic

intimidate

pragmatic

privation

perpetuate

astute

contralto

inequity

docile

stereotype

maxim

astute

imminent

preempt

coherent

personify

ameliorate

Identification and Significance

After studying Chapter 25 of *A People and a Nation,* you should be able to identify fully *and* explain the historical significance of each item listed below.

1. Identify each item in the space provided. Give an explanation or description of the item. Answer the questions *who, what, where,* and *when.*

2. Explain the historical significance of each item in the space provided. Establish the historical context in which the item exists. Establish the item as the result of or as the cause of other factors existing in the society under study. Answer this question: *What were the political, social, economic, and/or cultural consequences of this item?*

Marvin Montgomery

> Identification

> Significance

"Hoovervilles"

> Identification

> Significance

the Farmers' Holiday Association

> Identification

> Significance

the Bonus Expeditionary Force

> Identification

> Significance

the Communist party

> Identification

> Significance

the Socialist party

   Identification

   Significance

Herbert Hoover

   Identification

   Significance

Andrew Mellon

   Identification

   Significance

the President's Organization on Unemployment Relief

   Identification

   Significance

the Federal Farm Board

   Identification

   Significance

the Reconstruction Finance Corporation

> Identification

> Significance

the Hawley-Smoot Tariff

> Identification

> Significance

the Revenue Act of 1932

> Identification

> Significance

the Twenty-First Amendment

> Identification

> Significance

Franklin D. Roosevelt

> Identification

> Significance

Eleanor Roosevelt

    Identification

    Significance

the Brain Trust

    Identification

    Significance

the economics of scarcity

    Identification

    Significance

the 1932 presidential campaign and election

    Identification

    Significance

the Twentieth Amendment

    Identification

    Significance

Roosevelt's first inaugural address

     Identification

     Significance

national bank holiday

     Identification

     Significance

the Emergency Banking Relief Bill (March 9, 1933)

     Identification

     Significance

the Economy Act (March 20, 1933)

     Identification

     Significance

Roosevelt's fireside chats

     Identification

     Significance

the Beer-Wine Revenue Act (March 22, 1933)

    Identification

    Significance

parity

    Identification

    Significance

the Agricultural Adjustment Act (May 12, 1933)

    Identification

    Significance

the Farm Credit Act (June 16, 1933)

    Identification

    Significance

the Civilian Conservation Corps (March 31, 1933)

    Identification

    Significance

the Federal Emergency Relief Act (May 12, 1933)

>   Identification

>   Significance

the National Industrial Recovery Act (June 16, 1933)

>   Identification

>   Significance

the Public Works Administration

>   Identification

>   Significance

the National Recovery Administration

>   Identification

>   Significance

Section 7(a) of NIRA

>   Identification

>   Significance

the Federal Securities Act (May 17, 1933)

     Identification

     Significance

the Banking Act of 1933 (June 16, 1933)

     Identification

     Significance

the Tennessee Valley Authority (May 18, 1933)

     Identification

     Significance

the First Hundred Days

     Identification

     Significance

the Commodity Credit Corporation (October 18, 1933)

     Identification

     Significance

the Taylor Grazing Act (June 28, 1934)

    Identification

    Significance

interest-group democracy

    Identification

    Significance

the American Liberty League

    Identification

    Significance

the "Okies" and "Arkies"

    Identification

    Significance

the Dust Bowl

    Identification

    Significance

Father Charles Coughlin

    Identification

    Significance

Dr. Francis E. Townsend

    Identification

    Significance

Huey Long

    Identification

    Significance

the Communist Party of the United States of America

    Identification

    Significance

Schechter v. *U.S.* and *U.S.* v. *Butler*

    Identification

    Significance

the Second New Deal

    Identification

    Significance

the Emergency Relief Appropriation Act (April 8, 1935)

    Identification

    Significance

the Works Progress Administration

    Identification

    Significance

the Federal Theater, Federal Music, and Federal Writers' Projects

    Identification

    Significance

the Second Hundred Days

    Identification

    Significance

the National Labor Relations (Wagner) Act (July 5, 1935)

      Identification

      Significance

the Social Security Act (August 15, 1935)

      Identification

      Significance

the Wealth Tax Act (August 30, 1935)

      Identification

      Significance

the 1936 presidential election

      Identification

      Significance

the New Deal coalition

      Identification

      Significance

the Judiciary Reorganization Bill of 1937

>Identification

>Significance

NLRB v. *Jones and Laughlin Steel Corp.*

>Identification

>Significance

the recession of 1937–1939

>Identification

>Significance

the National Housing Act (September 1, 1937)

>Identification

>Significance

the Fair Labor Standards Act (June 25, 1938)

>Identification

>Significance

craft unions vs. industrial unions

    Identification

    Significance

John L. Lewis

    Identification

    Significance

the Congress of Industrial Organizations

    Identification

    Significance

the United Auto Workers' strike of 1936

    Identification

    Significance

the Memorial Day Massacre

    Identification

    Significance

Judge John J. Parker

    Identification

    Significance

the Scottsboro trials

    Identification

    Significance

A. Philip Randolph

    Identification

    Significance

the Harlem Tenants League

    Identification

    Significance

the Black Cabinet

    Identification

    Significance

Marian Anderson

    Identification

    Significance

the March on Washington Movement

    Identification

    Significance

Executive Order No. 8802 (June 25, 1941)

    Identification

    Significance

John Collier

    Identification

    Significance

the Indian Reorganization Act (June 18, 1934)

    Identification

    Significance

Mexican Americans and the Depression

    Identification

    Significance

the Farm Security Administration

    Identification

    Significance

It's Up to the Women

    Identification

    Significance

the "women's network"

    Identification

    Significance

the 1940 presidential election

    Identification

    Significance

Organizing Information

President and Mrs. Roosevelt engaged in such a flurry of activity to jump-start a nation in the throes of a deep depression and also to influence social attitudes that it is difficult to remember all they did to re-shape Americans' concept of the federal government. To get a handle on the Roosevelt initiatives and programs and forms of social as well as political and economic leadership, complete the following two charts about New Deal achievements and then a third chart about how the roles of federal government evolved under the influence of the Roosevelts.

Achievements of the First and Second New Deals

The charts on the following pages include the major achievements of the First and Second New Deals discussed in Chapter 25. They are arranged in the same manner as in the chart on page 707 in the textbook. Use the charts to compile and organize information about New Deal achievements and categorize those achievements. Since some of the acts listed are not dealt with extensively in the text, your professor may want you to do some library research to better identify and explain the historical significance of each.

First New Deal Achievements

Labor	Agriculture	Business and Industrial Recovery	Relief	Reform
1933 Section 7A of NIRA Identification Significance	Agricultural Adjustment Act Identification Significance Farm Credit Act Identification Significance	Emergency Banking Act Identification Significance Beer-Wine Revenue Act Identification Significance Banking Act of 1933 Identification Significance National Industrial Recovery Act Identification Significance	Civilian Conservation Corps Identification Significance Federal Emergency Relief Act Identification Significance Home Owners Refinancing Act Identification Significance Public Works Administration Identification Significance Civil Works Administration Identification Significance	TVA Identification Significance Federal Securities Act Identification Significance
1934 National Labor Relations Board Identification Significance	Taylor Grazing Act Identification Significance			Securities Exchange Act Identification Significance

Second New Deal Achievements

Labor	Agriculture	Business and Industrial Recovery	Relief	Reform
1935 National Labor Relations Act Identification Significance	Resettlement Administration Identification Significance Rural Electrification Administration Identification Significance		Works Progress Administration Identification Significance National Youth Administration Identification Significance	Banking Act of 1935 Identification Significance Social Security Act Identification Significance Public Utilities Holding Co. Act Identification Significance Revenue Act Identification Significance
1937	Farm Security Administration Identification Significance			National Housing Act Identification Significance
1938 Fair Labor Standards Act Identification Significance	Agricultural Adjustment Act Identification Significance			

Evolving Roles of the Federal Government

Each column heading in the chart "Roles the Federal Government Assumed or Expanded to Turn Itself Into 'The' Government" names a kind of role that is now associated with the Roosevelt administrations and that, according to many Americans, represents a Depression-Era expansion of the concept of what government is all about. Under each sub-topic in each column, record illustrative examples mentioned in Chapter 25. Of course, you have already looked at many of these examples to come up with your entries for the two New Deal charts.

Roles the Federal Government Assumed or Expanded to Turn Itself into "The" Government				
Booster of Morale and Morality	**Regulator of Production, Consumption, Marketplace**	**Provider of Economic Safety Net for Individuals**	**Guardian of National Economic/ Financial Stability**	**Redistributor of Wealth, Resources, Power, and Status**
Public Confidence	Money Supply and Credit	Dependent Children	Regulator, Protector of Financial Institutions	Wealth
Racism/Sexism	Business Competition	Elderly Disabled	Balanced Budget/Deficit Spending	*Power/Treatment of Minorities* • African Americans
Sale/Consumption of Alcoholic Beverages	Farm Production, Prices Imports/Exports	Unemployed		• Native Americans • Mexican Americans • Women

Interpreting Information

Using information you collected from Chapter 25 and your class notes and then organized in the three Organizing Information charts, plan and write a working draft of an essay in direct response to the following question:

> In what ways could it be said that the Roosevelts and the Roosevelt administrations transformed the American public's perception of the functions of the federal government and the federal government's role in protecting citizens from economic catastrophe and social unfairness.

Let the chart "Roles the Federal Government Assumed or Expanded to Turn Itself Into 'The' Government" guide you in categorizing the most relevant specific examples from all three charts of attitude-shaping activities the federal government took on in the Roosevelt Era. Of course, you will want to cite the strongest examples to illustrate each of the categories. (You might want to review the hints in Chapter 8 of this study guide about writing essays—or sections of essays—about types or categories.)

Ideas and Details

Objective 1

_____ 1. As a result of the Great Depression,
    a. the Communist party became a major political force at the national level.
    b. the divorce rate soared.
    c. the number of marriages declined and the birthrate fell.
    d. shortages of basic agricultural commodities caused famine.

Objective 2

_____ 2. The reactions of Americans to the Great Depression indicate which of the following?
    a. Most Americans blamed the depression on the policies of the federal government.
    b. Anger at the capitalist system placed society on the verge of anarchy.
    c. Disillusionment with the American system caused the masses to think seriously of revolution.
    d. Many Americans blamed themselves for the depression.

Objective 3

_____ 3. Hoover responded to the Bonus March by
    a. calling out troops to disperse the marchers.
    b. establishing a comprehensive pension plan for future army veterans.
    c. encouraging Congress to authorize the immediate payment of veterans' benefits.
    d. meeting with the marchers and negotiating a settlement.

Objective 3

_____ 4. The Reconstruction Finance Corporation was based on the theory that
   a. an increase in supply leads to a corresponding increase in demand.
   b. the government must not interfere in the natural economic laws governing society.
   c. aid made available at the top of the economic ladder will trickle down to those at the bottom.
   d. taxes are a disincentive to economic recovery.

Objectives 4 and 5

_____ 5. Franklin Roosevelt's actions as governor of New York demonstrate that he
   a. accepted the theory that government should engage in deficit spending to combat an economic depression.
   b. was willing to use the government to combat the depression.
   c. believed that government should embark on a new trustbusting program to end bigness in industry.
   d. rejected the extension of direct government aid to the poor.

Objective 6

_____ 6. Both the Agricultural Adjustment Act and the National Industrial Recovery Act were based on the belief that
   a. the problems of the depression could best be solved by dealing with the problem of overproduction.
   b. prices of industrial and agricultural goods had to be lowered.
   c. deficit spending would result in an economic rebound.
   d. the depression could best be dealt with by state and local authorities.

Objectives 6 and 12

_____ 7. As a result of Section 7(a) of the National Industrial Recovery Act,
   a. unemployment insurance was provided to workers.
   b. federally guaranteed pension plans were required by all major corporations.
   c. workers were guaranteed the right to unionize and bargain collectively.
   d. workers were required to join company-sponsored unions.

Objective 7

_____ 8. Conservative critics charged that the New Deal
   a. cooperated too closely with business interests.
   b. extended too little aid to the lower classes.
   c. exercised too little control over economic forces.
   d. destroyed individual initiative.

Objective 7

_____ 9. Through the Share Our Wealth program, Huey Long advocated that the government should
a. nationalize all major industry in the United States.
b. distribute free land to all families requesting it.
c. provide a guaranteed annual income to all American families.
d. create a national health insurance program.

Objective 8

_____ 10. In 1935, the Supreme Court ruled part of the NIRA unconstitutional because it
a. violated the First Amendment.
b. delegated excessive legislative power to the executive branch.
c. discriminated against small businesses.
d. violated the due process clause of the Fourteenth Amendment.

Objectives 6 and 9

_____ 11. The Second New Deal differed from the First in that it
a. adopted a more aggressive, less cooperative approach toward big business.
b. returned to the concept of laissez faire.
c. rejected the concept of deficit spending.
d. emphasized the importance of state action.

Objective 9

_____ 12. Which of the following is true of the Social Security Act?
a. It established an old-age insurance plan for all workers in the United States.
b. Through its enactment, the government acknowledged some responsibility toward the aged, the dependent, and the disabled.
c. It established a national health insurance program for all Americans.
d. All benefits were paid by employers and the government.

Objective 11

_____ 13. Roosevelt's 1937 decision to cut federal spending resulted in
a. a balanced budget.
b. a lowering of interest rates.
c. renewed spending by business on capital improvements.
d. a new recession.

Objective 12

_____ 14. During the 1930s the growth of organized labor was most impressive among
          a. skilled workers.
          b. industrial workers.
          c. farm workers.
          d. white-collar workers.

Objective 13

_____ 15. Analysis of the AAA, the FHA, the CCC, and TVA indicates which of the following?
          a. These measures were quite effective in bringing about a redistribution of wealth in the United States.
          b. Money spent on such programs went mainly to the wealthy.
          c. All of these programs extended benefits to people in the city but not to the people in rural areas.
          d. Some New Deal measures functioned in ways that were discriminatory toward black Americans.

Essay Questions

Objective 1

1. Discuss the impact of the Great Depression on the lives of Americans. What was the response of the American people to the Depression? Why did they respond as they did?

Objective 3

2. Explain President Hoover's response to the depression.

Objectives 3 and 5

3. Discuss the similarities and differences between Herbert Hoover and Franklin Roosevelt in terms of personality, governing style, and view of the role of government.

Objectives 6 and 9

4. Discuss the similarities and differences between the theoretical basis of the First New Deal and that of the Second New Deal, and explain in both cases how the legislation enacted reflected this theory.

Objective 12

5. Discuss the impact of the New Deal on organized labor.

Objective 13

6. Examine the impact of the depression and New Deal on African Americans.

CHAPTER 26

Peaceseekers and Warmakers: Americans in the World, 1920–1941

Learning Objectives

After you have studied Chapter 26 in your textbook and worked through this study guide chapter, you should be able to:

1. Explain the ideas of independent internationalism and isolationism, and discuss how these ideas were manifested in the various attempts by American citizens and the American government to create a stable international order during the interwar years.

2. Examine and discuss the objectives and consequences of the foreign economic policy of the United States from 1918 to 1941.

3. Discuss the impact of the Great Depression on international relations, and explain Secretary of State Cordell Hull's response to intensified economic nationalism.

4. Examine and evaluate the interests, methods, and results of United States policy toward Latin America during the 1920s and 1930s.

5. Explain Europe's descent into the Second World War.

6. Explain the nature and growth of isolationist sentiment in the United States, and discuss the Neutrality Acts as an expression of such sentiment.

7. Discuss the foreign-policy ideas and diplomatic leadership of President Franklin Roosevelt from 1933 to United States entry into the Second World War.

8. Examine the erosion of American neutrality toward the war in Europe between September 1939 and December 7, 1941.

9. Examine the deterioration of Japanese-American relations from the 1920s to the Japanese attack against Pearl Harbor, and discuss American entry into the Pacific theater of the Second World War.

Thematic Guide

In this chapter, the authors seek to explain the instability of the world order in the 1920s and the coming of world war in the 1930s. Involvement in disarmament talks and arms limitation treaties, acceptance of the Kellogg-Briand Pact outlawing war, and international economic expansion by the United States serve as examples of the independent internationalist approach to foreign policy undertaken by the United States during the 1920s. These examples also illustrate the drawbacks of such an approach. United States acceptance of arms limitations treaties that did not include some of the most dangerous weapons of the age—submarines, destroyers, and cruisers—meant the continuation of rearmament. Acceptance of a treaty that outlawed war but had no enforcement provisions served a useful educational purpose but did not prevent war. International economic expansion, high United States tariff rates, United States policies concerning war debts and reparations, and the onset of the Great Depression caused an upsurge of economic nationalism and destabilized the international economy. Although Secretary of State Cordell Hull's attempts to move in the direction of economic internationalism were positive, they did not have a dramatic short-term impact.

In the 1920s, the United States altered its policy toward Latin America. Blatant military intervention no longer seemed to preserve American interests and maintain the order and stability so important to those interests. A new approach favored support for strong native leaders, training of the national guard in Latin American countries, continued economic expansion, Export-Import Bank loans, and political subversion. The discussion of American policy toward the Dominican Republic, Nicaragua, Haiti, Cuba, and Puerto Rico during the 1920s and early 1930s provides evidence of this change of approach. The Good Neighbor policy enhanced American power throughout the region but did not bring to Latin America the stable, democratic governments that the United States professed to desire. Mexico was a special case. In response to the expropriation controversy, President Roosevelt decided compromise was the best course of action. The general success of Roosevelt's policy can be seen in the 1936 Pan American Conference in Buenos Aires and the Declaration of Panama in 1939.

As the depression, economic nationalism, and aggressive fascist states began slowly to carry Europe into the abyss of war, the United States continued to follow the policy of independent internationalism, as evidenced in American economic ties with the Soviet Union and diplomatic recognition of that country in 1933. At the same time, isolationist sentiment (the desire to remain aloof from European power struggles and war) increased. Such sentiment found expression in the investigations of the Nye Committee, which attempted to prove that business interests had selfishly pulled the United States into the First World War. Although it failed to prove this assertion, the Nye Committee did find evidence of discreditable business practices during the 1920s and 1930s designed to increase arms sales. Furthermore, the chapter includes evidence of American business ties to Nazi Germany and fascist Italy. The publicity generated by the Nye Committee was in part responsible for passage of the Neutrality Acts of 1935, 1936, and 1937. Although Roosevelt supported these acts, events in Europe gradually convinced him that they should be revised and finally repealed.

In "Japan, China, and a New Order in Asia," the authors discuss American interests in Asia and trace the deterioration of United States–Japanese relations during the 1920s and 1930s. This discussion leads to the final section, "On a Collision Course with Japan and Germany, 1939–1941," where the authors focus on events in Europe and explain President Roosevelt's policies, which carried the United States from neutrality to undeclared war. In the end of the chapter, the authors offer answers to questions such as: Could the United States have avoided going to war and why did the United States enter the war?

Building Vocabulary

Listed below are important words and terms that you need to know to get the most out of Chapter 26. They are listed in the order in which they occur in the chapter. After carefully looking through the list, refer to a dictionary and jot down the definition of words that you do not know or of which you are unsure.

eradicate

infrastructure

virulent

fervent

unilateralism

elusive

emasculate

gloat

discreet

aversion

carnage

opportune

ape (verb)

magnanimous

cataclysm

indemnity

doldrums

usurp

blatant

exploitative

permeate

abrogate

disparage

tutelage

expropriate

authoritarianism

punitive

apex

satiate

scuttle

covet

protocol

malcontents

diligently

discretionary

chastise

consummate

deviant

affront

vestige

harry

ignoble

pummel

ardent

dissipate

Identification and Significance

After studying Chapter 26 of *A People and a Nation,* you should be able to identify fully *and* explain the historical significance of each item listed below.

1. Identify each item in the space provided. Give an explanation or description of the item. Answer the questions *who, what, where,* and *when.*

2. Explain the historical significance of each item in the space provided. Establish the historical context in which the item exists. Establish the item as the result of or as the cause of other factors existing in the society under study. Answer this question: *What were the political, social, economic, and/or cultural consequences of this item?*

the Rockefeller Foundation's anti-mosquito campaign

Identification

Significance

independent internationalism

Identification

Significance

the American peace movement

    Identification

    Significance

the Washington Conference

    Identification

    Significance

the Five-Power Treaty, the Nine-Power Treaty, and the Four-Power Treaty

    Identification

    Significance

the Kellogg-Briand Pact of 1928

    Identification

    Significance

American economic and cultural expansion

    Identification

    Significance

the Webb-Pomerene Act and the Edge Act

    Identification

    Significance

the war debts and reparations issue

    Identification

    Significance

the Dawes Plan of 1924

    Identification

    Significance

the Young Plan of 1929

    Identification

    Significance

the Johnson Act of 1934

    Identification

    Significance

economic nationalism

    Identification

    Significance

Cordell Hull

    Identification

    Significance

the Reciprocal Trade Agreements Act

    Identification

    Significance

the most-favored-nation principle

    Identification

    Significance

the Export-Import Bank

    Identification

    Significance

the Good Neighbor policy

    Identification

    Significance

Rafael Leonidas Trujillo

    Identification

    Significance

César Augusto Sandino

    Identification

    Significance

General Anastasio Somoza

    Identification

    Significance

the occupation of Haiti

    Identification

    Significance

the Cuban Revolution of 1933

Identification

Significance

Ramón Grau San Martín

Identification

Significance

Fulgencio Batista

Identification

Significance

Puerto Rico

Identification

Significance

the Jones Act of 1917

Identification

Significance

Pedro Albizo Campos

>   Identification

>   Significance

Luis Muñoz Marín

>   Identification

>   Significance

the Mexican expropriation controversy

>   Identification

>   Significance

the 1936 Pan American Conference in Buenos Aires

>   Identification

>   Significance

the Declaration of Panama

>   Identification

>   Significance

fascism

    Identification

    Significance

the Rome-Berlin Axis and the Anti-Comintern Pact

    Identification

    Significance

the policy of appeasement

    Identification

    Significance

the Abraham Lincoln Battalion

    Identification

    Significance

the Munich Conference

    Identification

    Significance

the Nazi-Soviet Pact

    Identification

    Significance

the German invasion of Poland

    Identification

    Significance

diplomatic recognition of the Soviet Union

    Identification

    Significance

American isolationist sentiment

    Identification

    Significance

the Nye Committee

    Identification

    Significance

the Neutrality Acts of 1935, 1936, and 1937

    Identification

    Significance

Roosevelt's Chautauqua speech

    Identification

    Significance

repeal of the arms embargo (the Neutrality Act of 1939)

    Identification

    Significance

The Good Earth

    Identification

    Significance

Jiang Jieshi

    Identification

    Significance

Japanese seizure of Manchuria

     Identification

     Significance

the Stimson Doctrine

     Identification

     Significance

the Sino-Japanese War

     Identification

     Significance

Roosevelt's quarantine speech

     Identification

     Significance

the *Panay* incident

     Identification

     Significance

Japan's "New Order"

    Identification

    Significance

the fall of France

    Identification

    Significance

the destroyers-for-bases agreement

    Identification

    Significance

the Selective Training and Service Act

    Identification

    Significance

the Lend-Lease Act

    Identification

    Significance

the Atlantic Charter

    Identification

    Significance

the *Greer*, the *Kearny*, and the *Reuben James*

    Identification

    Significance

the Tripartite Pact

    Identification

    Significance

Japanese occupation of French Indochina

    Identification

    Significance

Operation MAGIC

    Identification

    Significance

the Japanese attack on Pearl Harbor

Identification

Significance

Organizing Information

Using information from Chapters 21, 23, and 26 and your class notes, plan and write the working draft of an essay comparing or contrasting the way Presidents Woodrow Wilson and Franklin D. Roosevelt led the country into participation in world war and enter it in your Reading Notebook.

Use the information already entered in the chart "Going To War—World War I and World War II" as a guide in collecting and organizing the information your essay should include. In the second column, list Roosevelt's responses to developments leading to war that offer striking parallels or contrasts to Wilson's responses to developments leading to war. Add any other parallels or differences you think are significant in the three blank rows.

Going to War—World War I and World War II	
Wilson	**Roosevelt**
Wilson kept America out of war for three years. During that time he tried to protect American trading interests, tried to improve the country's military posture, and lectured the belligerents.	
Wilson and his administration clearly had pro-Allied sympathies. Despite those sympathies and in an attempt to keep America distanced from the war, Wilson at first issued a proclamation of neutrality and asked Americans to refrain from taking sides. Privately, also, he said that the nation definitely had to remain neutral	
As early as 1915, Wilson began planning a military build-up, and then in 1916 he got the legislation passed to launch and pay for it.	
Wilson's campaign slogan for the 1916 election was "He kept us out of war."	
When 128 Americans lost their lives in the sinking of the *Lusitania* by a German U-boat and when the Germans attacked other Allied ships with Americans aboard, Wilson ruled out a military response and refused to ban American travel on belligerent ships.	

Going to War—World War I and World War II (concluded)	
Wilson	**Roosevelt**
Wilson responded to the direct threat to U.S. security posed by Germany's seeking an alliance with Mexico against the United States (the Zimmermann telegram) by asking Congress for "armed neutrality" to defend American lives and commerce.	
Under Wilson, the military draft came only after the United States declared war	

Interpreting Information

Using the entries you made in the Organizing Information chart "Presidents Moving Toward War—World War I and World War II" as your guide, compose the working draft of an essay in direct response to the following question:

> How was President Franklin D. Roosevelt's approach to American entry into World War II different from President Woodrow Wilson's approach to American entry into World War I? What factors account for the differences?

You may want to review the hints about composing comparison and contrast essays in Chapter 5 of this study guide (Volume I).

Ideas and Details

Objective 2

_____ 1. Secretary of State Charles Evans Hughes encouraged United States economic expansion abroad because he believed such expansion
   a. would promote world stability.
   b. would foster healthy competition and rivalry.
   c. would bring power and glory to the United States at the expense of the less-virtuous European nations.
   d. would promote economic nationalism.

Objective 1

_____ 2. As a result of the Five-Power Treaty,
   a. Britain, the United States, Japan, France, and Italy agreed to limits on the number of submarines that each nation could build.
   b. Britain, the United States, and Japan dismantled some capital ships to meet the tonnage ratio agreed to.
   c. provisions for the enforcement of the Open Door policy were accepted by Britain, the United States, Japan, France, and Italy.
   d. Britain, the United States, France, Italy, and the Soviet Union agreed to impose economic sanctions against Nazi Germany.

Objective 1

_____ 3. The Kellogg-Briand Pact
  a. placed limits on the number of submarines and destroyers to be built by the world's five major powers.
  b. called for an end to international arms sales.
  c. made the United States an official observer at the League of Nations.
  d. renounced war as an instrument of national policy.

Objective 2

_____ 4. Which of the following conclusions may be drawn from an examination of the war debts and reparations issue?
  a. The United States handled the issue in a selfless manner.
  b. The triangular arrangement that emerged was economically destabilizing in the long run.
  c. The European nations demonstrated a willingness to forgive Germany in the aftermath of the First World War.
  d. The German government used the issue to create tensions between the United States and Great Britain.

Objectives 2 and 3

_____ 5. In response to the Hawley-Smoot Tariff,
  a. European states raised tariffs against American imports, causing economic nationalism to gain momentum.
  b. European nations exported inexpensive goods to the United States in record numbers.
  c. European states pledged to support the Open Door policy.
  d. Japan imposed an embargo against all American-made goods.

Objectives 2 and 3

_____ 6. The central feature of the Reciprocal Trade Agreements Act of 1934 was
  a. the adoption of free trade by the United States.
  b. low-interest loans to foreign countries agreeing to buy American goods.
  c. the most-favored-nation principle.
  d. the establishment of a free trade zone in the Western Hemisphere.

Objective 4

_____ 7. The Good Neighbor policy meant that
  a. the United States would strictly adhere to the doctrine of nonintervention in Latin America.
  b. the United States would be less blatant in dominating Latin America.
  c. American businesses in Latin America would invest their profits there rather than in the United States.
  d. the United States would practice isolationism in Latin America.

Objective 4

_____   8. Both the Trujillo regime in the Dominican Republic and the Somoza regime in Nicaragua are evidence that
   a.   American concepts of government were planted in fertile soil in Latin America.
   b.   the United States was careful to support Latin American rulers who were strongly supported by the masses.
   c.   Latin American dictators often rose through the ranks of a United States-trained national guard.
   d.   the United States continued to live up to its own revolutionary tradition by supporting liberation movements in Latin America.

Objective 5

_____   9. As a result of the Munich Conference,
   a.   Britain and France accepted Hitler's seizure of the Sudeten region of Czechoslovakia.
   b.   Britain agreed to extend financial and military aid to France in the event of German aggression.
   c.   Britain, France, and the Soviet Union entered into a defensive alliance against Nazi Germany.
   d.   Germany and France agreed to withdraw their troops from Austria and the Rhineland, respectively.

Objectives 2 and 6

_____   10. Records from the 1920s and 1930s concerning American business practices abroad indicate that
   a.   all major American corporations strongly supported arms control in the belief that fewer armaments would generate peace and prosperity.
   b.   American petroleum exports to Italy increased after that country's attack on Ethiopia.
   c.   all major American corporations severed their business ties with Germany when the Nazis gained power.
   d.   all American firms severed economic ties with Germany after learning about the persecution of Jews.

Objective 6

_____   11. The Neutrality Acts of 1935 and 1936
   a.   were attempts to provide aid to the Allies while avoiding war with Hitler.
   b.   imposed a unilateral freeze on further deployment of destroyer-class vessels.
   c.   allowed the president to intervene in the Spanish Civil War.
   d.   prohibited arms shipments and loans to nations declared by the president to be in a state of war.

Objective 8

_____   12. As a result of the outbreak of war in Europe in September 1939,
              a. Roosevelt promised that the United States would involve itself in the conflict if British defeat seemed imminent.
              b. Congress, at Roosevelt's urging, approved arms exports on a cash-and-carry basis.
              c. the United States broke diplomatic relations with the Soviet Union.
              d. Roosevelt asked Congress for a declaration of war against Germany.

Objective 9

_____   13. In response to the Japanese invasion of Manchuria, the United States
              a. issued the Stimson Doctrine by which it refused to recognize any impairment of Chinese sovereignty.
              b. froze Japanese assets in this country.
              c. called for economic sanctions against Japan through the League of Nations.
              d. signed a defensive treaty of alliance with China.

Objective 8

_____   14. By the Lend-Lease Act,
              a. the United States traded fifty old destroyers to the British for leases to four British bases.
              b. the provisions of the Neutrality Acts were revoked.
              c. Roosevelt was authorized to ship war materiel to the British.
              d. the United States canceled Allied debts from the First World War.

Objective 9

_____   15. The Roosevelt administration
              a. plotted to start a war with Japan.
              b. was completely surprised by the Japanese decision in favor of war.
              c. was aware of Japanese war plans but did not conspire to leave Pearl Harbor vulnerable.
              d. expected a Japanese attack against the American mainland.

Essay Questions

Objective 1

1. Discuss the Washington Conference's treaty agreements and the Kellogg-Briand Pact as examples of the United States independent-internationalist approach to foreign policy during the 1920s, and explain the strengths and weaknesses of that approach.

Objectives 1 and 2

2. Explain and evaluate American handling of the war debts and reparations issue.

Objective 4

3. Discuss the dominant themes suggested by American policy toward the Dominican Republic, Nicaragua, Haiti, Cuba, and Puerto Rico during the 1920s and 1930s.

Objective 6

4. Explain the sources of isolationist thought in the United States in the 1920s and 1930s, and discuss the actions taken by Congress to prevent United States involvement in European power struggles.

Objective 8

5. Explain the process by which the United States moved from neutrality in 1939 to undeclared war with Germany in 1941.

Objective 9

6. Trace relations between the United States and Japan during the 1920s and 1930s, and explain the Japanese decision to bomb Pearl Harbor.

CHAPTER 27

The Second World War at Home and Abroad, 1941–1945

Learning Objectives

After you have studied Chapter 27 in your textbook and worked through this study guide chapter, you should be able to:

1. Describe the military strategy and the major military operations undertaken by the Allies in the European theater; discuss the disagreements that arose concerning strategy; and explain the resolution of these disagreements.

2. Discuss United States military strategy and the major military operations in the Pacific theater that brought America to the verge of victory by 1945.

3. Explain and evaluate President Truman's decision to use the atomic bomb.

4. Examine the impact of the Second World War on America's economic institutions, organized labor, agriculture, and the federal government, and discuss and assess the role played by the federal government in the war effort.

5. Discuss the impact of military life and wartime experiences on the men and women in the United States armed forces during the Second World War.

6. Examine and evaluate the civil liberties record of the United States government during the Second World War, and discuss the government's response to the Holocaust and to the plight of Jewish refugees.

7. Discuss the impact of the Second World War on African Americans, Mexican Americans, women, and the family.

8. Discuss the decline of political liberalism during the early 1940s, and examine the issues and personalities and explain the outcome of the 1944 presidential election.

9. Examine the relations, the issues debated, and the agreements reached among the Allies from the second-front controversy through the Yalta and Potsdam conferences, and discuss the issues left unresolved after Yalta and Potsdam.

10. Assess the impact of the Second World War on the world community of nations and on the world balance of power.

Thematic Guide

The first two sections of Chapter 27, "Winning the Second World War in Europe" and "The War in the Pacific," trace the European and Pacific theater campaigns that led to Allied victory in World War II. The undercurrent of suspicion among the Allies, obvious in the second-front controversy, provides the theme for discussion of the European campaigns. Discussion of the war in the Pacific focuses on America's wartime perception of Japan as the major enemy. The authors also consider the "island-hopping" strategy adopted by American forces after breaking the momentum of Japan's offensive at the Battle of Midway, and the American goal of crippling Japan's merchant marine. The success of these strategies led to the conventional bombing of Japan's cities and ultimately to the use of atomic bombs on Hiroshima and Nagasaki. Truman's rejection of suggested alternatives to the atomic bomb and the strategic, emotional, psychological, and diplomatic reasons for his decision to use it are explained at the end of the section on the war in the Pacific.

The focus of the chapter then shifts to a discussion of the impact of World War II on the home front. In the economic sphere the war brought (1) renewed government-business cooperation and an acceleration of corporate growth, (2) the growth of scientific research facilities through government incentives, (3) the growth of labor unions, and (4) increased mechanization of agriculture as part of a transition from family-owned farms to mechanized agribusiness. The Second World War, to an even greater extent than the First World War, was a total war, requiring not only military mobilization but mobilization of the home front as well. The responsibility for coordinating total mobilization fell on the federal government. As a result, the federal bureaucracy mushroomed in size.

Life in the military, life away from family, and the experience of war profoundly affected the men and women who served in the armed forces during the course of the Second World War. The frame of reference of many GIs was broadened by associations with fellow soldiers from backgrounds and cultures different from their own. Some men and women homosexuals found the freedom within the service to act upon their sexual feelings. As a consequence of the military's technical schools, many soldiers returned home with new skills and ambitions. But as GIs returned to civilian life, they quickly realized that life at home had continued without them; thus, many felt a sense of loss and alienation.

The war had a special impact on Japanese Americans, nonwhites, and women. The authors note that the treatment of Japanese Americans was the "one enormous exception" to the nation's generally creditable wartime civil liberties record; Japanese Americans were interned chiefly because of their ethnic origin. For African Americans, the war did provide some opportunities in the military and at home, but the Detroit riot of 1943 made clear that racism remained a shaping force in blacks' lives. The zoot-suit riot in Los Angeles in 1943 demonstrated that the same was true for Mexican Americans.

For women, the war became a turning point. More women, including more married women and mothers, entered the labor force than ever before. As some of the negative attitudes toward women working in heavy industry began to change, women experienced more geographic and occupational mobility. Although they continued to receive lower pay than men and were still concentrated in sex-segregated occupations, more women than ever were deciding to remain in the labor market. But even with those changes, home and family responsibilities continued to fall on their shoulders. In many cases, the wartime absence of husbands and fathers made women fully responsible for the family. The combination of these factors and experiences meant that many women gained a new sense of independence.

The political impact of the war is the theme of "The Decline of Liberalism and the Election of 1944." Then, in the last two sections of the chapter, the authors examine wartime foreign policy. The goals of the United States, embodied in the Atlantic Charter, were based to some extent on the memory of the post-First World War period. Continued suspicions among the Allies made cooperation to achieve these objectives difficult. Despite these suspicions and continued disagreement over Poland, Stalin and Churchill reached some agreements about Eastern Europe; and, though China's role was not determined, the Allies agreed in most other respects on the charter for a United Nations Organization.

After a brief discussion of American policy toward Jewish refugees—a policy characterized by anti-Semitism and fear of economic competition—the authors turn to the Yalta and Potsdam conferences. The Yalta Conference was "the high point of the Grand Alliance." The agreements reached there are explained in the context of the suspicions among the Allies, the goals of each of the Allies, and the positions of each of the Allied armies. The Potsdam Conference, on the other hand, revealed a crumbling alliance in which any sense of cooperation had given way to suspicions among competitive nation states. These suspicions, so obvious at Potsdam, were a portent concerning the post-war world.

Building Vocabulary

Listed below are important words and terms that you need to know to get the most out of Chapter 27. They are listed in the order in which they occur in the chapter. After carefully looking through the list, refer to a dictionary and jot down the definition of words that you do not know or of which you are unsure.

decipher

indispensable

capitulate

internment

balk

mollify

peripheral

amphibious

clandestine

saboteurs

titular

tenacious

deterrent

intimidate

elicit

exemplify

interdependence

abstraction

retrospect

instigate

obliterate

wantonly

enfeeble

novice

Identification and Significance

After studying Chapter 27 of *A People and a Nation,* you should be able to identify fully *and* explain the historical significance of each item listed below.

1.   Identify each item in the space provided. Give an explanation or description of the item. Answer the questions *who, what, where,* and *when.*

2.   Explain the historical significance of each item in the space provided. Establish the historical context in which the item exists. Establish the item as the result of or as the cause of other factors existing in the society under study. Answer this question: *What were the political, social, economic, and/or cultural consequences of this item?*

the Code Talkers

    Identification

    Significance

the "Europe first" formula

    Identification

    Significance

Winston Churchill

  Identification

  Significance

Josef Stalin

  Identification

  Significance

the second-front controversy

  Identification

  Significance

the battle for Stalingrad

  Identification

  Significance

the Teheran Conference

  Identification

  Significance

Operation Overlord

    Identification

    Significance

D-Day

    Identification

    Significance

the Battle of the Bulge

    Identification

    Significance

the Bataan Death March

    Identification

    Significance

the Battle of the Coral Sea and the Battle of Midway

    Identification

    Significance

Operation MAGIC

Identification

Significance

the "island-hop" strategy

Identification

Significance

the Battles of Iwo Jima and Okinawa

Identification

Significance

the bombing of Tokyo

Identification

Significance

the Manhattan Project

Identification

Significance

Hiroshima and Nagasaki

    Identification

    Significance

the Office of War Information

    Identification

    Significance

the Office of Price Administration

    Identification

    Significance

the War Production Board

    Identification

    Significance

the synthetic-rubber industry

    Identification

    Significance

government-business interdependence

     Identification

     Significance

American universities and war research

     Identification

     Significance

antibiotics and sulfa drugs

     Identification

     Significance

the no strike–no lockout pledge

     Identification

     Significance

the National War Labor Board

     Identification

     Significance

the War Labor Disputes (Smith-Connally) Act

   Identification

   Significance

agribusiness

   Identification

   Significance

post-traumatic stress disorder

   Identification

   Significance

homosexuals on active duty

   Identification

   Significance

the Alien Registration (Smith) Act

   Identification

   Significance

conscientious objectors

    Identification

    Significance

the internment of Japanese Americans

    Identification

    Significance

the 442nd Regimental Combat Team

    Identification

    Significance

the *Hirabayashi* ruling and the *Korematsu* case

    Identification

    Significance

the Commission on Wartime Relocation and Internment of Civilians

    Identification

    Significance

Colonel Benjamin O. Davis

    Identification

    Significance

the "Double V" campaign

    Identification

    Significance

the Congress of Racial Equality

    Identification

    Significance

Executive Order No. 8802

    Identification

    Significance

the Detroit riot of 1943

    Identification

    Significance

the *bracero* program

      Identification

      Significance

the zoot-suit riot

      Identification

      Significance

women's war work

      Identification

      Significance

Rosie the Riveter

      Identification

      Significance

latchkey children

      Identification

      Significance

the Lanham Act

    Identification

    Significance

Extended School Services

    Identification

    Significance

the 1942 congressional elections

    Identification

    Significance

the Economic Bill of Rights

    Identification

    Significance

Harry S Truman

    Identification

    Significance

Thomas E. Dewey

   Identification

   Significance

the presidential election of 1944

   Identification

   Significance

the Polish question

   Identification

   Significance

the Katyn Forest massacre and the Warsaw Uprising

   Identification

   Significance

the Dumbarton Oaks Conference

   Identification

   Significance

Jewish refugees from the Holocaust

      Identification

      Significance

the voyage of the *St. Louis*

      Identification

      Significance

the War Refugee Board

      Identification

      Significance

the Yalta Conference

      Identification

      Significance

the Potsdam Conference

      Identification

      Significance

The Best Years of Our Lives

Identification

Significance

Organizing Information

Collect information from Chapter 27 and your class notes about the successes and failures scored by the United States during World War II in reducing discrimination against women and minorities and extending full political, social, and economic rights to them. Record reminders of the information you find in the appropriate blocks in the chart "American Treatment of Minorities During World War II." You will not find information to put in every block.

American Treatment of Minorities During World War II					
Standard of Measurement	**Women**	**African Americans**	**Mexican Americans**	**Japanese Americans**	**Homosexuals**	**Jews and Other Refugees**
Acceptance in Armed Forces						
Degree of Integration into Activities of Dominant Group						
Job Opportunities and Wages/ Provision of Needed Job-Related Social Services						
Victimization in Riots or Other Violence						
Kind of Support Given or Denied in Immigration Policies and Diplomatic Efforts						

Interpreting Information

Referring to the entries you have made in the Organizing Information chart "American Treatment of Minorities During World War II, analyze the nation's wartime progress in the area of eliminating discrimination against women and minorities in American society. Based on your analysis, compose the working draft of an essay that responds directly to this question:

> Identify and discuss the advances and setbacks American women and members of minority groups experienced during and partly because of World War II in their on-going effort to combat political, economic, and social discrimination against them. How far were the contributions to the war effort by women and minorities rewarded by reduction in the various forms of discrimination from which these groups have traditionally suffered?

Ideas and Details

Objective 1

_____ 1. Roosevelt initially wanted to open a second front in 1942 because
   a. he wanted to check Russian power on the European continent.
   b. the North African campaign had been highly successful.
   c. Churchill insisted it was the only way to save England.
   d. he was afraid Russia might be defeated, leaving Hitler free to invade England.

Objective 1

_____ 2. As a result of the Teheran Conference, the Allies
   a. reached agreement on launching Operation Overlord.
   b. agreed to launch an attack against North Africa.
   c. reluctantly decided to recognize the pro-Nazi Vichy French regime in North Africa.
   d. made plans for the battle for Stalingrad.

Objective 2

_____ 3. As a result of the Battle of Midway,
   a. the United States destroyed Japan's merchant marine.
   b. Japanese momentum in the Pacific was broken.
   c. American naval losses made Hawaii more vulnerable to attack.
   d. President Roosevelt began to harbor private fears of Japanese victory in the Pacific.

Objective 3

_____ 4. Truman decided to drop the atomic bomb on Japan, in part, because
   a. he believed it was the only way the United States could win the war in the Pacific.
   b. a quick American victory against Japan would allow the United States to concentrate on defeating Hitler.
   c. the Allies decided collectively at Potsdam that it was the quickest and most humane way to defeat Japan.
   d. he wanted to prevent the Soviet Union from having a role in the reconstruction of postwar Asia.

Objective 4

_____ 5. The first task of the War Production Board was to
   a. vigorously enforce the nation's antitrust laws.
   b. minimize the cost of the war by ensuring competitive bidding on government contracts.
   c. oversee the conversion of industry from civilian to military production.
   d. analyze the military situation in order to determine what weapons needed to be produced and in what quantity.

Objective 4

_____ 6. The Smith-Connally Act
   a. reduced the powers of the NWLB.
   b. prohibited strikes and lockouts.
   c. guaranteed cost of living increases to workers in defense-related industries.
   d. authorized the president to seize and operate any strike-bound plant deemed necessary to the national security.

Objective 4

_____ 7. The Second World War affected America's basic economic institutions in which of the following ways?
   a. Large economic units were broken up by the government to increase competition.
   b. The trend toward bigness in industry and agriculture accelerated as a result of the war.
   c. The withdrawal of government money from the economy brought a restructuring of industry and agriculture.
   d. The banking industry was virtually nationalized to ensure the availability of money for the war effort.

Objective 5

_____   8. Those who served in the United States armed forces during the Second World War
   a. often found their horizons broadened because of associations with people of differing backgrounds.
   b. found that the technical training they received in the military was useless in civilian life.
   c. usually received no training before being sent into combat.
   d. were given no background information on the history and culture of the places to which they were sent.

Objective 6

_____   9. Which of the following is the major reason for the internment of Japanese Americans during the Second World War?
   a. Criminal behavior
   b. Evidence of disloyalty to the government of the United States
   c. Their ethnic origin
   d. Their economic challenge to white businesses

Objective 7

_____   10. During the Second World War, African Americans
   a. continued to move to northern cities, where they began to gain more political power.
   b. experienced equal opportunity in housing and employment.
   c. experienced a deterioration of their economic position.
   d. steadfastly refused to participate in the war effort.

Objective 8

_____   11. Which of the following is true of the 1944 presidential election?
   a. Roosevelt was elected to a fourth term by a popular-vote landslide.
   b. Fear of a postwar depression led many people to vote for Roosevelt.
   c. While Roosevelt won the election, the Republicans carried the South.
   d. Harry Truman won a narrow victory over Thomas Dewey in both the popular vote and the electoral vote.

Objective 6

_____   12. In response to Nazi persecution of the Jews, the United States
   a. did not act in a decisive manner until the creation of the War Refugee Board in 1944.
   b. relaxed immigration requirements in the mid-1930s in order to allow Jewish refugees free entry into the United States.
   c. cooperated closely with the British in opening Palestine to Jewish refugees.
   d. bombed the gas chambers at Nordhausen toward the end of the war.

Objective 9

_____ 13. A major factor that influenced the agreements at Yalta was
   a. Roosevelt's ill health.
   b. dissension between Roosevelt and Churchill over German reparations.
   c. the military positions of the Allies.
   d. Stalin's insistence that China be recognized as a major power.

Objective 10

_____ 14. Which of the following countries suffered the most casualties as a result of the Second World War?
   a. Great Britain
   b. the United States
   c. Japan
   d. the Soviet Union

Objective 10

_____ 15. Which of the following countries emerged from the Second World War more powerful than it had been when it entered the war?
   a. Great Britain
   b. the United States
   c. Japan
   d. Russia

Essay Questions

Objective 1

1. Discuss the disagreements within the Grand Alliance over the opening of a second front, and explain how these disagreements were ultimately resolved.

Objective 3

2. Examine and assess President Truman's decision to use the atomic bomb.

Objective 4

3. Discuss the various responsibilities assumed by the federal government as coordinator and overseer of America's war effort, and evaluate its performance.

Objective 4

4. Discuss the trend toward bigness in American industry, organized labor, and agriculture during the course of the Second World War.

Objective 7

5. Discuss the impact of the Second World War on nonwhite Americans.

Objective 8

6. Examine the issues and explain the outcome of the 1944 presidential election.

Objective 9

7. Discuss the similarities and differences between the "spirit of Yalta" and the "brawl at Potsdam," and explain and assess the agreements reached at these conferences.

CHAPTER 28

Postwar America: Cold War Politics, Civil Rights, and the Baby Boom, 1945–1961

Learning Objectives

After you have studied Chapter 28 in your textbook and worked through this study guide chapter, you should be able to:

1. Examine the domestic economic problems that faced the Truman administration during the immediate postwar period; explain Truman's actions concerning those problems; and discuss the consequences of those actions.

2. Explain the actions of the Eightieth Congress concerning major domestic issues; and discuss the consequences of those actions.

3. Examine the issues and personalities and explain the outcome of the 1948 presidential election.

4. Examine the issues and personalities and explain the outcome of the 1952 congressional and presidential elections.

5. Discuss the legacy of the Truman years, and assess the Truman presidency.

6. Discuss the 1950s as an age of consensus and conformity, and explain the beliefs associated with this consensus mood.

7. Discuss the domestic issues facing the Eisenhower administration; explain and evaluate the administration's handling of those issues; and discuss the consequences of those actions.

8. Discuss the legacy of the Eisenhower years, and assess the Eisenhower presidency.

9. Discuss the combination of forces and incidents that caused the postwar wave of anti-Communist hysteria, and examine the various ways in which this hysteria manifested itself.

10. Explain Senator Joseph McCarthy's rise to power and his ultimate decline, and discuss the impact of the postwar wave of anti-Communist hysteria on American society.

11. Discuss the gains of African Americans during the late 1940s and early 1950s, and examine the factors responsible for those gains.

12. Examine the reinvigoration of the civil rights movement during the 1950s; discuss the response of white southerners and of the federal government to the demands and actions of African Americans; and explain the extent to which African Americans were successful in achieving their goals.

13. Discuss the reasons for and indicate the extent of the postwar baby boom.

14. Examine the cornerstones of the postwar economic boom, and discuss the causes and consequences of the computer revolution.

15. Examine the forces that contributed to the growth of the Sunbelt, the growth of the suburbs, and the emergence of the megalopolis during the postwar period; indicate the characteristics associated with suburban life; and discuss the criticisms leveled against suburbia.

16. Discuss the concentration of ownership in industry, and explain how the merger wave of the 1950s and 1960s differed from previous merger waves.

17. Discuss the characteristics of and the trends within the labor movement and agriculture from 1945 to 1970.

18. Discuss the impact of the postwar economic boom on the environment.

19. Discuss American concepts about education and American attitudes about religion and sex during the 1950s.

20. Discuss changes in the American family, the role of women, and the concept of motherhood during the 1950s and 1960s.

21. Explain the characteristics of each of the following, and discuss their impact on American society in the 1940s, 1950s, and early 1960s:
    a. Television
    b. Advertising
    c. Motion pictures
    d. Popular music
    e. Fads
    f. the Beat writers

22. Examine the reasons for, extent of, and effects of poverty in America during the postwar era, and discuss the characteristics of the poor.

23. Examine the issues and personalities and explain the outcome of the 1960 presidential election.

Thematic Guide

After the Second World War, the United States experienced an uneasy and troubled transition to peace. The Truman administration was plagued by postwar economic problems, and the administration's handling of those problems led to widespread public discontent which in turn led to Republican victory in the 1946 congressional elections. However, the actions of the conservative Eightieth Congress worked to Truman's political advantage; and, to the surprise of most analysts, he won the presidential election of 1948.

During Truman's first elected term, he and the American people had to contend with the domestic consequences of the Korean War. Although the war brought prosperity, it also brought inflation and increased defense spending at the expense of the domestic programs of Truman's Fair Deal. Furthermore, both the nature and length of the Korean War led to disillusionment and discontent on the part of many Americans. These factors, coupled with reports of influence peddling in the Truman administration, caused the President's approval rating to plummet and led to a Republican triumph in the presidential and congressional elections of 1952.

After a discussion of the Truman legacy, the authors turn to a discussion of the "age of consensus"—a period in which Americans agreed on their stance against communism and their faith in economic progress. Believing in the rightness of the American system, many people viewed reform and reformers in a negative light and saw conflict as the product of psychologically disturbed individuals, not as the product of societal ills. President Dwight D. Eisenhower, sharing these beliefs, actively pursued policies designed to promote economic growth and to defeat communism at home and abroad.

In pursuit of economic growth, Eisenhower tried to reduce federal spending and the federal government's role in regulating the forces of the marketplace. Eisenhower's farm policies reflected these efforts, and his belief that government should actively promote economic development may be seen in the St. Lawrence Seaway project, the president's tax reform program, the Atomic Energy Act, and the Highway Act of 1956. Furthermore, Eisenhower's conservative fiscal policy, as well as his states' rights philosophy, may be seen in the Indian termination policy adopted during his administration. The authors relate these programs to Eisenhower's frame of reference and study their impact on American society.

Despite Eisenhower's fiscal conservatism, the administration's activist foreign policy and three domestic economic recessions caused increased federal expenditures, decreased tax revenues, and deficit spending. As a result, Eisenhower oversaw only three balanced budgets during his eight years in office. The Sherman Adams scandal and large Democratic gains in the congressional elections of 1958, meant that a beleaguered Eisenhower was on the defensive during his last two years in office.

During the late 1940s and early 1950s, the United States also witnessed a wave of anti-Communist hysteria. The tracing of events from the *Amerasia* case to Truman's loyalty probe, the Hiss trial, and the Klaus Fuchs case supports the view that (1) fear of communism, long present in American society, intensified during the postwar years; (2) the building of this fear in the late 1940s was in many ways a "top-down phenomenon"; (3) revelations gave people cause to be alarmed; and (4) McCarthy's name has been given to a state of mind that existed before he entered the scene. Further discussion supports the characterization of McCarthy as a demagogue, the idea that McCarthyism was sustained by events, and the contention that anti-Communist measures received widespread support.

Eisenhower's strong anti-Communist views are reflected in his broadening of the loyalty program, his actions in the Rosenberg case, and his support for the Communist Control Act of 1954. Furthermore, Eisenhower chose to avoid a direct confrontation with Senator Joe McCarthy. As a result, McCarthy proceeded to add more victims to his list of alleged subversives and continued to jeopardize freedom of speech and expression. Ultimately, McCarthyism did decline, with McCarthy himself being largely responsible for his own demise.

One group that challenged the consensus mood of the age was African Americans. Under Truman, the federal government, for the first time since Reconstruction, accepted responsibility for guaranteeing equality under the law—civil rights—to African Americans. Furthermore, work by the NAACP, aid by the Justice Department in the form of friend-of-the-court briefs, and decisions by the Supreme Court resulted in a slow erosion of the separate-but-equal doctrine and of black disfranchisement in the South. Then the Supreme Court's historic decision in *Brown* v. *Board of Education of Topeka* gave African Americans reason to believe that their long struggle against racism was beginning to pay off. However, white southerners reacted with hostility to that decision and actively resisted Court-ordered desegregation. This resistance led to the crisis in Little Rock, Arkansas, a crisis in which Eisenhower felt compelled to use federal troops to prevent violence in the desegregation of the city's public schools. But the Little Rock crisis was merely the tip of an emerging civil rights movement as can be seen through the discussion of the Montgomery bus boycott, the formation of the Southern Christian Leadership Conference, the sit-in movement, and organization of the Student Nonviolent Coordinating Committee.

After discussion of Cold War politics and the civil rights movement, we focus on the social and cultural development of American society between 1945 and 1961. This period is characterized by sustained economic growth and prosperity. One of the consequences of this prosperity was the "baby boom," which fueled more economic growth. This increase in population was especially important to the automobile and construction industries, two of the cornerstones of the economic expansion during the period. The third cornerstone, military spending, was sustained by the government.

As many white middle-class Americans made more money, bought more goods, and created more waste, they also continued a mass migration to the Sunbelt that had begun during the war. In addition, Americans increasingly fled from the cities to the suburbs. Drawn to the suburbs by many factors, including a desire to be with like-minded people and the desire for "family togetherness," life in suburbia was often made possible by government policies that extended economic aid to families making such a move. Federal, state, and local expenditures on highway construction also spurred the growth of suburbia and led to the development of the megalopolis. Although suburbia had its critics, most Americans seemed to prefer the lifestyle it offered.

Government aid also played a role in other developments that would have a momentous impact on American society. In the late 1940s, government aid to weapons research led to the development of the transistor, which brought the computer and technological revolution to American society. This revolution affected employment patterns, led to the third great merger wave (characterized by conglomerate mergers), and played a role in stabilizing union membership. Consolidation in industry was matched by consolidation in labor (the merging of the AFL and the CIO) and an acceleration of the trend toward bigness in American agriculture. As the cost of farm machinery, pesticides, fertilizer, and land soared, agribusiness presented more of a threat than ever to the family farm.

Economic growth inspired by government defense spending and by the growth of a more affluent population demanding more consumer goods and larger quantities of agricultural products had a negative impact on the environment. Automobiles and factories polluted the air. Human and industrial waste polluted rivers, lakes, and streams. Pesticides endangered wildlife and humans alike, as did the waste from nuclear processing plants. Disposable products marketed as conveniences made America a "throw-away society."

As both education and religion gained importance in American life during the postwar years, Americans were also, paradoxically, caught up in the materialistic values and pleasures of the era. This fact is revealed through a discussion of the effects of television on American society during the postwar era. The postwar economic boom also affected the family. The changes it brought included the influence of Dr. Benjamin Spock on the parent-child relationship and the conflicting and changing roles of women as more entered the labor market.

After a discussion of the influence of the pioneering work of Dr. Alfred Kinsey in the late 1940s and early 1950s on American attitudes toward sexual behavior, we look at the emergence of a youth subculture, the birth of rock 'n' roll, the fads of the era, and the critique of American society offered by the Beat Generation of the 1950s.

Prosperity did not bring about a meaningful redistribution of income in American society during the period under study. Therefore, many Americans (about 25 percent in 1962) lived in poverty. The authors provide a statistical picture of America's poor, who stood in decided contrast to the affluence around them. As before, the poor congregated in urban areas. African Americans, poor whites, Puerto Ricans, Chicanos, and Native Americans continued their movement to low-income inner-city housing, while the more affluent city residents—mostly whites—continued their exodus to the suburbs. Although low-interest government housing loans made life in suburbia possible for many middle-class whites, government programs such as "urban renewal" hurt the urban poor.

Within the context of a rapidly changing American society, Richard M. Nixon and John F. Kennedy became the standard-bearers for the Republican and Democratic parties in the presidential election contest of 1960. The chapter ends with a discussion of this election and the reason's for Kennedy's victory.

Building Vocabulary

Listed below are important words and terms that you need to know to get the most out of Chapter 28. They are listed in the order in which they occur in the chapter. After carefully looking through the list, refer to a dictionary and jot down the definition of words that you do not know or of which you are unsure.

indulgent

invincibility

constitute

volatile

reconversion

staunchly

quiescent

alienate

livid

vindicate

oblivious

spunk

bona fide

pretense

syntax

status quo

unabashedly

savvy

covert

conjunction

subservient

distraught

affront

malign

sully

aspirations

resurgence

tacitly

impede

perseverance

quell

apathetic

invigorate

befoul

castigate

atheistic

venerated

vicariously

boorish

psychic

flaunt

unsavory

tepid

Identification and Significance

After studying Chapter 28 of *A People and a Nation,* you should be able to identify fully *and* explain the historical significance of each item listed below.

1. Identify each item in the space provided. Give an explanation or description of the item. Answer the questions *who, what, where,* and *when.*

2. Explain the historical significance of each item in the space provided. Establish the historical context in which the item exists. Establish the item as the result of or as the cause of other factors existing in the society under study. Answer this question: *What were the political, social, economic, and/or cultural consequences of this item?*

postwar unemployment

  Identification

  Significance

postwar inflation

  Identification

  Significance

the threatened railroad strike of 1946

    Identification

    Significance

the Eightieth Congress

    Identification

    Significance

the Taft-Hartley Act

    Identification

    Significance

the Progressive party

    Identification

    Significance

the Dixiecrats

    Identification

    Significance

the presidential campaign and election of 1948

Identification

Significance

Korean War discontent

Identification

Significance

Dwight D. Eisenhower

Identification

Significance

the congressional and presidential elections of 1952

Identification

Significance

the age of consensus

Identification

Significance

"the vital center"

        Identification

        Significance

dynamic conservatism

        Identification

        Significance

the St. Lawrence Seaway

        Identification

        Significance

the Atomic Energy Act

        Identification

        Significance

the termination policy

        Identification

        Significance

the congressional elections of 1954

    Identification

    Significance

Lyndon B. Johnson

    Identification

    Significance

the Highway Act of 1956

    Identification

    Significance

the congressional and presidential elections of 1956

    Identification

    Significance

the congressional elections of 1958

    Identification

    Significance

the military-industrial complex

    Identification

    Significance

the *Amerasia* incident

    Identification

    Significance

Truman's loyalty program (Employee Loyalty Program)

    Identification

    Significance

the "Hollywood Ten"

    Identification

    Significance

redbaiting

    Identification

    Significance

the Alger Hiss case

>Identification

>Significance

Klaus Fuchs

>Identification

>Significance

Senator Joseph McCarthy

>Identification

>Significance

the Rosenbergs

>Identification

>Significance

the Internal Security Act of 1950

>Identification

>Significance

Dennis et al. v. *U.S.*

    Identification

    Significance

the Communist Control Act of 1954

    Identification

    Significance

the Army-McCarthy hearings

    Identification

    Significance

To Secure These Rights

    Identification

    Significance

the Employment Board of the Civil Service Commission

    Identification

    Significance

the Committee on Equality of Treatment and Opportunity in the Armed Services

Identification

Significance

Thurgood Marshall

Identification

Significance

Smith v. *Allwright* and *Morgan* v. *Virginia*

Identification

Significance

Shelly v. *Kramer*

Identification

Significance

An American Dilemma, Native Son, and *Black Boy*

Identification

Significance

Brown v. *Board of Education of Topeka*

    Identification

    Significance

White Citizens' Councils

    Identification

    Significance

the Little Rock crisis

    Identification

    Significance

Rosa Parks

    Identification

    Significance

Martin Luther King, Jr.

    Identification

    Significance

the Southern Christian Leadership Conference

Identification

Significance

the Montgomery bus boycott

Identification

Significance

the Civil Rights Act of 1957

Identification

Significance

the sit-in movement

Identification

Significance

the Student Nonviolent Coordinating Committee

Identification

Significance

John F. Kennedy

    Identification

    Significance

the baby boom

    Identification

    Significance

the housing boom

    Identification

    Significance

Arthur Levitt and Sons

    Identification

    Significance

the Highway Act of 1956

    Identification

    Significance

growth of the suburbs

> Identification

> Significance

the megalopolis

> Identification

> Significance

the Sunbelt

> Identification

> Significance

the computer revolution

> Identification

> Significance

conglomerate mergers

> Identification

> Significance

the postwar labor movement

       Identification

       Significance

agricultural consolidation

       Identification

       Significance

the environmental costs associated with economic growth

       Identification

       Significance

Silent Spring

       Identification

       Significance

"planned obsolescence"

       Identification

       Significance

William H. Whyte and C. Wright Mills

Identification

Significance

the GI Bill of Rights

Identification

Significance

the National Defense Education Act

Identification

Significance

the postwar religious revival

Identification

Significance

television

Identification

Significance

Dr. Benjamin Spock

    Identification

    Significance

Momism

    Identification

    Significance

the Kinsey reports

    Identification

    Significance

rock 'n' roll

    Identification

    Significance

Elvis Presley

    Identification

    Significance

Slinky, Silly Putty, 3-D movies, and hula hoops

Identification

Significance

Invisible Man

Identification

Significance

the Beat writers

Identification

Significance

inner-city and rural poverty

Identification

Significance

Operation Wetback

Identification

Significance

the National Housing Act of 1949

    Identification

    Significance

The Other America

    Identification

    Significance

the presidential campaign and election of 1960

    Identification

    Significance

Organizing Information

Enter " reminders" (notes) in the charts "Government's Confronting of the Issues 1945–1961" to help yourself identify key issues covered in Chapter 28 and organize the available information about those issues.

The Citizenry's Confronting of the Issues 1945–1961						
	The Key Issues			Outcomes		
Those Confronting the Issues	**Cold War and Anti-Communism (national security, McCarthyism)**	**Civil Rights (African Americans' rights, Native Americans' rights)**	**The Economy (business, labor, prices, federal budgets)**	**Effects on Elections**	**Progress (Achievements, Positive Effects on Later Events)**	**Failures (Losses, Negative Effects on Later Events)**
Executive Branch				1948	Truman Years	Truman Years
				1952		
				1956	Eisenhower Years	Eisenhower Years
				1960		
Legislative Branch				1948	Truman Years	Truman Years
				1952		
				1956	Eisenhower Years	Eisenhower Years
				1960		

Government's Confronting of the Issues 1945–1961						
Those Confronting the Issues	**The Key Issues**			**Outcomes**		
	Cold War and Anti-Communism (national security, McCarthyism)	**Civil Rights (African Americans' rights, Native Americans' rights)**	**The Economy (business, labor, prices, federal budgets)**	**Effects on Elections**	**Progress (Achievements, Positive Effects on Later Events)**	**Failures (Losses, Negative Effects on Later Events)**
Judicial Branch				1948	Truman Years	Truman Years
				1952		
				1956	Eisenhower Years	Eisenhower Years
				1960		
State Govern-ments Executive Legislative Judicial				1948	Truman Years	Truman Years
				1952		
				1956	Eisenhower Years	Eisenhower Years
				1960		

Government's Confronting of the Issues 1945–1961 (concluded)						
Those Confronting the Issues	**The Key Issues**			**Outcomes**		
	Cold War and Anti-Communism (national security, McCarthyism)	**Civil Rights (African Americans' rights, Native Americans' rights)**	**The Economy (business, labor, prices, federal budgets)**	**Effects on Elections**	**Progress (Achievements, Positive Effects on Later Events)**	**Failures (Losses, Negative Effects on Later Events)**
Rights Organizations and Other Protesters				1948	Truman Years	Truman Years
				1952		
				1956	Eisenhower Years	Eisenhower Years
				1960		
Unions				1948	Truman Years	Truman Years
				1952		
				1956	Eisenhower Years	Eisenhower Years
				1960		

Interpreting Information

Your goal in this exercise is to anticipate essay questions that might come up on your next history test by analyzing your entries in the Organizing Information charts for Chapter 28 and how they are or could be organized.

Study the organization of the two charts "Government's Confronting of the Issues 1945–1961" and "The Citizenry's Confronting of the Issues, 1945–1961" and the entries you made in them. Based on those two factors, what would you say are some questions that you could be asked on your next test? What would you ask if you were the professor? Do you see any potential comparison or contrast questions or causal analysis questions, for instance?

On the basis of your own analysis of the two charts, formulate several essay questions on major issues of the period between the end of World War II and the early 1960s that should appear on a test covering that period and compose working drafts of essays answering your two best questions. (One or two of the questions you formulate may appear among those listed at the end of this chapter in your study guide.)

Ideas and Details

Objectives 2 and 3

_____   1. Truman won the presidency in 1948 because
              a. the Dixiecrat and Progressive parties threw their support to Truman in the final weeks of the campaign.
              b. the Republican party was seriously divided over domestic issues and could not conduct a unified campaign.
              c. the Eightieth Congress offended many interest groups, which in turn threw their support to Truman.
              d. the electorate believed that the Republican party platform was too liberal.

Objective 6

_____   2. Which of the following was a characteristic of American thought in the 1950s?
              a. A belief that the faults of American society should be publicly debated
              b. A belief that reform was unnecessary
              c. An often-expressed fear that Americans could not withstand the pressures of the Cold War world
              d. A belief that people in positions of authority were to be questioned and forced to justify their decisions

Objective 7

_____ 3. As a result of the termination policy supported by the Eisenhower administration,
  a. Indian reservations were expanded and Indian culture further protected.
  b. Native Americans were successfully relocated to urban areas and assimilated into American society.
  c. federal benefits to Indian tribes were withdrawn, causing the displacement and impoverishment of many Indians.
  d. the federal government agreed to aid Indian reservations in the extraction of natural resources from tribal lands.

Objectives 9 and 10

_____ 4. Which of the following contributed to the emergence of McCarthyism?
  a. The use of redbaiting by politicians
  b. News of a treaty of alliance between Mexico and the Soviet Union
  c. The rapid increase in Communist party membership
  d. Discovery of a well-formed Communist conspiracy under the leadership of Henry Wallace

Objectives 7, 9, and 10

_____ 5. Which of the following is true of the Communist Control Act of 1954?
  a. The liberal senators who opposed the act were labeled Communist sympathizers.
  b. Liberal Republicans who opposed the act were expelled from the Republican party.
  c. The act was supported by liberals and conservatives and made membership in the Communist party illegal.
  d. Debate over the act split the Democratic party causing heavy losses in the congressional elections of 1954.

Objective 11

_____ 6. African Americans made gains in American society in the postwar period because
  a. Congress passed a strong voting rights bill.
  b. racist practices at home made it more difficult to compete with the Soviet Union for the support of nonaligned nations.
  c. Truman persuaded southern congressmen to support federal laws against lynching and against the poll tax.
  d. Congress took a decisive stand against racist organizations by outlawing the Ku Klux Klan.

Objective 12

_____ 7. In the Brown decision, the Supreme Court held that
  a. the poll tax was unconstitutional.
  b. segregation in public educational facilities was unconstitutional.
  c. black Americans had benefited from segregated public educational institutions.
  d. racial discrimination in public accommodations was unconstitutional.

Objective 12

_____ 8. Dr. Martin Luther King, Jr., urged his followers to adhere to the philosophy of
   a. accommodation.
   b. socialism.
   c. nonviolence.
   d. Black Power.

Objective 14

_____ 9. The economic basis of the consumer culture of postwar America was
   a. the rising value of stocks and bonds.
   b. the rise in GNP.
   c. credit.
   d. the computer.

Objective 13

_____ 10. Which of the following is true of the postwar baby boom?
   a. The boom had little impact on the American economy.
   b. The boom was largely due to an increase in the birthrate among immigrants and poor Americans.
   c. Ignorance concerning birth control and family planning was probably the most important reason for the boom.
   d. The boom was in part due to sustained economic growth and prosperity.

Objective 17

_____ 11. The decline of the family farm during the 1950s and 1960s was due in large part to
   a. the absence of technological improvements to reduce the drudgery of farm life.
   b. a decline in the value of farm output.
   c. the expense of land, machinery, and fertilizers necessary for modern farming.
   d. the decrease in farm labor productivity.

Objectives 15 and 20

_____ 12. The emphasis on family togetherness during the 1950s probably resulted from
   a. the Kinsey reports.
   b. the Great Depression and Second World War experiences of 1950s parents.
   c. television shows such as "Father Knows Best."
   d. the writings of David Riesman.

Objective 21

_____ 13. The Beats were important because they
    a. introduced the "bebop" style.
    b. introduced the new, sophisticated advertising techniques associated with the television era.
    c. were the first group to perform rock 'n' roll publicly.
    d. produced some important literary works in which they challenged the materialism of the 1950s.

Objective 22

_____ 14. In 1960, a woman was more likely than a man to be poor because
    a. occupational segregation limited the availability of well-paying jobs.
    b. the courts did not award child-support payments in divorce proceedings.
    c. women were generally overeducated for the 1960s job market.
    d. women were more likely to suffer from catastrophic illnesses.

Objective 22

_____ 15. Which of the following is true of the black population between 1940 and 1970?
    a. Most blacks moved from inner-city ghettos to the suburbs.
    b. The black population became increasingly urban.
    c. The south-to-north pattern of black movement was reversed during this period.
    d. Poverty among blacks decreased dramatically.

Essay Questions

Objective 11

1. Discuss the Truman administration's record on civil rights.

Objectives 9 and 10

2. Defend the following statement: "The Cold War heightened anti-Communist fears at home, and by 1950 they reached hysterical proportions. McCarthy did not create this hysteria; he manipulated it to his own advantage."

Objective 6

3. Defend or refute the following statement: "During the 1950s, Americans were confident to the verge of complacency about the perfectibility of American society, anxious to the point of paranoia about the threat of communism."

Objectives 12

4. Discuss the reaction of the southern states and the Eisenhower administration to the *Brown* decision.

Objective 12

5. Discuss the emergence of Dr. Martin Luther King, Jr., as the leader of the civil rights movement that emerged in the aftermath of the *Brown* decision and explain Dr. King's philosophy.

Objective 12

6. Discuss the successes and failures of the civil rights movement from the Montgomery bus boycott through the 1960 presidential election.

Objective 8

7. Discuss Dwight D. Eisenhower as a leader and evaluate his tenure as president of the United States.

Objectives 13 and 14

8. Discuss the baby boom, and explain its social and economic impact on American society.

Objective 17

9. Explain the trends in American agriculture from 1945 to 1970.

Objectives 15 and 20

10. Discuss the concept of the American family and American attitudes concerning gender roles during the 1950s and early 1960s.

Objective 20

11. Discuss the following statement: "A reason for woman's dilemma was the conflicting roles she was expected to fulfill."

Objective 22

12. Examine the reasons for and the extent of poverty in American society during the 1950s and early 1960s.

CHAPTER 29

The Cold War and American Globalism, 1945–1961

Learning Objectives

After you have studied Chapter 29 in your textbook and worked through this study guide chapter, you should be able to:

1. Examine and explain the sources of the Cold War.

2. Examine the reasons for the activist, expansionist, globalist diplomacy undertaken by the United States in the aftermath of the Second World War; and, during the course of the Cold War, explain the exaggeration of the Soviet threat by United States officials.

3. Discuss the similarities and differences between American and Soviet perceptions of major international problems and events from 1945 to 1961.

4. Explain the rationale behind the containment doctrine; examine the evolution of the doctrine from its inception in 1947 to the end of the Eisenhower administration in 1961; discuss the history, extent, and nature of criticisms of the doctrine; and evaluate the doctrine as the cornerstone of American foreign policy from 1947 to 1961.

5. Examine the nature and extent of the arms race between the United States and the Soviet Union from 1945 to 1961.

6. Examine, evaluate, and discuss the consequences of the defense and foreign policy views, goals, and actions of the Truman administration.

7. Discuss the reconstruction of Japan after that country's defeat in the Second World War, and discuss relations between the United States and Japan from 1945 to 1961.

8. Examine and evaluate the events and decisions that led to deepening United States involvement in Vietnam from 1945 to 1961, and discuss the course of the war from 1950 to 1961.

9. Discuss the nature and outcome of the Chinese Civil War, and examine United States policy toward the People's Republic of China from 1949 to 1961.

10. Discuss the origins of the Korean War; explain its outcome; and examine its impact on domestic politics and United States foreign policy.

11. Examine, evaluate, and discuss the consequences of the defense and foreign policy views, goals, and actions of the Eisenhower administration.

12. Discuss the rise of the Third World and explain the challenge the Third World posed to the United States from 1945 to 1961.

13.   Explain the U.S. view of the Third World and the obstacles to United States influence in the Third World.

14.   Discuss the various ways in which the United States attempted to counter nationalism, radical doctrines, and neutralism in the Third World.

15.   Examine the role of the CIA as an instrument of United States policy in the Third World during the 1950s.

Thematic Guide

Chapter 29 surveys the history of the bipolar contest for international power between the United States and the Soviet Union, a contest known as the Cold War, from 1945 to 1961.

We first examine the Cold War as the outgrowth of a complex set of factors. At the end of the Second World War, international relations remained unstable because of (1) world economic problems; (2) power vacuums caused by the defeat of Germany and Japan; (3) civil wars within nations; (4) the birth of nations resulting from the disintegration of empires; and (5) air power, which made all nations more vulnerable to attack. This unsettled environment encouraged competition between the United States and the Soviet Union, the two most powerful nations at the war's end.

Furthermore, both the United States and the Soviet Union believed in the rightness of their own political, economic, and social systems, and each feared the other's system. Their decisions and actions, based on the way each perceived the world, confirmed rather than alleviated these fears. For example, the American resolution to avoid appeasement and hold the line against communism, the American feeling of vulnerability in the air age, and American determination to prevent an economic depression led to an activist foreign policy characterized by the containment doctrine, economic expansionism, and globalist diplomacy. These factors, along with Truman's anti-Soviet views and his brash personality, intensified Soviet fears of a hostile West. When the Soviets acted on the basis of this feeling, American worries that the Soviet Union was bent on world domination intensified.

Despite the fact that the Soviet Union had emerged from the Second World War as a regional power rather than a global menace, United States officials were distrustful of the Soviet Union and reacted to counter what they perceived to be a Soviet threat. They did so because of (1) their belief in a monolithic communist enemy bent on world revolution; (2) fear that unstable world conditions made United States interests vulnerable to Soviet subversion; and (3) the desire of the United States to use its postwar position of strength to its advantage. When the actions of the United States brought criticism, the United States perceived this as further proof that the Soviets were determined to dominate the world.

The interplay of these factors provides the thread running through the examination of American-Soviet relations from 1945 to 1961. The action-reaction theme is evident throughout the chapter, and the events discussed serve as evidence to support the authors' interpretation of the sources of the Cold War. For example, in the discussion of the origins of the Korean War, we find that Truman acted out of the belief that the Soviets were the masterminds behind North Korea's attack against South Korea. However, closer analysis of the situation shows the strong likelihood that North Korea started the war for its own nationalistic purposes and secured the support of a reluctant Joseph Stalin only after receiving the support of Mao Zedong. We examine the conduct of the war, Truman's problems with General Douglas MacArthur, America's use of atomic diplomacy, and the war's domestic political impact. In the war's aftermath, the globalist foreign policy used to justify it became entrenched in U.S. policy. This, in turn, led to an increase in foreign commitments and military appropriations and solidified the idea of a worldwide Soviet threat.

President Dwight D. Eisenhower and his secretary of state, John Foster Dulles, accepted this view of a worldwide communist threat. During Eisenhower's administration, this belief and the fear of domestic subversives that accompanied it led to the removal of talented Asian specialists from the Foreign Service, an action that would have dire consequences later on. Meanwhile, a new jargon invigorated the containment doctrine and the U.S. undertook propaganda efforts to foster discontent in the Communist regimes of Eastern Europe. Despite Eisenhower's doubts about the arms race, as expressed in his 1953 "Atoms for Peace" speech, the president continued the activist foreign policy furthered during the Truman years and oversaw the acceleration of the nuclear arms race. Therefore, during the Eisenhower-Dulles years, the action-reaction relationship between the superpowers continued. Each action by one side caused a corresponding defensive reaction by the other in a seemingly endless spiral of fear and distrust. As a result, problems continued in Eastern Europe, Berlin, and Asia.

The process of decolonization begun during the First World War accelerated in the aftermath of the Second World War. As scores of new nations were born, the Cold-War rivalry between the United States and the Soviet Union began. Both superpowers began to compete for friends among the newly emerging nations of the Third World; however, both the United States and the Soviet Union encountered obstacles in finding allies among these nations. The factors that created obstacles for the United States in its search for Third World friends included:

1. America's negative view toward the nonaligned movement among Third World nations;
2. the way in which the United States characterized Third-World peoples;
3. embarrassing incidents in the United States in which official representatives of the Third World were subjected to racist practices and prejudices;
4. America's intolerance of the disorder caused by revolutionary nationalism; and
5. America's great wealth.

To counter nationalism, radical doctrines, and neutralism in the Third World, the United States undertook development projects and, through the United States Information Agency, engaged in propaganda campaigns. In addition, during the Eisenhower administration the United States began increasingly to rely on the covert actions of the Central Intelligence Agency, as demonstrated in the Guatemalan and Iranian examples. Moreover, the attitude of the United States toward neutralism and toward the disruptions caused by revolutionary nationalism may be seen in the discussion of America's deepening involvement in Vietnam and in the Eisenhower administration's reaction to the events surrounding the 1956 Suez Crisis. In the aftermath of that crisis, fear of a weakened position in the Middle East led to the issuance of the Eisenhower Doctrine, which in turn was used to justify American military intervention in Lebanon in 1958, thus expanding the nation's "global watch" approach to the containment of Communism.

Building Vocabulary

Listed below are important words and terms that you need to know to get the most out of Chapter 29. They are listed in the order in which they occur in the chapter. After carefully looking through the list, refer to a dictionary and jot down the definition of words that you do not know or of which you are unsure.

wisp

topography

indigenous

vie

appeasement

prostrate

ingratiating

nuance

ambiguity

resurgent

expedient

monolithic

coup

ostentatious

retort

manifesto

permeate

tentative

polarize

ensnare

schism

skirmish

renege

amphibious

rampant

contentious

procurement

vigilance

partisan

hector

obliteration

strident

incendiary

extol

tout

acrimony

bemoan

cavalcade

rife

garner

tutelage

ascribe

rebuff

servile

pusillanimous

benefactor

unsavory

expropriate

conspicuous

multifaceted

cajole

rail (verb)

Identification and Significance

After studying Chapter 29 of *A People and a Nation,* you should be able to identify fully *and* explain the historical significance of each item listed below.

1. Identify each item in the space provided. Give an explanation or description of the item. Answer the questions *who, what, where,* and *when.*

2. Explain the historical significance of each item in the space provided. Establish the historical context in which the item exists. Establish the item as the result of or as the cause of other factors existing in the society under study. Answer this question: *What were the political, social, economic, and/or cultural consequences of this item?*

Ho Chi Minh

    Identification

    Significance

the Cold War

    Identification

    Significance

the Third World

    Identification

    Significance

the Truman-Molotov encounter

    Identification

    Significance

Soviet actions in Poland, Romania, Hungary, and Czechoslovakia

    Identification

    Significance

atomic diplomacy

      Identification

      Significance

the Baruch Plan

      Identification

      Significance

the World Bank and the International Monetary Fund

      Identification

      Significance

the "long telegram"

      Identification

      Significance

Churchill's "Iron Curtain" speech

      Identification

      Significance

Henry A. Wallace

    Identification

    Significance

the Truman Doctrine

    Identification

    Significance

the Greek civil war

    Identification

    Significance

the "Mr. X" article

    Identification

    Significance

the containment doctrine

    Identification

    Significance

Walter Lippmann

    Identification

    Significance

the Marshall Plan

    Identification

    Significance

the National Security Act of 1947

    Identification

    Significance

the Fulbright Program

    Identification

    Significance

the Congress for Cultural Freedom

    Identification

    Significance

the Rio Pact and the Organization of American States

    Identification

    Significance

recognition of Israel

    Identification

    Significance

the Berlin blockade and airlift

    Identification

    Significance

the Point Four Program

    Identification

    Significance

the North Atlantic Treaty Organization

    Identification

    Significance

the hydrogen bomb

Identification

Significance

NSC-68

Identification

Significance

Japanese reconstruction

Identification

Significance

the Chinese civil war

Identification

Significance

Jiang Jieshi

Identification

Significance

Mao Zedong

    Identification

    Significance

the People's Republic of China

    Identification

    Significance

the China lobby

    Identification

    Significance

Vietnam's quest for independence

    Identification

    Significance

the Korean War

    Identification

    Significance

General Douglas MacArthur

    Identification

    Significance

the Inchon landing

    Identification

    Significance

Chinese entry into the Korean War

    Identification

    Significance

the POW question

    Identification

    Significance

the Korean armistice

    Identification

    Significance

John Foster Dulles

    Identification

    Significance

liberation, massive retaliation, and deterrence

    Identification

    Significance

the "New Look" military

    Identification

    Significance

brinkmanship

    Identification

    Significance

the domino theory

    Identification

    Significance

Eisenhower's use of the CIA

    Identification

    Significance

the principle of "plausible deniability"

    Identification

    Significance

the United States Information Agency and Radio Free Europe

    Identification

    Significance

the "kitchen debate"

    Identification

    Significance

the *Lucky Dragon*

    Identification

    Significance

Sputnik and the missile race

    Identification

    Significance

the "missile gap"

    Identification

    Significance

the nuclear triad

    Identification

    Significance

Eisenhower's 1953 critique of the nuclear arms race

    Identification

    Significance

the "atoms for peace" and "open skies" proposals

    Identification

    Significance

the Geneva disarmament talks and the Geneva summit

>Identification

>Significance

the Hungarian uprising

>Identification

>Significance

the Berlin crisis of 1958

>Identification

>Significance

the U-2 incident

>Identification

>Significance

the CORONA project

>Identification

>Significance

the Jinmen (Quemoy)-Mazu (Matsu) crisis

    Identification

    Significance

the Formosa Resolution

    Identification

    Significance

the "Japanese miracle"

    Identification

    Significance

the process of decolonization

    Identification

    Significance

the nonaligned movement

    Identification

    Significance

the Bandung Conference of 1955

    Identification

    Significance

the G. L. Mehta incident

    Identification

    Significance

United States "development" projects in the Third World

    Identification

    Significance

Stages of Economic Growth: A Non-Communist Manifesto

    Identification

    Significance

USIA propaganda campaigns

    Identification

    Significance

The Ugly American

    Identification

    Significance

Jacobo Arbenz Guzmán

    Identification

    Significance

Fidel Castro

    Identification

    Significance

Operation Bootstrap

    Identification

    Significance

Mohammed Mossadegh

    Identification

    Significance

Gamal Abdul Nasser

    Identification

    Significance

the Suez crisis

    Identification

    Significance

the Eisenhower Doctrine

    Identification

    Significance

Dienbienphu

    Identification

    Significance

the 1954 Geneva accords

    Identification

    Significance

SEATO

Identification

Significance

Ngo Dinh Diem

Identification

Significance

the National Liberation Front (the Vietcong)

Identification

Significance

Organizing Information

Before you tackle this exercise, it would be a good idea to jog your memory concerning the long-standing distrust between the United States and the Soviet Union. Some Americans may have found themselves fighting on the same side during the Spanish Civil War in the 1930s and the two countries may indeed have been allies of sorts during World War II, but their resentments and enmity were of longer standing. You might want to look into that by reviewing the discussion of American military intervention in the Soviet Union in 1918 (Chapter 23, pages 654–655).

To complete the current exercise, gather evidence of how much the United States feared the U.S.S.R. and of the effects of that fear on American policies and policy-makers and well as on the American public between the end of World War II and 1961. Record specific indications of American fear of the power and behavior of the Soviet Union during the Truman years and the Eisenhower years. Notice that your finished chart will give you a snapshot of the nation's Cold War mentality during the two presidents' administrations on American policies, attitudes, and expenditures for nearly half a century.

The United States and the Cold War *Evidence of American Fears of the USSR, 1945-1961*			
Areas in which Fear Could Be Reflected	**Truman Years**	**Eisenhower Years**	**Conclusion**
Arms Development and Buildup			
Signing "Entangling" Defense Alliances			
Attempts To Interfere in USSR's Sphere of Influence or Its Efforts to Maintain or Expand Its Sphere of Influence			
Use of Trade Policy and Dollar Diplomacy as Cold War Weapons			

The United States and the Cold War *Evidence of American Fears of the USSR, 1945-1961 (concluded)*			
Areas in which Fear Could Be Reflected	**Truman Years**	**Eisenhower Years**	**Conclusion**
Adoption of Covert Operations and Morally Questionable Methods of Influencing or Overthrowing Foreign Regimes			
Recognizing or Withholding Recognition of New Governments			
Domestic political discord or distrust			
Conclusions			

Interpreting Information

Using evidence of America's fear of the U.S.S.R. during the Cold War Era, which you have cited in your Organizing Information chart "The United States and the Cold War," plan and write the working draft of an essay answering the following question:

> Compare or contrast the effects of American distrust of its wartime ally, the Soviet Union, on important policies guiding the United States activities abroad and the political climate Americans found themselves experiencing at home during the Truman and Eisenhower administrations.

Ideas and Details

Objectives 1 and 2

_____   1. The fact that United States exports constituted about 10 percent of the gross national product in 1947 is evidence in support of which of the following ideas?
   a. American officials believed that an activist foreign policy was necessary for the economic well-being of the United States.
   b. The economic crisis in postwar Europe had no impact on American exports.
   c. The United States decided to abandon its prewar policy of economic expansionism.
   d. Few American products depended on foreign markets.

Objectives 1 and 3

_____   2. Which of the following was a major Russian objective in the aftermath of the Second World War?
   a. To oversee the rebuilding of a unified German nation
   b. To prevent encirclement of the Soviet Union by capitalist nations
   c. To share power with the United States in the reconstruction of Japan
   d. To create a strong, independent China

Objective 2

_____   3. In the immediate aftermath of the Second World War, the Soviet Union
   a. had the military power to overrun Western Europe.
   b. was economically powerful and had no reason to fear the West.
   c. was a regional power, not a global menace.
   d. had no territorial ambitions.

Objective 4

_____   4. The containment policy, expressed in the Truman Doctrine and George Kennan's "Mr. X" article, committed the United States to
    a. extend economic and medical aid to impoverished people throughout the world.
    b. help only those countries that showed a determination to help themselves.
    c. assist peoples throughout the world in resisting Communist expansion.
    d. create a more stable world through the use of diplomatic rather than military means.

Objectives 3, 6, and 9

_____   5. Which of the following is true of United States policy toward China during the Chinese civil war?
    a. The United States attempted to open diplomatic relations with Mao's forces but was rebuffed.
    b. United States officials recognized the nationalist origins of the struggle.
    c. The United States decided not to take sides in the struggle.
    d. Most United States officials supported Jiang Jieshi (Chiang Kai-shek) because of their belief that Mao was part of an international communist movement.

Objectives 4, 6, and 8

_____   6. For which of the following reasons did the United States refuse to recognize Vietnamese independence in 1945?
    a. The United States feared that such recognition would jeopardize negotiations with China.
    b. Ho Chi Minh had worked with the Japanese against the United States during World War II.
    c. FDR had guaranteed the return of French colonies at the end of the Second World War.
    d. Since Ho Chi Minh was a Communist, the United States chose to support the imperialist stance of its Cold War ally, France.

Objectives 3, 4, 6, and 10

_____   7. Truman's claim that the Soviet Union was the mastermind behind North Korea's invasion of South Korea is questionable because available evidence now indicates that
    a. the Soviet Union gave no aid to North Korea during the course of the war.
    b. President Kim Young-Sam undertook the war for his own nationalist objectives and drew a reluctant Stalin into the crisis.
    c. the Soviet Union was sending military aid to South Korea at the time of the invasion.
    d. North Korea was fiercely independent and had broken its ties with the Soviet Union.

Objective 10

_____ 8. President Truman fired General Douglas MacArthur because
   a. the general denounced the concept of limited war supported by President Truman and the Joint Chiefs of Staff.
   b. MacArthur refused to obey Truman's order to attack China with massive bombing raids.
   c. the United Nations Security Council demanded MacArthur's removal.
   d. the failure of the Inchon operation destroyed MacArthur's credibility.

Objective 11

_____ 9. The "New Look" military of the Eisenhower-Dulles years emphasized
   a. nuclear weapons rather than conventional military forces.
   b. a United Nations police force.
   c. conventional military forces.
   d. Soviet-American cooperation in space.

Objectives 4, 5, and 11

_____ 10. Which of the following is true in relation to the "missile gap"?
   a. Revelation of the inferiority of United States forces led to Soviet invasion of Hungary in 1956.
   b. Although there was a gap, it favored the United States rather than the Soviet Union.
   c. The superiority of Soviet ICBMs caused the United States to back down in the 1958 Berlin crisis.
   d. Eisenhower's reluctance to spend money on defense had allowed the Soviets dangerously to surpass the United States in missile technology.

Objectives 4, 5, and 11

_____ 11. As a result of the 1954 crisis concerning Jinmen (Quemoy) and Mazu (Matsu),
   a. the United States severed relations with Jiang Jieshi.
   b. the United States recognized the People's Republic of China.
   c. tactical nuclear weapons were installed on Formosa.
   d. Khrushchev called for "peaceful coexistence" with the United States.

Objectives 1, 2, and 12

_____ 12. Because of extensive investments abroad and its reliance on foreign trade, the United States
   a. was intolerant of the destabilizing influence of revolutionary nationalism in the Third World.
   b. suffered more than Western Europe from the worldwide post-war economic depression.
   c. enjoyed improved relations with developing nations during the 1950s.
   d. increased its commitment to and support for the United Nations.

Objective 13

_____ 13. The United States found it difficult to make friends in the Third World because
  a. the United States usually supported the propertied, antirevolutionary elements in the Third World.
  b. diplomats from Third World countries disliked America's pluralistic society.
  c. American business interests refused to invest in Third World countries.
  d. the Soviets were more adept at doing so.

Objectives 4, 11, 12, 13, 14, and 15

_____ 14. Upon learning that Cuba had signed a trade treaty with the Soviet Union in 1960, the Eisenhower administration responded by
  a. immediately cutting off all trade with Cuba.
  b. establishing a blockade of Cuba.
  c. ordering the CIA to plot Castro's overthrow.
  d. negotiating new trade agreements with Cuba designed to increase Cuban imports into the U.S.

Objectives 4, 11, 12, 14, and 15

_____ 15. What do Jacobo Arbenz Guzmán of Guatemala and Mohammed Mossadegh of Iran have in common?
  a. Both agreed to the deployment of Russian intermediate-range missiles in their respective countries.
  b. Both strongly supported United States interests in the Third World.
  c. Both were killed while observing the 1954 test of a 15-megaton H-bomb.
  d. Both threatened American investments in their respective countries and were overthrown in CIA-supported coups.

Essay Questions

Objectives 1, 2, 3, 4, and 5

1. Defend or refute the following statement: "Both the United States and the Soviet Union must share responsibility for the Cold War."

Objectives 3, 4, 7, 8, 9, and 10

2. Explain and evaluate the American perception of events in Asia between the end of the Second World War and North Korea's invasion of South Korea. What bearing did these perceptions have on the Truman administration's response to North Korean aggression?

Objective 10

3. Explain the impact of the Korean War on United States foreign policy.

Objective 5

4. Examine and evaluate the nuclear arms race and attempts at arms control between the United States and the Soviet Union from 1945 to 1961.

Objective 4

5. Examine the containment doctrine as the cornerstone of American foreign policy from 1945 to 1961.

Objective 8

6. Examine the deepening involvement of the United States in Vietnam from 1945 to 1961.

Objectives 12, 13, 14, and 15

7. Explain and evaluate the Eisenhower administration's perception of and response to nationalist movements in the Third World. Illustrate with examples from the Middle East and Latin America. Pay particular attention to the administration's response to Jacobo Arbenz Guzmán and Gamal Abdul Nasser.

Map Exercise

As part of the containment doctrine, the United States in 1949 formed the North Atlantic Treaty Organization (NATO), consisting of the United States, Great Britain, Canada, France, Belgium, the Netherlands, Luxembourg, Italy, Denmark, Norway, Iceland, and Portugal. Greece and Turkey joined NATO in 1952, and West Germany joined in 1954.

To counter NATO, in May 1955 the Soviet Union formed the Warsaw Pact, consisting of the Soviet Union, Albania,[1] Bulgaria, Czechoslovakia, East Germany, Hungary, Poland, and Romania. China did not sign but did pledge support.

In addition, the United States (1) entered into a military alliance with Latin American countries, the Rio Pact, in 1947; (2) sent military advisory missions to Latin America, Greece, Turkey, Iran, China, and Saudi Arabia; (3) activated an air base in Libya in 1948; (4) recognized the new state of Israel in May 1948; (5) entered into a mutual defense agreement, the ANZUS Treaty, with Australia and New Zealand in 1951; and (6) entered into a similar defense agreement in 1954, the Southeast Asia Treaty Organization (SEATO), that first included Britain, France, Australia, New Zealand, Pakistan, Thailand, and the Philippines, and was extended to include South Vietnam, Cambodia, and Laos.

Consider all such alliances, air bases, and military advisory missions in your answers to the following questions:

---

[1] Albania withdrew from the Warsaw Pact in 1968.

1. Using two markers of different colors, mark on the map on page 405 the nations allied with or friendly toward the United States in or around 1973 with one color, and those allied with or friendly toward the Soviet Union with the other color. (Refer to Chapters 29 and 31 in the text, to the map on page 830 in the text, and to an historical atlas.)

2. How successful was the alliance aspect of the containment doctrine as of 1973?

3. The Soviet Union complained of encirclement in the early 1950s and after. Was there reason to complain?

4. As of 1973, would you feel more secure as a citizen of the Soviet Union or as a citizen of the United States? Why?

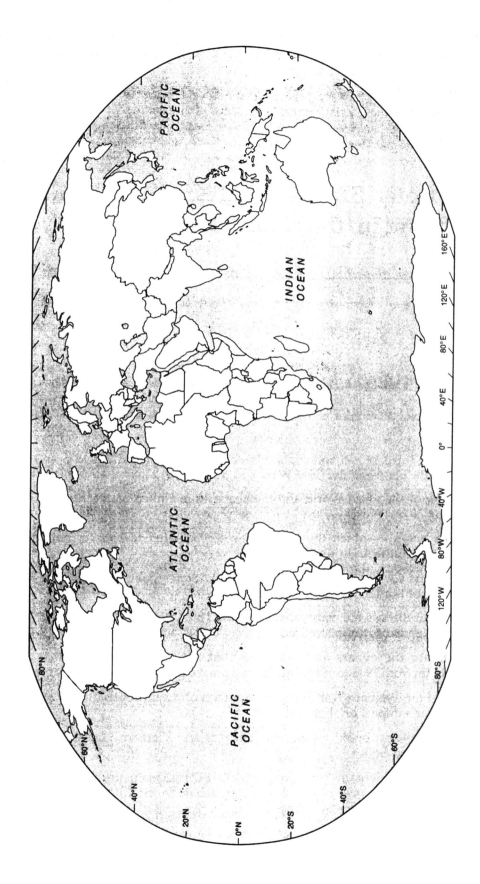

CHAPTER 30

Reform and Conflict at Home: A Turbulent Era, 1961–1974

Learning Objectives

After you have studied Chapter 30 in your textbook and worked through this study guide chapter, you should be able to:

1. Discuss John F. Kennedy's personal and political background; examine the goals and accomplishments of the Kennedy administration, and evaluate the legacy of the Kennedy presidency.

2. Discuss John F. Kennedy's assassination and its impact on American society.

3. Examine the goals and accomplishments of the Johnson administration, and evaluate the legacy of the Johnson presidency.

4. Discuss the issues and personalities and explain the outcome of the 1964 congressional and presidential elections.

5. Discuss the major rulings of the Warren Court, and explain the impact of these rulings on American life and society.

6. Discuss the accomplishments and failures of the black search for equality from 1961 to 1973; explain the transformation of the civil rights movement into the black power movement; and discuss the impact of black activism on American society.

7. Discuss the forces that gave rise to the New Left and the counterculture; examine the philosophy, goals, and actions of these two groups; and discuss their impact on American society.

8. Explain the emergence of the gay rights movement, and discuss the movement's goals and its impact on American society.

9. Examine the crises that sent shock waves through American society in 1968.

10. Discuss the issues and personalities and explain the outcome of the 1968 congressional and presidential elections.

11. Explain the emergence, characteristics, and goals of the feminist movement of the 1960s and 1970s, and discuss the successes and failures of this movement and its impact on American society.

12. Discuss the issues that faced the Nixon administration in the late 1960s and early 1970s; explain and evaluate the administration's actions concerning those issues; and discuss the consequences of those actions.

13. Examine the issues and personalities and explain the outcome of the 1972 congressional and presidential elections.

14. Discuss the illegal activities that constituted the Watergate scandal, and explain the threat these activities posed to constitutional government.

15. Examine the impact of the Watergate scandal on the American people, American society, and American institutions, and discuss and evaluate the reforms enacted in the scandal's aftermath.

Thematic Guide

In Chapter 30, we examine the crises that engulfed American society during the 1960s and early 1970s. As we learn from the first section, "Civil Rights and the New Frontier," the New Frontier was overly ambitious in light of the political distance between the new president's liberal agenda and a Congress dominated by a conservative coalition. When he attempted to deal with this conservative coalition, Kennedy at first failed to press forward on civil rights issues. At this point, violence began to have an impact on developments. In the face of violent challenges from southern segregationists to an expanding black civil-rights movement, the Kennedy administration gradually committed itself to a decisive stand in favor of black equality. But only because of continuing racial violence and Kennedy's assassination did Congress finally pass civil rights legislation.

The section "The Great Society and the Triumph of Liberalism" covers the legislative accomplishments of the Johnson administration—the most sweeping reform legislation since 1935. This legislation comprised the Civil Rights Act of 1964, establishment of the Equal Employment Opportunity Commission, the Economic Opportunity Act of 1964, the Voting Rights Act of 1965, and legislation associated with Johnson's War on Poverty. The authors look closely at the legislation that constituted the War on Poverty and discuss the problems and successes of this program.

The liberal decisions rendered by the Supreme Court during the 1960s and early 1970s matched the liberalism reflected in the progressive legislation of the Johnson years. The authors examine these rulings, the aspects of American life and American society they affected, and the praise and criticisms they evoked.

As the three branches of the federal government slowly began to deal with such long-standing American problems as poverty and minority rights, frustrations that had built up over generations of inaction manifested themselves. Events convinced civil-rights activists in the South that the "power structure" in American society was not to be trusted. Northern blacks began to reach the same conclusions. Both the civil-rights movement and Johnson's antipoverty programs had offered African Americans hope for a better day in American society. However, as discussion of the social, economic, and political plight of urban blacks reveals, that hope had not been fulfilled. Among other factors, unfulfilled expectations and the continued display of wealth and possessions in the consumer-oriented American society led to the urban riots of the 1960s. Militant black leaders gained prominence and questioned Martin Luther King's philosophy of nonviolence as well as his goal of integration. Malcolm X, Stokely Carmichael, and the Black Panther party called for "black power" within the context of black nationalism.

Along with this revolution of rising expectations among blacks, some whites involved in the civil rights movement began to become disillusioned with American society. Although their disillusionment stemmed from different sources than that of blacks, it led to the political and social activism associated with the New Left and the counterculture. The authors discuss the emergence, characteristics, and goals of both of these groups as well as the reaction of the middle class to their attacks on traditional values. In addition, the activism of blacks, the New Left and counterculture, and women gave rise to gay activism and to the gay rights movement. As the Vietnam War escalated and the New Left and the counterculture found common cause in their antiwar stance, the middle class became more and more convinced that traditional society was under siege.

The forces of frustration, rage, and anger born of racism, sexism, poverty, disillusionment, materialism, and the revolution of rising expectations practically ripped America apart in the tumult of 1968. After explaining the events of that year, the authors discuss the emergence, characteristics, and goals of both moderate and radical feminists. They also examine the problems encountered by many working women in the 1960s and note gains made by women against sexism in the late 1960s and early 1970s.

Continuation of chaos into the 1970s convinced President Nixon and many Americans that society was on the verge of anarchy. Nixon attempted to use the perceived danger to his political advantage by portraying critics, including the Democratic opposition, as Communist pawns and enemies of American society. These tactics gained Nixon little in the 1970 congressional elections, and publication of the *Pentagon Papers* fostered more distrust of government. As Nixon prepared for the 1972 presidential election, he turned to Keynesian economics to deal with the country's economic problems and opened relations with the People's Republic of China.

In "Nixon's Reelection and Resignation," the authors first examine the factors that contributed to Nixon's landslide victory in the 1972 election. These factors include the "southern strategy," Nixon's success in associating the Democratic party with groups and movements that threatened traditional values, the nature of George McGovern's campaign, division within the Democratic party, and Nixon's announcement that peace was at hand in Vietnam. Even though the voters overwhelmingly chose to return Nixon to the White House in 1972, they also chose to leave both houses of Congress in the hands of the Democrats.

Unfortunately, Nixon's landslide victory did not guarantee an end to the crisis atmosphere that had plagued the nation since the late 1960s. The Watergate scandal caused more disillusionment with government and increased the somber mood of the people, for it involved a series of illegal activities approved at the highest level of American government. Some of these activities, such as the break-in at Daniel Ellsberg's psychiatrist's office, had been undertaken to discredit political opponents; others, such as the paying of hush money to witnesses, were part of an elaborate cover-up.

Beyond the illegal actions, the Watergate scandal was a constitutional crisis; the "imperial presidency" threatened the balance-of-power concept embodied in the Constitution and the guarantees of individual rights embodied in the Bill of Rights. We see the constitutional nature of the crisis in the clash between the executive and judicial branches of government, the impeachment hearings undertaken by the House Judiciary Committee, and ultimately the resignation of the president. Unlike the scandals of previous administrations, the activities linked to Watergate were aimed not at financial gain but at monopolizing political power. After citing the events associated with Watergate, the authors outline and briefly evaluate congressional attempts to correct the abuses associated with the scandal.

Building Vocabulary

Listed below are important words and terms that you need to know to get the most out of Chapter 30. They are listed in the order in which they occur in the chapter. After carefully looking through the list, refer to a dictionary and jot down the definition of words that you do not know or of which you are unsure.

inextricably

volatility

vigilante

alienate

placate

capitulation

eradicate

perpetuate

censure

verve

indelible

oblivious

solicitous

remedial

random

debilitating

impropriety

altercation

furtive

rueful

hireling

empathy

defector

languish

mystique

effigy

disparity

incursion

coddle

pall

enunciate

espouse

benign

moratorium

expunge

diligent

feign

credible

capricious

caisson

_____

Identification and Significance

After studying Chapter 30 of A *People and a Nation*, you should be able to identify fully *and* explain the historical significance of each item listed below.

1. Identify each item in the space provided. Give an explanation or description of the item. Answer the questions *who, what, where,* and *when*.

2. Explain the historical significance of each item in the space provided. Establish the historical context in which the item exists. Establish the item as the result of or as the cause of other factors existing in the society under study. Answer this question: *What were the political, social, economic, and/or cultural consequences of this item?*

the Mississippi Freedom Democratic Party

Identification

Significance

Fannie Lou Hamer

Identification

Significance

John F. Kennedy

Identification

Significance

"the best and the brightest"

    Identification

    Significance

the New Frontier

    Identification

    Significance

Martin Luther King, Jr.

    Identification

    Significance

the Freedom Rides

    Identification

    Significance

Student Nonviolent Coordinating Committee

    Identification

    Significance

James Meredith

    Identification

    Significance

the March on Washington

    Identification

    Significance

Medgar Evers

    Identification

    Significance

Sixteenth Street Baptist Church bombing

    Identification

    Significance

the assassination of John Kennedy

    Identification

    Significance

Lee Harvey Oswald

    Identification

    Significance

Jack Ruby

    Identification

    Significance

the space program

    Identification

    Significance

the Kennedy aura

    Identification

    Significance

Lyndon B. Johnson

    Identification

    Significance

the Great Society

   Identification

   Significance

the Civil Rights Act of 1964

   Identification

   Significance

the Equal Employment Opportunity Commission

   Identification

   Significance

the Twenty-fourth Amendment to the Constitution

   Identification

   Significance

the Economic Opportunity Act of 1964

   Identification

   Significance

the presidential and congressional elections of 1964

  Identification

  Significance

the Medicare and Medicaid programs

  Identification

  Significance

the Elementary and Secondary Education Act

  Identification

  Significance

the Voting Rights Act of 1965

  Identification

  Significance

the Immigration and Nationality Act of 1965

  Identification

  Significance

the Civil Rights Act of 1968

    Identification

    Significance

the Indian Bill of Rights

    Identification

    Significance

the War on Poverty

    Identification

    Significance

the Warren Court

    Identification

    Significance

Baker v. *Carr*

    Identification

    Significance

the Supreme Court's school-prayer decision

    Identification

    Significance

Griswold v. *Connecticut*

    Identification

    Significance

Gideon v. *Wainwright, Escobedo* v. *Illinois,* and *Miranda* v. *Arizona*

    Identification

    Significance

J. Edgar Hoover

    Identification

    Significance

race riots of 1964

    Identification

    Significance

Watts race riot

    Identification

    Significance

Malcolm X

    Identification

    Significance

the Black Muslims

    Identification

    Significance

Stokely Carmichael

    Identification

    Significance

Black Power

    Identification

    Significance

the Black Panther party

    Identification

    Significance

the Free Speech Movement

    Identification

    Significance

Students for a Democratic Society

    Identification

    Significance

the Port Huron Statement

    Identification

    Significance

the New Left

    Identification

    Significance

the counterculture

       Identification

       Significance

Timothy Leary

       Identification

       Significance

Bob Dylan and Janis Joplin

       Identification

       Significance

Woodstock

       Identification

       Significance

"Hashbury"

       Identification

       Significance

the birth-control pill

    Identification

    Significance

Stonewall Inn riot

    Identification

    Significance

antiwar protests

    Identification

    Significance

the U.S.S. *Pueblo*

    Identification

    Significance

the assassination of Martin Luther King, Jr.

    Identification

    Significance

the assassination of Robert Kennedy

    Identification

    Significance

the 1968 Democratic convention

    Identification

    Significance

the presidential and congressional elections of 1968

    Identification

    Significance

George C. Wallace

    Identification

    Significance

The Feminine Mystique

    Identification

    Significance

American Women

      Identification

      Significance

the National Organization for Women (NOW)

      Identification

      Significance

radical feminism

      Identification

      Significance

occupational segregation

      Identification

      Significance

Title IX of the Educational Amendments of 1972

      Identification

      Significance

the Equal Rights Amendment

    Identification

    Significance

Roe v. *Wade*

    Identification

    Significance

Reed v. *Reed* and *Frontiero* v. *Richardson*

    Identification

    Significance

Kent State and Jackson State

    Identification

    Significance

the Attica prison revolt

    Identification

    Significance

stagflation

>   Identification

>   Significance

wage, price, and rent controls

>   Identification

>   Significance

revenue sharing

>   Identification

>   Significance

the modern environmental movement

>   Identification

>   Significance

Nixon's "southern strategy"

>   Identification

>   Significance

Swann v. *Charlotte-Mecklenburg*

      Identification

      Significance

the presidential and congressional elections of 1972

      Identification

      Significance

George McGovern

      Identification

      Significance

the Watergate scandal

      Identification

      Significance

CREEP and the Plumbers

      Identification

      Significance

John W. Dean III

    Identification

    Significance

the White House tapes

    Identification

    Significance

the Saturday Night Massacre

    Identification

    Significance

Spiro Agnew's resignation

    Identification

    Significance

Gerald R. Ford

    Identification

    Significance

Carl Bernstein and Bob Woodward

    Identification

    Significance

U.S. v. *Nixon*

    Identification

    Significance

the impeachment hearings of the House Judiciary Committee

    Identification

    Significance

Nixon's resignation

    Identification

    Significance

the pardon of Richard Nixon

    Identification

    Significance

the imperial presidency

    Identification

    Significance

the War Powers Act

    Identification

    Significance

the Congressional Budget and Impoundment Control Act

    Identification

    Significance

Organizing Information

Record reminders of the specific information provided in Chapter 30 concerning each of the groups listed in the first column in the chart "Social and Political Activism, 1961–1974"

    Try to insert your entries in a way that differentiates the various leaders and organizations in terms of the tactics they favored.

SOCIAL AND POLITICAL ACTIVISM, 1961–1974						
Cause	Leaders	Organi-zations	Favored Tactics	Landmark Events	Assessment of the Group As Activists	
					Failings	Strengths
African Americans						
Women						
Homo-sexuals						
Dissidents						

Interpreting Information

Consider each of the important groups fighting for social and political justice listed in the Organizing Information chart "Social and Political Activism, 1961–1974." Which do you consider to have been successful?

Referring to entries you made in the chart and additional information provided in Chapter 30 and your class notes— and considering your own estimation of how successful the groups were in advancing their causes— plan and compose the working draft of an essay that responds directly to this question:

In light of the amount of progress made between 1960 and 1975 by the most important or visible of the groups fighting social and political injustice in American society, do the differences in tactics and attitudes appear to affect activists' chances of achieving their groups' goals? How? Are a group's leaders more important than a groups tactics? Can a tactic such as nonviolence succeed if the forces against change are nonviolent also? What other important factors help explain the progress or lack of progress of activists in the Sixties and Seventies?

Ideas and Details

Objectives 1, 2, 3, and 6

_____   1. Passage of the Civil Rights Act of 1964 was in large part due to
  a. the work of the Freedom Riders.
  b. Kennedy's ability to push legislation through Congress.
  c. President Kennedy's assassination.
  d. mobilization of nationwide support by the Student Nonviolent Coordinating Committee.

Objective 3

_____   2. The 1965 Elementary and Secondary Education Act
  a. provided separate classes and increased funding for the teaching of the academically gifted.
  b. was the first general program of federal aid to education.
  c. required federal certification of all public school teachers.
  d. established a job placement service at the federal level for public school teachers in the United States.

Objectives 3 and 6

_____ 3. As a result of the Voting Rights Act of 1965,
  a. the right to vote was extended to eighteen-year-olds.
  b. the number of registered African American voters in the South dramatically increased.
  c. literacy tests were required of all voters in federal elections.
  d. eligible voters were legally required to register through federal registrars.

Objective 5

_____ 4. In the Supreme Court's 1962 ruling concerning school prayer, the Court held that
  a. public schools could require nondenominational prayer at the beginning of each school day.
  b. God had no place in the public schools of the United States.
  c. required prayers in public schools were unconstitutional.
  d. there could be no prayers in public schools.

Objective 5

_____ 5. Cases such as *Gideon* v. *Wainwright* and *Miranda* v. *Arizona* were controversial because they
  a. broadened the definition of religion.
  b. reinforced and expanded freedom of expression.
  c. transformed the criminal justice system by protecting the rights of criminal suspects.
  d. affected people's personal lives by dealing with sexual issues.

Objective 6

_____ 6. The urban race riots of the 1960s and the emergence of black nationalism in the voices of Malcolm X and Stokely Carmichael were the result of
  a. the deterioration of the social and economic conditions of many northern blacks.
  b. communist infiltration of civil rights groups.
  c. denial of the right to vote to northern blacks.
  d. a shift in the tactics of the SCLC from passive resistance to violent confrontation.

Objective 7

_____ 7. The counterculture differed from the New Left in which of the following ways?
  a. The counterculture completely condemned the use of drugs.
  b. The counterculture was more realistic in its goals than the New Left.
  c. The counterculture used music to attack the status quo.
  d. The counterculture was more supportive of the Vietnam War.

Objective 8

_____ 8. The Stonewall riot
  a. marked the beginning of the gay rights movement.
  b. occurred in Atlantic City when radical feminists disrupted the 1968 Miss America contest.
  c. was the result of overreaction by the Chicago police to street demonstrations at the Democratic national convention.
  d. was an expression of black rage over the assassination of Martin Luther King.

Objectives 9 and 10

_____ 9. The 1968 Democratic presidential candidate killed by an assassin's bullet was
  a. George Wallace.
  b. Robert Kennedy.
  c. Eugene McCarthy.
  d. Edmund Muskie.

Objective 11

_____ 10. In the late 1960s, radical feminists differed from the members of the National Organization for Women in which of the following ways?
  a. Radical feminists opposed the gay rights movement.
  b. Radical feminists were concerned with political issues, not social and economic issues.
  c. The radical feminist movement repudiated the work of Betty Friedan.
  d. Radical feminists turned to the tactic of direct action to accomplish their goals.

Objective 12

_____ 11. In an effort to help Republican candidates in the 1970 congressional elections, the Nixon administration
  a. advocated the passage of a national health insurance program.
  b. pledged an immediate end to the Vietnam War.
  c. announced the imposition of wage and price controls.
  d. tried to associate the Democratic party with radicalism and violence.

Objective 13

_____ 12. Nixon's 1972 victory was in large part due to
  a. the campaign proposals of his opponent, George McGovern.
  b. his support for extension of the Voting Rights Act of 1966, which gained him the black vote.
  c. public support for his economic policies, which had reduced the federal deficit and lowered inflation.
  d. his support for environmental protection legislation.

Objective 14

_____ 13. Which of the following authorized the payment of hush money to E. Howard Hunt to
prevent disclosures concerning the break-in at Democratic headquarters?
   a. James McCord
   b. John Mitchell
   c. Richard Nixon
   d. John Ehrlichman

Objective 15

_____ 14. As a result of its impeachment hearings, the House Judiciary Committee
   a. voted in favor of President Nixon's impeachment on three of five counts.
   b. declared President Nixon to be guilty of tax fraud.
   c. chose to make no recommendation concerning the impeachment of the president.
   d. declared President Nixon to be innocent of all charges of wrongdoing.

Objective 15

_____ 15. The War Powers Act required the president to
   a. consult with Congress "in every possible instance" before sending American troops
       into foreign wars.
   b. withdraw troops from any foreign assignment after ten days unless Congress
       specifically authorized otherwise.
   c. get approval from Congress before sending American troops to foreign territory.
   d. get a declaration of war from Congress before sending American soldiers into a
       foreign war.

Essay Questions

Objective 6

1. Explain the transformation of the civil rights movement in the mid-1960s and the impact of this
    transformation on African Americans and on American society.

Objective 3

2. Discuss the successes and failures of the War on Poverty.

Objectives 3, 4, 5, and 6

3. Explain the erosion of the liberal consensus in the years after 1964.

Objective 7

4. Explain the similarities and differences between the New Left and the counterculture.

Objectives 10, 12, and 13

5. Explain the political strategy of Richard Nixon and the Republican party in the 1968, 1970, and 1972 elections.

Objective 11

6. Explain the emergence of radical feminism, and discuss its impact on American society in the late 1960s and early 1970s.

Objectives 14 and 15

7. Discuss the Watergate scandal as a constitutional crisis, examine President Richard Nixon's role in the scandal, and explain the House Judiciary Committee's decision concerning the articles of impeachment against the President.

CHAPTER 31

Disaster and Détente: The Cold War, Vietnam, and the Third World, 1961–1989

Learning Objectives

After you have studied Chapter 31 in your textbook and worked through this study guide chapter, you should be able to:

1. Examine, evaluate, and discuss the consequences of the defense and foreign policy views, goals, and actions of the Kennedy and Johnson administrations.

2. Discuss Cuban-American relations from 1959 to October 1962; explain the causes, outcome, and consequences of the Cuban missile crisis; and evaluate President John Kennedy's handling of the crisis.

3. Examine and evaluate the events and decisions that led to deepening United States involvement in Vietnam from 1961 to 1965.

4. Discuss the nature of the Vietnam War, the characteristics of American soldiers who served in the war, and the war's impact on those soldiers.

5. Explain the factors that contributed to the emergence of anti-Vietnam War sentiment and protests within the United States.

6. Discuss the course of the Vietnam War from 1965 to 1975; explain the war's impact on Southeast Asia and American society; and discuss the debate in the United States over the meaning of the American experience in Vietnam.

7. Explain the theories on which the Nixon-Kissinger "grand strategy" was based; examine and evaluate the policies and actions inspired by those theories; and examine the international crises and issues that placed the grand strategy in jeopardy.

8. Examine, evaluate, and discuss the consequences of the defense and foreign policy views, goals, and actions of the Carter administration.

9. Examine, evaluate, and discuss the consequences of the defense and foreign policy views, goals, and actions of the Reagan administration.

10. Discuss the activities that constituted the Iran-contra scandal, and explain the scandal's impact on the presidency of Ronald Reagan.

Thematic Guide

Chapter 31 continues the survey of the Cold War, begun in Chapter 29, and carries the story from the inauguration of President John F. Kennedy in 1961 to the end of President Reagan's term in 1989. As can be seen in the discussion of U.S. foreign policy during this period, the containment doctrine, formulated during the Truman administration, continued to be the guiding force behind American foreign policy from the Kennedy administration through the Reagan administration. Furthermore, the action-reaction relationship between the United States and the Soviet Union that was so much a part of the early Cold War persists into the 1961 to 1989 period.

In its quest for friends in the Third World and ultimate victory in the Cold War, the Kennedy administration adopted the goal of nation building, to be accomplished, for example, through the Alliance for Progress and the Peace Corps as well as through the techniques of counterinsurgency. Such methods perpetuated an idea that had long been part of American foreign policy: that other people cannot solve their own problems and that the American economic and governmental model can be transferred intact to other societies. Historian William Appleman Williams believed that such thinking led to "the tragedy of American diplomacy," and historian Arthur M. Schlesinger, Jr., refers to it as "a ghastly illusion." The idea is further evidenced in the CIA's intervention in the Congo (Zaire) from 1960 to 1961 and in Brazil from 1962 to 1964.

Despite the strategic superiority of the United States over the Soviet Union in 1960, President Kennedy's presidential campaign was based, in part, on the false premise that the Eisenhower administration had allowed a "missile gap" to develop between the United States and its arch-rival. Once elected, President Kennedy oversaw a significant military buildup based on the principle of "flexible response," and his policies and actions in the field of foreign policy were shaped by his acceptance of the containment doctrine and his preference for a bold, interventionist foreign policy. His activist approach not only helped bring the world to the brink of nuclear disaster in the Cuban missile crisis but also led to a significant acceleration of the nuclear arms race—a trend that continued through the administration of Kennedy's successor, Lyndon B. Johnson.

The authors trace the course of American involvement in Vietnam from deepening U.S. involvement during the Kennedy administration to the collapse of South Vietnam in April 1975. This discussion is based on the thesis that disaster befell the United States in Vietnam because of the U.S. belief that it had a right to influence the internal affairs of Third World countries. This theme runs through the discussion of United States involvement in Vietnam in several variations: the United States decision to sabotage the Geneva accords (see Chapter 29), United States support of the overthrow of the Diem regime, Johnson's view of Vietnam as "this damn little pissant country," the arrogance of power on the part of the United States, and Nixon's "jugular diplomacy."

Several subthemes remind us of the sources of the Cold War, discussed in Chapter 29. It is within this context that the authors state: "Overlooking the native roots of the nationalist rebellion against France, and the long, tenacious Vietnamese resistance to foreign intruders, American presidents from Truman through Ford took a globalist view of Vietnam, interpreting events through a Cold War lens." And in a review of the material we find that the following sources of the Cold War discussed in Chapter 29 fit the war in Vietnam:

1.   The unsettled international environment at the end of World War II encouraged competition between the United States and the Soviet Union. Empires were disintegrating (France's attempt to reinstate its authority in Indochina ended in disaster at Dienbienphu); nations were being born (Ho Chi Minh attempted to create an independent Vietnam); and civil wars were raging within nations (the National Liberation Front emerged against Ngo Dinh Diem's South Vietnamese regime).

2. United States fear of the Soviet system led to economic expansionism (the United States recognized Southeast Asia as an economic asset) and globalist diplomacy (Southeast Asia seemed vital to the defense of Japan and the Philippines).

3. United States officials exaggerated the Soviet threat because of their belief in a monolithic communist enemy bent on world revolution. (American presidents from Truman through Nixon failed to recognize the nationalist roots of the problem in Vietnam. Instead, they saw Ho Chi Minh as a Communist and Vietnam as an "Asian Berlin," and they accepted the tenets of the domino theory.)

In the aftermath of the Vietnam War, Americans began to debate its causes and consequences. Just as they had disagreed over the course and conduct of the war, they were now unable to reach any real consensus on its lessons for the nation.

Although a great deal of energy was expended on questions relating to the Vietnam War during Richard M. Nixon's presidency, Nixon considered other foreign policy matters, especially the relationship between the United States and the Soviet Union, to be more important. In an attempt to create a global balance of power, Nixon and Henry Kissinger (Nixon's national security adviser and later his secretary of state) adopted a "grand strategy." By means of détente with the Soviet Union and the People's Republic of China, Nixon and Kissinger sought to achieve the same goals as those of the old containment doctrine, but through accommodation rather than confrontation. Despite détente, the United States still had to respond to crises rooted in instability. Nowhere was the fragility of world stability via the grand strategy more apparent than in the Middle East, where war again broke out between the Arab states and Israel in 1973. While the Soviet Union and the United States positioned themselves by putting their armed forces on alert, OPEC imposed an oil embargo against the United States. Kissinger was able to persuade the warring parties to agree to a cease-fire; OPEC ended its embargo; and, through "shuttle diplomacy," Kissinger persuaded Egypt and Israel to agree to a United Nations peacekeeping force in the Sinai. But many problems remained, and the instability of the region continued to be a source of tension between the United States and the Soviet Union.

President Nixon believed, just as previous presidents had believed, in America's right to influence the internal affairs of Third World countries. It was out of this belief and the concomitant belief that the United States should curb revolution and radicalism in the Third World, that Nixon accepted the Johnson Doctrine in Latin America, as evidenced by the overthrow of the Allende government in Chile.

As Nixon and Kissinger sought world order through the grand strategy, global economic issues highlighted the differences between the rich and poor nations of the world and heightened the animosity of Third World nations toward what they perceived to be the exploitive industrialized nations of the world. The United States, the richest nation on Earth, exports large quantities of goods to developing nations as well as importing raw materials from those nations. This important trade, along with America's worldwide investments, in part explains the interventionist nature of United States foreign policy, a policy accepted and continued by Presidents Nixon and Gerald Ford, and by their foreign-policy overseer, Henry Kissinger. Therefore, during the Nixon-Ford-Kissinger years America's global watch against forces that threatened its far-flung economic and strategic interests continued.

When Jimmy Carter assumed the presidency in 1977, he and Secretary of State Cyrus Vance at first pledged a new course for the United States. However, this course was challenged by Carter's national security adviser Zbigniew Brzezinski, by Democratic and Republican critics, and by the Soviet Union, which reacted in anger and fear to the human rights aspect of Carter's policies. The Cold War seemed to have its own momentum. Despite the Carter administration's successful negotiation of the SALT-II treaty and its achievements in the Middle East, Africa, and Latin America, it was overwhelmed by critics at home, the Iranian hostage crisis, and the Soviet invasion of Afghanistan. The grain embargo, the 1980 Olympics boycott, and the Carter Doctrine all seemed more reminiscent of the containment doctrine and the sources of the Cold War than of a new course in American foreign policy. Furthermore, the excesses in which the United States had engaged in the past in its attempts to create stability, protect American economic interests, and contain the Communist threat rained down on the Carter administration in the form of the Iranian hostage crisis. In this crisis America's missiles, submarines, tanks, and bombers ultimately meant nothing if the lives of the hostages were to be saved. But many Americans wished for a return to the immediate postwar world, a world in which the United States had a monopoly on economic and military power. In this spirit of nostalgia, the electorate chose Ronald Reagan as its president in the 1980 election.

Ronald Reagan's election in 1980 marked a return to foreign-policy themes rooted in America's past and reminiscent of the early days of the Cold War. As a result, relations between the United States and the Soviet Union deteriorated and arms talks between the two nations broke down. The questioning of U.S. intervention in Third World nations, so apparent in the immediate aftermath of the Vietnam disaster, was absent in the Reagan administration. Fearing communism, Reagan simplistically blamed unrest in the world on the Soviets, failed to see the local roots of problems, and formed alliances with antirevolutionary regimes, which tended to be unrepresentative. American relations with the Third World during the 1980s evoke memories of the sources of the Cold War, of the containment policy, and of attempts to protect American economic interests against the force of revolutionary nationalism. Therefore, in the name of protecting private American companies, the Reagan administration rejected the Law of the Sea Treaty. In the same vein, American policies toward El Salvador and Nicaragua recall phrases used to describe American policy in previous eras; and Reagan's desire for victory rather than negotiation, seen especially in his policies toward Central America, brings to mind the early years of the Kennedy administration. However, since the Kennedy years the American people had been through the traumas of Vietnam and Watergate, and the power of Congress, relative to that of the president, had increased. Therefore, Congress in the mid-1980s was much more willing to play an active role in foreign policy decisions than it had been in the 1960s. But Congress, reflecting the debate among the American people over the nation's policy toward Nicaragua, vacillated between ending aid to the contras in mid-1984 and again extending aid in 1986. During the period when aid was prohibited, the executive branch of the government, through the National Security Council and the Central Intelligence Agency, acted to circumvent the will of Congress. These actions came to light in 1986 in the Iran-contra scandal, a scandal that deeply wounded Ronald Reagan's ability to lead during his last two years in office.

From this discussion of the Iran-contra scandal, the authors turn their attention to continuing problems in the Middle East, the problem of terrorism against United States citizens and property, America's ill-fated 1983 mission in Lebanon, and to a discussion of Congress's ability to force the Reagan administration to alter its policy of "constructive engagement" toward South Africa. At the close of the 1980s major problems continued to face the United States in the Third World as the famine in Africa and the debt problems of the Third World indicate.

Public concern over the Reagan administration's anti-Soviet stance and propensity toward confrontation led to international concern and to massive support for a freeze in the nuclear arms race. Public pressure, combined with other forces, led to a resumption of arms talks in 1985. In the same year Mikhail Gorbachev assumed power in the Soviet Union. Perhaps President Reagan was right when he said that he was "dropped into a grand historical moment," because under Gorbachev's leadership the Soviet Union undertook an ambitious domestic reform program and Soviet foreign policy underwent significant changes. These dramatic changes helped reduce international tensions and, in 1987, led to a Soviet-American agreement to eliminate intermediate-range nuclear missiles in Europe.

Building Vocabulary

Listed below are important words and terms that you need to know to get the most out of Chapter 31. They are listed in the order in which they occur in the chapter. After carefully looking through the list, refer to a dictionary and jot down the definition of words that you do not know or of which you are unsure.

imbue

protracted

subterfuge

acrimonious

diffuse

abet

quell

exacerbate

bequeath

provocative

conciliatory

bipolar

ardent

disparaging

attrition

sodomize

precarious

litany

macabre

volatile

aghast

ignobly

vengeful

quash

excoriate

venerable

derogatory

prowess

codify

tenacious

languish

visceral

malevolent

intransigence

embroil

strident

Identification and Significance

After studying Chapter 31 of A *People and a Nation*, you should be able to identify fully *and* explain the historical significance of each item listed below.

1. Identify each item in the space provided. Give an explanation or description of the item. Answer the questions *who, what, where,* and *when.*

2. Explain the historical significance of each item in the space provided. Establish the historical context in which the item exists. Establish the item as the result of or as the cause of other factors existing in the society under study. Answer this question: *What were the political, social, economic, and/or cultural consequences of this item?*

John F. Kennedy

    Identification

    Significance

the concept of nation building

    Identification

    Significance

the Alliance for Progress

    Identification

    Significance

the Peace Corps

    Identification

    Significance

the doctrine of counterinsurgency

    Identification

    Significance

Patrice Lumumba and João Goulart

    Identification

    Significance

the principle of flexible response

    Identification

    Significance

the 1961 Berlin crisis

    Identification

    Significance

the Bay of Pigs invasion

    Identification

    Significance

Operation Mongoose

    Identification

    Significance

the Cuban missile crisis

Identification

Significance

the Treaty on the Nonproliferation of Nuclear Weapons

Identification

Significance

Project Beef-up

Identification

Significance

the Strategic Hamlet Program

Identification

Significance

the Tonkin Gulf incident and the Tonkin Gulf Resolution

Identification

Significance

Johnson's bombing campaign in Laos

      Identification

      Significance

Operation Rolling Thunder

      Identification

      Significance

Agent Orange

      Identification

      Significance

the My Lai massacre

      Identification

      Significance

"the body-count nonsense" during the Vietnam war

      Identification

      Significance

draft resisters

    Identification

    Significance

the Tet offensive

    Identification

    Significance

the gold crisis

    Identification

    Significance

the Nixon Doctrine

    Identification

    Significance

Vietnamization

    Identification

    Significance

the invasion of Cambodia

    Identification

    Significance

the *Pentagon Papers*

    Identification

    Significance

the Christmas bombing

    Identification

    Significance

the Vietnam cease-fire agreement

    Identification

    Significance

the fall of Saigon

    Identification

    Significance

the "boat people"

>Identification

>Significance

Vietnam syndrome

>Identification

>Significance

the War Powers Act of 1973

>Identification

>Significance

post-traumatic stress disorder

>Identification

>Significance

Henry A. Kissinger

>Identification

>Significance

the Nixon-Kissinger grand strategy

      Identification

      Significance

détente

      Identification

      Significance

the SALT-I agreements

      Identification

      Significance

MIRVs

      Identification

      Significance

the Helsinki Accords

      Identification

      Significance

Nixon's China trip

    Identification

    Significance

the Six-Day War

    Identification

    Significance

the Palestine Liberation Organization

    Identification

    Significance

the 1973 Middle East war

    Identification

    Significance

the OPEC oil embargo

    Identification

    Significance

shuttle diplomacy

    Identification

    Significance

Salvador Allende

    Identification

    Significance

Nixon's policy toward Africa

    Identification

    Significance

the New International Economic Order

    Identification

    Significance

the "dollar glut" of the early 1970s

    Identification

    Significance

economic competition with Japan

    Identification

    Significance

the 1972 environmental conference in Stockholm

    Identification

    Significance

Jimmy Carter

    Identification

    Significance

Carter's human rights policy

    Identification

    Significance

Zbigniew Brzezinski vs. Cyrus Vance

    Identification

    Significance

the SALT-II treaty

    Identification

    Significance

the Soviet invasion of Afghanistan

    Identification

    Significance

the Carter Doctrine

    Identification

    Significance

the Camp David Accords

    Identification

    Significance

the Iranian hostage crisis

    Identification

    Significance

the Iranian rescue mission

Identification

Significance

the Panama Canal treaties of 1977

Identification

Significance

Ronald Reagan

Identification

Significance

Reagan's "devil theory"

Identification

Significance

the Reagan Doctrine

Identification

Significance

the Law of the Sea Treaty

    Identification

    Significance

the Reagan defense buildup

    Identification

    Significance

the Salvadoran civil war

    Identification

    Significance

the contra war in Nicaragua

    Identification

    Significance

the Iran-contra scandal

    Identification

    Significance

the Lebanese crisis of 1982–1983

    Identification

    Significance

intifadah

    Identification

    Significance

the policy of constructive engagement

    Identification

    Significance

famine in Africa

    Identification

    Significance

the Third World debt crisis

    Identification

    Significance

the nuclear weapons debate

    Identification

    Significance

the nuclear freeze movement

    Identification

    Significance

the Catholic Bishops' Pastoral letter

    Identification

    Significance

"nuclear winter"

    Identification

    Significance

the 1985 Geneva summit

    Identification

    Significance

Mikhail S. Gorbachev

    Identification

    Significance

perestroika and glasnost

    Identification

    Significance

the 1987 INF treaty

    Identification

    Significance

Organizing Information

You have two organizing jobs to do in this exercise, the first a continuation of the Organizing Information exercise for Chapter 29 in which you gathered information about the impact of American fears of the Soviet Union and the second the job of organizing information from Chapter 31 concerning Americans' changing political ideology on the home front.

American Fears of the Soviet Union

Gather evidence from Chapter 31 and your class notes concerning how much the United States continued to fear the U.S.S.R. from 1961 through 1989, how it showed its fear, and how its fear affected American policies and the attitudes of both the American public and the nation's policy-makers. Record specific indications of American fear of the power and behavior of the Soviet Union during the specific periods suggested by the column headings.

In the bottom or final row of the chart, draw a conclusion about how much and in what way the country's activities on the world stage reflected the national concern about the power, influence, and threat of the Soviet Union. (Does the concern seem reasonable to you?)

In the chart's final column, draw a conclusion about whether American fears of the Soviet Union seemed to be increasing or decreasing and the significance of the increase or decrease in terms of the kinds of activities the United States was focusing on abroad as the 1990s opened.

The United States and the Cold War Evidence of American Fears of the USSR, 1961-1989					
Areas in which Fear Could Be Reflected	**Kennedy and Johnson Years**	**Nixon and Ford Years**	**Carter Years**	**Reagan Years**	**Conclusion**
Arms Development and Buildup					
Signing "Entangling" Defense Alliances					
Attempts To Interfere in USSR's Sphere of Influence or Its Efforts to Maintain or Expand Its Sphere of Influence					
Use of Trade Policy and Dollar Diplomacy as Cold War Weapons					

The United States and the Cold War Evidence of American Fears of the USSR, 1961-1989 (concluded)					
Areas in which Fear Could Be Reflected	Kennedy and Johnson Years	Nixon and Ford Years	Carter Years	Reagan Years	Conclusion
Adoption of Covert Operations and Morally Questionable Methods of Influencing or Overthrowing Foreign Regimes					
Recognizing or Withholding Recognition of New Governments					
Other					
Conclusions					

America's Political Ideology

Now turn to a consideration of Americans' political climate at home. Record reminders of evidence presented in Chapter 31 of the ideological shift the United States underwent in the Sixties and Seventies in the chart "Ideological Shifts in the Turbulent Era, 1961–1974."

Ideological Shifts in the Turbulent Era, 1961–1974				
Administration				
Areas in Which Shifts Might Occur	**Kennedy** **House (D)** **Senate (D)**	**Johnson** **House (D)** **Senate (D)**	**Nixon/Ford** **House (D)** **Senate (D)**	**Overall Trend**
Democratic Party (makeup, attitudes)				
Republican Party (makeup, attitudes)				
Presidential Philosophy and Initiatives (social, economic, fiscal, diplomatic)				
Legislation and Resolutions Passed by Congress				

Ideological Shifts in the Turbulent Era, 1961–1974 (concluded)

Areas in Which Shifts Might Occur	Administration			
	Kennedy House (D) Senate (D)	Johnson House (D) Senate (D)	Nixon/Ford House (D) Senate (D)	Overall Trend
Supreme Court Replacements (makeup)				
Supreme Court Rulings				
Public Concerns and Political Activity				
Other				
Conclusions				

Interpreting Information

American Fears of the Soviet UnionUsing evidence of America's fear of the U.S.S.R. during the Cold War Era, which you have cited in your Organizing Information charts for both Chapter 31 and Chapter 29 ("The United States and the Cold War") plan and write the working draft of an essay answering the following question:

> What might lead objective observers of American behavior and attitudes from 1945 through the early 1990s to conclude that Americans' fear of the Soviet Union during the Cold War Era was perhaps unreasonable and certainly dominated the nation's attention and sapped its energies and resources?

Looking ahead, you might want to see how some of what the authors of your textbook have to say about the Cold War in Chapter 33 (pages 952–954) squares with your own conclusions.

America's Political Ideology

Using the evidence you found in Chapter 31 and your class notes, and which you recorded in the chapter's Organizing Information exercise, plan and write a working draft of an essay in which you answer this question:

> What in the political events and atmosphere of the Sixties and early Seventies suggests that both America's political leaders and the public at large were shying away from liberalism and adopting more and more conservative attitudes?

As you move on to other chapters in *A People and a Nation*, look for indications of whether the trend being established in the Sixties and Seventies continued throughout the rest of the twentieth century.

Ideas and Details

Objective 1

_____   1. The concept of nation building was based on the idea that
   a. the industrialized nations of the world should pool their resources to aid Third World nations.
   b. the United States could win the friendship of Third World countries by helping them as they struggled through the infant stages of nationhood.
   c. the European states should demonstrate their acceptance of self-determination by allowing their colonies to become independent nations.
   d. a nation's social, political, and economic system must be based on its own unique historical experience.

Objective 1

_____   2. Kennedy chose to adopt the policy of flexible response because
           a. he wanted to streamline the decision-making process in the executive branch.
           b. it would allow subtle shifts in domestic policy statements to match the changing mood of the electorate.
           c. he wanted the United States to be able to respond to any kind of warfare.
           d. the policy would enable the United States to reduce its nuclear arsenal.

Objectives 1 and 2

_____   3. In the aftermath of the Bay of Pigs invasion, the United States government
           a. attempted to overthrow the government of Fidel Castro.
           b. apologized to the Cuban people for infringing on their national sovereignty.
           c. reestablished trade with the Castro regime.
           d. restored diplomatic relations with Cuba.

Objective 2

_____   4. As a result of the Cuban missile crisis,
           a. the Soviet Union made new demands in Berlin.
           b. the United States agreed to dismantle its missiles in Western Europe.
           c. the Soviet Union embarked on a program to match the nuclear strength of the United States.
           d. the United States conducted air strikes against Cuba and destroyed the missile bases on the island.

Objectives 1 and 3

_____   5. In the Gulf of Tonkin Resolution, Congress
           a. publicly questioned President Johnson's escalation of the Vietnam War.
           b. gave virtually a free hand to President Johnson in conducting the war in Vietnam.
           c. condemned the My Lai massacre.
           d. declared war against North Vietnam.

Objective 5

_____   6. In the late 1960s, growing numbers of Americans began to question United States involvement in the Vietnam War in large part because they
           a. were frightened by China's threat to launch a nuclear attack against the United States.
           b. accepted the Republican party's assessment that the United States should abandon the corrupt government of South Vietnam.
           c. recognized the democratic nature of Ho Chi Minh's regime in North Vietnam.
           d. saw the ugliness of the war each evening on the nightly news.

Objectives 4, 5, and 6

_____ 7. Which of the following is, in part, an explanation for atrocities such as the My Lai massacre?
   a. Soldiers who engaged in such atrocities were drug addicts.
   b. Soldiers who engaged in such atrocities had learned to view the Vietnamese as less than fully human.
   c. High-ranking Pentagon officials ordered such atrocities.
   d. CIA operatives disguised as Vietcong engaged in such atrocities.

Objectives 5 and 6

_____ 8. As a result of the Tet offensive,
   a. the Soviet union sent troops to Vietnam.
   b. the Joint Chiefs of Staff advised American withdrawal from Vietnam.
   c. the North Vietnamese were driven to the north of the Demilitarized Zone and requested peace negotiations.
   d. President Johnson, realizing the Vietnam War was unwinnable, decided to open negotiations with the North.

Objective 6

_____ 9. Under the Nixon-Kissinger policy of "Vietnamization,"
   a. stability slowly returned to Indochina as the Vietnam War de-escalated.
   b. withdrawal of American troops was accompanied by increased bombing of the North and the invasion of Cambodia.
   c. the South Vietnamese army proved that it was an effective fighting force.
   d. a coalition government was established in Hanoi and the war quickly drew to a close.

Objective 6

_____ 10. In the aftermath of the Vietnam War, Americans
   a. disagreed over the lessons to be drawn from the experience.
   b. withdrew from the United Nations.
   c. vowed to support Third World revolutions.
   d. agreed to increase the powers of the president in foreign policy.

Objectives 7

_____ 11. The 1972 SALT I agreements
   a. left the United States with a disadvantage in deliverable nuclear warheads.
   b. allowed each side to construct antiballistic missile systems.
   c. placed no restriction on the number of independently targetable warheads that could be placed on each missile.
   d. failed to freeze the number of offensive nuclear missiles each side could have.

Objective 7

_____ 12. As a result of Kissinger's "shuttle diplomacy,"
   a. an autonomous Palestinian state under United Nations protection was created.
   b. the Palestine Liberation Organization recognized Israel's right to exist.
   c. OPEC agreed to reduce oil prices.
   d. Egypt and Israel agreed to a United Nations peacekeeping force in the Sinai.

Objectives 9 and 10

_____ 13. In defending its policies in El Salvador, the Reagan administration warned that
   a. the Soviets were installing nuclear missiles in El Salvador.
   b. the rebel forces in El Salvador would continue to grow if the United States ignored the plight of impoverished Salvadoran peasants.
   c. Communists would soon be at the Texas border if they were not stopped in El Salvador.
   d. the United States should abandon right-wing governments that lacked mass popular support.

Objective 9

_____ 14. What was the Reagan administration's goal in Nicaragua?
   a. To persuade the Sandinista government to hold elections
   b. To remove the Sandinista government from power
   c. To reduce foreign military bases and advisers in that country
   d. To bring about a negotiated settlement between the Sandinista government and the contras

Objective 9

_____ 15. The improvement in Soviet-American relations during Reagan's second term may be attributed, in part, to
   a. Reagan's apology for his "Evil Empire" rhetoric.
   b. the Reagan administration's agreement to limit research on the Strategic Defense Initiative.
   c. cooperation between the United States and the Soviet Union to combat international terrorism.
   d. Gorbachev's decision to reduce Soviet military expenditures and decrease foreign aid.

Essay Questions

Objective 1 and 2

1. Discuss the causes and consequences of the Cuban missile crisis and evaluate President John Kennedy's handling of the crisis.

Objectives 3 and 6

2.   Examine the course of the Vietnam War under President Johnson and President Nixon. To what extent did President Nixon live up to his 1968 campaign pledge to end the war?

Objectives 1, 3, and 6

3.   Debate the following statement: "The belief in the right of the United States to influence the internal affairs of other countries led to disaster in Southeast Asia."

Objective 4

4.   Discuss the characteristics of soldiers who served in the Vietnam War; explain their war-related experiences; and discuss the impact of those experiences on their lives.

Objective 6

5.   Discuss the domestic debate over the meaning of the American experience in Vietnam.

Objective 7

6.   Explain how events in the Middle East placed the Nixon-Kissinger "grand strategy" in jeopardy.

Objective 8

7.   Discuss President Carter's foreign policy objectives, and explain his accomplishments and failures in attempting to achieve those objectives.

Objectives 7, 8, and 9

8.   Define *nationalism*; discuss its role in international affairs in the 1970s and 1980s; and explain the response of the United States to revolutionary nationalism.

Objective 9

9.   Explain the following statement: "Ronald Reagan's foreign policy was driven by beliefs rooted in America's past."

Objective 9

10.   Discuss and evaluate the Reagan administration's policy toward Third World nations, paying particular attention to its policy toward Central America.

Objectives 1, 7, 8, and 9

11. Examine the nuclear arms race and attempts at arms control between the United States and the Soviet Union from 1961 to 1989.

Objective 9

12. Defend or refute the following statement: "The turnaround in Soviet-American relations which began in 1985 stemmed more from changes abroad than from President Reagan's decisions."

Map Exercise

Refer to the map on page 904 of the textbook to complete this exercise. You may also find it helpful to refer to a historical atlas. You will need three pens of different colors to complete this exercise. (Highlight pens may be used.)

Label each of the following on the map of the Middle East that follows.

Countries	*Bodies of Water*	*Territories*	*Capital Cities*
• Egypt	• Gulf of Aqaba	• Gaza Strip	• Amman
• Iran	• Gulf of Suez	• Golan Heights	• Beirut
• Iraq	• Jordan River	• Sinai Peninsula	• Baghdad
• Israel	• Mediterranean Sea	• West Bank	• Cairo
• Jordan	• Persian Gulf		• Damascus
• Lebanon	• Red Sea		• Jerusalem
• Saudi Arabia	• Sea of Galilee		• Riyadh
• Syria	• Suez Canal		• Tehran

Color the map as follows:

• Use one color to denote the Jewish state after the partition of Palestine, 1947

• Use a second color to denote the territory Israel gained as a result of the War of 1948–1949

• Use a third color to denote the territory controlled by Israel after the Six-Day War, 1967

• Place backward slashes (\\\\\\) in the Sinai Peninsula to denote that by the Egyptian-Israeli Agreements of 1975 and 1979 Israel withdrew from the Sinai in 1982.

  Do not put backward slashes in the area known as the Gaza Strip. That area was not returned to Egypt when Israel withdrew from the Sinai.

• Place forward slashes (//////) in the Golan Heights to denote that Israel annexed this area in 1981.

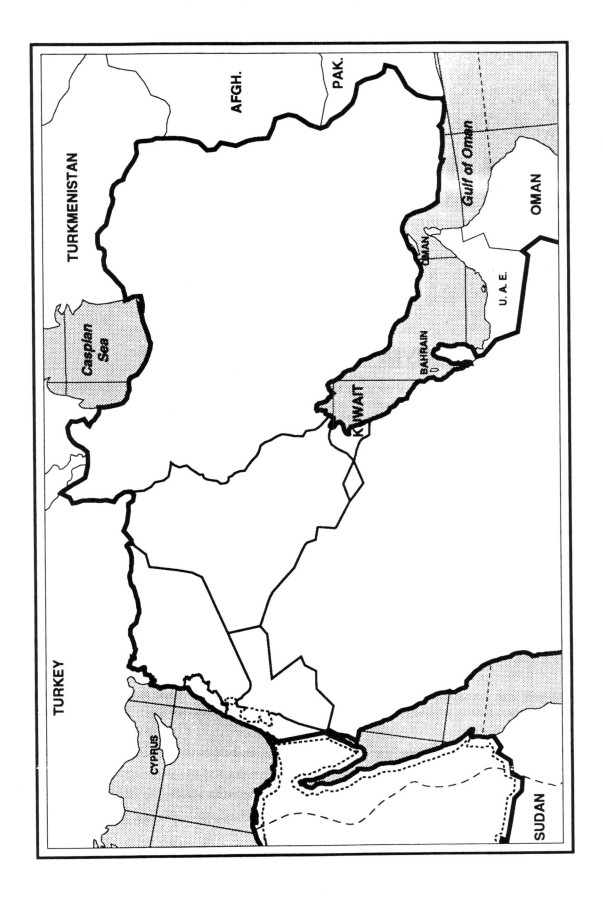

CHAPTER 32

The End of the Postwar Boom: Stagflation, Immigration, and the Resurgence of Conservatism, 1974–1989

Learning Objectives

After you have studied Chapter 32 in your textbook and worked through this study guide chapter, you should be able to:

1. Discuss the causes, characteristics, and consequences of the economic and energy crises of the 1970s, and explain and evaluate the attempts by the Ford and Carter administrations to deal with these crises.

2. Examine the issues and personalities and explain the outcome of the 1976 presidential election.

3. Discuss Jimmy Carter's personal and political background; examine the domestic issues and political problems that faced the Carter administration; and explain and evaluate the administration's actions concerning those issues and problems.

4. Examine the emergence, characteristics, goals, and accomplishments of the new conservative coalition, and discuss the impact of this coalition on the election of 1980.

5. Discuss Ronald Reagan's personal and political background, and explain his political, social, and economic views.

6. Examine the issues and personalities and explain the outcome of the 1980 congressional and presidential elections.

7. Examine Ronald Reagan's economic policies in relation to federal spending, federal income taxes, and federal environmental, health, and safety regulations; explain Congress's reaction to these policies; and assess the impact of these policies on the United States.

8. Discuss the causes and consequences of the 1981–1983 economic recession.

9. Examine the issues and personalities and explain the outcome of the 1984 presidential election.

10. Discuss the problems that nonwhites, immigrants, and women faced in American society during the 1970s and 1980s; explain their approaches to those problems; and discuss the extent to which they were successful in achieving their goals.

11. Discuss the emergence, characteristics, and goals of the antifeminist and anti-abortion movements, and discuss their impact on American society during the 1970s and 1980s.

12. Examine the forces that caused increased polarization of American society during the 1980s.

13.   Examine the reasons for, the extent of, and the effects of poverty in America during the 1970s and 1980s, and discuss the characteristics of the poor.

14.   Discuss the drug epidemic and the AIDS epidemic; explain their impact on the American people and American society; and assess the government's response to the threats posed by these epidemics.

15.   Examine the domestic economic challenges that faced the Reagan administration during its second term; explain Reagan's actions concerning those challenges; and discuss the consequences of those actions.

16.   Explain the reaction of the American people to the Iran-contra scandal and hearings; discuss the revelations concerning Reagan's management style; and examine the scandal's impact on President Reagan's ability to govern.

17.   Discuss the political problems faced by Ronald Reagan during his last two years in office.

18.   Examine the issues and personalities and explain the outcome of the 1988 presidential election.

Thematic Guide

The nation's disillusionment with its government—disillusionment produced by the crises of the 1960s and early 1970s—intensified further when governmental leaders could not deal successfully with the disruptive economic forces of the 1970s. In "Economic Crisis and Ford's Response," we examine the nature of the economic crisis and its causes. This section also covers President Ford's responses to the economic and energy crises, the nuclear power debate, and the fiscal crisis experienced by some of the nation's cities.

An apathetic electorate elected Jimmy Carter to the presidency in the 1976 election. Although Carter did score some notable domestic accomplishments, his unwillingness to compromise alienated congressional representatives of both parties, and his fiscal conservatism put him at odds with the liberal wing of the Democratic party. In addition, Carter was plagued by political and economic forces beyond his control; his popularity declined dramatically, and he became politically impotent.

As the American people became more and more deeply troubled and frightened by changes and forces over which they and their government seemed to have little control, they became more distrustful of government and of those groups that continued to advocate change within society. This conservative mood was buttressed by the uniting of conservative politicians of the "old right" with evangelical Christians of the "new right." The channeling of these forces into a new conservative coalition, plus a distrust of government born of a decade of chaos produced America's "turn to the right" in 1980 and led to Ronald Reagan's victory in the presidential election of that year.

With widespread support from the American people, President Ronald Reagan, the standard-bearer of a new conservative coalition and a strong advocate of supply-side economic theory, persuaded Congress to enact two major aspects of his conservative agenda: (1) deep spending cuts in social and health programs and (2) a five-year, $750 billion tax cut that primarily benefited the wealthy. In addition, out of the belief that government regulations reduced business profits and slowed economic growth, the Reagan administration launched an attack against federal environmental, health, and safety regulations.

Although inflation and interest rates declined during Reagan's first two years in office, these successes resulted from the Federal Reserve Board's policies, a decline in oil prices, which had a ripple effect throughout the economy, and a massive recession lasting from mid-1981 to late 1983. The recession affected both industrial and agricultural workers; and, in spite of an economic recovery that began in 1984, poverty increased to pre-Great Society levels. The one group that did not experience increased poverty levels was the elderly, a group that had more political power than ever before. Although Reagan promised to maintain a "safety net" for the most needy in American society, when faced with a mounting federal deficit, he reduced welfare and social programs, maintained his tax cuts, and increased defense spending for a major military buildup. Using these issues to their advantage, the Democrats picked up twenty-six seats in the House of Representatives in the 1982 congressional elections but were unable to take control of the Senate.

However, issues that ordinarily would have posed severe political liabilities for an incumbent during a presidential election year had little impact on the voters' perceptions of President Reagan. Although in many cases the voters disagreed with the president's policies, they liked Reagan personally and seldom seemed to hold him responsible for the failures of his administration. These and other factors led to Reagan's landslide victory over his Democratic opponent in the 1984 presidential election.

From this discussion of the attempts by successive administrations to deal with the nation's domestic problems during the 1970s and 1980s, the focus of the chapter shifts to an analysis of the impact of the economic and energy crises on various groups in American society. The increase in poverty accompanying the stagnant economy of the 1970s and the recession of the early 1980s occurred most often among nonwhites, children, and female heads of households. Although many Americans accepted traditional beliefs that blamed the victims of poverty for their distress, economic reality meant that occupational opportunities, especially for unskilled workers, were severely limited.

While poor unskilled blacks languished in poverty, the black middle class expanded. In spite of increased opportunities for some blacks, the resurgence of white racism, the problems encountered by Indians, and the struggle of Hispanics and other immigrants make clear that the divisive elements long present in pluralistic America were worsened by the political, social, and economic crises of the 1970s and 1980s.

Divisiveness also continued in the form of sexism. Although women had made gains in American society, they still faced barriers. In "Feminism, Antifeminism, and Women's Lives," the authors discuss the emergence, characteristics, and aims of the antifeminist forces that gained strength in the 1970s. Although, according to feminist scholar Barbara Ehrenreich, the appeal of the *Playboy* lifestyle was a major factor in the soaring divorce rate of the 1960s and 1970s, most antifeminists blamed the revolt against marriage on feminists. Arguing in favor of "traditional" American values in the midst of a rapidly changing society, antifeminists successfully stalled ratification of the Equal Rights Amendment and began to campaign actively against legalized abortion. The recession also affected women adversely. Occupational segregation continued, and many women found themselves caught in "the Superwoman Squeeze."

The domestic problems faced by the United States continued to mount during Reagan's last four years in office, and the polarization and tensions within pluralistic America increased. As the gap widened between rich and poor, a variety of factors increased the severity of poverty. Nonwhite minorities, immigrants, and women continued to face the discrimination accompanying racism, nativism, and sexism. The crack epidemic and the AIDS epidemic continued to plague, and divide, the American people. Furthermore, despite the "feel-good" campaign conducted by Reagan in 1984, once reelected he and Congress were forced to grapple with the economic problems posed by the spiraling federal deficit. Reagan also began to make his mark on the Supreme Court and oversaw enactment of a sweeping tax reform bill in 1986. Revelations related to the Iran-contra scandal and the fact that Reagan was a lame-duck president combined to cause a decline in Reagan's ability to lead during his last two years in office. However, thawing of relations between the United States and the Soviet Union and a six-year economic recovery led the American electorate to elect George Bush to the presidency in 1988. President Bush and the American people faced difficult choices as the United States prepared to enter the decade of the 1990s.

Building Vocabulary

Listed below are important words and terms that you need to know to get the most out of Chapter 32. They are listed in the order in which they occur in the chapter. After carefully looking through the list, refer to a dictionary and jot down the definition of words that you do not know or of which you are unsure.

distraught

augur

resurgence

reverberate

formidable

scapegoat

credence

gibe

fetter

catapult

genial

anomaly

amnesty

jettison

assail

scourge

inane

Identification and Significance

After studying Chapter 32 of A *People and a Nation*, you should be able to identify fully *and* explain the historical significance of each item listed below.

1. Identify each item in the space provided. Give an explanation or description of the item. Answer the questions *who, what, where,* and *when.*

2. Explain the historical significance of each item in the space provided. Establish the historical context in which the item exists. Establish the item as the result of or as the cause of other factors existing in the society under study. Answer this question: *What were the political, social, economic, and/or cultural consequences of this item?*

OPEC price increases of 1973

    Identification

    Significance

recession in the auto industry

      Identification

      Significance

stagflation

      Identification

      Significance

Keynesianism

      Identification

      Significance

deindustrialization

      Identification

      Significance

annual productivity growth, 1966–1980

      Identification

      Significance

easy credit

>   Identification

>   Significance

WIN (Whip Inflation Now)

>   Identification

>   Significance

the 1974 congressional elections

>   Identification

>   Significance

the nuclear-power debate

>   Identification

>   Significance

Brown's Ferry and Three Mile Island

>   Identification

>   Significance

the New York City financial crisis

    Identification

    Significance

the 1976 presidential election

    Identification

    Significance

Jimmy Carter

    Identification

    Significance

the Federal Reserve Board's policies, 1979–1980

    Identification

    Significance

the "discomfort index"

    Identification

    Significance

the environmental "superfund"

    Identification

    Significance

the Moral Majority

    Identification

    Significance

the 1980 federal census

    Identification

    Significance

population shift to the Sunbelt

    Identification

    Significance

Ronald Reagan

    Identification

    Significance

the 1980 congressional and presidential elections

　　Identification

　　Significance

Reaganomics

　　Identification

　　Significance

supply-side economics

　　Identification

　　Significance

the 1981 tax cuts

　　Identification

　　Significance

Reagan's policies toward regulatory agencies

　　Identification

　　Significance

organized labor in the 1980s

    Identification

    Significance

the recession of the early 1980s

    Identification

    Significance

the "safety net" for the "truly needy"

    Identification

    Significance

John W. Hinkley, Jr.

    Identification

    Significance

the 1982 congressional elections

    Identification

    Significance

Walter Mondale

    Identification

    Significance

Geraldine Ferraro

    Identification

    Significance

the 1984 presidential election

    Identification

    Significance

the 1981 Children's Defense Fund survey concerning African American children

    Identification

    Significance

the African American middle class in the 1980s

    Identification

    Significance

white backlash

    Identification

    Significance

Bakke v. *University of California* and *Richmond* v. *Croson*

    Identification

    Significance

the Miami and Chattanooga race riots of 1980

    Identification

    Significance

Sandra Day O'Connor

    Identification

    Significance

the seizure of the Pine Ridge Reservation trading post

    Identification

    Significance

the dual status of Native Americans

Identification

Significance

the Indian Claims Commission

Identification

Significance

Hispanic immigrants

Identification

Significance

"brown power"

Identification

Significance

United Farm Workers

Identification

Significance

the "new immigrants" of the 1970s and 1980s

Identification

Significance

the Immigration Reform and Control (Simpson-Rodino) Act

Identification

Significance

the Equal Credit Opportunity Act

Identification

Significance

the antifeminist ("profamily") movement

Identification

Significance

Barbara Ehrenreich

Identification

Significance

the Equal Rights Amendment

> Identification

> Significance

the anti-abortion ("prolife") movement

> Identification

> Significance

the Hyde Amendment

> Identification

> Significance

Webster v. *Reproductive Health Services*

> Identification

> Significance

the gender gap

> Identification

> Significance

the comparable-worth issue

    Identification

    Significance

"the Superwoman Squeeze"

    Identification

    Significance

poverty in the 1970s and 1980s

    Identification

    Significance

the homeless

    Identification

    Significance

the "crack" epidemic

    Identification

    Significance

the AIDS epidemic

    Identification

    Significance

"Safe Sex" campaigns

    Identification

    Significance

Bowers v. *Hardwick*

    Identification

    Significance

the federal deficit

    Identification

    Significance

the Gramm-Rudman bill

    Identification

    Significance

the Tax Reform Act of 1986

    Identification

    Significance

William Rehnquist and Antonin Scalia

    Identification

    Significance

the Iran-contra scandal

    Identification

    Significance

the Teflon-coated presidency

    Identification

    Significance

George Bush

    Identification

    Significance

Michael Dukakis

    Identification

    Significance

Jesse Jackson

    Identification

    Significance

the 1988 presidential election

    Identification

    Significance

Organizing Information

To get a good look at what, if anything, distinguished the Democratic approaches to economic and social problems besetting the country in the Seventies and Eighties from Republican approaches, enter reminders of relevant information from Chapter 32 and your class notes in the chart "Democratic and Republican Approaches to Key Domestic Problems, 1974–1989." After you have your chart completed, review the key steps taken by Presidents Ford, Carter, and Reagan to confront major issues facing their administrations.

Democratic and Republican Approaches to Key Domestic Problems, 1974–1989				
Area of Activity	Ford	Carter	Reagan	Conclusion
Inflation, Credit				
Jobs, Productivity				
Taxes				
Budget, Deficit				
Energy				
Transportation				

Democratic and Republican Approaches to Key Problems, 1974–1989 (concluded)				
Area of Activity	Ford	Carter	Reagan	Conclusion
Health, Welfare				
Ethnic, Racial, Class Divisions				
Budget, Deficit				
Unions/Strikes				
Other				
Conclusions				

Interpreting Information

Study the entries you have made in your Organizing Information chart and then compose the working draft of an essay on the following question:

> Using the efforts of President Jimmy Carter and Presidents Gerald Ford and Ronald Reagan as your examples, compare or contrast Democratic and Republican approaches to promoting the social and economic welfare of the people in the Seventies and Eighties.

Ideas and Details

Objective 1

_____ 1. As a result of the dramatic increase in energy prices in the early 1970s,
   a. the United States faced double-digit inflation in 1974.
   b. multinational oil companies prospered.
   c. automobile and related industries suffered a lingering recession.
   d. all of the above were true.

Objective 1

_____ 2. As a result of the slowing of growth in productivity during the 1970s,
   a. workers realized they could no longer expect the wage increases they had enjoyed during the 1960s.
   b. interest rates declined.
   c. American products became less competitive in the marketplace.
   d. business investments increased.

Objective 3

_____ 3. Which of the following created difficulties for the Carter administration?
   a. Carter alienated members of his own party as a result of his stand on deregulation of certain industries.
   b. The decrease in the number of political action committees made it difficult for Carter to raise campaign funds.
   c. Carter was not prepared to deal with the increase in the power of the president relative to the power of Congress.
   d. Carter's veto of legislation to impose a windfall-profits tax on the oil companies alienated the Republican-controlled Congress.

Objectives 4 and 6

_____ 4. The emergence of a powerful political network consisting of evangelical Christians and members of the Hoover Institute indicate that
   a. conservatism was the dominant political mood in the late 1970s.
   b. there was a resurgence of political power in the frostbelt in the late 1970s.
   c. economic issues dominated the political scene in the late 1970s.
   d. Americans were no longer concerned with the threat of Communist expansion.

Objective 5

_____ 5. As governor of California, Ronald Reagan
   a. dismantled the state's welfare system.
   b. signed one of the nation's most liberal abortion laws.
   c. proposed the legalization of marijuana.
   d. instituted a statewide healthcare program.

Objective 7

_____ 6. Which of the following benefited the most from the 1981 tax reductions?
   a. The poor
   b. The wealthy
   c. The middle class
   d. Married couples

Objective 7

_____ 7. President Reagan's appointees to the National Labor Relations Board
   a. actively encouraged companies to declare bankruptcy as a way of canceling union contracts.
   b. questioned the right of union members to strike.
   c. consistently voted in favor of management.
   d. campaigned in favor of the closed shop.

Objectives 7 and 8

_____ 8. A major reason for the dramatic decline in inflation from 1980 to 1982 was
   a. increasing productivity among American workers.
   b. the deepening recession during that period.
   c. increased spending by Americans.
   d. the rise in GNP from increased investment spending.

Objectives 8 and 10

_____ 9. As a result of changes in the job market in the 1980s,
   a. occupational segregation by sex slowly disappeared.
   b. the number of blue-collar jobs increased dramatically.
   c. the unskilled and poorly educated found it increasingly difficult to find work.
   d. organized labor became more interested in unskilled laborers.

Objective 10

_____ 10. Which of the following was true of African Americans during the 1970s and 1980s?
   a. The number of African Americans attending college decreased during the decade.
   b. The gap between poor African Americans and middle-class African Americans increased.
   c. The number of African American families with a female head of household decreased.
   d. Increasing numbers of African Americans fell out of the middle class into the ranks of the poor.

Objectives 10 and 12

_____ 11. Black civil rights leaders denounced the Reagan administration because it
   a. encouraged local school districts to defy court-ordered busing.
   b. stood against renewing intact the Voting Rights Act of 1965.
   c. sought repeal of fair-housing laws.
   d. secured the passage of legislation outlawing affirmative action.

Objectives 4 and 11

_____ 12. Antifeminist forces were able to prevent ratification of the Equal Rights Amendment by
   a. successfully organizing a nationwide strike of working women.
   b. persuading the Senate to rescind its approval of the amendment.
   c. publishing a study that proved gender-based discrimination to be nonexistent in the United States.
   d. frightening people with false claims about what would happen if it were ratified.

Objective 14

_____ 13. Which of the following caused caution to replace the liberated sexual practices associated with the sexual revolution?
   a. The threat of sexually transmitted diseases
   b. The health risks associated with the use of birth-control pills
   c. The graying of America
   d. The influence of TV evangelists

Objectives 7, 8, 9, and 15

_____ 14. An issue of growing public concern throughout the Reagan presidency concerned
   a. the nation's weakening defense posture.
   b. Reagan's opposition to abortion.
   c. the federal deficit.
   d. America's lack of influence over Israel.

Objective 16

_____ 15. As a result of the Iran-contra hearings,
   a. it became clear that President Reagan clearly instructed his national security aide Robert McFarlane not to sell arms to Iran.
   b. evidence proved that President Reagan had full knowledge of the diversion of profits from the sale of arms to Iran to the contras in Nicaragua.
   c. it was revealed that President Reagan always instructed his advisors to respect the role of Congress in the making and implementation of foreign policy.
   d. many political observers argued that President Reagan was an unengaged and uninformed leader.

Essay Questions

Objective 1

1. Discuss the economic problems of the United States in the 1970s, and evaluate the attempts by Presidents Ford and Carter to deal with those problems.

Objectives 1 and 3

2. Discuss the domestic successes and failures of the Carter presidency, and explain why it may be said that many of Carter's problems were not of his own making.

Objectives 7, 8, 10, 12, 13, and 15

3. Discuss the economic policies of the Reagan administration, and examine the impact of these policies on the United States.

Objectives 9, 10, 12, and 13

4. Identify the major groups during the course of the 1980s that opposed Reagan administration policies and actions, and discuss the reasons for their opposition.

Objective 10

5. Discuss the economic, social, and political position of Hispanic Americans during the 1970s and 1980s.

Objective 11

6. Explain the emergence and evaluate the goals of the antifeminist movement.

Objectives 12 and 13

7. Examine the reasons for and the extent of poverty in the United States in the 1980s. What groups were most affected? Why?

Objective 14

8. Discuss the extent of the AIDS epidemic, and explain the impact of the epidemic on the sexual behavior and attitudes of Americans.

Objectives 15, 16, and 17

9. Discuss the following statement: "The main challenge of Reagan's last two years in office was to reassert his leadership and avoid becoming a lame-duck president." How successful was President Reagan in meeting this challenge? Explain.

CHAPTER 33

Prosperity, Power, and Peril: America in the 1990s

Learning Objectives

After you have studied Chapter 33 in your textbook and worked through this study guide chapter, you should be able to:

1. Discuss George Bush's personal and political background; examine the domestic issues and political problems that faced the Bush administration; and explain and evaluate the administration's actions concerning those issues and problems.

2. Discuss the nomination of Clarence Thomas to the Supreme Court; explain the issues addressed by the Senate Judiciary Committee in its confirmation hearings; and discuss the reaction of the American people to those hearings.

3. Discuss the multiplicity of factors that led to the collapse of the Soviet empire in Eastern Europe, the disintegration of the Soviet Union, and the reunification of Germany.

4. Explain the reasons for the end of the Cold War, and discuss the war's legacy for the United States, the former Soviet Union, and the world community of nations.

5. Examine, evaluate, and discuss the consequences of the defense and foreign policy views, goals, and actions of the Bush administration in relation to:
   a. global environmental issues
   b. the START talks
   c. China
   d. NAFTA
   e. Central America
   f. South Africa
   g. Somalia

6. Discuss the causes and consequences of the Persian Gulf War.

7. Discuss the scandals that plagued Congress between 1988 and 1992, and explain the reaction of the American people to these scandals.

8. Discuss both the immediate and underlying causes of the Los Angeles riots of April 1992.

9. Examine the issues and personalities and explain the outcome of the 1992 presidential and congressional elections.

10. Discuss Bill Clinton's personal and political background; examine the domestic issues and political problems that faced the Clinton administration; and explain and evaluate the administration's actions concerning those issues and problems.

11. Examine the issues and personalities and explain the outcome of the 1994 congressional elections.

12. Examine the sources for the antigovernment sentiment felt by many Americans in the 1990s.

13. Discuss the causes and consequences of the "gender gap" of the 1990s.

14. Examine the issues and personalities and explain the outcome of the 1996 presidential and congressional elections.

15. Examine, evaluate, and discuss the consequences of the defense and foreign policy views, goals, and actions of the Clinton administration in relation to:
   a. the end of the Cold War.
   b. ethnic wars in former Yugoslavia.
   c. the Middle East.
   d. genocide in Rwanda.
   e. Haiti and Cuba.
   f. China.
   g. international economic and financial issues.
   h. Japan.
   i. weapons proliferation.
   j. global environmental issues.
   k. human rights for women.
   l. the United Nations.

16. Discuss the causes and consequences of the globalization of American culture in the 1990s.

17. Examine Kenneth Starr's investigation of alleged scandals involving President Clinton.

18. Examine relations between President Clinton and Congress; explain the reasons for the President's impeachment; and explain the President's acquittal by the Senate.

19. Examine the issues and personalities of the 2000 presidential campaign.

Thematic Guide

The mood of the American people in the 1990s is variously described in Chapter 33 as one of apathy, disgust, anger, anxiety, and hostility. It is within the context of these feelings that the authors discuss the array of domestic and international problems facing the United States in the decade preceding the new millennium.

In 1988 George Bush rode into the presidency on the back of peace and prosperity. Although he presented himself as the heir of his conservative predecessor, Ronald Reagan, in deed and action he seemed indecisive and out of touch. Although he most certainly wanted to *be* president, he seldom seemed to know what he wanted to achieve *as* president. Therefore, rather than leading in a decisive and positive direction, he engaged in crisis management as he attempted to maintain the status quo. Wanting an unchanging America over which he could be caretaker, President Bush instead inherited an America in which economic and social problems abounded. Although the American people had been told, and many believed, that government was the problem, a significant number still expected government to respond with meaningful solutions to the real national problems that existed. In this America George Bush's aversion to active government made him seem to be out of place and out of step.

After Bush's election to the presidency in 1988, the economy slowly drifted into stagnation and recession. As businesses "downsized" in an effort to deal with overwhelming debt burdens, unemployment rose. Rejecting the advice to call Congress into special session to deal with mounting economic problems, the Bush administration remained passive. Passivity was also the order of the day in dealing with the real problems that plagued the American system of public education and in dealing with the many social problems left over from the 1980s. In addition, Bush had pledged to be the "environmental" president, but allowed the Council on Competitiveness to gut the Clean Air Act; and, although he pledged in the 1988 presidential campaign that he would not raise taxes, he entered into a deal with the Democratic-controlled Congress in which the Democratic leaders agreed to cut spending and Bush endorsed a tax hike. As criticism of the administration mounted in these areas, the Clarence Thomas–Anita Hill confrontation galvanized many Americans, especially women, and increased opposition to the Republican party.

During his first three years as president, George Bush witnessed the collapse of communism in Eastern Europe, the reunification of Germany, the disintegration of the Soviet Union, and Mikhail Gorbachev's fall from power—all of which signaled the end of the Cold War. After examining the trends that brought an end to the Cold War and discussing the START treaties, the authors turn to a discussion of the impact of the Tiananmen Square massacre on U.S.-Chinese relations.

Despite the end of the Cold War and an end to civil strife in Nicaragua, El Salvador, and Guatemala, United States relations with the Third World remained turbulent, as can be seen in the discussion of the U.S. invasion of Panama and the Persian Gulf War. A theme that runs through the discussion of the economic and political problems of the Third World is the contribution of the United States to problems that led to turmoil. From the U.S.-financed contra war in Nicaragua to military aid to Somalia's dictatorial regime, to the extension of U.S. aid to the drug-trafficking dictator of Panama, Manuel Noriega, the story is much the same. Often in the name of "containment" of Communism and always in the name of national security, United States military aid often engendered the very instability the United States sought to prevent.

Nowhere was this clearer than in Panama and Iraq, two areas in which the United States ultimately used military force to deal with the excesses of dictators it had previously supported. Although Manuel Noriega was removed from power in Panama, the United States had few resources to help rebuild the devastated country. And although Iraq was decisively and humiliatingly defeated in the Persian Gulf War, its dictator Saddam Hussein remained in power and continued to repress the peoples of his war-ravaged nation.

As President Bush prepared for a reelection bid in 1992, the country was mired in economic recession. As unemployment mounted and personal income stagnated, the president remained inactive. Furthermore, the Los Angeles riots of 1992 were a shocking reminder that racial tensions continued to plague the nation, and the Bush administration's passivity in dealing with the plight of the urban poor and the problems associated with their plight led to still more criticism.

Although many Americans became increasingly critical of the Republican president, they were just as critical of the scandal-ridden Democratic-controlled Congress. As the 1992 election approached, the American people seemed genuinely dissatisfied with "Washington gridlock" and ready for change. They were also ready for the government to act in solving many long-standing problems. It was this desire for change and this readiness for action that fueled the campaigns of the independent presidential candidate Ross Perot and the Democratic candidate Bill Clinton.

Bill Clinton's election to the presidency in 1992 signaled that the American people wanted a change from the passivity of the Bush years. But the pluralistic America of the 1990s was a fragmented America in which consensus on solutions to long-standing problems was difficult. President Clinton would soon discover in both the gays-in-the-military issue and in the response to his economic proposals just how difficult it was to lead an American people who were deeply divided over their own vision of the nation's future, a division reflected in the lobby groups that vied with each other over control of the national agenda. Although the President and Congress did find consensus in some areas, which produced some legislative successes, the attack of interest-group lobbyists against the President's healthcare reform proposals prevented substantive reform in that area.

Questions about the President's character, which had been part of the 1992 presidential campaign, persisted throughout Clinton's tenure in the Oval Office, and controversy also surrounded the First Lady, Hillary Rodham Clinton. These questions coupled with questions about Clinton's management ability caused American voters in 1994 to show again their disillusionment with government, this time by giving Republicans majorities in both houses of Congress for the first time since 1954. But as the 104th Congress attempted to enact the Republican "Contract with America," political stalemate persisted, leading to government shutdowns and increased anger and disgust among the electorate.

In looking at the American past, one can readily see that the American people have historically had a hostility toward and a distrust of government. The authors point to the American Revolution, the Civil War, and antigovernment movements that expressed hatred against certain "out-groups" as evidence of this hostility. A primary source for the hostility toward the federal government in the 1990s is found in the 1960s. The authors also point to a link between the student radicals of the 1960s and the conservatives of the 1990s, pointing out that both groups wanted to be free from government restraints. Scandals such as Watergate, Iran-contra, and those associated with the Clinton White House caused a further deepening of this distrust of government. President Reagan also contributed to this distrust through his antigovernment rhetoric and through the quadrupling of the federal debt during the Reagan-Bush years, a factor which put severe restraints on the financial ability of government to fund additional programs.

The distrust of government that built up over a thirty-year period led to an American public "deeply alienated from politics" and "deeply cynical." Within this atmosphere, many predicted that voters in 1996 would direct their anger against President Clinton and return a Republican to the White House. But Clinton positioned himself as the protector of certain federal programs that the Republican-dominated 104th Congress attacked. In doing so, he gained the support of women and of those who benefited from such programs. Furthermore, the Republican willingness to allow government shutdowns in their quest for a balanced budget convinced many that Bill Clinton was reasonable and moderate while Congress was "ideologically inflexible." Therefore, despite hints of scandal in the White House and continued Republican attacks against President Clinton on the character issue, Clinton easily defeated his challengers and became the first Democrat to be reelected to the presidency since Franklin D. Roosevelt in 1936.

As the United States tried to gain its footing in the post-Cold War world, international issues related to ethnic wars, weapons proliferation, global environmental concerns, and women as a world-wide human rights issue caused continuing debate among the American people over the proper role of the United States in the new world of the 1990s. In the meantime, little American aid flowed to Haiti, Nicaragua, El Salvador, and Panama to help rebuild economies devastated by years of internal strife. Furthermore, as indicated in the Helms-Burton Act, the United States still felt the need to "contain" Castro's Cuba; but, as events in Rwanda in 1994 indicated, the United States remained unable to adequately "discipline" the peoples of the Third World.

Realizing that U.S. prosperity depended, to a great extent, on foreign trade, the Clinton administration focused on stabilizing economically and politically troubled nations, opening foreign markets to American products, and reducing the nation's trade deficit. Believing, as President Bush had before him, that friendly relations with the hard-line Chinese government were in the best interests of the United States, President Clinton granted China most-favored-nation trading status and spoke of the need to "decouple trade and human rights issues." Relations with Japan continued to be conditioned, in large measure, by economic competition between the two nations, and trade was an issue in the reopening of normal trade and diplomatic relations with Vietnam.

After discussing the globalization of American culture, the authors turn to a discussion of the Whitewater investigation, the expansion of that investigation, the president's impeachment by the House of Representatives for matters relating to the Monica Lewinsky affair, and his ultimate acquittal by the Senate. The chapter ends with a discussion of the issues and likely candidates in the 2000 presidential election.

Building Vocabulary

Listed below are important words and terms that you need to know to get the most out of Chapter 33. They are listed in the order in which they occur in the chapter. After carefully looking through the list, refer to a dictionary and jot down the definition of words that you do not know or of which you are unsure.

abjure

philandering

chameleon

punster

acquiescence

protagonist

icon

interdiction

sordid

mettle

pummel

caricature

pundit

impunity

paradoxical

obtuse

portend

gaffe

conflagration

inimical

libertarian

tout

disconsolate

scrutiny

eschew

fruition

intrastate

fissure

pander

nettlesome

virulent

lackluster

emasculation

tawdry

tribulation

contrite

denigrate

Identification and Significance

After studying Chapter 33 of A *People and a Nation*, you should be able to identify fully *and* explain the historical significance of each item listed below.

1. Identify each item in the space provided. Give an explanation or description of the item. Answer the questions *who, what, where,* and *when.*

2. Explain the historical significance of each item in the space provided. Establish the historical context in which the item exists. Establish the item as the result of or as the cause of other factors existing in the society under study. Answer this question: *What were the political, social, economic, and/or cultural consequences of this item?*

the Columbine massacre

  Identification

  Significance

George Bush

  Identification

  Significance

"gridlock" in the federal government

  Identification

  Significance

Bush's "No-new-taxes" pledge

    Identification

    Significance

Bush's education policies

    Identification

    Significance

Bush's environmental policies

    Identification

    Significance

the Clean Air Act

    Identification

    Significance

the Council on Competitiveness

    Identification

    Significance

the Americans with Disabilities Act

      Identification

      Significance

Clarence Thomas

      Identification

      Significance

Anita Hill

      Identification

      Significance

health-care problems

      Identification

      Significance

"outsourcing" and "downsizing"

      Identification

      Significance

the collapse of communism in Eastern Europe

    Identification

    Significance

the disintegration of the Soviet Union

    Identification

    Significance

"imperial overstretch"

    Identification

    Significance

START I and START II

    Identification

    Significance

the Tiananmen Square Massacre

    Identification

    Significance

anti-immigrant sentiment

     Identification

     Significance

the North American Free Trade Agreement

     Identification

     Significance

the "drug war"

     Identification

     Significance

General Manuel Antonio Noriega

     Identification

     Significance

Operation Just Cause

     Identification

     Significance

apartheid in South Africa

    Identification

    Significance

Nelson Mandela

    Identification

    Significance

the Persian Gulf War

    Identification

    Significance

Operation Restore Hope

    Identification

    Significance

the Republican coalition

    Identification

    Significance

economic recession, 1989–1992

    Identification

    Significance

scandals in Congress, 1988–1992

    Identification

    Significance

the Twenty-seventh **Amendment**

    Identification

    Significance

Bill Clinton

    Identification

    Significance

Albert Gore

    Identification

    Significance

Ross Perot

Identification

Significance

the Los Angeles riots of 1992

Identification

Significance

the 1992 Republican convention

Identification

Significance

the politics of cultural conservatism

Identification

Significance

the presidential and congressional elections of 1992

Identification

Significance

the pardon of Iran-contra figures

    Identification

    Significance

the gays-in-the-military issue

    Identification

    Significance

Clinton's 1993 economic plan

    Identification

    Significance

the "motor-voter" act

    Identification

    Significance

the Family and Medical Leave Act

    Identification

    Significance

gun control legislation

    Identification

    Significance

Clinton's crime bill

    Identification

    Significance

Ruth Bader Ginsburg and Stephen Breyer

    Identification

    Significance

Planned Parenthood v. *Casey, U.S.* v. *Virginia,* and *Romer* v. *Evans*

    Identification

    Significance

health-care reform

    Identification

    Significance

Hillary Rodham Clinton

    Identification

    Significance

Newt Gingrich

    Identification

    Significance

the "Contract with America"

    Identification

    Significance

the Republican Revolution

    Identification

    Significance

antigovernment feelings and movements of the 1990s

    Identification

    Significance

the Oklahoma City bombing

    Identification

    Significance

decline in the federal deficit

    Identification

    Significance

"Reagan's revenge"

    Identification

    Significance

Proposition 187

    Identification

    Significance

the 104th Congress

    Identification

    Significance

government shutdowns, 1995 and 1996

    Identification

    Significance

the line-item veto

    Identification

    Significance

the Telecommunications Act of 1996

    Identification

    Significance

the Freedom to Farm Act of 1996

    Identification

    Significance

the Personal Responsibility and Work Opportunity Act

    Identification

    Significance

the gender gap of the 1990s

    Identification

    Significance

Bob Dole

    Identification

    Significance

the presidential and congressional elections of 1996

    Identification

    Significance

ethnic wars in the former Yugoslavia

    Identification

    Significance

START-III

    Identification

    Significance

the Middle East peace process, 1991–1997

Identification

Significance

genocide in Rwanda

Identification

Significance

the Haitian crisis

Identification

Significance

the Helms-Burton Act

Identification

Significance

U.S. trade with China

Identification

Significance

the World Trade Organization

      Identification

      Significance

Japanese-American relations, 1980s and 1990s

      Identification

      Significance

nuclear proliferation

      Identification

      Significance

the Comprehensive Nuclear-Test-Ban Treaty of 1996

      Identification

      Significance

the Chemical Weapons Convention

      Identification

      Significance

the "greenhouse effect"

        Identification

        Significance

Clinton's environmental policies

        Identification

        Significance

the 1995 Fourth World Conference on Women in Beijing

        Identification

        Significance

the debate over the role of the United States in the United Nations

        Identification

        Significance

the globalization of American culture

        Identification

        Significance

information warfare

      Identification

      Significance

Whitewater investigation

      Identification

      Significance

the Monica Lewinsky affair

      Identification

      Significance

the impeachment and acquittal of President Clinton

      Identification

      Significance

the 1998 congressional elections

      Identification

      Significance

Organizing Information

Record reminders of evidence from Chapter 33 and your class notes of a continuation of the nation's ideological shifting to the right or of readjustments to such shifting in the Sixties and Seventies in the chart "More Ideological Shifting as the Century Ends?"

Compare your finished chart and your entries in the chart "Ideological Shifts in the Turbulent Era, 1961–1974" (See Interpreting Information exercise, Chapter 31, in this Study Guide.)

More Ideological Shifting as the Century Ends?					
Administration					
Areas in Which Shifts Might Occur	Ford House (D) Senate (D)	Carter House (D) Senate (D)	Bush House (D) Senate (D)	Clinton House (D) (R) Senate (D) (R)	Overall Trend
Democratic Party (makeup, attitudes)					
Republican Party (makeup, attitudes)					
Presidential Philosophy and Initiatives (social, economic, fiscal, diplomatic)					
Legislation and Resolutions Passed by Congress					
Supreme Court Makeup (replacements)					

More Ideological Shifting as the Century Ends?					
Administration					
Areas in Which Shifts Might Occur	Ford House (D) Senate (D)	Carter House (D) Senate (D)	Bush House (D) Senate (D)	Clinton House (D) (R) Senate (D) (R)	Overall Trend
Supreme Court Rulings					
Public Concerns and Political Activities					
Other					
Conclusions					

Interpreting Information

This exercise has two parts, the first based on the information concerning trends in American ideological trends that you entered in the Organizing Information exercise and the other concerning America's Cold War foreign policy.

Exercise A

American Ideological Trends

Using your entries in the Organizing Information chart "More Ideological Shifting as the Century Ends?" for guidance, plan and write a working draft of an essay in which you answer this question:

> Did the shift away from liberalism and toward conservatism begun in the Sixties continue as the twentieth century drew to a close? Support your answer with specific, concrete evidence.

Exercise B

America's Cold War Foreign Policy

1. The containment doctrine was the cornerstone of American foreign policy from the time of the Truman Doctrine and George Kennan's "Mr. X" article of 1947 to 1991. How has the focus of American foreign policy changed during the post-Cold-War era?

2. Consider the following three statements related to the Cold War.
    a. The Soviets emerged from the Second World War with a weak military establishment, a hobbled economy, and obsolete technology. "The Soviet Union was a regional power in Eastern Europe, not a global menace."
    b. Some Americans fixed their attention, as they had since the Bolshevik Revolution of 1917, on "the utopian Communist goal of world revolution rather than on actual Soviet behavior."
    c. President Reagan believed in "a devil theory." In other words, he believed that "a malevolent Soviet Union" was the source of the world's troubles.

    How do these statements relate to the crumbling of the Soviet empire in Eastern Europe and the disintegration of the Soviet Union? To what extent was American policy during the Cold War based on reality? To what extent was it based on myth?

3. Another cornerstone of American foreign policy since the presidency of Woodrow Wilson is the concept of self-determination—the idea that a nation has the right to determine its own destiny without outside interference. From the beginning of the Cold War to its end, the United States and the NATO alliance consistently chastised the Soviet Union for not allowing self-determination in the nations in Eastern Europe under Soviet domination. Under Gorbachev, the Soviet Union reversed its totalitarian policies and allowed self-determination. As a result, the Eastern European nations under Soviet domination during the course of the Cold War have undergone democratic revolutions and have begun to restructure their economic systems.

What opportunities and problems do these changes in Eastern Europe pose for the world community of nations, the NATO alliance, and the United States?

Problems:

Opportunities:

4. Yugoslavia broke with the Soviet Union in 1948 and traveled an independent Communist path.
   a. What impact did the democracy movements and the collapse of Communism in the Soviet Union and Eastern Europe have on Yugoslavia?
   b. What problems did the changes in the former Yugoslavia pose for the world community of nations, the NATO alliance, and the United States?

5. Soon after Mikhail Gorbachev came to power, he said to the United States: "We will deny you an enemy." What did he mean by that statement? Did he fulfill that promise?

6. Redbaiting has been a dominant feature of American political campaigns since the Second World War. Did the absence of the Soviet Union as an enemy affect the way the presidential candidates ran their campaigns during the 1990s? Did it affect the outcome of the 1992 presidential campaign? Explain.

Ideas and Details

Objective 1

_____ 1. In response to economic and social problems during his administration, President Bush
   a. favored an active government.
   b. did little.
   c. proposed an increase in welfare benefits to the working poor.
   d. supported the funding of public-works projects to reduce unemployment.

Objectives 1 and 9

_____ 2. Which of the following was a result of the 1990 budget negotiations between the White House and Congress?
   a. Congress agreed to pass legislation giving the President a line-item veto.
   b. President Bush agreed to a tax hike while the Democrats agreed to budget cuts.
   c. Congress agreed to allow debate on a balanced-budget amendment to the Constitution while Bush agreed to release impounded funds.
   d. President Bush and the Democrats agreed to increase the federal debt limit.

Objective 1

_____ 3. Which of the following is true of the Council on Competitiveness?
   a. It instituted a quality-control program in the automobile industry to make American cars more competitive in world markets.
   b. It suggested government subsidies to American businesses that adopted Japanese management practices.
   c. It gutted enforcement of the Clean Air Act of 1990 while arguing that environmental regulations slowed economic growth.
   d. It charged the Japanese with unfair trade practices and suggested protective tariffs against all Japanese imports.

Objective 2

_____ 4. As a result of Anita Hill's testimony before the Senate Judiciary Committee,
   a. many women vowed that they would oppose the Republican party in the 1992 elections.
   b. the Bush administration withdrew its nomination of Clarence Thomas to the Supreme Court.
   c. the full Senate failed to confirm Clarence Thomas to the Supreme Court.
   d. legislation was passed making it easier for women to file sexual harassment charges.

Objective 4

_____ 5. Which of the following is a reason for the end of the Cold War?
   a. The ability of the United States to finance its military arsenal without diverting money from domestic social programs ultimately caused the collapse of the Soviet system.
   b. Most Third World nations openly allied with the West, depriving the Soviet Union of much needed raw materials.
   c. The burden of a monolithic empire consisting of dependent states in Eastern Europe, Africa, and Asia so drained the Soviet Union of its wealth and resources that the Soviet system collapsed.
   d. The emergence of the Third World challenged bipolarism.

Objective 9

_____ 6. Which of the following was most likely to vote for Republican presidential candidates in the 1970s and 1980s?
   a. An advocate of the Equal Rights Amendment
   b. An advocate of strict enforcement of the Clean Air Act
   c. An advocate of abortion
   d. An advocate of "family values"

Objective 7

_____ 7. In the House banking scandal it was revealed that
   a. representatives were regularly allowed to overdraw on their accounts with no penalties.
   b. the manager of the House bank had secretly loaned money to noncongressional friends and colleagues.
   c. Vice-President Dan Quayle was allowed to write checks against the House bank even though he had no actual account there.
   d. money was secretly withdrawn from the bank to finance covert CIA operations.

Objective 8

_____ 8. The immediate cause of the Los Angeles riots of 1992 was the
   a. enactment of a city ordinance that forbade sleeping on park benches.
   b. shooting of three unarmed black teenagers by a white police officer.
   c. closing of a city-operated recreational center in Watts.
   d. acquittal of four police officers charged with beating a black motorist.

Objective 9

_____ 9. As a result of the 1992 elections,
   a. the Republicans gained control of the Senate.
   b. women gained more seats in both houses of Congress.
   c. the Republicans retained control of the presidency.
   d. nonwhites lost representation in both houses of Congress.

Objective 10

_____ 10. In response to his original plan to lift the ban on homosexuals in the military, President Clinton
   a. received the support of over 75 percent of the American people.
   b. was criticized by Vice President Al Gore.
   c. won the support of key leaders in the Republican party.
   d. was criticized by high-ranking military officials.

Objective 10

_____ 11. The economic plan that President Clinton sent to Congress in February 1993 called for
        a. an energy tax.
        b. lower taxes on the middle class.
        c. tax breaks for the wealthy.
        d. lower corporate taxes.

Objective 14

_____ 12. As a result of the Brady bill,
        a. discrimination in hiring on the basis of sexual orientation was prohibited.
        b. a short waiting period was required for persons wanting to buy a handgun.
        c. the sale of assault weapons was banned in the United States.
        d. the use of Medicaid funds for abortions was prohibited.

Objective 14

_____ 13. In response to the government shutdowns of 1995 and 1996, most Americans
        a. reacted with indifference.
        b. blamed the crisis on President Clinton.
        c. blamed themselves for having elected a mixed government.
        d. perceived the Republican-controlled Congress as ideologically inflexible.

Objective 15

_____ 14. According to the Japanese, which of the following hurts the competitiveness of United States products in the world marketplace?
        a. The poor education of American workers
        b. The nation's low wage-scale for industrial workers
        c. American marketing techniques
        d. Overemphasis by American producers on robotics and other high-tech production techniques

Objective 18

_____ 15. After the House of Representatives voted to impeach President Clinton, public-opinion polls showed that a majority of Americans
        a. did not believe that partisan politics played a role in the decision by the House.
        b. strongly disapproved of the President's job performance.
        c. did not want the President removed from office.
        d. blamed Monica Lewinsky for the President's problems.

Essay Questions

Objective 1

1. Examine the causes of the economic recession during the Bush administration, discuss the consequences of this recession, and explain President Bush's handling of the recession.

Objective 2

2. Examine the controversy surrounding President Bush's nomination of Clarence Thomas to the Supreme Court and discuss the impact of the Senate Judiciary Committee's confirmation hearings on the American electorate.

Objectives 9 and 10

3. Explain the healthcare problems in the United States in the 1980s and 1990s and discuss how the federal government addressed these problems.

Objectives 3 and 4

4. Discuss the factors that brought an end to the Cold War, and discuss the legacy of the war for the United States, the Soviet Union, and the world community of nations.

Objective 4

5. Explain the improvement in Soviet-American relations in the post-Cold-War world, and discuss the tangible results of this improvement.

Objective 5

6. Discuss the causes and consequences of the 1989 U.S. invasion of Panama.

Objective 6

7. Discuss the causes and consequences of the Persian Gulf War.

Objective 7

8. Discuss the scandals that plagued Congress in the years prior to the 1992 presidential election, and discuss the reaction of the American people to these scandals.

Objective 9

9. Examine the issues and personalities in the 1992 presidential election, and explain the election's outcome.

Objective 10

10. Discuss the gays-in-the-military issue and assess how President Clinton handled that issue.

Objective 11

11. Examine the 1994 congressional elections and assess the actions of the 104th Congress.

Objective 12

12. Examine the sources of the anger and apathy felt by many Americans toward the federal government in the 1990s.

Objective 13

13. Discuss the causes and consequences of the "gender gap" of the 1990s.

Objective 14

14. Examine the issues and personalities and explain the outcome of the 1996 presidential and congressional elections.

Objective 15

15. Discuss the Clinton administration's policy toward the ethnic wars in the former Yugoslavia.

Objective 15

16. Examine the debate in the United States in the post-Cold War era over the proper role for the nation in the Third World and in the United Nations.

Objectives 17 and 18

17. Explain the impeachment of President Clinton by the House of Representatives and his subsequent acquittal in the Senate. What implications did Clinton's impeachment have for the future?

Answers

Chapter 16

Interpreting Information

The value of most of the Interpreting Information exercises in this study guide lies in your working out interpretations for yourself and composing your own "answer"; therefore, the answer provided below is purposely incomplete.

What you see below is the essay's plan—for convenience sake, presented as a traditional outline—and a rough or working draft of one sub-section of the body of the mock essay.

The plan represents the structure and sequencing of the whole essay suggested by the questions and the way they are grouped in the exercise. As you can see, Section I.A., which is more detailed than other sections of the outline, represents the part of the plan that you see developed in the illustrative partial "answer."

What follows the outline is an excerpt from a mock essay. It is, of course, too long to serve as a quarter or a third of an essay written in an examination situation. When responding to such a broad essay question during a test, you would naturally drop the least important points and examples as well as some of the transitional devices. On the other hand, if the question on the test ended up being "What was the role of the presidency in influencing how and how far voting and other rights were extended during Reconstruction?", then including all of the points and examples in the excerpt below would be appropriate.

Outline

Thesis* _____

_____

_____

_____

_____

I.   Role of the federal government in the turmoil over voting rights
    A.   Role of Presidents Lincoln, Johnson, and Grant
        1.   Lincoln's attitudes about extending voting
        2.   Johnson's attitudes about extending voting rights to particular groups
           a.   Former Confederate officials and leaders
           b.   African Americans
        3.   Johnson's actions supporting or hindering the extension of voting rights
           a.   Former Confederate officials and leaders
           b.   African Americans
        4.   Grant's attitude and actions regarding the extension of voting rights
    B.   Role of Congress
    C.   Role of the Supreme Court

II. Effect of public attitudes concerning the extension or possible extension of voting rights
   A. The degree to which voting rights were extended to particular groups
     1. Former Confederate officials and leaders
     2. African Americans
     3. Women
     4. Immigrants
   B. Indicators of public attitudes about whether voting rights would be extended
     1. Indications of public attitudes in the South
     2. Indications of public attitudes in the North
   C. The relationship between public attitudes and the degree to which voting rights were extended during the period

Excerpt from a Mock Essay

(Development of Section I.A. in Outline)

During the Reconstruction era (1865–1877), Presidents Abraham Lincoln, Andrew Johnson, and Ulysses S. Grant encouraged the re-establishment of the voting rights of those who had been the Union's former enemies, the men who had led the Confederacy. In contrast, however, they hindered the extension of voting rights to African Americans and, for all practical purposes, did not even consider extending voting rights to women.

Because he was killed before Reconstruction got under way, President Lincoln's role was more that of a vague background influence than as a real shaper of policy. As a part of his 10 Percent Plan for reconstruction following the war, Lincoln had recommended granting the right to vote to some African Americans but to how many and under what conditions is not clear. The role of the presidency in the extension of voting rights during Reconstruction was thus left primarily to Presidents Johnson and Grant.

In the case of President Johnson, the only two groups whose voting rights were in question were former Confederate officials and leaders and African Americans. From Johnson, neither group would have been justified in expecting much support. Johnson had a long history of antipathy toward the planter class from which the Confederate leadership had come; and, although he said he favored African American suffrage, he was in fact a white supremacist, as is indicated by his explanation of his veto of the Civil Rights Bill of 1866. He was also a states' rightist, which meant that he thought states—and to him the southern states were just that, states, not territories— rather than the federal government should decide who should vote. Of course, if it were left up to the old order in the former Confederate states, the right to vote would not be extended to African Americans.

Johnson's actions promoted the quick re-establishment of voting rights for former Confederate officials and leaders but discouraged the extension of voting rights to African Americans. Surprisingly, he was liberal in his granting of pardons, and that made many former Confederates eligible to vote for and/or be delegates to the state constitutional conventions. Furthermore, in defiance of the will of Congress, military officers in the South who were enforcing the provisions of the Reconstruction Act of 1867 that barred certain former Confederate leaders from voting were replaced by Johnson with officers who allowed such people to vote. As a result, the former Confederate leaders could exert major influence on the selection of delegates to the state constitutional conventions and the political leadership of the South. As for African Americans, the sincerity of Johnson's declaration of support for black suffrage was not borne out in his actions. He opposed, and in fact vigorously campaigned against, ratification of the Fourteenth Amendment. That amendment granted citizenship to freedmen and, although it did not extend the right to vote to African Americans, it did at least encourage southern states to do so by rewarding them with increased political representation in Congress if they did.

President Grant was another story. Unlike Johnson who said one thing and did another, Grant tacitly said one thing and actually did nothing. By supporting the Republican platform in the election of 1868, Grant tacitly said he supported black suffrage, at least in the southern states. In office, though, he did nothing to push it and very little to protect blacks' civil rights in general. Grant rarely used federal troops to back the Enforcement Acts of 1870 and 1871 or an anti-Klan law, even when military force was clearly called for, such as an 1875 Mississippi case. After the Greeley-Liberal Republicans' challenge in the election of 1872, Grant was, if anything, less willing to take action that would foster any extension of voting rights to African Americans or to protect their civil rights.

Multiple-Choice Questions

1a.   No. Although Johnson demonstrated a considerable amount of sympathy toward the South, he did not go so far as to promise federal aid to rebuild the region. See pages 436–437.

1b.   Correct. At first it appeared that Johnson's Reconstruction plan would prevent the prewar southern elite from returning to power. But Johnson freely gave pardons to ex-Confederates whom southerners had defiantly elected to Congress. This caused Congress to question Johnson's plan. See pages 436–437.

1c.   No. Congress supported the requirement in Johnson's plan that the Confederate war debt be repudiated. Congress was angered when two southern states defiantly refused to abide by this requirement. See pages 436–437.

1d.   No. The Johnson plan stipulated that most white southern males, including yeoman farmers, could gain the right to vote by swearing an oath of loyalty to the United States government. See pages 436–437.

2a.   No. Although some of the southern states were reluctant to admit that slavery was a thing of the past, the black codes did not require that freedmen pay "freedom dues" to their former masters. See pages 437–438.

2b.   No. The black codes did not extend political rights to any freedmen. See pages 437–438.

2c.   Correct. The black codes, adopted by most southern state legislatures immediately after the war, were in large measure restatements of the old slave codes. Those responsible for enacting the codes intended permanently to relegate blacks to a subservient position in southern society. See pages 437–438.

2d.   No. The black codes did not indicate acceptance of the Thirteenth Amendment and did not protect the civil rights of the freedmen. See pages 437–438.

3a.   No. The Constitution stipulates that treaties must be ratified by the Senate, but Congress (the Senate and the House) did not base its claim that it had a right to have a voice in the Reconstruction process on this constitutional grant of power to the Senate. See page 438.

3b.   No. The Constitution does grant Congress the power to declare war, but this was not the basis for Congress's claim that it had a right to a voice in the Reconstruction process. See page 438.

3c.   Correct. Article IV, Section 4, of the Constitution states: "The United States shall guarantee to every State in this Union a republican form of government." It was on the basis of this statement that Congress claimed its right to have a voice in Reconstruction. See page 438.

3d.   No. The Preamble to the Constitution states that one of the purposes of the government is to "promote the general welfare," but this was not the section of the Constitution on which Congress based its claim to a voice in the Reconstruction process. See page 438.

4a.   No. Most conservative and moderate Republicans believed that voting was a privilege, not a right. They did not ally with the Radical Republicans out of the belief that full political rights should be extended to blacks. See page 438.

4b.   No. Most conservative and moderate Republicans viewed property rights as sacred. They rejected the contention by the Radical Republicans that a redistribution of southern land was necessary. See page 438.

4c.   Correct. All those who questioned Johnson's program, even conservatives and moderates, were labeled as "radical" by Johnson and the Democrats. Therefore, to make changes they thought necessary, conservative and moderate Republicans were forced into an alliance with the Radicals. See page 438.

4d.   No. The Radical Republicans held views that most northerners rejected. For example, some Radicals went beyond advocating equality under the law for freedmen by advocating political, social, and economic equality as well. See page 438.

5a.   No. After the Civil War, Jefferson Davis, former president of the Confederacy, was arrested in Georgia and imprisoned from 1865 to 1867. Although he was indicted for treason in 1866, a trial was never held. He was released on bail from prison in 1867. Therefore, Jefferson Davis was not elected to the Senate after the Civil War. See page 440.

5b.   No. President Johnson did not appoint Alexander Stephens, former vice-president of the Confederacy, to his cabinet. However, Stephens was elected to the Senate under Johnson's Reconstruction plan, and this convinced many northerners that President Johnson's Reconstruction plan was too lenient. See page 440.

5c.   No. President Johnson's Reconstruction plan called for the repudiation of the Confederate war debt. Northerners did, however, become convinced that Johnson's Reconstruction plan was too lenient when two former Confederate states refused to repudiate the Confederate war debt and some refused to repudiate secession. See page 440.

5d.   Correct. In 1866, northerners began to read daily newspaper accounts of violence against blacks in the South. Especially disturbing were reports of antiblack riots in Memphis and New Orleans in which the police aided mobs in their attacks. Such revelations convinced the northern public and Republicans in Congress that Johnson's Reconstruction plan was too lenient. See page 440.

6a.   No. The Fourteenth Amendment allowed the southern states to decide whether or not to extend voting rights to freedmen. If a state denied voting privileges to its black citizens, the state's delegation to the House of Representatives would be reduced proportionately. This provision was never enforced. See pages 440–441.

6b.   No. Johnson condemned the Fourteenth Amendment. He actively worked against the amendment by urging northerners to reject it and southern state legislatures to vote against ratification. See pages 440–441.

6c.   No. The Fourteenth Amendment ignored women. See pages 440–441.

6d.   Correct. Conservative and moderate Republicans disagreed with Radical Republicans over extension of voting rights to freedmen. The second section of the Fourteenth Amendment clearly indicates a compromise favoring the conservative/moderate view on this question. See pages 440–441.

7a.   Correct. Only one southern state (Tennessee) had initially accepted and been reconstructed under the Fourteenth Amendment. However, under the Reconstruction Act of 1867, the southern states were required to ratify the amendment before returning to the Union. See pages 441–442.

7b.   No. Although most Radical Republicans called for redistribution of southern land, most people rejected the idea as being beyond the power of the federal government and as unwarranted interference in private property. See pages 441–442.

7c.   No. The act stipulated that the ten southern states to which it applied had to guarantee freedmen the right to vote in elections for state constitutional conventions and in subsequent state elections, but it did not guarantee freedmen the right to vote in federal elections. See pages 441–442.

7d.   No. The Reconstruction Act of 1867 did not stipulate a definite time period during which the Reconstruction process would take place. See pages 441–442.

8a.   No. Johnson's impeachment by the House and subsequent trial in the Senate rendered him almost totally powerless as president. See pages 443–444.

8b.   Correct. The Radical Republicans who led the prosecution of Johnson in his Senate trial advanced the belief that impeachment was political in nature. The Senate's acquittal of Johnson was a rejection of that idea. See pages 443–444.

8c.   No. The Senate fell only one vote shy of the two-thirds majority necessary to convict Johnson of the charges brought against him. This is not an indication that northern opinion toward Johnson and the South had softened. See pages 443–444.

8d.   No. The Senate's failure to convict Johnson did not cause a rift between the House and the Senate. See pages 443–444.

9a.   Correct. By eliminating property qualifications for voting, the new state constitutions made the South more democratic and brought the South in line with the rest of the nation. See pages 446–447.

9b.   No. Although these state constitutions extended more rights to women, women's suffrage, advocated by some black delegates, was considered radical and was not adopted. See pages 446–447.

9c.   No. The new constitutions did provide for public schools, but attendance to these schools was not compulsory. See pages 446–447.

9d.   No. Yearly reapportionment of legislative districts was not made mandatory by the new state constitutions. See pages 446–447.

10a.   Correct. Southern Republicans quickly restored the voting rights of former Confederates. This meant that the Republican party would face defeat if it could not gain white support. In courting the white vote, the Republican party abandoned its most loyal supporters—blacks. See page 447.

10b.   No. Although the southern Republicans appealed for support from a broad range of groups in the South, they were never able to build a broad popular base for the party. See page 447.

10c.   No. In the first place, southern Democrats were not more "liberal" than the southern Republicans. Furthermore, freedmen themselves supported restoration of the voting rights of former Confederates. See page 447.

10d.   No. The evidence does not indicate that congressional Republicans were embarrassed by the decision of southern Republicans to restore the voting rights of former Confederates. See page 447.

11a.   No. The evidence indicates that freedmen throughout the South, and especially those participating in Reconstruction governments, were very interested in participating in the political process and did so with great dignity and distinction. See pages 448–449.

11b.   Correct. Charges of "black domination" and "Negro rule" are examples of the racist propaganda used by white conservatives to discredit the Reconstruction governments. See pages 448–449.

11c.   No. Those blacks who participated in Reconstruction governments were practical and realistic in their approach to power. They extended the right to vote to former Confederates, did not insist on an integrated school system, and did not insist on social equality. See pages 448–449.

11d.   No. The evidence indicates that those blacks participating in Reconstruction governments were not vindictive toward their former masters. Their actions demonstrate their belief in "the Christian goal of reconciliation." See pages 448–449.

12a.   No. The evidence indicates that after 1867 the terrorist activities against blacks became more organized and purposeful, and the campaign of terror in Alamance and Caswell counties clearly fits this characterization. See pages 449–450.

12b.   No. The campaign of terror in the North Carolina counties of Caswell and Alamance was organized by the wealthy and the powerful. See pages 449–450.

12c.   Correct. Terrorist campaigns by the Klan were organized and purposeful after 1867. This was clearly the case in these North Carolina counties where the wealthy and powerful organized the campaign of terror for the purpose of regaining political control. See pages 449–450.

12d.   No. Blacks and whites of the yeoman class were allies in Alamance and Caswell counties, and the Klan successfully used racism to destroy this coalition. See pages 449–450.

13a.   No. Although the Reconstruction governments were able to effect some reform in the South, they chose not to demand redistribution of land. This decision is one of the main reasons that these governments were not able to alter the social structure of the region. See pages 450–451.

13b.   No. The success of the Klan's terrorist campaign in Alamance and Caswell counties in North Carolina is evidence that there was not a lasting alliance between blacks and whites of the yeoman class. See pages 450–451.

13c.   No. Blacks were given the right to vote, but it was naive to believe that the ballot was an adequate weapon in the struggle by African Americans for a better life. See pages 450–451.

13d.   Correct. The Reconstruction governments did not demand and Congress did not bring about a redistribution of land in the South. As a result, blacks were denied economic independence and remained economically dependent on hostile whites. See pages 450–451.

14a.   Correct. John Campbell argued that the Fourteenth Amendment brought individual rights under federal protection by making the Bill of Rights applicable to the states. The Court disagreed and said that state citizenship and national citizenship were separate, with the former being more important. See page 453.

14b.   No. The Court ruled that the Fourteenth Amendment protected only those rights that went along with national citizenship, and the Court narrowly defined those rights. See page 453.

14c.   No. Although the Court later ruled that corporations were legal persons protected under the Fourteenth Amendment (the 1886 *Santa Clara* case), this was not its ruling in the *Slaughter-House* cases. See page 453.

14d.   No. The Court ruled that, of the two, state citizenship was more important than national citizenship. See page 453.

15a.   No. The monetary issue aroused a great deal of interest during the 1870s, especially among farmers, who tended to favor an inflationary policy. However, by the 1876 election a "sound money" policy had basically won out. See page 454.

15b.   No. William H. Seward was secretary of state from 1861 to 1869. His policies had no direct bearing on the outcome of the disputed presidential election of 1876. See page 454.

15c.   Correct. The fact that both candidates in this disputed election favored removal of federal troops from the South and an end to Reconstruction indicates that the electorate had lost interest in Reconstruction. This is especially important in relation to the northern electorate. See page 454.

15d.   No. Since the end of the Civil War, the government had been injecting money into the economy and extending indirect aid to business interests. Most people favored a continuation of this practice, which had spurred industrial growth, especially in the North. See page 454.

Chapter 17

Finding the Main Idea

Exercise A

The first sentence is a transition sentence from a discussion of the mining frontier to a discussion of the lumbering frontier. Although it points out that the two industries were similar in that both were extractive, it implies a difference between the two industries by saying that lumbering required vast stretches of land.

1.   *Paragraph topic:* Methods by which the lumber industry gained land.

2.   *Main idea:* The main idea is developed in the first two sentences.
       a.   Lumber production required vast stretches of land.
       b.   Lumber companies exploited an act of Congress for their own purposes rather than adhering to the intent of the act.
             Lumber companies exploited the Timber and Stone Act to obtain the vast stretches of land required in lumber production.

3.   *Supporting details:*
       a.   The Timber and Stone Act was passed by Congress in 1878 to stimulate western settlement. Provisions of the act are noted to provide evidence that the intent of the act was to stimulate western settlement and to establish that the act was intended for "private citizens."
             The point about Congress's intent in passing the Timber and Stone Act—to aid the settlement and development of the frontier—is an underlying theme in this chapter's discussions of natural resources, ranching, and farming.
       b.   Lumber companies hired seamen to register claims to timberland; these claims were then turned over to the lumber companies. The point provides further evidence of exploitation.
       c.   Most of the 3.5 million acres bought by 1900 under the Timber and Stone Act belonged to corporations.

Exercise B

Paragraph 1   The first paragraph establishes the theme for the two-paragraph series and develops the first part of that theme.

1.   *Paragraph topic:* The establishment of racial categories by white settlers in the West

2.   *Main idea:* White settlers separated people in the West into racial categories and used those categories to control labor and social relations.

3.   *Supporting details:* The details used in this paragraph support the first part of the theme for the two-paragraph series. The first part of the theme is: White settlers separated people in the West into racial categories.
       a.   White settlers in the West established four nonwhite racial categories
       b.   All such nonwhites were considered inferior by white settlers using these categories

Paragraph 2   The second part of the theme established in the first paragraph is developed in the second paragraph of this two-paragraph series. The second part of the theme is: Racial categories were used by white settlers in the West to control labor and social relations.

1.   *Paragraph topic:* The development of a two-tiered labor system in western communities

2.   *Main idea:* Race was used by white western settlers to determine whether a person was in the top tier or the bottom tier of a two-tiered labor system.

3.   Supporting details:
       a.   Whites were to be in the top tier as managers and skilled laborers.
       b.   Racial minorities occupied the bottom tier of this labor system
              (1)   Work done by the Irish, Chinese, and Mexicans
              (2)   Work done by blacks
       c.   All nonwhites plus the Irish experienced prejudice
              (1)   Experience of the Chinese who went into commercial fishing or agriculture
              (2)   Experience of the Mexicans

Multiple-Choice Questions

1a.   No. Much of the life of Plains Indians centered on the buffalo, but they did not rely solely on the buffalo for subsistence. See pages 461–462.

1b.   No. Although the western Indian tribes traded with whites and with other Indians, they did so mainly to obtain necessities and not for reasons of profit. Furthermore, they did not believe that they could depend only on trade and crop raising to achieve subsistence. See pages 461–462.

1c.   No. The western Indians were not part of a market economy in which they sold items for the purpose of obtaining money to buy food and other necessities. See pages 461–462.

1d.   Correct. Although western Indian tribes differed culturally, they all depended on a balance among four main economic activities to achieve subsistence—crop raising; livestock raising; hunting, fishing, and gathering; and raiding. This system depended on an ecological balance that was destroyed as whites moved west. See pages 461–462.

2a.   No. Indians of the Great Plain depended on the buffalo for food, clothing, and tools. Because of the importance of the buffalo in their lives, they did not encourage whites to slaughter the buffalo. See page 463.

2b.   No. Since animal diseases such as anthrax and brucellosis were brought into the Plains by white-owned livestock, whites did not slaughter the buffalo to prevent the spread of such diseases to sheep and goat herds. Of course, these animal diseases spread to the buffalo and caused many to die. See page 463.

2c.   Correct. Slaughter of the buffalo by whites was simply one a many factors that doomed the buffalo to near extinction. Other factors were: increased buffalo kills by Indians, competition with humans for space and water, lethal animal diseases, and competition for grazing land with Indian and white-owned livestock. See page 463.

2d.   No. The process that led to the virtual extinction of the buffalo began before whites began to slaughter the buffalo in the late 1800s. See page 463.

3a.   Correct. The subsistence culture of the Northwestern Indians was centered on salmon. Therefore, the decline of the salmon population due to the actions of white commercial fishermen and canneries, undermined the subsistence culture of Northwestern Indians. See page 463.

3b.   No. The Northwestern Indians were not affected by the slaughter of the buffalo because the buffalo was not important to their subsistence. See page 463.

3c.   No. Lack of irrigation facilities did not undermine the subsistence culture of Northwestern Indians. See page 463.

3d.   No. Animal diseases were not an important factor in the undermining of the subsistence culture of Northwestern Indians. See page 463.

4a.   No. White settlers to the Great Plains did not assume that the federal government would bar African American workers from settling in that area. See pages 463–464.

4b.   No. White settlers who moved into the Great Plains in the 1870s and 1880s generally carried with them the ethnocentric frame of reference of the age. Those settlers assumed that there would be equality of opportunity among white males; but, because of their prejudices against nonwhites, they did not apply that concept to other ethnic groups. See pages 463–464.

4c.   Correct. White settlers to the Great Plains in the 1870s and 1880s held white-racist and white-superiority beliefs and tended to see Indians as "barbarians." As a result, these white settlers generally assumed that they had a right to settle wherever they pleased. See pages 463–464.

4d.   No. White settlers to the Great Plain in the 1870s and 1880s had little or no concern for Indian cultures and did not generally believe that they had to respect the land rights of Native Americans. See pages 463–464.

5a.   Correct. The reservation policy was designed to "civilize" the Indian tribes. Three major problems characterized the policy: (1) the Indians had no say over their own affairs; (2) it was impossible to keep reservations isolated; and (3) the government disregarded variations among tribes. See pages 465–466.

5b.   No. Many Indians, in order to preserve their own culture, resisted involvement in a market economy. Furthermore, the trade relationships that emerged were generally imposed on the Indians, were beneficial to whites, and made Indians more dependent on whites. See pages 465–466.

5c.   No. Under the reservation policy, the government, in an effort to engage the Indians more completely in the market economy, promised to provide natives with food, clothing, and necessities. As Indians concentrated on producing trade items demanded by whites, many were forced to give up crop production. See pages 465–466.

5d.   No. Although the government, through the reservation policy, promised the Indians protection from white encroachment, in the long run it was impossible to keep the reservations isolated. Therefore, since whites continued to seek Indian land for their own purposes, they continued to encroach on that land. See pages 465–466.

6a.   No. A boarding-school program was established by the Dawes Severalty Act in an attempt to "civilize" Indian children. However, most did not reject their culture and returned to their reservations. See pages 467–468.

6b.   No. Under the Dawes Act the Indian Bureau did establish religious schools among the Indians in an attempt to Christianize them. However, most Indians continued to practice their native religions. See pages 467–468.

6c.   Correct. The Dawes Act attempted to "civilize" western Indians by dissolving tribal, or community-owned, lands and dividing this land among individual families. The policy was ineffective, was misused by whites, and was abandoned. See pages 467–468.

6d.   No. Indians had no voice in United States Indian policy as established under the Dawes Act and carried out by the Indian Bureau. The United States government assumed a paternalistic attitude and assumed that it knew what was best for Indians. See pages 467–468.

7a.   No. In the earliest stages of development one sees the individual prospector in relation to the mining frontier, the individual rancher and cowboy in relation to open-range ranching, and, to some extent, the individual timberman. Such individuals did not need large outlays of capital. See pages 470, 484.

7b.   No. Misuse of this act was important in the development of the lumber industry but not in the development of the mining and ranching industries. See pages 470, 484.

7c.   Correct. Corporate interests had the capital necessary for profitable long-term development of these industries and replaced the individual lumberman, prospector, and cowboy. See pages 470, 484.

7d.   No. Those involved in the development of these frontiers were usually more interested in profit than in conservation or planned use of natural resources. See pages 470, 484.

8a.   No. Passage of immigration laws in 1881 and 1882 to exclude Chinese immigrants and additional evidence noted on pages 471–472 do not support the conclusion that ethnic minorities were welcomed into the frontier communities.

8b.   Correct. Although there was an ethnic mixture in many of the frontier communities, ethnic minorities such as blacks, Chinese, Mexicans, and Indians experienced abuse as a result of white prejudice. See pages 471–472.

8c.   No. Undoubtedly some opportunities were available to ethnic minorities in the frontier communities, but the evidence does not support the conclusion that "opportunities abounded." See pages 471–472.

8d.   No. Blacks, Indians, Mexicans, and Chinese did not usually gain economic or political power in the frontier communities. See pages 471–472.

9a.   No. Although some individual railroad companies turned to central business offices to keep track of equipment, freight, rates, and schedules, the railroads did not collectively coordinate all their schedules through a "central clearing house." See page 477.

9b.   No. The idea of daylight-saving time was first suggested by the resourceful and pragmatic Benjamin Franklin in the eighteenth century. The railroads did not request government establishment of this in 1883. See page 477.

9c.   No. Railroad companies generally accepted the philosophy of laissez-faire capitalism. Therefore, believing that property owners should be free to make their own economic decisions without government interference, the railroads did not ask for the creation of the ICC. See page 477.

9d.   Correct. Because of the difficulties posed by the hodgepodge of times throughout the United States, the railroads established four standard time zones for the whole country in 1883. They did so without consulting anyone in government. See page 477.

10a.   Correct. The railroads were given some 180 million acres of land by the federal government (page 476). Much of this land was used as security for bonds or sold for cash. Ranchers often bought land bordering streams and allowed their cattle to graze on adjacent public domain (page 482).

10b.   No. Although farmers became dependent on the railroad for transportation of goods, they bitterly complained about railroad abuses. Many farmers also complained about ranchers who denied them the use of fenced-in pastureland. See pages 476, 482.

10c.   No. There is no indication from the evidence given that either the cattle industry or the railroad industry respected the rights and culture of Indians. See pages 476, 482.

10d.   No. Both the railroad industry and the cattle industry objected to government regulation. See pages 476, 482.

11a.   No. The Great Plains is characterized by climatic extremes. See page 479.

11b.   No. Because of the absence of timber in the Great Plains, many farm families had to build their houses of sod and use buffalo and cow chips for fuel. See page 479.

11c.   Correct. One of the hardships of farm life on the Great Plains was the periodic grasshopper plagues of the 1870s and 1880s. See page 479.

11d.   No. Although rainfall in the Plains was unpredictable and often inadequate during the fall and summer, the area was often plagued by flooding during March and April. These characteristics are not descriptive of a desert area. See page 479.

12a.   No. Plains settlers were not so much in competition with each other as with their environment. At any rate, a competitive frontier spirit was not the cause of social isolation on the Plains. See page 479.

12b.   No. A plain is by definition an area of flat, level land. Therefore, the Great Plains region of the United States is not an area in which travel is difficult because of "rugged terrain." See page 479.

12c.   No. The authors of the text state that increased use of farm machinery made conquering the Plains possible. Therefore, farm machinery was widely used in the Great Plains. See page 479.

12d.   Correct. Settlers acquired 160-acre rectangular plots of land under the Homestead Act if they agreed to *live on* and improve the land. This restriction prevented European-style villages from emerging and led to social isolation. See page 479.

13a.   No. Railroad expansion in the late nineteenth century linked farmers of the Great Plains with an international marketplace, but the railroad did not relieve the loneliness of farm life. See page 480.

13b.   No. Commercial radio broadcasts did not begin until 1920. In addition, most rural areas did not have electricity until the 1940s. See page 480.

13c.   No. Since the majority of farm families did not have electricity until the 1940s, the telegraph did not lessen farm isolation in the late nineteenth century. See page 480.

13d.   Correct. The availability of RFD after 1896 meant farmers could receive letters, newspapers, advertisements, and catalogues at home on a daily basis. See page 480.

14a.   Correct. Machines, increasing productivity and reducing the time and cost of farming various crops, made the extension of the farming frontier possible. See page 481.

14b.   No. Truly effective and selective pesticides were not used on a wide scale until the mid-twentieth century. See page 481.

14c.   No. Although scientists in the nineteenth century began to identify the nutrients necessary for plant growth, commercial fertilizers did not become widely available until the twentieth century. See page 481.

14d.   No. Extensive use of migrant labor did not make the extension of the farming frontier possible. See page 481.

15a.   No. Carver worked as a botanist and an instructor at Tuskegee Institute from 1896 until his death in 1943. His agricultural research was not subsidized by the federal government. See page 481.

15b.   Correct. The Hatch Act of 1887 provided for agricultural experiment stations in every state, thus encouraging the advancement of farming technology. See page 481.

15c.   No. Luther Burbank, noted plant breeder and horticulturist, never headed the research division of the Department of Agriculture. See page 481.

15d.   No. The federal government did not fund a vast irrigation network in the Great Plains. See page 481.

Chapter 18

Interpreting Information

Since the value of collecting information and composing a mock essay based on it lies in the doing, what follows is not a complete "answer" to the hypothetical essay test question.

What you see first is the notes entered in the blanks for the third Evidence Set.

Following the notes is a the portion of a working draft of an essay in which the expanded notes have been incorporated. Notice that the student-writer's conclusion is expressed in the opening sentence. (Your conclusion for Evidence Set Three does not have to be exactly the same conclusion as the one presented here. As long as your conclusion is a logical derivative of the evidence you have offered in your essay and if you have not ignored significant contradictory evidence, then your conclusion is acceptable.)

If your notes and entire working draft resemble what you see here, that's enough.

The "answer" for the Interpreting Information exercise in Chapter 18 has been provided mainly to help you understand what is called for in most of the remaining Interpreting Information exercises in this study guide. Many of those exercises will not include a series of questions directing you to specific bits of information as the exercise for Chapter 18 does. What you will be given instead are aids (usually tables) like the one in the Organizing Information exercise for Chapter 17. You will have to ask yourself the questions that will direct you to the relevant, concrete, and specific information you will need in your essays. The "answer" to Chapter 18's exercise illustrates the use of notes in the abbreviated form you will need to use when you enter them in the tables. For more complex tables, your notes will have to be even more abbreviated, just topics really.

Evidence Set 3 (Sample Notes)

Did the cost of living increase or decrease during the Machine Age? How much? Did incomes change in the same direction? As fast and as much as the cost of living?

> **Notes** Cost of living rose faster than wages. Avg. yearly wage up from $486 to $630 between 1890 and 1910. Cost of living up 47% from 1889 to 1913 for typical working-class family of four.

How did economic conditions affect the number and ages of persons in a working class family who worked outside the home for pay?

> **Notes** Women and children in families took jobs to boost family income by somewhere between 33% and 50%.

How did the nature of working class families' expenditures change during the Machine Age? What items formerly considered luxuries, if any, were becoming necessities and what items formerly considered necessities, if any, were becoming luxuries?

> **Notes** Working-class families still had to spend disproportionate amount of family income on necessities, such as food (p. 524). About half of primary wage earner's pay bought food. Expenditures increased for life insurance, amusements, alcoholic beverages, and union dues, though. Bought more on credit when companies like International Harvester and Singer Sewing Machine introduced innovative financing schemes for customers. Bought more clothing ready-made rather than producing clothing themselves or doing without extra outfits. Bought more perishable fruits and vegetables because of advances in canning and refrigeration.

What important technological innovations and scientific discoveries affected the healthfulness of and variety in the diet of American factory workers from 1877–1920? Did the diet of American workers and their families improve or decline? Were perishable foods and foods produced in other parts of the country more or less readily available to working class families? Why?

> **Notes** Working class families were not subjected to extreme malnutrition. Institution of big food chains like A&P meant food could be bought more cheaply than previously. Refrigeration, including home ice boxes, and canning technology, including an improved tin can, made perishable foods—including meat—available to just about everybody in greater variety (because what couldn't be produced locally could be brought in from great distances) than ever before. New, nutritious foods, such as Kellogg's Corn Flakes and Post Grape-Nuts , peanut butter, and condensed milk (Borden) developed as knowledge about vitamins and nutritional principles spread.

How did death rates and life expectancy change during the Machine Age? How did disease-caused deaths change? How did suicide, homicide, and vehicular death rates change?

> **Notes** From 1900 to 1920, life expectancy rose by six years and death rate fell 24%. Some dread diseases, such as typhoid, TB, intestinal ailments caused fewer deaths. Illnesses that would affect older people more than younger people—such as heart disease and cancer—resulted in more deaths.

What changes in technology affected sanitation in the American home and the privacy of individuals in the home during the Machine Age? Did sanitation and privacy increase or decrease?

> **Notes** Indoor toilets and private bath tubs both increased both privacy and sanitation. Greater understanding of germ theory made people more concerned about sanitation. Advances in refrigeration and canning reduced food spoilage.

What innovations affected the amount and kinds of clothing working class families had and who produced it? What was the effect of these innovations?

Notes In 1850s Elias Howe and Isaac Singer perfected sewing machine enough to make it widely used in manufacturing. Increasingly clothing was mass produced for retail sale in years following Civil War. Clothing for middle and lower classes became more stylish and more comfortable partly because of department stores, which multiplied from end of Civil war and the turn of the century. Men's clothing—other than laborers' work clothes—became more lightweight and more seasonal. Work clothes for industrial workers did not change much....

What, if any, opportunities opened up during the Machine Age that would make it reasonable for factory workers to think they or their children could move upward into the middle or upper economic classes? Were there any signs that people who might be seen as trapped on the lowest rungs of the economic ladder were taking advantage of whatever opportunities for their own or their children's advancement were available?

Notes Two paths to upward mobility gave hope: public education through high school and compulsory attendance laws gave many working-class youngsters a head start their parents did not have and the opening up of new service-industry clerical jobs offered better working conditions and sometimes opportunities for advancement. The Women's Trade Union league pushed for apprenticeship programs and other educational programs to help women break into skilled trades.

Conclusion for Evidence Set 3

How did the overall quality of life change for the factory worker during the Machine Age (1877–1920)? Would it be reasonable for large numbers of such workers to look to the future with hope and optimism?

Notes Improvements in the standard of living resulting primarily from technological and marketing advances made living conditions—not counting those associated with the job—better during the Machine Age than they had been earlier.

**Sample Section of the Working Draft of an Essay
(Based on Notes for Evidence Set Three)**

Conditions off the job improved on the whole. Although wages did not keep pace with the cost of living, family income often did. The 47% rise in the cost of living experienced by a typical working-class family of four between 1890 and 1913 may not look good next to the improvement between 1890 and 1910 of only a little over 29% in the average yearly wage (from $486 to $630), but in many working-class families the pay of working women and children in the family boosted family income somewhere between 33 percent and 50 percent, and rent from boarders often helped, too. Working-class families still had to spend a disproportionate amount of the family income on necessities, about half the primary wage earner's pay going to food, for example, but they were also spending more for things that most people would not call necessities, such as amusements and alcoholic beverages. Instead of making their own clothing or making do with the same old clothes for both weekday and Sunday wear, they were buying ready-made clothes—widely available because of the quickly multiplying department stores and more likely to be within their means because of mass production fostered by the spreading use in manufacturing of the Howe and Singer-improved sewing machine. And the food they bought was more varied and nutritious. Improvements in canning and refrigeration and the advent of innovations in marketing, such as chain grocery stores like the A&P, made more perishable fruits, vegetables, and meats both more available and more affordable. Advances in nutrition and sanitation meant that working-class families were likely to be healthier, too. Between 1900 and 1920 life expectancy rose by six years, and deaths caused by dread diseases such as TB and typhoid declined. More and more people understood the relationship between germs and disease, and the same sort of advances in technology that provided refrigeration and canning to reduce food spoilage also provided indoor toilets and bath tubs to advance both privacy and sanitation. Finally, working-class families began to enjoy the luxury of hope. The availability of public education through high school for their children and compulsory attendance laws and the opening up of opportunities to move into white-collar clerical positions gave parents and young people a vision of a better future.

Multiple-Choice Questions

1a.   No. The use of precision machinery to make interchangeable parts was first seen as part of the "American system of manufacturing" during the first half of the nineteenth century. Therefore, the manufacture and use of interchangeable parts was well established long before the Ford Motor Company began operation in 1903. See page 491.

1b.   No. The machine-tool industry—the mass manufacture of specialized machines for various industries—was born in the 1820s, long before the Ford Motor Company opened for operation in 1903. See page 491.

1c.   Correct. When the Ford Motor Company began operation in 1903, it utilized mass production and, through use of the electric conveyor belt, introduced the moving assembly line at its Highland Park plant in 1913. This drastically reduced the time and cost of producing cars. See page 491.

1d.   No. Team production suggests that a team of workers is responsible for making and assembling the entire automobile. The Ford Motor Company was not organized in this way when it began operation in 1903. See page 491.

2a.   No. To increase efficiency in the work place, work was divided into specific tasks. A worker could then specialize in the repetitious performance of a given task in as little time as possible. Such a process does not increase the value of skilled labor. See page 494.

2b.   No. Efficiency in the production of a product can lead to decreased production costs, higher profits, and higher wages. See page 494.

2c.   No. In many cases efficiency in production leads to a reduction in the work force. For example, after studying the shoveling of ore, Frederick Taylor designed fifteen different shovels and outlined the proper motions for using each. As a result, a work force of 600 was reduced to 140. See page 494.

2d.   Correct. Systems of efficiency, such as those espoused by Frederick Taylor, equated time with money. As a result, the time taken to perform specific tasks became as important as the quality of the end product. See page 494.

3a.   No. Many workers of the late nineteenth century were very dissatisfied with the wage system because they believed it was weighted in favor of the employer. Theoretically the wage system was based on the idea that workers were free to negotiate with the employer for the highest wages possible. However, this theory was based on the worker and the employer having equal power in such negotiations. In fact, this was not true and many workers felt at the mercy of employers. See pages 497–498.

3b.   No. Competition for jobs among workers did not cause the base pay of all workers to rise steadily during the late nineteenth century, and most wage earners did not see the wage system in this way. See pages 497–498.

3c.   No. Although some forward-looking thinkers of the late nineteenth century may have believed that Congress should establish a minimum wage, such a concept was beyond the frame of reference of most workers of the era. See pages 497–498.

3d.   Correct. Many employers of the late nineteenth century believed in the "iron law of wages." In other words, they believed that labor is sold in the marketplace and, like any other commodity, its price (wages in this case) should be dictated by the law of supply and demand. It was further held that if workers are paid unnaturally high wages they will simply be able to support more children. That, in turn, will lead to an increase in the supply of workers and to more unemployment. Therefore, many employers held that they were actually doing workers a favor by keeping wages at a low level, in accordance with the "natural" economic law of supply and demand. In such a system, most wage earners felt trapped and exploited in a system controlled by employers. See pages 497–498.

4a.   No. This was not a distinction made by the Court in cases involving limitations on working hours. See page 499.

4b.   No. In striking down a maximum-hours law for bakers, the Court in *Lochner* v. *New York* held that the law violated the Fourteenth-Amendment guarantee that no state may deprive any person of property (wages) without due process of law. In this way, the Court applied the Fourteenth Amendment to state action. See page 499.

4c.   Correct. The Court's decisions in the *Holden, Lochner,* and *Muller* cases demonstrated a narrow interpretation of what constituted a dangerous job and, therefore, of which workers needed protection. See page 499.

4d.   No. The *Lochner* v. *New York* case is evidence that the Court did not always uphold the regulatory powers of the states. See page 499.

5a.   No. Neither the Knights of Labor nor the American Federation of Labor advocated the use of violence against corporate power. See pages 500, 502, 504.

5b.   No. Many of the goals of the Knights of Labor were long range, abstract, and vague. The objectives of the American Federation of Labor, in contrast, were much more specific and pragmatic. See pages 500, 502, 504.

5c.   No. The Knights of Labor generally opposed strikes. See pages 500, 502, 504.

5d.   Correct. The Knights of Labor welcomed all workers into its ranks, including women, blacks, and immigrants, and including both skilled and unskilled workers. In contrast, the AFL allowed only skilled workers, was openly hostile to women, and often excluded immigrants and blacks. See pages 500, 502, 504.

6a.   No. This answer suggests that Congress was receptive to organized labor and to its demands at the time of the Haymarket riot in 1886. Reread the section on the union movement on pages 500–504.

6b.   No. Although the Haymarket riot was falsely identified in the newspapers and in the minds of many people as an "anarchist riot," the government did not respond by putting military forces on alert. See pages 500–501.

6c.   Correct. As a result of strikes and labor unrest, a sense of crisis existed at the time of the Haymarket riot (May 1886) and increased as a result of the riot. This led to the consequences stated in the choice. See pages 500–501.

6d.   No. As a result of its association with the Haymarket riot, the Knights of Labor was weakened rather than strengthened. See pages 500–501.

7a.   Correct. Initially, the WTUL was dominated by middle-class as opposed to working-class women. However, this changed in the 1910s. See pages 503–504.

7b.   No. The leadership of the WTUL accepted the idea that women needed protection from exploitation. On these grounds it supported protective legislation for women and argued against a constitutional amendment guaranteeing equal rights to women. See pages 503–504.

7c.   No. The WTUL worked for women's suffrage. See pages 503–504.

7d.   No. The WTUL did join with the Ladies Garment Workers Union in a strike against New York City sweatshops, but it did not advocate a war against capitalist society. Gradually, the union even backed away from active union organization. See pages 503–504.

8a.   No. The data indicate that the wages of working-class wage earners increased between 1890 and 1920. See pages 505–506.

8b.   No. The data indicate that wages increased for farm laborers, factory workers, and middle-class workers. See pages 505–506.

8c.   Correct. Although the income of factory workers, farm laborers and middle-class workers rose in the period from 1890 to 1920, the cost of living rose as well and usually outpaced wage increases. See pages 505–506.

8d.   No. We are not given enough data on the income of professionals to determine the rate of increase from 1890 to 1920. We cannot logically infer from the data supplied that inflation caused professionals to suffer more than industrial workers. See pages 505–506.

9a.   No. Most bathrooms have mirrors and mirrors make people conscious of personal appearance, but mirrors were available before indoor bathrooms. See page 507.

9b.   Correct. Americans began to see bodily functions in a more unpleasant light as a result of two factors: (1) the germ theory of disease, which raised fears about the link between human pollution and water contamination, and (2) the indoor bathroom's association with cleanliness and privacy. See page 507.

9c.   No. Although there is a certain amount of truth in this choice, it is important to remember two factors: (1) in the late nineteenth century few Americans could afford to stay in hotels; and (2) there is not sufficient evidence in the text to support this choice. See page 507.

9d.   No. The fact that indoor bathrooms became more and more common in American society in the late nineteenth and early twentieth centuries indicates that Americans were concerned about human waste as a source of infection and water contamination. See page 507.

10a.   No. Although that was the task of the traditional salesperson, it is not the task of the advertiser in a society of abundance. See page 509.

10b.   Correct. In a society of abundance, supply often outstrips demand. In such a society, it is the task of advertisers to *create* demand by convincing groups of consumers that they need a particular product. It is in this way that "consumption communities" are created. See page 509.

10c.   No. The task of advertisers goes far beyond simply displaying products in an attractive way. See page 509.

10d.   No. Advertisers are not necessarily concerned with the quality of the product with which they are dealing or with the price, except as those factors relate to their primary task. See page 509.

11a.   Correct. Both centralized management, in the form of trusts, and centralized ownership, in the form of holding companies, were means by which business leaders of the late nineteenth century attempted to deal with the uncertainties of the business cycle. See pages 510–511.

11b.   No. Trusts and holding companies were "devices of control" within a particular industry. Businesspeople did not turn to such devices out of a desire to be more responsive to the needs of consumers. See pages 510–511.

11c.   No. Trusts and holding companies did not separate the management of production from the management of finances and were not used by businesspeople to achieve that end. See pages 510–511.

11d.   No. Trusts, which brought several companies under centralized management, and holding companies, which brought several companies under centralized ownership, did not create a more open market. See pages 510–511.

12a.   No. Social Darwinists believed that there would always be people within society who were less "fit" than others. Because of this belief, they argued that poverty would always be present. See page 513.

12b.   Correct. Social Darwinists believed that human society should be allowed to operate in accordance with natural laws, with "survival of the fittest" being one of those laws. Therefore, they believed, wealth and power would flow into the hands of the "most capable." See page 513.

12c.   No. Social Darwinists believed that if natural laws were allowed to operate freely, wealth would continue to be maldistributed. They did not desire, nor did they advocate, an equal distribution of wealth. See page 513.

12d.   No. Social Darwinists believed that people are aggressive by nature. Therefore, if natural laws were allowed to operate freely, this aggressiveness would continue to be part of human society. See page 513.

13a.   No. Since most businesspeople accepted the ideas of Social Darwinism and laissez-faire conservatism, they believed that extending help to the disadvantaged was beyond the proper sphere of government. See page 513.

13b.   No. In accepting the tenets of laissez-faire conservatism, most businesspeople believed that the use of government power to regulate prices would threaten the right of the producer to charge the highest price the market would bear. See page 513.

13c.   No. In accepting the tenets of laissez-faire conservatism, most businesspeople stood against organized labor as a threat to the rights of both factory owners and factory workers. See page 513.

13d.   Correct. Although business leaders argued against government aid to the disadvantaged, to labor unions, or to consumers, they advocated government aid to business interests in the form of protective tariffs, government loans, and the like. See page 513.

14a.   Correct. Ward challenged the determinism of Social Darwinism by arguing that human beings, unlike other animals, are not at the mercy of natural laws. On the contrary, they can, through cooperative activities, create a better society. See pages 513–514.

14b.   No. Lester Ward did not accept the theory, espoused by Social Darwinists, that human institutions and corporate structures are the product of an evolutionary process that follows the dictates of natural law. See pages 513–514.

14c.   No. Lester Ward did not accept the idea that a society's economy should be allowed to operate in accordance with natural economic laws, and he rejected the notion that tampering with such laws would have disastrous consequences. See pages 513–514.

14d.   No. Lester Ward believed that government, as the agent of the people, could act as a positive force for good in human society. This, he believed, entailed more than merely providing for the national defense. See pages 513–514.

15a.   No. The Court did not declare all trusts to be illegal in this case involving the so-called Sugar Trust. See page 514.

15b.   No. The case did not involve the Interstate Commerce Commission, which was established by Congress in 1887 to regulate the rail industry. See page 514.

15c.   Correct. In this case the Court narrowly interpreted Congress's power to regulate interstate commerce by ruling that manufacturing (in this case the refining of sugar) took place within a state and did not fall under congressional control. See page 514.

15d.   No. The *E. C. Knight Co.* case did not deal with organized labor. See page 514.

Chapter 19

Multiple-Choice Questions

1a.   No. Long-term mortgage financing did not become widely available until the early twentieth century; therefore, it was not the "primary agent" in making suburban life practical and possible. See pages 520–521.

1b.   No. The automobile revolutionized American life and was ultimately a factor in the success of suburban development, but the first suburbs were well established by the time the Model T began to come off the assembly line. Therefore, the automobile was not the "primary agent" in making suburban life practical and possible. See pages 520–521.

1c.   No Since shopping centers followed successful suburban development, the success of the suburbs did not depend on shopping centers. See pages 520–521.

1d.   Correct. Development of an inexpensive and efficient mass-transit system, such as the electric trolley, made it possible for people of the late nineteenth and early twentieth centuries to commute from a suburban home to an inner-city job. See pages 520–521.

2a.   No. In the late nineteenth and early twentieth centuries, urban death rates declined, but so did urban birthrates. Therefore, although some urban growth may be attributed to natural increase, it was not the most important factor in such growth. See page 521.

2b.   No. Although an urban area can grow by merging with surrounding areas (e.g., Manhattan's merger with four boroughs in 1898), such mergers were not the most important cause of urban population growth in the late nineteenth and early twentieth centuries. See page 521.

2c.   Correct. Of the three ways by which the population of a place may grow, migration and immigration contributed most to urban population growth in the late nineteenth and early twentieth centuries. See page 521.

2d.   No. Annexation of outlying areas is one of the ways in which a place may grow, but it was not the most important source of urban population growth in the late nineteenth and early twentieth centuries. See page 521.

3a.   No. Most foreign immigrants were male, but most black migrants were women. Most jobs available to blacks in the cities were in domestic and personal service, and such jobs were traditionally held by women. See page 523.

3b.   No. Blacks, like foreign immigrants, came from a peasant background. In other words, both had been small farmers or farm laborers in the areas from which they moved. See page 523.

3c.   Correct. Blacks found it more difficult than foreign immigrants to find employment in northern factories. As a result, many went into the lower-paying service sector. See page 523.

3d.   No. One characteristic that black migrants and foreign immigrants had in common was that both generally moved for economic reasons. See page 523.

4a.   Correct. Since most of the new immigrants came from eastern and southern Europe, they were usually non-Protestants. See pages 524–525.

4b.   No. Family bonds were strong for both old and new immigrants. See pages 524–525.

4c.   No. Both old and new immigrants settled mainly in the cities. See pages 524–525.

4d.   No. The new immigrants were no more likely to be escaping from persecution than were the old immigrants, and most immigrants, old and new, sought opportunity in the United States. See pages 524–525.

5a.   No. The description of immigrant communities as "urban borderlands" does not support the idea that most immigrants quickly shed their Old World attitudes and beliefs. See pages 527–528.

5b.   No. Although many immigrants wanted to retain their native language, the fact that English was taught in the schools and necessary on the job made this virtually impossible. See pages 527–528.

5c.   No. The statement that immigrants "practiced religion as they always had" is later qualified by the statements that churches ultimately "had to appeal more broadly to the entire nationality in order to survive" and that groups accommodated their faiths to the new environment. This clearly implies change in the area of religion. See pages 527–528.

5d.   Correct. Although immigrants kept many Old World customs, the evidence supports the conclusion that as they interacted with the diversity of peoples and ideas in American society, they were forced to change their traditional habits and attitudes. See pages 527–528.

6a.   No. Private investors, whether as individuals or collectively, were not willing to build housing for low-income residents because they would have to accept lower profits on such units. See page 531.

6b.   Correct. Traditional attitudes about the role of government often restricted what local government could do or was willing to do to solve urban problems, but some states did take action by legislating light, ventilation, and safety codes for new tenement buildings. See page 531.

6c.   No. Most Americans did not believe it was either the responsibility of the federal government or within the government's power to legislate a national housing code. See page 531.

6d.   No. People's beliefs and perceptions concerning the role of government placed restrictions on the response of local, state, and national governments to housing problems. It was believed that government subsidies would undermine private enterprise. See page 531.

7a.   No. Most Americans believed that factors other than luck were responsible for a person's socioeconomic position. See page 533.

7b.   No. Although some reformers, most notably welfare workers, believed that poverty could be eliminated by changing the environment in which people lived, most Americans did not agree with this view of poverty. See page 533.

7c.   Correct. Most Americans believed that the poor were unfit, weak, and lazy. By the same token, they believed that anyone could escape poverty through hard work, thrift, and clean living. See page 533.

7d.   No. Most Americans of the late nineteenth and early twentieth centuries did not believe it to be the responsibility of the federal government to assist the poor. See page 533.

8a.   No. Statistics showing that the rate of upward mobility among manual laborers in Atlanta, Los Angeles, and Omaha was one in five do not support the conclusion that American society was static and offered little chance for occupational advancement. See pages 534–535.

8b.   No. Although there were instances of people traveling the rags-to-riches path, this most certainly did not apply to 10 percent of the population of the United States. See pages 534–535.

8c.   No. The evidence indicates that in general the rates of upward mobility were almost always double those of downward mobility. This would hold true in urban areas because that is where most opportunities for advancement existed. See pages 534–535.

8d.   Correct. The evidence indicates that movement along the path from "poverty to moderate success" was relatively common among white males. See pages 534–535.

9a.   Correct. Rapid city growth created governmental chaos from which political machines emerged. Machine politicians gained and retained power by getting to know new urban voters and responding to their needs. See pages 536–537.

9b.   No. Machine politicians often engaged in bribery, thievery, and extortion. They did not gain and retain their power because they brought honesty to city government. See pages 536–537.

9c.   No. Urban political machines were not efficient or cost effective. Bosses solved many urban problems, but they often did so in a way that was costly to taxpayers. See pages 536–537.

9d.   No. Urban political bosses granted "favors" to their supporters. Therefore, favors were not evenly distributed to all groups and classes. See pages 536–537.

10a.   No. Civic reform leaders of the late nineteenth and early twentieth centuries saw political bosses as irresponsible leaders and a threat to American society. See pages 537–538.

10b.   Correct. In an effort to remove politics from government, most civic reform leaders concentrated on structural changes. They focused only on the waste and corruption associated with political bosses and failed to recognize that bosses succeeded because they used government to meet people's needs. See pages 537–538.

10c.   No. Most civic reform leaders wanted to make city government more businesslike and efficient. Only a few reformers, such as Thomas L. Johnson, attempted to make government responsive to the social ills of society. See pages 537–538.

10d.   No. Most civic reform leaders supported citywide election of government officials and were opposed to the district representation associated with the ward system. See pages 537–538.

11a.   No. Although settlement-house founders worked with immigrants, acting as an employment and housing agency for immigrants was not their primary focus. See page 538.

11b.   No. Settlement-house founders were not primarily concerned with "street people." See page 538.

11c.   No. It was not the aim of settlement-house founders to establish city-run, tax-supported social welfare agencies. See page 538.

11d.   Correct. Settlement-house founders believed that they could improve the lives of working class people by providing education, job training, childcare, and other benefits to the residents of working-class neighborhoods. See page 538.

12a.   No. Although boarding sometimes provided extra income to middle- and working-class families, it was not a means by which people *found* employment. See page 541.

12b.   Correct. Although housing reformers complained that boarding caused overcrowding and lack of privacy, it provided many young people who had left home with the semblance of a family environment. Therefore, it was a transitional stage between dependence and total independence. See page 541.

12c.   No. Boarding was not important as a provider of childcare for working mothers. See page 541.

12d.   No. Housing reformers charged that boarding caused overcrowding and a loss of privacy. This may have been true, but it does not indicate the importance of boarding, which was useful to many people. See page 541.

13a.   No. Since both sexes could participate in bicycling, it was instrumental in bringing men and women together. This was especially true of the bicycle-built-for-two. (The most popular song of 1892 was "Daisybelle.") See page 544.

13b.   No. There is no indication that bicycling groups demanded lighted suburban streets. See page 544.

13c.   Correct. Bicycling was an important sport for both men and women. In order to ride, women's garments had to be less restrictive than the traditional Victorian fashions. The freer styles necessary for cycling gradually influenced everyday fashions. See page 544.

13d.   No. Stop and go lights were a response to the advent of the automobile in the 1920s and were not installed because of the popularity of bicycling. See page 544.

14a.   Correct. Burt Williams mainly played stereotypical roles. *The Birth of a Nation* presents blacks in a stereotypical way. Therefore, information about both supports the inference that blacks were subjected to prejudicial stereotyping in popular entertainment in the United States. See page 546.

14b.   No. Ethnic humor was often gentle and sympathetic, allowing people to laugh at the human condition. However, such an inference about ethnic humor cannot be drawn from information about Burt Williams's career or from *The Birth of a Nation.* See page 546.

14c.   No. The statement that show business provided economic opportunities to immigrants is a true statement. However, it is not an inference that is logically derived from the information about Burt Williams's career or from *The Birth of a Nation.* See page 546.

14d.   No. Although vaudeville was the most popular form of entertainment in early-twentieth-century America, this statement is not supported by the information about Burt Williams's career or by *The Birth of a Nation.* See page 546.

15a.   Correct. Urbanization in the late nineteenth century created a culturally pluralistic society. In such a society, politics became important as the arena in which different interest groups were competing for power, wealth, and status. See page 548.

15b.   No. The idea of a society in which ethnic groups had blended into one, unified people is an expression of the "melting pot" idea. Such a society was not created by the urbanization in America in the late nineteenth century. See page 548.

15c.   No. The discussion of urban growth in Chapter 19 deals with overcrowding, inadequate housing, urban poverty, urban crime and violence, ethnic prejudice, and governmental confusion. These topics do not suggest the emergence of a "smoothly functioning society." See page 548.

15d.   No. Although some Americans attempted to use government as an agent for moral reform, the evidence does not support the conclusion that urbanization created a society in which most Americans accepted this as the proper role of government. See page 548.

Chapter 20

Multiple-Choice Questions

1a.   Correct. Since voters were evenly divided between the two political parties, neither party was the "majority party" during the period from 1877–1897. As a result, there were frequent power shifts that prevented the passage of effective, lasting legislation. See page 553.

1b.   No. Americans generally accepted a passive federal government that did not involve itself in economic and social matters. See page 553.

1c.   No. This was an age in which party identification was important; voters were interested in politics, believed their votes were important, and voted in large numbers. See page 553.

1d.   No. Politics was a popular form of mass entertainment and people formed strong loyalties to politicians and political parties. Consequently, political contests were often deeply personal. See page 553.

2a.   No. Although the Supreme Court placed responsibility for the regulation of interstate commerce in the hands of Congress through the *Wabash* case, the Court did not broadly interpret those powers in cases arising under the Interstate Commerce Act. See page 556.

2b.   No. The Interstate Commerce Act did not extend government aid to private industry; therefore, the Court did not rule on this issue in cases arising under the Interstate Commerce Act. See page 556.

2c.   Correct. Through the *Wabash* case, the Court ruled that only Congress could limit railroad rates involving interstate commerce. But in cases arising under the Interstate Commerce Act, the Court reduced the regulatory powers of the Interstate Commerce Commission. See page 556.

2d.   No. In the *Wabash* case the Court accepted the principle of government regulation of industry by holding that only Congress could limit railroad rates involving interstate commerce. This decision was not overturned by the Court in cases arising under the Interstate Commerce Act. See page 556.

3a.   No. The Dingley Tariff was passed in 1897 and raised tariff rates to an average level of 57 percent. The passage of the tariff was not referred to as the "Crime of '73." See pages 557–558.

3b.   Correct. Congress passed legislation in 1873 that demonetized silver and stopped the coining of silver dollars. The United States thus went to the gold standard. This policy did not meet the demands of debtors who wanted to expand the money supply and was denounced as the "Crime of '73." See pages 557–558.

3c.   No. The Sherman Silver Purchase Act was passed by Congress in 1878 and required the U.S. Treasury to buy between $2 million and $4 million of silver per month. This law was an attempt by Congress to pacify groups calling for the "free coinage of silver" and was not referred to as the "Crime of '73." See pages 557–558.

3d.   No. The Pendleton Act was passed by Congress in 1882 and created the Civil Service Commission. It was not referred to as the "Crime of '73." See pages 557–558.

4a.   No. The presidents during the Gilded Age were not "inspiring" figures to most of the electorate. See page 558.

4b.   No. The presidents during the Gilded Age were hardworking men and may not accurately be described as lazy. See page 558.

4c.   Correct. The presidents during the Gilded Age did not evoke much of an emotional response from the electorate, but they were honorable, proper, and honest. See page 558.

4d.   No. Believing that it was their job to execute the laws passed by Congress, the presidents during the Gilded Age may not be described as forceful or active. See page 558.

5a.   Correct. Partly as a result of bribery and vote fraud, the Republicans carried Indiana by 2,300 votes and New York by 14,000 votes. See page 560.

5b.   No. The British minister, to the delight of the Republicans, said that Democrat Grover Cleveland's election would be good for England. This offended Irish Democrats and weakened Cleveland's campaign. See page 560.

5c.   No. Grover Cleveland is not known to have told ethnic jokes offensive to Irish Catholics. See page 560.

5d.   No. Grover Cleveland was against high tariffs, and, even though he was convinced to temper his attacks against tariffs for political reasons, he never called for higher tariffs. See page 560.

6a.   No. The question of pensions to Civil War veterans and their widows concerned Union veterans only. Congress never considered pensions for Confederate veterans. See page 560.

6b.   No. The events leading to congressional action on pensions for Civil War veterans and their widows make it obvious that the memories of the war were still alive and affected the decisions of Congress. See page 560.

6c.   No. By providing generous pensions to Union veterans and their widows, Congress made one of the largest welfare commitments it has ever made. See page 560.

6d.   Correct. Although angered by tactics of lobbyists for the Grand Army of the Republic, congressmen still voted in favor of providing generous pensions for Union veterans and their widows. They did so, in large measure, because of pressure from this politically powerful interest group. See page 560.

7a.   No. The contention that women will demand national disarmament was not the most common argument against giving women the right to vote. See page 563.

7b.   Correct. The most common argument in the Senate against the extension of the right to vote to women was the contention that it would interfere with their family responsibilities and ruin female virtue. See page 563.

7c.   No. The contention that women were not well enough educated to vote was not the most common argument used by senators opposed to the extension of the vote to women. See page 563.

7d.   No. The contention that women were too emotional was not the most common argument used by senators opposed to the extension of the vote to women. See page 563.

8a.   No. The crop-lien system did not make it possible for southern farmers to increase the prices of their agricultural products. See pages 563–564.

8b.   Correct. The operation of the crop-lien system forced many farmers into perpetual debt and into a state of helpless peonage. See pages 563–564.

8c.   No. The crop-lien system was at the heart of sharecropping and tenant farming and did not create the opportunity for more southern farmers to become landowners. See pages 563–564.

8d.   No. The growing of traditional cash crops, especially cotton, was emphasized rather than agricultural diversification. See pages 563–564.

9a.   No. Although farmers complained about the cost of farm machinery, they did not see the subtreasury system as a way to lower those costs. See pages 565–566.

9b.   No. The subtreasury system was not proposed as an agency that would make second mortgages available to farmers facing bankruptcy. See pages 565–566.

9c.   Correct. The subtreasury system would give farmers a place to store their crops while waiting for higher prices, and it would allow them to borrow subtreasury notes amounting to 80 percent of the value of their crops. Through this system, farmers hoped to solve their cash and credit problems. See pages 565–566.

9d.   No. The subtreasury system was not a means by which transportation costs could be lowered. See pages 565–566.

10a.   No. Although the Omaha platform called for increased government regulation of trusts, it did not call for the nationalization of the oil and steel industries. See page 567.

10b.   No. Although Populists did call for a more active federal government in the Omaha platform, they did not advocate a welfare program for destitute farmers. They believed that an expansive money supply, brought about by the free coinage of silver, would solve farmers' monetary problems. See page 567.

10c.   No. The Populists clearly recognized the debt problems of farmers but did not call for a moratorium on debts in the Omaha platform. They believed that a graduated income tax, the creation of a postal savings bank, and the free coinage of silver would solve farmers' monetary problems. See page 567.

10d.   Correct. Farmers believed that railroads had been built on public land with public funds, and it angered them that railroads were operated for the private enrichment of a few individuals. Therefore, the Omaha platform called for government ownership of the railroad lines. See page 567.

11a.   Correct. The national economy had reached the point where business failures in one area had a ripple effect throughout the economic system, causing failures in other areas. See page 569.

11b.   No. In some measure, the depression of the 1890s was due to overspeculation in certain industries, but it was not due to overspeculation in the stock market. See pages 568–569.

11c.   No. Although the Sherman Silver Purchase Act had a psychological impact that led to the dwindling of the nation's gold reserves, it was not the reason for the broad-based nature of the depression. In addition, repeal of the act did not halt the run on the Treasury. See pages 568–569.

11d.   No. The impact of the depression of the 1890s on other countries and the subsequent withdrawal of foreign investments from the United States are indications of the broad-based nature of the depression. However, this withdrawal did not cause the depression to be broad-based. See pages 568–569.

12a.   No. Jacob Riis (pages 531–532) was a New York journalist and the author of *How the Other Half Lives*, published in 1890. The book exposed the horrors of life in the slums of New York. Although Riis was an active reformer, he was not a socialist. See page 570.

12b.   Correct. Eugene Debs, president of the American Railway Union, was jailed in 1894 for defying a federal court injunction against the Pullman strike. While in jail, Debs became a socialist and, after his release, became the leading spokesperson for American socialism. See page 570.

12c.   No. Ignatius Donnelly (page 568) was a leading Minnesota Populist during the 1890s and was not the leading spokesperson for American socialism. See page 570.

12d.   No. Leonidas Polk (page 568) was president of the Southern Alliance in 1891 and a leading North Carolina Populist. See page 570.

13a.   No. Although Jacob Coxey was a wealthy businessman from Ohio, his plan for dealing with the depression did not include government aid to business. See page 570.

13b.   No. The United States was already on the gold standard in 1894 when Coxey's "commonweal army" marched on the nation's capital. Coxey believed that the government's insistence on backing currency with gold was prolonging the depression. See page 570.

13c.   No. The nation did not have a federal income tax in 1894, and Jacob Coxey did not advocate tax cuts as a way to end the depression. See page 570.

13d.   Correct. Jacob Coxey advocated that the government purposefully cause inflation by pumping $500 million of paper money into the economy through a federal jobs program. See page 570.

14a.   No. The Socialist Party's ideology was attractive primarily to disaffected workers while Populism primarily attracted farmers. In other words, the two parties attracted different groups with different grievances, and the Socialist Party did not endorse Populist Party candidates. See pages 560–561 and page 571.

14b.   No. Although some Populists attempted to forge an alliance between poor southern whites and blacks, southern Populists did not call for equality under the law for African Americans. See pages 560–561 and page 571.

14c.   Correct. Out of fear that a biracial Populist coalition would jeopardize their power in the South, southern white Democrats disfranchised southern African Americans. The removal of African Americans from southern politics thus prevented the emergence of a coalition of southern whites and blacks. See pages 560–561 and page 571.

14d.   No. Although some voters may have labeled the Populists extremists, it was not because the Populist Party endorsed Coxey's demand for a public-works relief program. See pages 560–561 and page 571.

15a.   Correct. Free silver was attractive to many farmers of the West and South, but its promise of inflation was not attractive to city dwellers and factory workers. As a result, Bryan was never able to build an urban-rural coalition. See page 574.

15b.   No. McKinley conducted a "front-porch" campaign that can hardly be called "spirited." See page 574.

15c.   No. When the Democrats nominated Bryan and endorsed many Populist ideas, the Populists decided to nominate Bryan for the presidency and Tom Watson of Georgia for the vice-presidency. See page 574.

15d.   No. Bryan was not endorsed by the Socialist party. See page 574.

Chapter 21

Multiple-Choice Questions

1a.   No. Voter loyalty to political parties began to decline during the Progressive era. See page 581.

1b.   No. These organizations were not responsible for introducing charismatic personalities to political campaigns. See page 581.

1c.   No. These organizations often served to stimulate debate on urban issues rather than stifle it. See page 581.

1d.   Correct. Organizations such as those mentioned lobbied for their own interests and, as a result, caused politics to become more fragmented. At the same time, however, their attempts to educate the public stimulated debate and made politics more issue-oriented. See page 581.

2a.   No. Progressives disliked professional politicians and the fact that they often selected candidates through the party caucus. It was for this reason that Progressives advocated the use of direct primaries to nominate candidates. See page 581.

2b.   No. Although middle-class progressive reformers advocated direct primaries as a way of returning government to "the people," they often meant middle-class people like themselves, excluding the working classes, blacks, and women from their definition of "the people." See page 581.

2c.   Correct. Most middle-class progressive reformers were opposed to party politics, which they believed had been corrupted by political machines and political bosses. Therefore, the reforms they advocated were intended to improve government by reducing the power of political parties. See page 581.

2d.   No. The direct primary was advocated as a way to nominate political candidates for office and does not demonstrate the belief that government should respect the rights of the individual. See page 581.

3a.   No. Progressives were not necessarily against compromise, but they disliked the bargaining associated with "old style" politics. See page 581.

3b.   Correct. Professionals of the new middle class generally formed the progressive movement's leadership. They believed that practices important in their professions, such as systematic investigation and application of the scientific method, could be used by government to plan, control, and predict, thus achieving the goal of social and political efficiency. See page 581.

3c.   No. Although the evidence indicates that progressives wanted political reforms designed to make government more responsive to "the people" by correcting the ills of "boss-ridden" party politics, progressives did not advocate literacy tests as a requirement for voting. See page 581.

3d.   No. Although progressives advocated political reforms designed to make politicians more responsive to "the people," they did not suggest requiring full financial disclosure by all political candidates. See page 581.

4a.   No. Evidence indicates that most middle-class progressives were interested in political reform (the initiative, referendum, and recall), and most working-class progressives were interested in social reform (improvements in housing, safe factories, workers' compensation). See page 582.

4b.   No. By advocating reforms that would shorten working hours and ensure safe factories, working-class progressives demonstrated their belief that government should ensure the safety and welfare of the worker by regulating the work place. See page 582.

4c.   No. Working-class progressives usually rejected moral reforms such as prohibition and Sunday closing laws. See page 582.

4d.   Correct. In their belief that government should be responsible for alleviating many of the problems associated with urban-industrial growth, working-class progressives realized that political bosses could be useful and that they were not necessarily enemies of reform. See page 582.

5a.   No. Eugene Debs's personality is not the reason that most progressives rejected socialist ideology. See page 582.

5b.   Correct. Most progressives of the middle and working classes accepted the capitalist system, had relatively comfortable economic and social positions within that system, and had too much of a stake in that system to advocate its overthrow. See page 582.

5c.   No. A nationalist appeal is one that emphasizes devotion to country and nation. Progressives had a strong sense of devotion to the United States and often saw socialism as a radical attack against the nation's fundamental principles. See page 582.

5d.   No. Progressives rejected the basic tenets of the laissez-faire philosophy as outdated and obsolete in an age of urban-industrial growth. See page 582.

6a.   Correct. La Follette believed that corporate involvement in politics was a source of political corruption and that corporations had amassed power at the expense of the people. Therefore, he advocated that corporations be driven out of politics. See page 584.

6b.   No. Although this was a belief held by Eugene Debs (the leader of the Socialist party), La Follette, a progressive, did not share this belief. See page 584.

6c.   No. La Follette's program (known as the "Wisconsin Idea") involved the establishment of regulatory commissions staffed with experts. See page 584.

6d.   No. Although La Follette advocated regulation of railroad rates, he did not advocate nationalization (government ownership) of the railroads. See page 584.

7a.   No. Dewey did not believe that the teaching of moral principles should be the primary concern of public education. Furthermore, when such principles were dealt with, Dewey, who rejected the idea of moral absolutes, believed that they should be subjected to scientific inquiry. See page 587.

7b.   No. Dewey did not propose the accreditation of public school teachers by a national accreditation agency. See page 587.

7c.   No. Dewey rejected the idea that there was a fixed body of knowledge to be conveyed to students. He favored the "student-centered" as opposed to the "subject-centered" school. See page 587.

7d.   Correct. Dewey believed that education should be related to the interests of students and that the subjects taught should relate directly to their lives. See page 587.

8a.   No. It is incorrect to say that Washington believed that black Americans should "passively" accept their position in American society. See pages 591–592.

8b.   Correct. Washington argued that while temporarily accepting their inferior position in American society, blacks should prove themselves worthy of equal rights by adopting a strategy of self-help. See pages 591–592.

8c.   No. Washington believed that actively demanding and fighting for their political and social rights would prove to be counterproductive for black Americans. See pages 591–592.

8d.   No. Although it is true that Washington secretly contributed money to support legal challenges to discriminatory legislation, he did not believe that black Americans should challenge such legislation in an open, direct, or active manner. See pages 591–592.

9a.   No. Although the suffrage crusade grew out of the 1830s abolitionist argument in favor of equal rights for all Americans, the idea was rejected by many Americans in the 1910s just as it had been rejected in the 1830s. See page 596.

9b.   No. Since most Americans accepted traditional gender roles and the restrictions such roles placed on women, some suffragists used a traditionalist view (that women have "unique" qualities) to defend female suffrage. However, use of this argument was not "the most decisive factor" in the extension of the vote to women. See page 596.

9c.   Correct. The efforts of women during the First World War were probably the most decisive factor in convincing legislators to extend the vote to women. See page 596.

9d.   No. Although Carrie Chapman Catt organized women at the precinct level so that pressure could be put on male politicians who opposed the extension of the vote to women, she is considered a moderate and did not engage in militant tactics. See page 596.

10a.   No. Roosevelt's policy toward the Northern Securities Company and his support of the Hepburn Act, the Pure Food and Drug Act, and the Meat Inspection Act demonstrate his rejection of the idea that business must be allowed to organize and operate without government interference. See pages 597–598.

10b.   Correct. Roosevelt preferred cooperation between government and business and preferred that business regulate itself. However, he was willing to prosecute trusts that unscrupulously exploited the public and refused to regulate themselves. See pages 597–598.

10c.   No. Roosevelt, recognizing that business consolidation could bring efficiency, did not see bigness as bad in and of itself. See pages 597–598.

10d.   No. Roosevelt's handling of the trusts does not indicate that he believed in using the tax power of the government (which was minimal since there was no income tax) to punish irresponsible corporations. See pages 597–598.

11a.   Correct. Roosevelt's handling of the trusts, his labor policy, and his actions on the issue of conservation indicate an assertion of presidential power. On the other hand, Taft's handling of the tariff issue and his inability to publicize issues he supported indicate caution and restraint. See pages 597–600.

11b.   No. Although Roosevelt preferred cooperation between business and government to confrontation, he often offended business leaders by speaking against their unscrupulous abuse of power. In contrast, although Taft supported federal regulation of business, he was quieter and his accomplishments were less publicized. See pages 597–600.

11c.   No. On the contrary, Roosevelt was far more willing to bend the law to his purposes than was Taft, who believed in the strict restraint of the law. See pages 597–600.

11d.   No. Both Roosevelt and Taft were sympathetic to reform. See pages 597–600.

12a.   No. Neither Roosevelt nor Wilson called for the "destruction" of big business. See pages 601–602.

12b.   No. Neither Roosevelt nor Wilson called for a restoration of the laissez-faire philosophy. See pages 601–602.

12c.   Correct. Roosevelt called for federal regulatory commissions to establish cooperation between big business and big government, thereby protecting citizens' interests; but Wilson emphasized breaking up monopolies, returning to open competition, and using government to accomplish both. See pages 601–602.

12d.   No. Both Roosevelt and Wilson supported equality of economic opportunity. See pages 601–602.

13a.   No. Wilson's support of the Clayton Antitrust Act and creation of the FTC demonstrates his acceptance of the fact that a return to free competition was impossible. See pages 602–603.

13b.   No. Neither the Clayton Antitrust Act nor the bill creating the FTC was passed as a consequence of Supreme Court rulings. Therefore, they do not indicate a challenge by Wilson to the Court. See pages 602–603.

13c.   No. The Democratic leadership in Congress favored passage of the Clayton Act and the bill creating the FTC. See pages 602–603.

13d.   Correct. As president, Wilson realized that economic concentration had gone so far that a return to free competition was impossible. With this realization, Wilson accepted expansion of the government's regulatory powers to deal with the reality of economic concentration in the hands of big business. Wilson's acceptance of this principle is demonstrated by his support of the Clayton Anti-Trust Act and creation of the FTC. See pages 602–603.

14a.   Correct. By reducing tariffs and thus encouraging imports, the Underwood Tariff encouraged free competition and free trade. See page 603.

14b.   No. President Wilson proposed and actively supported passage of the Underwood Tariff, including the income-tax provision. See page 603.

14c.   No. The Underwood Tariff imposed a graduated income tax on residents of the United States; the maximum rate was 6 percent, and that rate was applied to incomes over $500,000. See page 603.

14d.   No. Since the Underwood Tariff dramatically reduced tariff rates on imports, it did not lead to a trade war. See page 603.

15a.   No. The strength of opposition to reform, court rulings against progressive legislation, and shortcomings of regulatory agencies are a few indications that, in many respects, progressives failed to bring about a redistribution of power. In 1920 government remained under the influence of business and industry. See page 604.

15b.   No. Use of such devices as the initiative, the referendum, and the recall by special interests indicates that business and industrial interests still had influence and power at the state level, and the shortcomings of regulatory agencies indicate the same was true at the national level. See page 604.

15c.   Correct. By gaining public support for trust-busting and for legislation such as the Pure Food and Drug Act and the Meat Inspection Act, Progressives established the principle that government power could be used for the common good by ensuring fairness, health, and safety. See page 604.

15d.   No. Progressives stressed different themes and different causes and often worked at cross-purposes. See page 604.

Chapter 22

Multiple-Choice Questions

1a.   No. The American public has not traditionally paid a great deal of attention to nor been well educated on foreign policy issues. As a result, foreign policy, unlike domestic policy, is not usually "shaped" by the people. See page 610.

1b.   No. Although the business community has a hand in the shaping of foreign policy, it is a mistake to say that the business community alone was "largely" responsible for foreign policy decisions. See page 610.

1c.   Correct. The foreign policy elite, made up of "opinion leaders" from many areas of American society (business, politics, the military, labor, agriculture), were instrumental in the late nineteenth century, as they are instrumental today, in shaping American foreign policy. See page 610.

1d.   No. Although military leaders have a hand in the shaping of foreign policy, it is a mistake to say that such policy in the late nineteenth century was "shaped largely" by this one group. See page 610.

2a.   No. American farm leaders did not seek an expansionist foreign policy for the purpose of learning new agricultural techniques from foreign agricultural specialists. See pages 610–611.

2b.   Correct. In the final third of the nineteenth century, depressions affected the U.S. economy about once a decade. Many business and farm leaders believed overproduction was a major cause of economic declines and advocated expansion into foreign markets as a preventive measure. See pages 610–611.

2c.   No. The expansionist sentiment of the late nineteenth century was not fueled by the belief that domestic labor problems could be solved by increasing the number of immigrants. See pages 610–611.

2d.   No. Although United States economic and political influence increased in Latin America in the late nineteenth century, especially after the Spanish-American War, the states of Latin America did not want the United States to exert political control over them. See pages 610–611.

3a.   Although some religious leaders doubtless criticized American foreign policy in the late nineteenth century, it is a mistake to say that "most" did so. Certainly, Reverend Josiah Strong was not critical of American imperialism in *Our Country*. See pages 612–613.

3b.   Correct. In his book, Reverend Josiah Strong stated the belief that the Anglo-Saxon race was superior to and was destined to lead others. See pages 612–613.

3c.   No. *Our Country* does not provide evidence that late nineteenth-century American foreign policy was based on the principle of self-determination. See pages 612–613.

3d.   No. Although it is true that the American diplomatic corps was one of the worst in the world in the late nineteenth century, this was not a topic that Reverend Josiah Strong dealt with in his book. See pages 612–613.

4a.   No. Seward's vision of an American empire included Iceland, Greenland, Hawaii, and certain Pacific islands as well as expansion throughout the Americas. See pages 615–616.

4b.   Correct. Seward advocated a canal through Central America as essential to the unity of the large American empire that he envisioned. See pages 615–616.

4c.   No. Seward believed that other peoples would find the republican principles of American society attractive. Therefore, they would naturally gravitate toward the United States, making expansion by military means unnecessary. See pages 615–616.

4d.   No. Although in 1867 Seward signed a treaty with Denmark to buy the Danish West Indies, the treaty was not ratified by the Senate. The Danish West Indies did not become part of the American empire until 1917. See pages 615–616.

5a.   No. Andrew Carnegie was founder of the Carnegie Steel Company, which controlled most of the steel production in the United States by 1900. Although he supported the concept of the "New Navy" and signed a lucrative naval contract in 1883, he was not responsible for "popularizing" the New Navy. See page 618.

5b.   No. Ulysses Grant was not responsible for popularizing the New Navy. See page 618.

5c.   No. Hamilton Fish, secretary of state under President Grant, was not responsible for popularizing the New Navy. See page 618.

5d.   Correct. Alfred T. Mahan argued that a modern, efficient naval force was essential for any nation that aspired to great-power status. Through his lectures and published works, he had an enormous impact on the successful drive to modernize the United States Navy, popularly known as the "New Navy." See page 618.

6a.   No. Grover Cleveland was an expansionist who recognized the economic advantages of annexing the Hawaiian islands. His opposition to annexation was not based on economic questions. See page 619.

6b.   No. Cleveland's opposition to the annexation of Hawaii was not based on racial questions. See page 619.

6c.   Correct. Cleveland supported economic expansion but did not believe it should lead to imperialism. (See pages 608–609 for the distinction between economic expansion and imperialism.) The facts of the Hawaiian revolution, revealed to him through an investigation he ordered, convinced the new president that annexation was being forced on the Hawaiians and was, therefore, imperialistic. See page 619.

6d.   No. Cleveland's opposition to the annexation of Hawaii was not based on fear that it would lead to war. See page 619.

7a.   Correct. The boundary dispute between Venezuela and Great Britain was settled by an Anglo-American arbitration board that barely consulted Venezuela in its deliberations. By disregarding Venezuela's rights and sensibilities in this manner, the United States displayed an imperialistic attitude. See pages 619–620.

7b.   No. The crisis did not center on the question of the type of government Venezuela had. See pages 619–620.

7c.   No. The United States sent a strong protest to the British concerning their actions in Venezuela. The British stalled at first but then, not wanting war, bowed to American pressure. As a result, the Monroe Doctrine was strengthened and the United States and Great Britain began to form closer ties. See pages 619–620.

7d.   No. The United States Navy did not become involved in the Venezuelan crisis of 1895. See pages 619–620.

8a.   No. The Teller Amendment did not announce American intentions to annex Cuba. See page 621.

8b.   No. The Teller Amendment, passed by the U.S. Congress, was related to the Spanish-American-Cuban-Filipino War, but it was not a reason for the war. See page 621.

8c.   No. The Teller Amendment did not have the effect of expanding the Spanish-American-Cuban-Filipino War to the South Pacific. See page 621.

8d.   Correct. After passing resolutions declaring Cuba to be free, Congress adopted the Teller Amendment, which disclaimed any intention by the United States to annex Cuba. See page 621.

9a.   No. Although there was a humanitarian aspect to United States entry into the Spanish-American War, it cannot be said that "in the final analysis" this was the reason Americans accepted the war. See page 622.

9b.   No. Although religious leaders supported the war and Protestant clergymen envisioned doing missionary work in Catholic Cuba, it is incorrect to say that "in the final analysis" Americans accepted the war because of a desire to carry the Christian message to other people. See page 622.

9c.   Correct. Since the spirit of expansionism had many sources, it may be labeled "multifaceted." Moreover, in dealing with the reasons for the war, each reason may be analyzed separately; but, "in the final analysis," we are left with multiple causation. See page 622.

9d.   No. Although many imperialists supported the war because it offered an opportunity to fulfill the "large policy," most Americans had no idea of what that policy was. Therefore, it is a mistake to say that "in the final analysis" this was why Americans accepted the war. See page 622.

10a.   Correct. Of the over 5,400 Americans who died in the war, only 379 died in combat. All others died from malaria or yellow fever. See page 622.

10b.   No. In the destruction of the Spanish fleet outside Santiago harbor, the Spanish suffered 474 killed and wounded, and the United States suffered one killed and one wounded. This does not constitute "most" of the 5,400 Americans who lost their lives in the Spanish-American War. See page 622.

10c.   No. In the Battle of Manila Bay (May 1, 1898) Spanish losses numbered 381 killed, and American casualties consisted of 8 wounded. See page 622.

10d.   No. In the charge up San Juan Hill, the Rough Riders lost about 89 men. This does not constitute "most" of the 5,400 Americans who lost their lives in the Spanish-American War. See page 622.

11a.   No. The anti-imperialists used a variety of arguments in their campaign against the Treaty of Paris. See page 623.

11b.   Correct. The anti-imperialists came from many different interest groups in American society. Each group looked at domestic issues differently and also found it impossible to speak with one voice on foreign policy issues. Therefore, they were hindered by the inconsistency of their arguments. See page 623.

11c.   No. Although Mark Twain and Andrew Carnegie spoke against the Treaty of Paris, the treaty passed by a 57-to-27 vote in the Senate. See page 623.

11d.   No. Believing it best to end the war and then push for Filipino independence, William Jennings Bryan supported the Treaty of Paris. However, his support for the treaty did not aid the anti-imperialist campaign. The treaty passed by a 57-to-27 vote. See page 623.

12a.   No. As an ideology rather than just a policy, the Open Door was not based on the preservation of the self-determination of other nations. See page 624.

12b.   Correct. The ideology expressed in the Open Door was that the United States required exports; therefore, any area closed to American products, citizens, or ideas threatened the survival of the United States. See page 624.

12c.   No. As an ideology rather than just a policy, the Open Door was not based on the idea that freedom of the seas would lead to the economic expansion of the world community of nations. See page 624.

12d.   No. As an ideology rather than just a policy, the Open Door was not based on the belief that all nations of the world should be considered equals. See page 624.

13a.   Correct. The Filipinos felt betrayed by the Treaty of Paris and, under the leadership of Emilio Aguinaldo, fought for their independence in the Philippine Insurrection. American forces finally suppressed the insurrection in 1901, leaving 5,000 Americans and 200,000 Filipinos dead. See pages 624–626.

13b.   No. The Philippines were not granted independence until 1946. See pages 624–626.

13c.   No. The United States assumed that it knew what was best for the Filipino people and held no referendum. See pages 624–626.

13d.   No. The United States held sovereignty over the Philippines for forty-eight years. Although it attempted to establish democratic government over the years, the United States did not guarantee to the Filipino people the same rights enjoyed by American citizens. See page 626.

14a.   No. The United States did not extend aid to French colonies in Indochina in the early twentieth century. See page 627.

14b.   No. In its efforts to protect American interests in the Pacific (especially in the Philippines), the United States made concessions to Japan—the dominant power in Asia. Therefore, in the Taft-Katsura Agreement of 1905 the United States recognized Japanese hegemony in Korea and, in return, the Japanese pledged not to interfere with American interests in the Philippines. See page 627.

14c.   No. The United States did not want either Russia or Japan to become dominant in Asia but wanted each to balance the power of the other. Therefore, the U.S. remained neutral in the conflict and President Roosevelt, at the request of the Japanese, agreed to mediate the crisis. See page 627.

14d.   Correct. In an effort to increase American influence in Manchuria, President Taft was able to gain agreement on the inclusion of a group of American bankers in a four-power consortium to build a Chinese railway. In response (and in defiance of the Open Door policy), Japan signed a treaty with Russia by which the two staked out spheres of influence in China for themselves. This strengthened Japan's position in Manchuria and caused more friction between the U.S. and Japan. See page 627.

15a.   No. Both the Roosevelt Corollary and United States actions in Latin America support the idea that in the late nineteenth and early twentieth centuries the United States believed in the rightness of its political system for Latin America. See page 629.

15b.   Correct. The United States believed that the debts-default crisis in Latin America invited intervention by European powers acting to protect the financial interests of European banks. President Roosevelt deemed this to be a threat to the security of the United States and its interests in the region, which included not only American commercial and investment interests, but the Panama Canal as well. Therefore, the United States, to preserve its own security, believed that financial and political stability were essential in Latin America Both the Roosevelt Corollary and United States behavior in the region demonstrate that the United States was willing to be the policeman of the region to protect its economic interests, its dominance, and to establish order. See page 629.

15c.   No. Although the United States has shared some of its wealth and resources with the people of Latin America, this clearly is not the rationale behind the Roosevelt Corollary. See page 629.

15d.   No. The Roosevelt Corollary to the Monroe Doctrine was an attempt to prevent European intervention in Latin America, not encourage it. See page 629.

Chapter 23

Multiple-Choice Questions

1a.   No. When Russia mobilized its armies to aid Serbia, Germany first declared war against Russia and then against France, Russia's ally. Through all of this, Austria-Hungary did not invade Russia and Britain did not declare war. See pages 635–636.

1b.   No. The act of terrorism that led to war was that of a Serbian nationalist against Archduke Franz Ferdinand, heir to the Austro-Hungarian throne. But Great Britain did not enter the war in response to this act of terrorism. See pages 635–636.

1c.   No. Serbia did not invade Austria-Hungary. See pages 635–636.

1d.   Correct. When Austria-Hungary declared war against Serbia and Germany declared war against Russia and France, Great Britain hesitated. Only when Germany invaded Belgium, whose neutrality was guaranteed by Great Britain, did Britain enter the war. See pages 635–636.

2a.   No. Woodrow Wilson was sincere in his desire to keep the United States out of the war in Europe. See page 637.

2b.   No. The print media had not built broad-based sympathy for Serbian nationalism in the United States. Moreover, Serbian nationalism was not the major issue in the minds of most Americans. See page 637.

2c.   Correct. Wilson's appeal for neutrality clashed with three realities: (1) ethnic groups in the United States took sides; (2) economic links with the Allies made neutrality difficult; and (3) administration officials were sympathetic to the Allies. See page 637.

2d.   No. Secretary of State William Jennings Bryan insisted on a policy of strict neutrality. See page 637.

3a.   No. Wilsonianism held that all diplomatic agreements among nations, including all alliance systems, should be openly negotiated. See page 637.

3b.   No. It is true that an army made up of soldiers from fourteen allied nations, including the United States, was sent to Russia and assisted anti-Bolshevik forces. It is also true that Wilson refused to recognize the Soviet government. But, Wilson was instrumental in persuading the Allies to abandon their attempt to overthrow the Bolshevik regime. Furthermore, one of his Fourteen Points stated that Russia should be allowed to determine its own form of government and its own national policy. Therefore, Wilson never explicitly included in the Fourteen Points a provision to form a collective security agreement for the purpose of containing communism. See page 637.

3c.   No. Wilsonianism advocated reducing world armaments. See page 637.

3d.   Correct. Wilsonianism advocated decolonization (the breaking up of empires) and the principle of self-determination (the right of all people to determine their own future without outside interference. See page 637.

4a.   Correct. Bryan believed that Germany had a right to prevent contraband from going to the Allies and faulted Great Britain for using passenger ships to carry such contraband. When Wilson rejected Bryan's advice that Americans not be allowed to travel on belligerent ships, Bryan resigned. See pages 638–639.

4b.   No. Although Bryan protested Great Britain's blockade of Germany, no great public outcry led to his resignation. See pages 638–639.

4c.   No. Bryan believed that the United States should remain strictly neutral in its relations with the European belligerents. See pages 638–639.

4d.   No. Bryan did not advocate American entry into the war. See pages 638–639.

5a.   No. Wilson broke diplomatic relations with Germany on February 3, 1917, in response to Germany's resumption of unrestricted submarine warfare on February 1. Thus, relations were severed before the Zimmermann note was given to the United States ambassador to Great Britain on February 24. See page 640.

5b.   No. The Zimmermann telegram proposed an alliance between Germany and Mexico and did not cause Wilson to rethink his position on the application of international law to the submarine. See page 640.

5c.   Correct. Mexican-American relations were strained in 1917, and Wilson saw this proposal of a Mexican-German alliance as proof of a German conspiracy against the United States. Soon after he learned of the telegram, Wilson asked Congress for "armed neutrality." See page 640.

5d.   No. American troops began to withdraw from Mexico in January 1917 and were fully withdrawn by February 5. Therefore, Wilson decided to change his policy toward Mexico before learning of the Zimmermann telegram on February 24. Furthermore, this change did not constitute "support" for the Mexican Revolution. See page 640.

6a.   No. Although Wilson referred to the group of senators responsible for filibustering the bill to death as that "little group of willful men," there is no evidence that he ever contemplated asking the Senate to censure them. In fact, such a request from the executive branch would most likely have angered the Senate. See page 640.

6b.   No. Wilson did not respond to the defeat of the bill by ordering the navy to escort American commercial ships. See page 640.

6c.   Correct. After some twelve senators used the filibuster to defeat the armed-ship bill, Secretary of State Robert Lansing advised President Wilson that he had the authority under statute law to arm merchant vessels without congressional approval. Therefore, Wilson proceeded to use that authority. See page 640.

6d.   No. The armed-ship bill was defeated on March 4, 1917, and Wilson did not deliver his war message to Congress until April 2, 1917. See page 640.

7a.   No. The training of recruits was not the responsibility of the Commission on Training Camp Activities. See page 643.

7b.   Correct. The government created this commission to coordinate the efforts of private organizations in providing "wholesome" recreational activities to soldiers. In an added effort to preserve soldiers' morals, the commission declared five-mile "sin-free" zones around military bases. See page 643.

7c.   No. The Commission on Training Camp Activities did not suggest the integration of military units. See page 643.

7d.   No. No such spy network existed. See page 643.

8a.   No. It was not Pershing's fear that he would lose control over American soldiers that led to his refusal to allow American soldiers to become part of Allied units. See page 643.

8b.   No. Although General Pershing was concerned about the virtue of American soldiers, it was not for this reason that he refused to allow American soldiers to become part of Allied units. See page 643.

8c.   Correct. Pershing refused to subject American soldiers to the horrors of trench warfare. For this reason the United States declared itself an Associated power and American soldiers did not become part of Allied units. See page 643.

8d.   No. General Pershing had tremendous faith in the ability of American soldiers. See page 643.

9a.   No. Antitrust laws were virtually suspended during the war. For example, the Webb-Pomerene Act granted immunity from antitrust legislation to companies that combined to operate in the export trade. See page 646–647.

9b.   No. Although the government did not institute a wage and price freeze during the war, it did fix prices on raw materials rather than on finished products. As a result, it lost control of inflation, and workers saw little improvement in their economic standing. See page 646–647.

9c.   Correct. Although government tax policies were designed to bring into the Treasury some of the profits reaped by business, the overall relationship between government and business was one of partnership. See page 646–647.

9d.   No. The government did not demand cost-of-living increases for workers in war-related industries. See page 646–647.

10a.   No. Men protested that women were undermining the wage system by working for *lower* pay than that received by men. See page 650.

10b.   Correct. Men complained that the higher productivity rate of women destabilized the work environment. In other words, men felt that their jobs were threatened by women who worked at a faster pace. See page 650.

10c.   No. Although women moved into jobs formerly reserved for men, they were discriminated against when it came to promotions. See page 650.

10d.   No. Except for unions organized by women, organized labor was male dominated and openly hostile toward women. See page 650.

11a.   No. Blacks served in all-black units in the army. Some served in combat units, but most were relegated to menial jobs. Although racism was obvious in the military, military leaders did not suggest integration of units as a solution. See page 651.

11b.   No. The northward migration of blacks created problems for southern white landowners and businessmen because it reduced their supply of cheap laborers. The problem was further complicated by the fact that white laborers were also moving away. See page 651.

11c.   No. Blacks continued to experience racial discrimination at home during and after the First World War. See page 651.

11d.   Correct. The massive influx of blacks into the North during the First World War caused anxiety among white northerners. This anxiety found expression in northern race riots in which whites terrorized blacks. See page 651.

12a.   Correct. The CPI was organized to mobilize American opinion behind the war effort. Through its efforts it portrayed antiwar dissenters as being dangerous to national security and encouraged patriotic Americans to spy on their neighbors and report any "suspicious" behavior. See page 652.

12b.   No. The CPI was established by Wilson in 1917 as a propaganda agency. As such, the CPI did not encourage Americans to debate openly the American war effort. See page 652.

12c.   No. The CPI, established in 1917 by President Wilson, was interested in good propaganda. This goal did not always coincide with the dissemination of accurate war news. See page 652.

12d.   No. President Wilson established the CPI in 1917 as a propaganda agency. The committee often found that exaggeration and rumor worked to its advantage. See page 652.

13a.   No. There was no law requiring members of the Socialist party to register with the government. See page 654.

13b.   Correct. The Court, in a unanimous opinion, upheld the Espionage Act as constitutional. In doing so, the Court applied the "clear and present danger" test to free speech in time of war. See page 654.

13c.   No. The Court upheld the constitutionality of the Sedition Act by a 7 to 2 vote in *Abrams* v. *U.S.* (1919). See page 654.

13d.   No. The *Schenck* case did not involve the teaching of foreign languages in public schools. See page 654.

14a.   No. Although political and business leaders believed a conspiracy existed among American radicals, the evidence indicates that the American left was badly divided and not capable of a "well-organized conspiracy" against the United States government. See page 656.

14b.   Correct. In the Palmer Raids, government agents were authorized by Attorney General Palmer to break into meeting halls, poolrooms, and homes without search warrants. Those arrested and jailed were denied legal counsel. These actions demonstrate a disregard for civil liberties. See page 656.

14c.   No. Although the New York State legislature expelled five Socialist legislators, the expulsion was not done on instructions from President Wilson. See page 656.

14d.   No. Although some believed that the Boston police strike and the steel strike indicated radical infiltration of the union movement in the United States, labor organizations were not declared illegal. See page 656.

15a.   Correct. The argument at the core of the debate over the treaty concerned the question of collective security versus America's traditional unilateralism. Those who opposed the Treat of Versailles rejected the idea of collective security contained in Article 10. See page 661.

15b.   No. Although some of the treaty's opponents charged that Wilson had compromised his stated principles of decolonization and self-determination by accepting the mandate system, opposition to the treaty did not rest on this issue. See page 661.

15c.   No. Those who opposed the Treaty of Versailles had no problem with the "war guilt clause," which placed most of the blame for the war on Germany and its allies. See page 661.

15d.   No. The treaty contained a provision that a reparations commission would determine the amount Germany was to pay the Allies. This figure was later set at $33 billion. See page 661.

Chapter 24

Multiple-Choice Questions

1a.   Correct. The judicial branch of the government, along with the legislative and executive branches, took a probusiness, antireform, and antiregulatory stance in the 1920s. The *Bailey* case serves as an example of this stance. See page 667.

1b.   No. The *Bailey* case did not deal with the issue of consumer protection, and the Court's stand did not indicate that its views were more liberal. See page 667.

1c.   No. The *Bailey* case did not deal with the issue of government aid to industry. See page 667.

1d.   No. The *Bailey* case did not deal with organized labor's right to strike. See page 667.

2a.   No. Corporations, large and small, continued to see organized labor as a threat to property rights. See pages 667–668.

2b.   No. The Court continued to demonstrate hostility toward organized labor. In cases such as *Coronado Coal Company* v. *United Mine Workers* (1922), the Court ruled that a striking union, like a trust, could be prosecuted for illegal restraint of trade. See pages 667–668.

2c.   No. Union membership fell from 5.1 million in 1920 to 3.6 million in 1929. See pages 667–668.

2d.   Correct. Large corporations continued their hostility toward organized labor, but they attempted to neutralize the appeal of unions by offering pension plans and other amenities. This policy is known as welfare capitalism. See pages 667–668.

3a.   No. President Coolidge supported allocation of funds by Congress for construction of a national highway system. See page 669.

3b.   Correct. Coolidge and Congress disagreed over how to respond to the plight of farmers. Coolidge, devoted to the concept of laissez faire, twice vetoed bills that would have established government-backed price supports for staple crops. See page 669.

3c.   No. Coolidge and Congress agreed in the area of foreign policy. See page 669.

3d.   No. Military spending was not a major issue during the Coolidge administration, and Coolidge and Congress did not disagree on this issue. See page 669.

4a.   No. During the 1920s women were criticized when they sought gainful employment. Indian women were not criticized for refusing to enter the labor force. See page 670.

4b.   Correct. Many Indian women refused to send their children to boarding schools and were criticized by reformers for that decision. See page 670.

4c.   No. Most Indian women attempted to protect and preserve Indian culture. Therefore, they did not encourage their children to abandon their tribes and land and move to urban areas. See page 670.

4d.   No. Most Indian women refused to abandon their cultural traditions and, as a result, were criticized for refusing to adopt lifestyles and homemaking methods associated with white middle-class women. See page 670.

5a.   Correct. Marcus Garvey preached the idea that blacks have an African heritage of which they should be proud, and he asserted that blackness symbolizes strength and beauty. He taught racial pride in an era in which white racism found expression in race riots and lynchings. See page 674.

5b.   No. Marcus Garvey was opposed to the assimilation of blacks into white American society. See page 674.

5c.   No. Marcus Garvey encouraged blacks to take advantage of the free enterprise system by sharpening their management skills and opening businesses. See page 674.

5d.   No. Although Marcus Garvey preached that blacks could gain respect by lifting their native Africa to world-power status, he did not advocate the use of violence to obtain his objectives. See page 674.

6a.   No. The new technology did not cause a new sense of responsibility toward household management on the part of husbands and children. In fact, by decreasing the need for servants, the new technology placed the burden of household management more squarely on the shoulders of the wife herself. See pages 676–677.

6b.   Correct. The urban housewife of the 1920s was no longer the producer of food and clothing that her female ancestors had been. However, it was still her responsibility to feed and clothe the family. Therefore, she became the family's chief consumer. See pages 676–677.

6c.   No. The new technology eliminated the need for servants in many cases. This placed more of the responsibility for childcare on the wife herself. See pages 676–677.

6d.   No. The new technology did not relieve most housewives of a wide variety of responsibilities, and in many cases the "labor-saving" machines added new responsibilities. See pages 676–677.

7a.   No. Newspaper circulation did not increase in the 1920s as a result of children being kept in school longer. See page 679.

7b.   No. Consumption of consumer goods increased in the 1920s. See page 679.

7c.   Correct. Children were kept in school longer as a result of child-labor laws and compulsory-school-attendance laws. As a consequence, the influence of the peer group in socializing children increased and the role of the family decreased. See page 679.

7d.   No. Child-labor laws and compulsory-school-attendance laws did not cause a severe labor shortage. See page 679.

8a.   No. The number of women working in factories showed very little increase during the decade of the 1920s. See page 679.

8b.   No. Sex segregation in the workplace showed no signs of decline during the 1920s. See page 679.

8c.   No. In 1920 there were some 10.4 million women in the work force, and by 1930 there were 10.8 million gainfully employed women. This meant that women constituted 22 percent of the total labor force in 1930, a 1.6 percent increase over 1920. See page 679.

8d.   Correct. Largely because of "need," as defined in the new consumer age, married women joined the work force in increasing numbers during the 1920s. The number of married women who were gainfully employed rose from 1.9 million in 1920 to 3.1 million in 1930. See page 679.

9a.   No. Although the "new" Klan of the 1920s was founded by William J. Simmons of Atlanta, its power spread into all regions of the country and by 1923 the organization claimed some 5 million members. See page 681.

9b.   No. The new mood of nationalism and militancy among African Americans in the 1920s was more pronounced in the North than in the South. Furthermore, the "new" Klan of the 1920s gained power in the South. See page 681.

9c.   Correct. The "new" Klan of the early 1920s was more broadly based than the first Klan, and it also directed its brand of hatred toward groups other than blacks. See page 681.

9d.   No. Although the Klan operated through terrorism and fear, it was not outlawed by Congress as a terrorist organization. See page 681.

10a.   No. The case demonstrates that the fear of radicalism, which was an important aspect of the Red Scare, was still very much alive. See page 682.

10b.   No. The Sacco and Vanzetti case is an indication of anti-immigrant sentiment in the United States during the early 1920s. See page 682.

10c.   No. The case did not involve blacks being tried in the South. See page 682.

10d.   Correct. Modern ballistics studies suggest that Sacco was probably guilty, Vanzetti probably innocent. However, the evidence used in the 1920 trial was questionable, and the conviction and sentencing of the two men was based largely on their immigrant background and anarchist beliefs. See page 682.

11a.   Correct. The age of mass consumerism robbed experiences and objects of their uniqueness, and as individuals became more anonymous and less significant in the fast-moving, materialistic world, they turned to "heroes" as a way of identifying with the unique. See pages 685–686.

11b.   No. In the first place, how one defines a "great" actor is a matter of judgment. In addition, Rudolph Valentino is the only actor among the three people listed. See pages 685–686.

11c.   No. Although "Babe" Ruth may be considered a "great" baseball player, this is not true of Jack Dempsey (boxer) or Rudolph Valentino (actor). See pages 685–686.

11d.   No. The three people listed were not engaged in "lawless" acts. See pages 685–686.

12a.   No. Prohibition was born out of the Puritan value system, which emphasized hard work and sobriety. Americans did not "completely" reject this value system. See page 687.

12b.   No. Rather than "foisting" illegal liquor on the public, organized crime provided it to a public that wanted to buy it. See page 687.

12c.   No. Although prohibition caused people in the legal liquor industry to lose their jobs, its negative economic impact was not the reason for its failure. See page 687.

12d.   Correct. Although most Americans continued to accept the Puritan value system on which prohibition was based, more and more Americans found the new diversions of "the age of play" attractive. Therefore, many willingly broke the law in favor of fun and personal freedom. See page 687.

13a.   No. Many of the writers of the Harlem Renaissance spoke with pride of the African past of black Americans. See pages 687–688.

13b.   No. Most of the writers associated with the Harlem Renaissance were not advocates of black nationalism and did not advocate the return of black Americans to Africa. See pages 687–688.

13c.   Correct. In addressing identity issues, black writers of the Harlem Renaissance rejected white culture and took pride in their African heritage. Instead of advocating assimilation into white society, they urged blacks to find their identity in the richness and uniqueness of black culture. See pages 687–688.

13d.   No. The black writers of the Harlem Renaissance were concerned with issues relating to the reality of the black experience in white American society. They were not concerned primarily with economic issues. See pages 687–688.

14a.   Correct. By carrying the nation's twelve largest cities, the Democratic party demonstrated that it was gaining power in the urban areas of the country. See page 690.

14b.   No. Al Smith, the Democratic presidential nominee in 1928, carried eight states to Herbert Hoover's forty. Six of these were southern states from which he gained 69 of his 87 electoral votes. See page 690.

14c.   No. The election indicated that Republicans had actually lost support in areas that were becoming more important in presidential elections. See page 690.

14d.   No. The Republican party was still the majority party—that is, a majority of the people who were registered to vote were registered as Republicans. See page 690.

15a.   No. The Hoover administration, like the Harding and Coolidge administrations, adhered to the laissez-faire philosophy and did not "impose" regulations on businesses. See page 692.

15b.   No. The government followed a policy of lowering income-tax rates, especially on the wealthy. Therefore, the tax policies of the government did not take large sums of money out of circulation. Furthermore, between 1920 and 1929, the after-tax income of the wealthiest 1 percent rose 75 percent as opposed to the average per-capita increase of 9 percent. This extra disposable income in the hands of the wealthy tended to fuel speculation in the stock market. See page 692.

15c.   Correct. The Board's easy-credit policy before 1931 fueled speculation in the stock market, and its shift to a tight-money policy after 1931 denied the economy of funds needed for economic recovery. See page 692.

15d.   No. The government did not give aid to organized labor. Furthermore, economic distress among farmers, factory layoffs, technological unemployment, and low wages caused production to outstrip demand. See page 692.

Chapter 25

Multiple-Choice Questions

1a.   No. Despite the hardships endured by Americans during the Great Depression, most people did not blame "the system" and they did not turn to radical movements as a solution to their despair. See page 698.

1b.   No. Divorce rates declined from 206,000 in 1929 to 164,000 in 1932. See page 698.

1c.   Correct. As a result of the Great Depression people postponed marriage. Furthermore, married couples postponed having children, causing the birthrate to fall from 21.3 live births per 1,000 in 1930 to 18.4 in 1933. See page 698.

1d.   No. As amazing as it seems, although many Americans suffered from malnutrition and others died of starvation, a surplus of basic agricultural commodities piled up in the Farm Belt. Although overproduction caused low food prices, unemployed Americans lacked money to buy food. See page 698.

2a.   No. Although government policies contributed to the crash and to the Great Depression, most people did not blame the government for the depression. See page 698.

2b.   No. In spite of the fact that the Great Depression may be seen as a major crisis within the capitalist system, Americans continued to accept capitalism and did not, as a general rule, lash out against that system in a violent way. See page 698.

2c.   No. Although there was disillusionment, the failure of both the Communist and Socialist parties to make major gains indicates that most Americans did not turn to ideologies that might advocate revolution and that the masses did not seriously contemplate revolution. See page 698.

2d.   Correct. In spite of the fact that the capitalist system was "on its knees," most Americans continued to believe in that system, continued to demonstrate loyalty to their government, and blamed themselves for the Great Depression. See page 698.

3a.   Correct. Hoover saw the Bonus marchers as extremists, refused to meet with them after Congress defeated the Bonus Bill, and finally called out the army to attack and disperse the Bonus Expeditionary Force encamped in Washington. See pages 698–699.

3b.   No. Hoover remained steadfast in his belief in limited government, in individual initiative, and in self-help. He never suggested establishing a comprehensive pension plan for future veterans. See pages 698–699.

3c.   No. President Hoover urged Congress to defeat the Bonus Bill. See pages 698–699.

3d.   No. Hoover refused to meet with leaders of the Bonus Expeditionary Force. See pages 698–699.

4a.   No. The RFC was not based on the basic assumption of "supply-side" economics. See page 700.

4b.   No. Hoover's reluctant support for the chartering of the RFC indicates that Hoover had gradually moved toward the idea of a more active federal role in dealing with the economic crisis and that by 1932 he was willing to accept limited federal "interference." See page 700.

4c.   Correct. The RFC is an example of "trickle-down" economic theory: money in the hands of the wealthy will trickle down to the masses. See page 700.

4d.   No. The RFC was not a tax measure and was not based on the theory that taxes are a disincentive to economic recovery. See page 700.

5a.   No. When governor of New York, Roosevelt did not believe in deficit spending, and his actions as governor do not indicate such a philosophy. See page 702.

5b.   Correct. Some of Roosevelt's actions and suggestions as governor of New York indicated a willingness to use government to combat the depression and, in doing so, to experiment in finding solutions to the problems posed by the depression. See page 702.

5c.   No. Roosevelt's actions as governor of New York do not indicate that Roosevelt wanted to embark on a trust-busting program. See page 702.

5d.   No. Roosevelt believed that it was the responsibility of government to extend direct relief to the jobless. His support for New York's Temporary Emergency Relief Administration is an indication of that belief. See page 702.

6a.   Correct. An assumption on which the AAA and the NIRA were based was that overproduction was the major factor preventing economic recovery. Therefore, through centralized national planning, farmers and industries would be encouraged to produce less. See pages 704–705.

6b.   No. The AAA sought to raise the prices of farm goods, and the NIRA attempted to do the same for manufactured goods. See pages 704–705.

6c.   No. Neither the AAA or the NIRA called for deficit spending. See pages 704–705.

6d.   No. Both the AAA and the NIRA demonstrated Roosevelt's willingness to deal with problems from the national level. See pages 704–705.

7a.   No. Unemployment insurance was first provided to some workers through the Social Security Act of 1935. See page 705.

7b.   No. Pension plans were not required under the NIRA. See page 705.

7c.   Correct. Because of concessions given to businesses under the NIRA, employers in turn had to accept the right of workers to unionize and bargain collectively. See page 705.

7d.   No. Section 7(a) of the NIRA did not require workers to join company-sponsored unions. See page 705.

8a.   No. Many conservative critics were business leaders. Rather than complaining about the close relationship between government and industry, they complained that there was too much government regulation of business. See page 709.

8b.   No. Conservatives were critical of relief programs such as the CCC and the FERA and claimed that such programs were based on socialist ideology. See page 709.

8c.   No. Conservatives, who believed that the economy should be allowed to operate in accordance with natural economic laws, criticized the Roosevelt administration for centralized economic planning. See page 709.

8d.   Correct. Conservatives believed that people should overcome personal hardships through self-reliance and individual initiative. Therefore, they charged that programs like the CCC and the FERA destroyed individual initiative. See page 709.

9a.   No. Although Long believed that the New Deal was too closely allied with business interests, he did not advocate nationalizing all major industry in the United States. See page 711.

9b.   No. Long proposed a homestead *allowance* of $5,000, but did not propose actually giving land. Furthermore, families did not have to request the allowance. See page 711.

9c.   Correct. Long proposed that the government provide a guaranteed annual income of $2,000 to every American family. See page 711.

9d.   No. Although Long proposed a free college education for every American, he did not propose a national health insurance program. See page 711.

10a.   No. The First Amendment deals with freedom of religion, speech, and the press and the right to assemble peacefully and petition the government for redress of grievances. The Court did not find that the NIRA abridged these rights. See page 711.

10b.   Correct. One of the grounds on which part of the NIRA was declared unconstitutional was that it delegated excessive legislative power to the executive branch of the government. See page 711.

10c.   No. The Court held part of the NIRA to be unconstitutional because it regulated businesses that were wholly involved in intrastate commerce, but it did not hold that the act discriminated against small businesses. See page 711.

10d.   No. The Court did not rule that the NIRA was in violation of the Fourteenth Amendment. See page 711.

11a.   Correct. Roosevelt believed that business leaders had placed their own interests above those of the nation. Therefore, during the Second New Deal, Roosevelt abandoned business-government cooperation and, to "cut the giants down to size," moved to enforce antitrust laws. See page 712.

11b.   No. Both the First and the Second New Deals reflect Roosevelt's belief that the government could act as a positive force in American society. Therefore, he did not return to the idea of passive government embodied in the laissez-faire philosophy. See page 712.

11c.   No. Although Roosevelt remained a fiscal conservative and was committed to a balanced budget, deficit spending characterized both the First and the Second New Deals. See page 712.

11d.   No. Both the First and the Second New Deals strengthened the role of the federal government. However, state and local governments were given the task of implementing much of the legislation passed under both New Deals. See page 712.

12a.   No. Although the Social Security Act established an old-age insurance program, the law did not apply to all workers. See page 713.

12b.   Correct. Although the law was a relatively conservative measure and did not apply to all workers, it established the idea of government responsibility toward the aged, dependent, and disabled. See page 713.

12c.   No. The Social Security Act authorized money grants to the states for public health work, but it did not establish a national health insurance program. See page 713.

12d.   No. The measure is considered relatively conservative because benefits were to be paid by workers and employers, not by the government. See page 713.

13a.   No. Although Roosevelt's intention in cutting federal spending was to achieve a balanced budget, this was not the end result. See pages 713–714.

13b.   No. At the same time that Roosevelt cut spending, the Federal Reserve Board tightened credit, causing interest rates to rise. See pages 713–714.

13c.   No. At the same time that Roosevelt cut federal spending, the Federal Reserve Board tightened credit. This, in turn, caused business to cut back on spending for capital improvements. See pages 713–714.

13d.   Correct. The massive spending cuts ordered by Roosevelt in 1937, along with the tightening of credit by the Federal Reserve Board, caused a recession. As a result, Roosevelt returned to deficit spending, which brought some economic recovery by 1939. See pages 713–714.

14a.   No. Skilled workers were already heavily involved in the labor movement through the American Federation of Labor. See page 714.

14b.   Correct. Workers in many major industries began to organize in industrial unions, such as the UMW and the UAW. See page 714.

14c.   No. Organized labor did not consist of farm workers. See page 714.

14d.   No. White-collar workers were not organizing in the 1930s. See page 714.

15a.   No. These measures did not bring about a redistribution of wealth. See pages 719–720.

15b.   No. Money spent on these programs tended to benefit middle- and lower-income groups, not the wealthy. See pages 719–720.

15c.   No. The AAA and TVA helped people in rural areas more than people in urban areas, and the FHA and CCC benefited people in both areas. See pages 719–720.

15d.   Correct. In operation, all of these acts indicate an antiblack bias and demonstrate that although blacks benefited from the New Deal, they did not get their fair share. See pages 719–720.

Chapter 26

Multiple-Choice Questions

1a.   Correct. Secretary of State Hughes accepted the philosophy that economic expansion was necessary for world peace. As a result, he supported passage of legislation intended to foster international trade. See page 731.

1b.   No. Secretary of State Hughes did not focus on the competition and rivalry that would accompany economic expansion. See page 731.

1c.   No. Secretary of State Hughes did not encourage economic expansion abroad out of a desire to increase the power of the United States at the expense of "less virtuous" European nations. See page 731.

1d.   No. Secretary of State Hughes did not encourage economic expansion abroad as a means by which the United States could promote economic nationalism. See page 731.

2a.   No. None of the treaties negotiated at the Washington Conference placed limits on the construction of submarines, destroyers, or cruisers—the most destructive weapons of the age. See page 733.

2b.   Correct. As one of a total of three treaties that came out of the Washington Conference, the Five-Power Treaty provided for a ten-year moratorium on the construction of capital ships and established a ratio of capital ships. Britain, the United States, and Japan had to dismantle some ships to meet the ratio. See page 733.

2c.   No. In the Nine-Power Treaty, all the nations represented at the Washington Conference agreed to respect Chinese sovereignty and to accept the Open Door principle. See page 733.

2d.   No. The Five-Power Treaty was drafted at the Washington Conference of 1921–1922. The Nazis were not in power in Germany at that time. See page 733.

3a.   No. No treaty signed during the 1920s placed limits on the number of submarines and destroyers to be built by the five major powers. See page 733.

3b.   No. No limits were placed on international arms sales during the 1920s. See page 733.

3c.   No. Although it is true that the United States began to send observers to League conferences, this was not accomplished by the Kellogg-Briand Pact. See page 733.

3d.   Correct. The Kellogg-Briand Pact, signed by sixty-two nations in 1928, condemned war as a way of solving international problems and renounced war as an instrument of national policy. See page 733.

4a.   No. Even though it worked a hardship on the debtor nations, the United States insisted that they pay their debts in full. This does not indicate a selfless handling of the war-debt issue. See page 736.

4b.   Correct. American loans to Germany, German reparations payments to the Allies, and Allied war-debt payments to the United States created a triangular arrangement that depended on German borrowing in the United States and was economically destabilizing. See page 736.

4c.   No. The Allies forced Germany to accept guilt for the First World War and insisted that Germany pay the $33 billion reparations bill levied by the Allies. See page 736.

4d.   No. The idea that the German government used the war-debt and reparations issue to create tensions between the United States and Great Britain is not a logical inference that can be drawn from the evidence presented. See page 736.

5a.   Correct. This tariff measure raised rates an average of 8 percent. As a result, many European nations were priced out of the United States market. In response, the European nations retaliated by raising tariff rates against American imports. See pages 736–737.

5b.   No. European imports to the United States declined as a result of the Hawley-Smoot Tariff. See pages 736–737.

5c.   No. The Hawley-Smoot Tariff was a general tariff measure and did not deal specifically with the Open Door policy, which applied to China. See pages 736–737.

5d.   No. Since most American imports came from Europe, the Hawley-Smoot Tariff primarily affected trade relations with that area. Therefore, this tariff did not give Japan a reason to impose an embargo against American products. See pages 736–737.

6a.   No. Although this act authorized the president to lower American tariffs by as much as 50 percent through special agreements with foreign countries, the United States did not adopt a free trade position. Such a position would have meant repealing all tariffs. See page 737.

6b.   No. This act did not offer low-interest loans to countries agreeing to buy American goods. See page 737.

6c.   Correct. Any nation entering into regular trade agreements with the United States would be given tariff rates matching those given to the "most-favored nation." This principle was important because it brought an overall lowering of tariff rates and fostered economic internationalism. See page 737.

6d.   No. This act moved toward freer trade but did not establish a free trade zone within the Western Hemisphere. See page 737.

7a.   No. In spite of the Good Neighbor Policy, the United States saw order in Latin American as vital to its national interests. As a result, it was not willing to "strictly adhere" to the doctrine of nonintervention. See pages 739–740.

7b.   Correct. Some methods used by the United States to maintain its influence in Latin America had become counterproductive. Therefore, the Good Neighbor Policy was an attempt to use less controversial and less blatant means to accomplish the same end. See pages 739–740.

7c.   No. In spite of the Good Neighbor Policy, American businesses in Latin America continued to take their profits out of the region and invest them elsewhere (a process known as decapitalization). See pages 739–740.

7d.   No. The Good Neighbor Policy certainly did not mean that the United States would practice isolationism in Latin America. Rather, it included ways for the United States to stay involved in more subtle ways. See pages 739–740.

8a.   No. Trujillo and Somoza ruled as dictators in their respective nations. This does not indicate the acceptance and growth of American concepts of government. See pages 739–740.

8b.   No. Trujillo and Somoza, who were supported by the United States government, ruled through the use of fraud and intimidation. They did not have the support of the masses of people in their respective countries. See pages 739–740.

8c.   Correct. Trujillo and Somoza became leaders of a United States-trained national guard in their respective countries, and each used that position to gain dictatorial powers. See pages 739–740.

8d.   No. The United States was interested in order, not in national liberation movements, in Latin America. See pages 739–740.

9a.   Correct. Britain and France, following the policy of appeasement, accepted Hitler's seizure of the Sudetenland in September 1938. Hitler proceeded to take the rest of Czechoslovakia in March 1939. Then, in September 1939, when German forces attacked Poland, Britain and France declared war on Germany. See page 742.

9b.   No. The British made no such pledge to France in the years leading up to the Second World War. See page 742.

9c.   No. The Munich Conference did not result in a defensive alliance among Britain, France, and the Soviet Union against Nazi Germany. See page 742.

9d.   No. At the time of the Munich Conference, Germany had seized the Rhineland (March 1936) and Austria (March 1938). Germany did not withdraw its troops from either area as a result of the conference. See page 742.

10a.   No. Hearings by the Nye Committee indicate that some United States corporations lobbied against arms control and attempted to increase arms sales to foreign nations during the 1920s and 1930s. See page 744.

10b.   Correct. After Italy's invasion of Ethiopia, Roosevelt invoked an arms embargo against Italy as required by the Neutrality Act of 1935. The act did not require a ban on petroleum, copper, and iron and steel scrap exports; and, despite Roosevelt's call for a moral embargo on these products, exports of these items to Italy increased. See page 744.

10c.   No. Records indicate that twenty-six of the top one hundred United States firms still had contractual agreements with Germany in 1937, four years after Hitler and the Nazis came to power. See page 744.

10d.   No. Many United States firms continued to maintain lucrative economic ties with Germany after learning about the persecution of Jews. One exception was the Wall Street firm of Sullivan and Cromwell, which severed economic ties with Germany to protest Hitler's anti-Semitic practices. See page 744.

11a.   No. The intent of the Neutrality Acts was to prevent the United States from being drawn into war, not to provide aid to the Allies. See page 744.

11b.   No. The Neutrality Acts contained no arms-control provisions. See page 744.

11c.   No. In 1937, the United States declared itself neutral in the Spanish Civil War and Roosevelt embargoed arms shipments to both sides. See page 744.

11d.   Correct. Congress believed that bankers and munitions-makers had dragged the United States into the First World War. To prevent this from recurring, Congress passed the Neutrality Acts, which required a mandatory arms embargo against and forbade loans to all belligerents. See page 744.

12a.   No. Although Roosevelt was sympathetic toward the British and saw Germany, Italy, and Japan as "bandit nations," he did not respond to the outbreak of war by promising American involvement if British defeat seemed imminent. See page 745.

12b.   Correct. In spite of strong lobbying efforts by isolationists and the presence of strong opposition in Congress, the arms embargo, at Roosevelt's urging, was repealed in November 1939 and the sale of arms was placed on a cash-and-carry basis. See page 745.

12c.   No. Although the United States condemned Russia's nonaggression pact with Hitler and the subsequent Russo-German conquest and partition of Poland, Washington did not break diplomatic relations with the Soviet Union. See page 745.

12d.   No. In response to the outbreak of war in Europe, President Roosevelt declared the United States to be a neutral nation. See page 745.

13a.   Correct. President Hoover, who was grappling with the problems of the Great Depression and who realized that the United States did not have the naval power to risk a Pacific war, refused to authorize anything stronger than the Stimson Doctrine, which was a moral condemnation of the Japanese. See pages 746–747.

13b.   No. The United States did not take definitive economic action against Japan in response to that nation's 1931 invasion of Manchuria, and Japanese assets were not frozen until after the Japanese occupation of southern Indochina in July 1941. See pages 746–747.

13c.   No. President Hoover refused to cooperate with the League in imposing economic sanctions on Japan. See pages 746–747.

13d.   No. The United States continued to follow a foreign policy characterized by nonalignment with foreign nations. See pages 746–747.

14a.   No. In September 1940, in the midst of the Battle of Britain, Roosevelt concluded the Destroyer-Bases Agreement with Great Britain. By this agreement, the United States traded fifty old destroyers to the British for ninety-nine-year leases to eight British bases in Newfoundland and the Caribbean. See page 750.

14b.   No. The Neutrality Acts of 1935, 1936, and 1937 were slightly modified in 1939; and, although the Lend-Lease Act may be considered a further modification, it did not "revoke" the provisions of the Neutrality Acts. See page 750.

14c.   Correct. Designed primarily to aid the British, who were running out of money, the Lend-Lease Act (March 1941) authorized the president to transfer, sell, exchange, lend, or lease war materiel to any country whose defense was considered vital to the United States. See page 750.

14d.   No. In 1931–1932, President Hoover and Congress refused to cancel Allied debts incurred during the First World War. As a result, European nations were forced to default, but that happened some ten years before the Lend-Lease Act. See page 750.

15a.   No. After the Japanese occupation of Indochina, Roosevelt's advisers, acting on the president's advice, tried to prolong talks with the Japanese so that the Philippines could be fortified and the fascists checked in Europe. See pages 752–753.

15b.   No. The United States had broken the Japanese code and knew by December 1 that Japan had decided on war with the United States if the oil embargo was not lifted. See pages 752–753.

15c.   Correct. The United States government knew of Japan's war plans but did not know where or when Japan would strike. When the location was learned, the telegram informing the base commanders at Pearl Harbor was delayed. See pages 752–753.

15d.   No. The United States government and the base commanders at Pearl Harbor expected an attack at British Malaya, Thailand, or the Philippines. See pages 752–753.

Chapter 27

Multiple-Choice Questions

1a.   No. The Soviet Union, the United States, and Great Britain were allies against Nazi Germany in the Second World War. Although Roosevelt might have had some concern about future Russian expansion, that concern did not initially cause him to want to open a second front in 1942. See page 761.

1b.   No. The North African campaign, which began in November 1942, was undertaken at Churchill's insistence and meant the postponement of a second front. See page 761.

1c.   No. Churchill assertively argued against the opening of a second front in Europe in 1942. See page 761.

1d.   Correct. In the European land war in 1942, Russia continued to suffer the brunt of the German onslaught. In light of this, Roosevelt was concerned that Russia might sue for a separate peace, leaving Germany free to invade England. See page 761.

2a.   Correct. Meeting at Teheran in December 1943, the Allies agreed, at the insistence of Roosevelt and Stalin, to open the long-delayed second front. In return, Stalin agreed that Russia would enter the war in the Pacific once Germany was defeated. See page 763.

2b.   No. The North Africa campaign began in November 1942 and ended in Allied victory in May 1943. The Teheran Conference was held in December 1943. See page 763.

2c.   No. Although it is true that General Eisenhower recognized the pro-Nazi Vichy regime in French North Africa, he did so at the time of the Allied invasion of North Africa, which was some thirteen months prior to the Teheran Conference. See page 763.

2d.   No. The battle for Stalingrad ended in Russian victory in January 1943, eleven months before the Teheran Conference. See page 763.

3a.   No. The United States did not destroy Japan's merchant marine as a result of the Battle of Midway. See page 763.

3b.   Correct. As a result of Operation Magic, American experts deciphered the secret Japanese code. With prior knowledge of Japanese plans, American forces sank four of Japan's aircraft carriers in the Battle of Midway and broke the enemy's momentum in the Pacific. See page 763.

3c.   No. The Battle of Midway did not make Hawaii more vulnerable to attack. See page 763.

3d.   No. The Battle of Midway did not cause Roosevelt to harbor fears of Japanese victory. See page 763.

4a.   No. Truman knew that victory over Japan was virtually assured and did not totally depend on use of the atomic bomb. See page 767.

4b.   No. Germany surrendered on May 8, 1945, three months before the first atomic bomb was dropped on Hiroshima on August 6. See page 767.

4c.   No. The decision to use the atomic bomb was made unilaterally by the United States. Not only did the United States not consult the Allies, but at Potsdam Truman chose not to tell the Soviet Union of the successful atomic test in the New Mexico desert. See page 767.

4d.   Correct. Truman decided to drop the bomb for several reasons: (1) it would save American lives by ending the war quickly; (2) it might deter future aggression; (3) it might prevent Soviet entry into the war in the Pacific, thus preventing the Soviet Union from having a role in the reconstruction of postwar Asia; and (4) in the face of United States power, it might cause the Soviet Union to make concessions in Eastern Europe. See page 767.

5a.   No. Cooperation between government and business was essential for successful execution of the war effort. As a result, the government guaranteed that companies would be exempt from antitrust prosecution during the war. See page 768.

5b.   No. Since the government had to produce war materiel in the shortest time possible, competitive bidding was usually not possible. Although some attempts were made to award contracts to small businesses, most government contracts were awarded to big businesses. See page 768.

5c.   Correct. Factories had to be converted from production of consumer goods to production of war materiel. This was the WPB's first task, a task at which it was very successful. See page 768.

5d.   No. The WPB was not responsible for analyzing the military situation. The efforts of the WPB were more concentrated on the home front. See page 768.

6a.   No. Under the Smith-Connally Act, the NWLB's powers were broadened to include the legal authority to settle labor disputes until the end of the war. See page 770.

6b.   No. Although the act established a mandatory thirty-day cooling-off period before a strike could be called in a war-related industry, it did not prohibit strikes and made no reference to lockouts (the shutdown of a plant to bring workers to terms). See page 770.

6c.   No. The Smith-Connally Act did not guarantee cost-of-living increases in defense-related industries. See page 770.

6d.   Correct. This act, passed over President Roosevelt's veto, broadened the power of the president in handling labor disputes in war-related industries. See page 770.

7a.   No. The Second World War did not lead to a more vigorous enforcement of antitrust laws by the government and did not bring about the breakup of large economic units. See pages 768–770.

7b.   Correct. Since most government contracts were awarded to big corporations, the dominance of those corporations increased. Furthermore, the expense of farm machinery brought a decline in the number of family farms and led to agricultural consolidation. See pages 768–770.

7c.   No. During the Second World War the government poured massive sums of money into the economy. This may be seen by the increase of the national debt from $49 billion in 1941 to $259 billion in 1945. See pages 768–770.

7d.   No. The banking industry remained in private hands. See pages 768–770.

8a.   Correct. Many soldiers who had never seen the world beyond their own cities, farms, and neighborhoods came into contact with other Americans and with peoples from other cultures. See pages 771–772.

8b.   No. In many instances, the technical training that soldiers received in the military served to foster their ambitions and to give them skills that made them more employable in the postwar years. See pages 771–772.

8c.   No. Soldiers went through basic training in which they learned skills basic to combat. In addition, many received advanced training in specialty areas through the military's technical schools. See pages 771–772.

8d.   No. Many soldiers were given orientation lectures and booklets that introduced them to the historical backgrounds and social customs of the foreign nations in which they served. See pages 771–772.

9a.   No. The evidence does not support the conclusion that Japanese Americans were interned because of criminal behavior. As the authors point out: "Charges of criminal behavior were never brought against any Japanese Americans; none was ever indicted or tried for espionage, treason, or sedition." See page 772.

9b.   No. Japanese Americans were not engaged in treasonable activities and did not display disloyalty toward the United States government. See page 772.

9c.   Correct. Japanese Americans, most of whom were native-born citizens, were interned in "relocation centers" because of their Japanese descent. See page 772.

9d.   No. Although many of those who were engaged in economic competition with Japanese Americans spoke in favor of internment, this competition was not the major reason for that action. See page 772.

10a.   Correct. The movement of some 1.5 million blacks to industrial cities in the North and West, where they could exercise the right to vote, increased the political power of blacks in national, state, and local elections. See page 775.

10b.   No. Blacks continued to experience political, economic, and social discrimination during World War II. See page 775.

10c.   No. Overall, the economic position of African Americans improved during World War II. See page 775.

10d.   No. African Americans eagerly participated in and supported the American war effort. See page 775.

11a.   No. Roosevelt's victory in 1944 may be considered a landslide in terms of the electoral vote (432 to 99), but his margin of victory in the popular vote was his narrowest ever. See page 780.

11b.   Correct. Victory was in sight in 1944, but many people were apprehensive about the postwar domestic economy. Remembering New Deal relief programs, they preferred Roosevelt over Dewey as a kind of insurance against hard times. See page 780.

11c.   No. The South remained solidly Democratic in the 1944 election. See page 780.

11d.   No. Roosevelt, not Truman, was the Democratic standard-bearer in the 1944 presidential election. See page 780.

12a.   Correct. Both United States immigration policy and the voyage of the *St. Louis* indicate reluctance by the United States to deal decisively with the Jewish refugee problem. Decisive action was not taken until 1944, when Roosevelt created the War Refugee Board. See pages 781–782.

12b.   No. The United States refused to relax its immigration rules and restrictions. As a result many Jewish refugees were turned away because they did not have the legal documents required. See pages 781–782.

12c.   No. The British refused to open Palestine to Jewish refugees. See pages 781–782.

12d.   No. The death camp at Nordhausen was not bombed by U.S. forces. See pages 781–782.

13a.   No. Although Roosevelt was physically ill while attending the Yalta Conference, the evidence indicates that he was mentally alert and that his health was not a factor in the decisions reached. See page 782.

13b.   No. Stalin, rather than Churchill, argued in favor of German reparations. The United States and Russia, without British acceptance, agreed to a rough figure of $20 billion "as a basis for discussion in the future." See page 782.

13c.   Correct. Because of the military positions of the Allied armies, the United States and Great Britain still needed the Soviet Union to win the war. This, and the fact that Russia occupied Eastern Europe, greatly affected decisions at Yalta. See page 782.

13d.   No. Recognition of China as a major power was an American demand, not a Russian demand. See page 782.

14a.   No. About 357,000 Britons died as a result of the Second World War, but the British did not suffer the highest number of casualties in the war. See page 784.

14b.   No. About 405,000 Americans died as a result of the Second World War, but this figure was far lower than the number of war dead in other countries. See page 784.

14c.   No. Although the Japanese lost some 2 million people in the war, this loss was ten times less than the casualties experienced by the country with the highest number of war dead. See page 784.

14d.   Correct. The Soviet Union lost some 20 million people in the Second World War. As a result, security was Russia's primary interest in the postwar era. See page 784.

15a.   No. Great Britain came out of the Second World War with far less power than when it entered the war. As a result, the British empire was quite vulnerable. See page 784.

15b.   Correct. The United States was the only power to emerge from the Second World War more powerful than when it entered. See page 784.

15c.   No. Japan lay in ruins at the end of World War II. See page 784.

15d.   No. The Soviet Union suffered enormously as a result of the war and emerged less powerful than when it entered. See page 784.

Chapter 28

Multiple-Choice Questions

1a.   No. Both the Progressive party candidate (Henry Wallace) and the Dixiecrat candidate (Strom Thurmond) continued their independent campaigns for the presidency through election day. See pages 791–792.

1b.   No. The Democratic party, not the Republican party, was divided in 1948. See pages 791–792.

1c.   Correct. The Eightieth Congress (1947–1949), dominated by Republicans, rejected most of Truman's proposals. Even when they were called into special session and told to enact the planks in the Republican party platform, they balked. As a result, they alienated many interest groups. See pages 791–792.

1d.   No. The Republican party had taken a conservative stance on most issues and was perceived by the electorate as more conservative than the Democratic party. See pages 791–792.

2a.   No. During the 1950s, most Americans paid little attention to the "faults" of American society, shunned idealistic causes, and saw society's critics as maladjusted. See page 794.

2b.   Correct. During the 1950s, most Americans unquestioningly accepted American society. Their belief that the country was engaged in a moral crusade against communism led most Americans to believe liberal reform was unnecessary. See page 794.

2c.   No. During the 1950s, most Americans were convinced of their ability to stand against any foe. See page 794.

2d.   No. During the 1950s, most Americans trusted and respected those in positions of authority and seldom questioned their decisions. See page 794.

3a.   No. The intent of the termination policy was to dissolve Indian reservations, not expand them. See page 795.

3b.   No. Although one in eight Indians left the reservations between 1954 and 1960, it cannot be said that they were either "successfully relocated" or "successfully assimilated." See page 795.

3c.   Correct. In this attempt to dissolve reservations and end federal services to Native Americans, many Indians were displaced and many joined the ranks of the urban poor. See page 795.

3d.   No. This was not a program designed to aid Indians in the extraction of natural resources from tribal lands. See page 795.

4a.   Correct. Although McCarthy was probably the most successful redbaiter in the country, conservative and liberal politicians, labor leaders, religious leaders, and others used the public's fear of communism against their opponents. They all contributed to the anti-Communist hysteria known as McCarthyism. See pages 796–797.

4b.   No. There was no such treaty. See pages 796–797.

4c.   No. Communist party membership declined from 83,000 in 1947 to 25,000 in 1954. See pages 796–797.

4d.   No. Henry Wallace was a liberal Democrat, not a Communist, and no such conspiracy existed. See pages 796–797.

5a.   No. The bill passed the Senate unanimously. See page 800.

5b.   No. No Republicans were expelled from the party for having opposed this act. See page 800.

5c.   Correct. This act, which made membership in the Communist party illegal, was passed with no dissenting votes by the Senate and with only two dissenting votes by the House. This indicates that both liberals and conservatives shared in the anti-Communist consensus of the age. See page 800.

5d.   No. There was little disagreement within either party over passage of this act. Furthermore, the Democrats retained control of both houses of Congress in the 1954 elections. See page 800.

6a.   No. Congress did not pass effective voting rights legislation until 1965. See page 801.

6b.   Correct. The gap between American ideals and the realities of American society made it difficult to compete with the Soviet Union among the Third World nonaligned nations. To win the support of these nations, the United States had to begin to live up to its ideals. See page 801.

6c.   No. Although Truman sent a special message to Congress in February 1948 calling for federal antilynching and anti-poll tax laws, southern congressmen were openly opposed to such legislation and Congress never formally responded to the message. See page 801.

6d.   No. Congress did not outlaw the Klan. See page 801.

7a.   No. The *Brown* decision did not declare the poll tax to be unconstitutional. Use of the poll tax to abridge a citizen's right to vote was not made illegal nationally until ratification of the Twenty-fourth Amendment in 1964. See pages 802–803.

7b.   Correct. The NAACP's legal campaign against desegregation scored a major victory when the Court ruled separate educational facilities to be "inherently unequal." See pages 802–803.

7c.   No. In the *Brown* decision, the Supreme Court found that black Americans had suffered from segregated public educational institutions. See pages 802–803.

7d.   No. It was not until 1964 that the Civil Rights Act of that year made discrimination in public accommodations illegal. This was upheld by the Court in the same year. See pages 802–803.

8a.   No. The policy of accommodation is associated with Booker T. Washington, not with Martin Luther King, Jr. See pages 803–804.

8b.   No. Martin Luther King, Jr., did not urge his followers to accept a socialist philosophy. See pages 803–804.

8c.   Correct. King had studied and was impressed by the nonviolent philosophy of Mahatma Gandhi of India. See pages 803–804.

8d.   No. Black Power was a concept put forward by Stokely Carmichael in the late 1960s. See pages 803–804.

9a.   No. Although stocks and bonds rose in value, most Americans did not invest heavily in the stock market. Furthermore, rising stock values do not automatically translate into real money or increased purchasing power. See page 805.

9b.   No. Although the nation's GNP rose from $286.5 billion in 1950 to $506.5 billion in 1960, this rise was a *consequence* of the consumer culture rather than the economic *basis* of that culture. See page 805.

9c.   Correct. Americans were able to purchase consumer goods because of the availability of credit. See page 805.

9d.   No. The computer, although an important technological achievement of the age, did not put money into the hands of consumers, allowing them to purchase consumer goods. Therefore, the computer was not the economic basis of the consumer culture. See page 805.

10a.   No. The number of births exceeded 4 million per year through the 1950s and into the 1960s. All these extra people had a ripple effect throughout the economy. See page 806.

10b.   No. The urban middle class, consisting of professionals, white-collar workers, and college graduates, contributed disproportionately to the baby boom. See page 806.

10c.   No. Many people having second, third, and fourth children had demonstrated in the past that they knew how to practice birth control, but during the 1950s they chose not to do so. See page 806.

10d.   Correct. Prosperity during the 1950s and early 1960s created a mood of optimism in American society. Because of this optimism, many Americans chose to have more children. See page 806.

11a.   No. Farming methods continued to be revolutionized by the introduction of new machines. See page 810.

11b.   No. The value of farm output increased by 120 percent from 1945 to 1970. See page 810.

11c.   Correct. The increase in land values and in the cost of machinery and fertilizers meant that farming became more expensive. As a result, there was a movement toward agricultural consolidation and away from the family farm. See page 810.

11d.   No. Farm-labor productivity increased threefold between 1945 and 1970. See page 810.

12a.   No. The Kinsey reports deal with sexual behavior among American men and women and do not emphasize "family togetherness." See page 811.

12b.   Correct. Many parents of the 1950s had suffered economic deprivation during the 1930s and separation from their families during the 1940s. As a result, they emphasized family togetherness in the 1950s. See page 811.

12c.   No. Television shows often reflected the emphasis that society placed on family togetherness, but they were not the primary cause of that emphasis. See page 811.

12d.   No. Riesman, a sociologist, was a critic of suburban living and of the isolation that families experienced as a result of the emphasis on "family togetherness." See page 811.

13a.   No. The "bebop" style is associated with developments in jazz during the 1940s and 1950s, when musicians such as Dizzy Gillespie began to experiment with complicated chord patterns. See page 815.

13b.   No. The Beats are not associated with new advertising techniques. See page 815.

13c.   No. The Beats were not rock-'n'-roll performers. See page 815.

13d.   Correct. The Beats challenged the consensus of the 1950s by questioning the materialism of consumer culture. They openly flaunted their sexual freedom and consumption of drugs. Their writings and lifestyle inspired the counterculture of the 1960s. See page 815.

14a.   Correct. In 1960 the median annual earnings for full-time women workers were 60 percent of men's earnings. One reason for this disparity was occupational segregation of women into low-paying "women's jobs." See pages 815–816.

14b.   No. Many husbands failed to pay child support and were seldom prosecuted for nonpayment; nevertheless, the courts still awarded child-support payments in divorce proceedings. See pages 815–816.

14c.   No. Although more women were getting more education, "overeducation" was not the reason a woman was more likely than a man to be poor. See pages 815–816.

14d.   No. Women were not more likely to suffer from catastrophic illnesses than men. See pages 815–816.

15a.   No. Black Americans generally continued to suffer from economic discrimination and particularly from discrimination in housing practices. As a result, blacks continued to congregate in the inner-city ghettos. See page 816.

15b.   Correct. Although the black population was 48.6 percent urban in 1940, by 1970 it was 81.3 percent urban. See page 816.

15c.   No. Blacks continued to move from the South to the North. See page 816.

15d.   No. Although economic expansion and anti-poverty programs caused an overall decline in the number of poor, black Americans continued to experience economic discrimination, and poverty among blacks did not decrease "dramatically." See page 816.

Chapter 29

Multiple-Choice Questions

1a.   Correct. The data indicate that the economic well-being of the United States depended on maintaining the flow of United States goods into foreign markets. An activist foreign policy was a means by which to protect and expand foreign trade. See page 824.

1b.   No. The economic devastation of Europe seriously jeopardized America's export trade. See page 824.

1c.   No. The evidence supports the conclusion that the United States continued its policy of economic expansion. See page 824.

1d.   No. The automobile, steel, and machine-tool industries depended heavily on foreign trade. Furthermore, some 50 percent of American wheat was exported, and surplus tobacco and cotton were sold abroad. See page 824.

2a.   No. The Soviet Union saw a unified Germany as a threat to its security. See page 825.

2b.   Correct. Although the Soviet Union was allied with Great Britain and the United States during World War II, it remained suspicious that the West wanted to destroy its communist government and prevent its expansion. Therefore, as the United States began to build "situations of strength" throughout the world in the aftermath of the Second World War, the Soviet Union expressed fear of "capitalist encirclement" and acted to prevent such an occurrence. See page 825.

2c.   No. Had the Soviet Union played a substantial role in the Pacific War it could have claimed a right to share in the reconstruction of Japan. However, the use of the atomic bomb against Japan prevented the Soviets from playing such a role, and the United States monopolized Japan's reconstruction. See page 825.

2d.   No. A strong independent China was seen as a security risk to the Soviet Union. See page 825.

3a.   No. The Soviet Union emerged from World War II with a weakened military establishment and did not have the power to overrun Western Europe. See page 825.

3b.   No. The Soviet Union emerged from the Second World War with its economy in ruins. Furthermore, in the twentieth century, Russia had twice been invaded by Germany. As a result, Russia was fearful of the West. See page 825.

3c.   Correct. With its military establishment weakened, its economy hobbled, and its technology obsolete, Russia did not have the power to dominate the world in 1945. A logical inference that may be drawn from these facts is that Russia was a regional power, not a global menace in the years immediately after the war. See page 825.

3d.   No. Taking into consideration certain facts about the Russian past and the Soviet Union's view of the world in 1945, it would not be logical to conclude that the Soviet Union had no territorial ambitions in the immediate aftermath of World War II. See page 825.

4a.   No. The containment policy did not include a commitment to extend aid to the impoverished. See pages 827–828.

4b.   No. The containment policy did not make American aid conditional on a country's demonstration of its determination to help itself. See pages 827–828.

4c.   Correct. The containment policy, as expressed by Truman and Kennan, pledged unconditional aid to peoples resisting Communist expansion. See pages 827–828.

4d.   No. The containment doctrine did not emphasize the use of diplomacy in international relations. See pages 827–828.

5a.   No. Many American officials became convinced that Mao was a Soviet puppet. Therefore, when Mao made secret overtures to the United States to begin diplomatic talks in 1945 and 1949, he was rebuffed by American officials. See page 832.

5b.   No. Most American officials saw the Chinese civil war as part of the East-West conflict and did not recognize the nationalist nature of Mao's struggle against Jiang. See page 832.

5c.   No. The United States did take sides in the struggle between Jiang Jieshi and Mao Zedong. See page 832.

5d.   Correct. Most American officials believed Mao was part of an international Communist conspiracy and failed to see him as an independent Communist fighting for a China free from outside interference, and, therefore, free to control its own future. See page 832.

6a.   No. Although the United States was attempting to negotiate a cease-fire in the Chinese civil war in 1945, recognition of Vietnamese independence would not have jeopardized those negotiations. See page 833.

6b.   No. During the Second World War, Ho Chi Minh, a Vietnamese nationalist, worked with the American Office of Strategic Services against Japanese domination of his country. See page 833.

6c.   No. FDR never made such a pledge to France. See page 833.

6d.   Correct. American leaders failed to see Ho Chi Minh as a nationalist seeking independence from foreign domination. They could see him only as a Communist. See page 833.

7a.   No. The Soviet Union did give aid to North Korea during the course of the Korean War. See page 834.

7b.   Correct. The collapse of the Soviet Union led to the opening of previously classified Soviet documents. These documents reveal that North Korean President Kim Il Sung initiated the North Korean attack against South Korea in an attempt to achieve his own nationalist objectives. Stalin, in fact, only reluctantly approved the attack, and his support for North Korea remained lukewarm throughout the war. See page 834 and the "How Do Historians Know" section on page 835.

7c.   No. The Soviet Union was not sending military aid to South Korea. See page 834.

7d.   No. Although Kim Il Sung, the Communist leader of North Korea, probably decided to invade South Korea for nationalistic reasons and Joseph Stalin only reluctantly approved the attack, North Korea had not broken its ties with the Soviet Union. See page 834.

8a.   Correct. After MacArthur began publicly to question President Truman's war policies, Truman, with the backing of the Joint Chiefs of Staff, fired him for insubordination. See page 836.

8b.   No. MacArthur demanded that Truman allow an attack on China, but Truman never agreed to the policy because he was sure it would widen the war. See page 836.

8c.   No. MacArthur was not removed at the insistence of the U.N. Security Council. See page 836.

8d.   No. The Inchon landing (September 1950) was successful for the United Nations forces under McArthur's command and led to the liberation of Seoul, the South Korean capital. See page 836.

9a.   Correct. Eisenhower's desire to trim federal spending led to the New Look military. Based on the policies of "massive retaliation" and "deterrence," the New Look emphasized nuclear weaponry rather than conventional forces. See pages 838–839.

9b.   No. Eisenhower's New Look military did not involve a United Nations police force. See pages 838–839.

9c.   No. Eisenhower's New Look military de-emphasized conventional military force. See pages 838–839.

9d.   No. The New Look military did not involve Soviet-American cooperation in space. In 1957, the Soviets launched *Sputnik*, to the shock and surprise of many Americans. In response, the United States created the National Aeronautics and Space Agency in 1958. See pages 838–839.

10a.   No. The Soviet Union responded to an uprising against its power in Hungary by sending troops and tanks to crush the rebellion. This was not done because of American weakness, but the United States could not aid the rebels without risking war. See page 841.

10b.   Correct. The idea of a "missile gap" was a false notion used by partisan opponents of the Eisenhower administration. At the end of the 1950s, the United States continued to enjoy an overwhelming strategic advantage over the Soviet Union. See page 841.

10c.   No. The United States did not "back down" in the 1958 Berlin crisis. Furthermore, the United States was testing its own ICBMs and had more nuclear warheads than the Soviets. See page 841.

10d.   No. The Eisenhower administration quickly responded to *Sputnik* by creating the National Aeronautics and Space Agency. The Russians never "dangerously surpassed" the United States in missile technology. See page 841.

11a.   No. The islands were bombarded by the People's Republic of China, and this led to the signing of a mutual defense treaty between the United States and Nationalist China (Formosa) on December 2, 1954. The treaty was ratified by the Senate in February 1955. See page 842.

11b.   No. The United States continued to refuse to recognize the People's Republic of China as the legitimate Chinese government. See page 842.

11c.   Correct. In reaction to the crisis, the United States signed a mutual defense treaty with Formosa (December 2, 1954), Congress passed the Formosa Resolution (January 1955), and the United States installed tactical nuclear weapons on Formosa (1957). See page 842.

11d.   No. In response to Cold War pressures that increased the likelihood of a nuclear confrontation, Khrushchev called for "peaceful coexistence" between the United States and the Soviet Union. This was not in direct response to the Formosa crisis. See page 842.

12a.   Correct. The United States economy was dependent on exports of finished products, imports of strategic raw materials, and foreign investments. Therefore, disorder caused by nationalist revolutions in the Third World were seen as a threat to the American standard of living and partially explain why America was hostile toward such revolutions. See page 846.

12b.   No. Western Europe was economically devastated by the Second World War while the United States was not. In fact, in order to prevent economic discontent in Western Europe from leading to the emergence of extremists, the United States financed a massive European recovery program known as the Marshall Plan. See page 846.

12c.   No. Extensive American investments abroad did not cause improved relations with developing nations. See page 846.

12d.   No. The United States did not increase its commitment to the United Nations because of extensive American investments abroad. See page 846.

13a.   Correct. The United States stood against Third World revolutions that threatened the interests of America's allies and threatened American investments and markets. As a major world power interested in its own security, the United States desired order and stability. See page 846.

13b.   No. Racism in American society, rather than a negative reaction by diplomats to America's pluralistic society, made it difficult for the United States to make friends in the Third World. See page 846.

13c.   No. American business interests engaged in economic expansion and invested heavily in Third World countries. In 1959 over one-third of America's private foreign investments were in Third World countries. See page 846.

13d.   No. The Soviet Union enjoyed only a slight edge, if any, in the race to win friends in the Third World. See page 846.

14a.   No. In response to the trade treaty between Cuba and the Soviet Union, the United States cut off all economic aid to Cuba and drastically cut U.S. purchases of Cuban sugar. However, President Eisenhower did not cut off all trade with Cuba. See page 847.

14b.   No. The United States imposed an embargo on all exports to Cuba except food and medicine in the fall of 1960, but the United States did not establish a blockade of Cuba. See page 847.

14c.   Correct. After learning in February 1960 of the trade treaty that Cuba entered into with the Soviet Union, President Eisenhower ordered the CIA to organize an invasion force made up of Cuban exiles for the purpose of overthrowing the Castro government. In addition, President Eisenhower drastically cut U.S. purchases of Cuban sugar. See page 847.

14d.   No. The Eisenhower administration did not negotiate new trade agreements with Cuba after learning of the trade treaty between Cuba and the Soviet Union in February 1960. See page 847.

15a.   No. Neither Arbenz of Guatemala nor Mossadegh of Iran agreed to the deployment of Russian missiles in their countries. See pages 847–848.

15b.   No. Both Arbenz of Guatemala and Mossadegh of Iran were strongly nationalist in their views. As nationalists, they tended to view American interests in the Third World as exploitative. See pages 847–848.

15c.   No. You may be thinking of the 1954 test that destroyed the island of Bikini and caused the death of a crew member aboard the *Lucky Dragon.* See pages 847–848.

15d.   Correct. Both Arbenz of Guatemala and Mossadegh of Iran threatened the interests of American-owned companies operating in their countries. As a result, the CIA, through covert actions, aided in the overthrow of these men. See pages 847–848.

Chapter 30

Multiple-Choice Questions

1a.   No. Although the work of the "Freedom Riders" in 1961 raised the national consciousness concerning civil rights, their work did not lead directly to passage of the Civil Rights Act of 1964. See page 858.

1b.   No. Kennedy had to deal with a Congress controlled by conservative Republicans and southern Democrats. As a result, he was not very successful in getting Congress to act on his programs. See page 858.

1c.   Correct. Although black activism and television news programs raised the national consciousness concerning civil rights, it took the tragedy of President Kennedy's assassination to convince reluctant politicians that action on civil rights was necessary. See page 858.

1d.   No. Although SNCC's involvement in the sit-ins, the Freedom Rides, and voter registration drives in the South did raise the national consciousness concerning civil rights, it did not lead directly to passage of the Civil Rights Act of 1964. See page 858.

2a.   No. These were not provisions of the 1965 Elementary and Secondary Education Act. See page 860.

2b.   Correct. This act, which granted $1.3 billion to school districts on the basis of the number of needy children, was the first general program of federal aid to education. See page 860.

2c.   No. This was not a provision of the 1965 education bill, and such certification is still left in the hands of the states. See page 860.

2d.   No. The establishment of a federal job-placement service for teachers was not a provision of the 1965 education bill. See page 860.

3a.   No. The right to vote was extended to eighteen-year-olds by the Twenty-sixth Amendment, ratified in 1971. See page 860.

3b.   Correct. Whereas only 29 percent of the South's black population was registered to vote in 1960, around 66 percent was registered by 1969. See page 860.

3c.   No. Literacy and other voter tests were suspended by the Voting Rights Act of 1965 in those states where such tests had been used to bar qualified people from the voting rolls and where less than half of the voting-age residents were registered. See page 860.

3d.   No. The act authorized federal supervision of voter registration in areas where less than half of the voting-age minority residents were registered, but it did not require all eligible voters to register through federal registrars. See page 860.

4a.   No. The Court did not sanction required nondenominational prayers in public schools. See page 862.

4b.   No. The Court did not rule that God has no place in the public schools. See page 862.

4c.   Correct. The Court held that the state could not require the reciting of an official prayer in public schools. See page 862.

4d.   No. The Court did not ban all prayers in public schools. See page 862.

5a.   No. These cases did not deal with religious issues and did not broaden the definition of religion. See page 863.

5b.   No. Freedom of expression was not at issue in these cases. See page 863.

5c.   Correct. These criminal cases extended coverage of the Fourteenth Amendment to include the right of a poor person charged with a felony to a state-appointed lawyer and the right of a suspect to be informed of his or her rights. See page 863.

5d.   No. These cases did not deal with sexual issues. See page 863.

6a.   Correct. The civil rights movement had been largely southern in focus and did not deal with the deteriorating conditions of blacks in inner-city ghettos. Black frustration was expressed through urban riots and in the voices of black nationalism. See pages 863–866.

6b.   No. There is no evidence to support the contention that there was "communist infiltration" of civil rights groups and that such infiltration caused the urban race riots of the 1960s and the emergence of black nationalism. See pages 863–866.

6c.   No. Northern blacks had long had and exercised the right to vote. See pages 863–866.

6d.   No. The SCLC, under the direction of Martin Luther King, Jr., continued to use the nonviolent tactic of passive resistance. See pages 863–866.

7a.   No. The drug culture of the 1960s is associated more with the counterculture than with the New Left. See pages 867–868

7b.   No. The counterculture's desire to build a "Woodstock nation" based on love, drugs, and rock music was not very realistic. Furthermore, the New Left was not a single movement with a single set of goals. See pages 867–868.

7c.   Correct. Although the New Left tended to be political in its orientation and used direct-action tactics, the counterculture used music to attack the status quo. See pages 867–868.

7d.   No. Student activists, the New Left, and the counterculture were united in their opposition to the Vietnam War. See pages 867–868.

8a.   Correct. The riot that erupted between police and the gay patrons of the Stonewall Inn is considered to be the beginning of the gay rights movement. See pages 868–869.

8b.   No. The Stonewall riot did not occur in Atlantic City and was not undertaken by radical feminists. See pages 868–869.

8c.   No. The Stonewall riot occurred in New York City and was not associated with the 1968 Democratic Convention in Chicago. See pages 868–869.

8d.   No. The Stonewall riot was not related to King's assassination. See pages 868–869.

9a.   No. George Wallace ran for president under the banner of the American Independent Party in 1968. In 1972 he was a candidate for the Democratic presidential nomination and was seriously wounded by a would-be assassin. See page 870.

9b.   Correct. With polls showing him as the leading presidential candidate among Democrats and having just won the California primary, Robert Kennedy was assassinated on June 5, 1968. See page 870.

9c.   No. McCarthy challenged President Johnson's war policies in 1968, and his victory in the New Hampshire primary was a factor in Johnson's decision to withdraw as a candidate. But McCarthy was not assassinated. See page 870.

9d.   No. Edmund Muskie was not a Democratic candidate for the presidency in 1968. See page 870.

10a.   No. In the late 1960s radical feminists were more likely to support the gay rights movement than were members of NOW. See pages 871–872.

10b.   No. Radical feminists were concerned with the political, social, and economic inequality of women. They also challenged women's legal inequality and sex-role stereotyping. See pages 871–872.

10c.   No. Although Friedan inspired the founding of NOW, she was not repudiated by the radical feminists. See pages 871–872.

10d.   Correct. While NOW concentrated on lobbying for legislation and testing laws through the courts, radical feminists became involved in direct action to achieve their goals. See pages 871–872.

11a.   No. Nixon did not advocate national health insurance and even strongly opposed expansion of Medicare, which applied only to the elderly. See page 874.

11b.   No. Nixon had instituted his Vietnamization policy; but, while American ground troops were being withdrawn, the air war widened. See page 874.

11c.   No. Nixon imposed wage and price controls in August 1971, nine months after the November 1970 congressional elections. See page 874.

11d.   Correct. The speeches of Vice President Agnew provide evidence that the Nixon administration deliberately tried to associate the Democratic party with radicalism and violence prior to the 1970 congressional elections. See page 874.

12a.   Correct. Middle-class Americans were frightened by McGovern's proposals and demonstrated their fear at the polls. See pages 876–877.

12b.   No. Nixon's attorney general, John Mitchell, worked to prevent extension of the Voting Rights Act of 1965 and, in the process, pleased many southerners. See pages 876–877.

12c.   No. Although Nixon had run as a fiscal conservative in 1968, he had authorized large budget deficits. See pages 876–877.

12d.   No. Much of the environmental-protection legislation that passed in the early 1970s was due to the support of Congress, not necessarily that of Nixon. See pages 876–877.

13a.   No. James McCord, one of the defendants in the Watergate break-in and a former security coordinator of CREEP, revealed in a letter to Judge Sirica that the defendants had been pressured to plead guilty and that perjury was committed at the trial. See page 877.

13b.   No. John Mitchell, who resigned as Nixon's attorney general to head the President's reelection campaign, knew of the payments but did not authorize them. See page 877.

13c.   Correct. President Nixon authorized CREEP to pay over $460,000 to keep Hunt and others from implicating the White House in the Watergate burglary. See page 877.

13d.   No. John Ehrlichman, Nixon's adviser on domestic affairs, had knowledge of the payments but did not authorize them. See page 877.

14a.   Correct. The committee voted for impeachment on three counts: obstruction of justice, defiance of a congressional subpoena, and abuse of power through the improper use of the CIA, FBI, and IRS. See page 879.

14b.   No. The article of impeachment accusing Nixon of demeaning the office of the presidency by misconduct of his personal financial affairs was voted down by a vote of 26 to 12. Furthermore, one cannot be declared guilty as the result of impeachment hearings. See page 879.

14c.   No. The committee voted on the articles of impeachment brought against Nixon and made a recommendation to the full House. See page 879.

14d.   No. The committee held hearings to determine if there was just cause to refer articles of impeachment to the full House, not to determine Nixon's guilt or innocence. See page 879.

15a.   Correct. The act, in an attempt to put some restrictions on the president's war-making powers, required the president to consult with Congress "in every possible instance" before sending troops into foreign wars. See page 880.

15b.   No. In an effort to put restrictions on the president's war-making powers, the act required the chief executive to withdraw troops after sixty days (as opposed to 10 days) unless Congress authorized otherwise. See page 880.

15c.   No. The president, as commander-in-chief of the armed forces, still had the authority to respond to threats to national security and send troops to foreign territory. See page 880.

15d.   No. The president, as commander-in-chief of the armed forces, still had the authority to respond to threats to national security and send troops into a foreign war without getting a declaration of war from Congress. See page 880.

Chapter 31

Multiple-Choice Questions

1a.   No. The concept of nation building did not envision a collective effort by the industrialized nations of the world to aid the Third World. See pages 885–886.

1b.   Correct. Nation building was undertaken with the belief that American capitalism and democracy could be transferred to the Third World. As this was done, it was believed, Third World countries would be brought into the American orbit. Presidential adviser Arthur Schlesinger later called this notion "a ghastly illusion." See pages 885–886.

1c.   No. The concept of nation building did not insist on decolonization by European countries. See pages 885–886.

1d.   No. Nation building did not pay much attention to the unique historical experiences of other nations. See pages 885–886.

2a.   No. The policy of flexible response is not associated with the decision-making process in the executive branch of the government. See page 887.

2b.   No. The Kennedy administration did not "track" the mood of the electorate with the frequency and sophistication of modern tracking (frequent scientific polling of the electorate's stand on particular issues), and "flexible response" was not an electioneering tool. See page 887.

2c.   Correct. In rejecting Eisenhower's policy of massive retaliation, Kennedy oversaw a military build-up based on the policy of flexible response. This policy held that the United States should be able to meet the threat of guerrilla warfare and the threat of a nuclear confrontation. See page 887.

2d.   No. Although Kennedy disagreed with the Eisenhower administration's emphasis on nuclear weapons, he did not envision and did not achieve a reduction of the nation's nuclear arsenal. In fact, from 1961 to mid-1964 there was a 150 percent increase in the nation's nuclear arsenal. See page 887.

3a.   Correct. After the failure of the Bay of Pigs invasion, the Kennedy administration authorized Operation Mongoose. Through this project, as well as programs of diplomatic and economic isolation, the United States government worked to overthrow the government of Fidel Castro. See page 888.

3b.   No. Kennedy recognized the Bay of Pigs invasion as a mistake because it was a defeat, not because it infringed on Cuban sovereignty. The president never apologized to the Cuban people. See page 888.

3c.   No. The United States continued its attempt to isolate Cuba economically. See page 888.

3d.   No. The United States continued its attempt to isolate Cuba diplomatically and did not restore diplomatic relations. See page 888.

4a.   No. The Soviet Union made demands concerning Berlin in the summer of 1961. The Cuban missile crisis occurred in the fall of 1962. See page 890.

4b.   No. Although Kennedy informally agreed to withdraw outdated missiles from Turkey at a future date, he did not agree to dismantle missiles in Western Europe. See page 890.

4c.   Correct. The Soviets decided that they would never again allow themselves to be humiliated because of military and nuclear weakness. Therefore, they embarked on a military build-up program and by the late 1960s achieved nuclear parity with the United States. See page 890.

4d.   No. Suggestions that the United States destroy the Cuban missiles through a surprise air attack were rejected. See page 890.

5a.   No. Congress did not question Johnson's escalation of the Vietnam War through the Tonkin Gulf Resolution. See pages 893–894.

5b.   Correct. With only two dissenting votes, Congress authorized the president to "take all necessary measures" to defend American forces and "prevent further aggression." In accepting the resolution, Congress, in effect, surrendered its foreign policy powers. See pages 893–894.

5c.   No. The Gulf of Tonkin resolution was passed in 1964; the My Lai massacre occurred in March 1968 and was not made public until twenty months later. See pages 893–894.

5d.   No. The Tonkin Gulf Resolution was not an official declaration of war. See pages 893–894.

6a.   No. Although the People's Republic of China joined the nuclear club in 1964, it was generally understood that it did not have the launchers (missiles) necessary to wage nuclear war. Furthermore, China was preoccupied with the internal disorder caused by the Cultural Revolution in the late 1960s. See page 895.

6b.   No. The Republican party stood staunchly behind the government of South Vietnam. See page 895.

6c.   No. Ho Chi Minh's regime in North Vietnam was a totalitarian regime and was not democratic in nature. See page 895.

6d.   Correct. As many Americans watched the horrors of the Vietnam War each evening on the nightly news, they began to question the United States involvement in the conflict. See page 895.

7a.	No. Although many American soldiers smoked marijuana and about one-third became addicted to opium and heroin, those who participated in atrocities such as the My Lai massacre were not necessarily addicts. See pages 895–896.

7b.	Correct. An interplay of several factors is seen as an explanation for My Lai and other acts of atrocities on the part of American soldiers in Vietnam. One of those factors was that the Vietnamese had been dehumanized in the eyes of these soldiers and were seen as little more than animals. See pages 895–896.

7c.	No. Although saturation-bombing of the North was ordered by such officials, they did not order American soldiers to commit atrocities such as that at My Lai. See pages 895–896.

7d.	No. Atrocities such as that at My Lai were committed by American soldiers, not by CIA operatives. See pages 895–896.

8a.	No. The Soviet Union did not send troops to Vietnam as a result of the Tet offensive. See pages 898–899.

8b.	No. The chairman of the Joint Chiefs of Staff, General Earle Wheeler, persuaded General Westmoreland to request an additional 206,000 soldiers. Furthermore, he favored calling the army and marine reserves to active duty. See pages 898–899.

8c.	No. Although the Vietcong and North Vietnamese suffered heavy losses in the Tet offensive, they still had not been defeated and did not retreat to North Vietnam. See pages 898–899.

8d.	Correct. The Tet offensive demonstrated that three years of search-and-destroy tactics had not destroyed the power of the Vietcong and North Vietnamese. As a result, Johnson announced an end to the bombing of most of the North and requested that Hanoi open peace negotiations. See pages 898–899.

9a.	No. Nixon's policy of Vietnamization was accompanied by other policies that further destabilized Indochina. See pages 899–900.

9b.	Correct. The policy of Vietnamization brought, among other things, a widening of the war into Cambodia, increased bombing of North Vietnam, and the mining of Haiphong harbor. See pages 899–900.

9c.	No. The South Vietnamese army proved itself a rather ineffective fighting force, incapable of defending the South. See pages 899–900.

9d.	No. Vietnamization did not bring about a coalition government, and the war did not quickly draw to a close. See pages 899–900.

10a.	Correct. Some Americans pointed to the war as an example of the softening of American resolve against communism; others questioned, among other things, the containment doctrine. See pages 900–901.

10b.	No. The United States did not withdraw from the United Nations in the aftermath of the Vietnam War. See pages 900–901.

10c.	No. In fact, many leaders talked of a Vietnam syndrome—a mood that would prevent the United States from becoming involved in any foreign entanglements. See pages 900–901.

10d.	No. Some Americans blamed the Vietnam experience on the "imperial presidency" and insisted that Congress retake the foreign policy power it had relinquished to the executive branch. See pages 900–901.

11a.	No. Although the Soviets had more launchers (missiles), the United States had more deliverable nuclear warheads. See pages 902–903.

11b.   No. Limits were placed on the construction of ABM systems. Each side could build only two—one to protect the capital and one to protect an ICBM field. See pages 902–903.

11c.   Correct. Each launcher (missile) could be MIRVed; and, since no restriction was placed on MIRVs, the nuclear build-up continued. See pages 902–903.

11d.   No. The treaties placed only a five-year freeze on the number of offensive nuclear missiles that each side could have. See pages 902–903.

12a.   No. Kissinger's "shuttle diplomacy" did not lead to the creation of a Palestinian state. See page 903.

12b.   No. In spite of Kissinger's "shuttle diplomacy," the PLO continued to refuse to recognize Israel's right to exist. See page 903.

12c.   No. Although Kissinger's diplomatic missions brought an end to the OPEC oil embargo, they did not lead to an OPEC agreement to reduce oil prices. See page 903.

12d.   Correct. Kissinger, acting as mediator by shuttling back and forth between Egyptian and Israeli officials, obtained an agreement between the two nations establishing a United Nations peacekeeping force in the Sinai. See page 903.

13a.   No. Although the Reagan administration warned that Nicaragua was supplying the El Salvadoran rebels with Soviet-made weapons, it did not warn that the Soviets were installing nuclear missiles in El Salvador. See page 911.

13b.   No. Although the Reagan administration at times demonstrated some concern for the impoverished conditions in El Salvador, its policies in the region relied on military solutions. Therefore, it did not defend its policies by emphasizing the relationship between the insurgency and impoverished conditions. See page 911.

13c.   Correct. By and large, the Reagan administration relied on military solutions to the problems in El Salvador. Therefore, to defend those policies, it relied on the old and discredited domino theory. See page 911.

13d.   No. The Reagan administration, in keeping with the policies of previous administrations, viewed right-wing governments in Latin America as better than governments with leftist leanings. Therefore, the administration supported right-wing governments even if they did not have mass popular support. See page 911.

14a.   No. Although the administration criticized the Sandinistas for not holding elections, when elections were held in November 1984, the administration called them a "sham." See page 911.

14b.   Correct. The economic embargo against Nicaragua, covert activities by the CIA, and United States aid to the contras all indicate that the administration wanted to topple the Nicaraguan government. See page 911.

14c.   No. Although the Reagan administration criticized the presence of Cuban advisers and Soviet arms in Nicaragua, it wanted more than simply a reduction of foreign military bases and advisers. In fact, it rejected the Contadora peace plan which would have reduced foreign bases and advisers in Nicaragua. See page 911.

14d.   No. The Reagan administration's actions toward Nicaragua do not indicate a desire for a negotiated settlement. In fact, two peace plans were put forward during the 1980s by representatives of Latin American countries. The administration's out-of-hand rejection of both the Contadora peace plan and the Arias peace plan is further indication that a negotiated settlement was not Reagan's goal in Nicaragua. See page 911.

15a.   No. Reagan never apologized for his statement that the Soviet Union was the source of evil in the world. See page 914.

15b.   No. The Reagan administration did not agree to limit research on the Strategic Defense Initiative. See page 914.

15c.   No. There were no obvious signs of cooperation between the United States and the Soviet Union to combat international terrorism. See page 914.

15d.   Correct. When Gorbachev assumed power and embarked on a reform program in the Soviet Union in 1985, he reduced military expenditures and expenditures on foreign aid. Therefore, he reduced the Soviet Union's armed forces and withdrew Soviet troops from Afghanistan. Largely because of these policies, Soviet-American relations improved. See page 914.

Chapter 32

Multiple-Choice Questions

1a.   No. The increase in oil prices caused double-digit inflation in 1974, but this is not the best answer. See pages 919–920.

1b.   No. The 350 percent increase in oil prices in 1973 slowed overall economic growth, but this is not the best answer. See pages 919–920.

1c.   No. The high cost of oil caused a lingering recession in the automobile and related industries, but this is not the best answer. See pages 919–920.

1d.   Correct. The 350 percent increase in oil prices from January 1973 to January 1974 brought double-digit inflation, slowed overall economic growth, and led to a recession in the automobile and related industries. See pages 919–920.

2a.   No. Despite the slow growth in productivity, many workers continued to expect wage increases that would give them more purchasing power each year. See page 921.

2b.   No. The slow growth in productivity did not lead to a decline in interest rates. See page 921.

2c.   Correct. The slow growth in productivity was one reason that American goods cost more than comparable foreign goods. High prices made American goods less competitive in foreign markets. See page 921.

2d.   No. The slow growth in productivity did not cause an increase in business investments. See page 921.

3a.   Correct. Most liberal Democrats believed that regulation of such industries as the airline industry was to the advantage of the consumer. Carter's stand in favor of deregulation angered these Democrats and made it more difficult for Carter to work with Congress. See pages 923–924.

3b.   No. The number of PACs quadrupled between 1974 and 1980. See pages 923–924.

3c.   No. From 1961 to 1981, no president was elected to two terms. During this same period the nation experienced the traumas of Vietnam and Watergate. The combination of these factors caused power to flow into the hands of Congress and presidential authority to decline. See pages 923–924.

3d.   No. President Carter supported imposing a windfall-profits tax on oil companies; Republicans were generally opposed to it. Furthermore, Democrats controlled both houses of Congress during the Carter administration. See pages 923–924.

4a.   Correct. The alliance between evangelical Christians and members of the Hoover Institute (a conservative think-tank) are associated with the swing toward conservatism in the late 1970s. See page 924.

4b.   No. As people continued to move from the Frostbelt to the more politically and socially conservative Sunbelt, the latter became more important politically. See page 924.

4c.   No. Although it is true that economic issues were very important in the late 1970s, the three pieces of evidence offered do not support the inference that economic issues were dominant. See page 924.

4d.   No. The passage of Proposition 13 and the emergence of evangelical Christians and the Hoover Institute as political forces do not indicate that Americans were unconcerned about Communist expansion. See page 924.

5a.   No. Although Reagan denounced welfare, after he became governor of California he presided over reform of the welfare bureaucracy in the state. Therefore, he did not dismantle the state's welfare system. See page 926.

5b.   Correct. Before the prochoice and prolife arguments became major political issues, Governor Ronald Reagan had signed one of the nation's most liberal abortion laws. See page 926.

5c.   No. Ronald Reagan did not propose the legalization of marijuana when he was governor of California. See page 926.

5d.   No. Ronald Reagan did not institute a statewide healthcare program for California during his two four-year terms as governor of that state. See page 926.

6a.   No. Those in the poorest fifth received essentially no tax cut, and by 1984 the after-tax income of those in the second-poorest fifth increased by only 1.4 percent. See page 928.

6b.   Correct. Wealthy people gained the most from the 1981 tax reductions. See page 928.

6c.   No. Although the after-tax income of those Americans in the middle fifth increased by 2.8 percent by 1984, another group's after-tax income increased by a higher percentage. See page 928.

6d.   No. Among the groups listed, married couples did not save the most as a result of the 1981 income-tax reductions. See page 928.

7a.   No. Although this practice was used by companies and was declared constitutional by the Supreme Court, Reagan's appointees to the NLRB did not *actively* encourage companies to declare bankruptcy as a way of canceling union contracts. See page 928.

7b.   No. The right of union members to strike was not questioned by Reagan's appointees to the NLRB. See page 928.

7c.   Correct. Reagan's appointees on the NLRB demonstrated their hostility toward organized labor by consistently voting in favor of management. See page 928.

7d.   No. A closed shop or union shop is a business whose employees are required to be union members. Reagan's appointees to the NLRB did not favor the closed shop. See page 928.

8a.   No. During 1981 and 1982 there was less than a 1 percent increase in the rate of productivity. See pages 928–929.

8b.   Correct. The recession brought soaring unemployment, severe economic hardship to many farmers, and an overall increase in the poverty rate. As a result, the inflation rate and, in some cases, prices declined. See pages 928–929.

8c.   No. An increase in spending by Americans did not cause prices to decline. See pages 928–929.

8d.   No. Both the GNP and investment spending fell during this period. See pages 928–929.

9a.   No. Occupational segregation continued as the shift from an industrialized to a service-oriented economy took place. See page 931.

9b.   No. The shifting occupational structure meant the loss of many blue-collar jobs and an increase in skilled, white-collar, high-technology jobs. See page 931.

9c.   Correct. As the economy shifted from an industrial to a service orientation, jobs that had traditionally been available to the unskilled and impoverished disappeared. The labor demand was in the area of skilled, white-collar, high-technology jobs. See page 931.

9d.   No. The shift from an industrialized to a service-oriented economy, and the resulting shift in labor demand, caused unions to devote more energy to organizing white-collar workers. See page 931.

10a.   No. The number of blacks attending college increased dramatically during the 1970s and 1980s. See page 931.

10b.   Correct. Since the plight of poor blacks worsened and the black middle class expanded, it is logical to conclude that the gap between poor blacks and middle-class blacks widened during the 1970s and 1980s. In fact, because of this widening gap, the sociologist William Julius Wilson spoke of the emergence of two black Americas. See page 931.

10c.   No. In the period from 1960 to 1975 the number of fatherless black families rose 130 percent. See page 931.

10d.   No. The black middle class expanded during the 1970s and 1980s. See page 931.

11a.   No. Although the Reagan administration did express opposition to court-ordered busing, it did not openly encourage local school districts to defy court orders under which they operated. See page 932.

11b.   Correct. Although the Voting Rights Act was in large measure responsible for the increased political power of African Americans, especially in the South, and was extended by Congress in 1971 and 1975, the Reagan administration stood against renewing the act intact. See page 932.

11c.   No. Although the Reagan administration was criticized for lax enforcement of fair-housing laws, it did not seek repeal of those laws. See page 932.

11d.   No. Although the Reagan administration was opposed to affirmative action, it did not gain passage of legislation outlawing it. See page 932.

12a.   No. A nationwide strike by working women was not a tactic employed by the antifeminist forces in their efforts to prevent ratification of the Equal Rights Amendment. See page 935.

12b.   No. The Senate did not rescind its approval of this amendment. See page 935.

12c.   No. Antifeminist leaders such as Phyllis Schlafly refused to acknowledge the existence of gender-based discrimination, but no such study was ever conducted and the facts do not support such a conclusion. See page 935.

12d.   Correct. Antifeminist forces used scare tactics, for the most part, as part of an emotional campaign against ratification of the Equal Rights Amendment. This had the desired effect, and the ERA fell three states short of ratification. See page 935.

13a.   Correct. The threat of AIDS and other sexually transmitted diseases caused many Americans to be more cautious about their sexual practices. See page 940.

13b.   No. Although there were some concerns about the possibility that health risks were associated with the use of birth-control pills, these concerns were not relatively minor and were not a primary cause for Americans to become more cautious about their sexual practices. See page 940.

13c.   No. The fact that Americans were living longer and that the number of elderly Americans was increasing was not a reason for Americans to become more cautious about their sexual practices. See page 940.

13d.   No. Although TV evangelists preached against the practices associated with the sexual revolution, their influence was not a major cause for Americans to become "more cautious" about their sexual practices. See page 940.

14a.   No. President Reagan oversaw a multi-trillion-dollar defense-spending program that favored building the B-1 bomber, enlarging the navy, increasing the production of poison gas, deploying the MX missile, and deploying an antimissile defense system in space. See page 940.

14b.   No. Although Reagan's opposition to abortion did concern some people, this was not of major concern to most people and did not generally cause "growing public concern." See page 940.

14c.   Correct. Although candidate Reagan promised to balance the federal budget, President Reagan oversaw the accumulation of more new debt than the combined deficits of all previous presidents. See page 940.

14d.   No. Although the United States certainly did not dictate to Israel, there was not a "lack of influence" either. See page 940.

15a.   No. The evidence indicated that President Reagan was aware of the sale of arms to Iran and that he did not instruct Robert McFarlane not to engage in such a sale. See page 941.

15b.   No. The evidence is inconclusive on this point, but it is likely that Reagan did not know about the diversion of funds from the Iranian arms sales to the Nicaraguan contras. See page 941.

15c.   No. The evidence indicated an attempt on the part of the Reagan administration to subvert the will of Congress on certain foreign policy issues. See page 941.

15d.   Correct. In assessing the evidence presented in the Iran-contra hearings, many political observers, both inside and outside the Reagan administration, argued that President Reagan practiced a "hands-off" management style and that he was an unengaged and uninformed leader. See page 941.

Chapter 33

Multiple-Choice Questions

1a.   No. President Bush did not believe that the federal government should play an active role in responding to economic and social problems. See pages 950, 958–959.

1b.   Correct. Although some of President Bush's advisers suggested that Bush call a special session of Congress to deal with the stagnant economy, Bush did not heed their advice. Furthermore, he did little to respond to the rise in unemployment and poverty that accompanied the economic downturn and did not respond in any meaningful way to the 1992 Los Angeles riots. See pages 950, 958–959.

1c.   No. Rather than responding to the stagnant economy by proposing an increase in welfare benefits to the working poor, President Bush defended tax breaks for the rich and opposed extending relief payments to the long-term unemployed. See pages 950, 958–959.

1d.   No. President Bush did not suggest nor did he support the funding of public-works projects to reduce unemployment. See pages 950, 958–959.

2a.   No. Although President Bush had consistently asked Congress to pass legislation allowing a line-item veto, Congress never agreed to such legislation. See page 951.

2b.   Correct. Although candidate Bush had pledged that he would not raise taxes, President Bush agreed to a tax hike when the Democrats who controlled Congress agreed to budget cuts. See page 951.

2c.   No. Bush was not impounding funds appropriated by Congress and the budget negotiations did not produce an agreement by Congress that there would be a debate on a balanced-budget amendment. See page 951.

2d.   No. Although the federal debt limit was increased during the Bush administration, the agreement to do this did not come out of the 1990 budget negotiations. See page 951.

3a.   No. The Council on Competitiveness did not show concern over the quality of American automobiles. See page 951.

3b.   No. The Council on Competitiveness did not attempt to persuade American businesses to adopt Japanese management practices. See page 951.

3c.   Correct. Headed by Vice President Dan Quayle, the Council on Competitiveness used the argument that environmental regulations slowed economic growth to justify gutting enforcement of the Clean Air Act of 1990. See page 951.

3d.   No. The Council on Competitiveness did not suggest protective tariffs against Japanese imports. See page 951.

4a.   Correct. The Senate's disregard of Anita Hill's testimony so angered many women that they vowed to oppose the Republican party in 1992. See page 952.

4b.   No. The Bush administration did not withdraw its nomination of Thomas to the Supreme Court. See page 952.

4c.   No. Despite Anita Hill's testimony, the Senate confirmed Thomas's nomination to the Supreme Court. See page 952.

4d.   No. The Senate did not pass such legislation. See page 952.

5a.   No. Throughout the history of the Cold War the United States often diverted money from domestic social programs to finance its military arsenal. This is most obvious during the administrations of Lyndon Johnson and Ronald Reagan. See pages 953–954

5b.   No. Throughout the history of the Cold War Third World nations often attempted to remain neutral. By doing so they could play the United States and the Soviet Union against each other. Therefore, most Third World nations did not openly ally with the United States and the Soviet Union was not deprived of essential raw materials. See pages 953–954.

5c.   No. The Soviet Union never built a "monolithic" empire. See pages 953–954.

5d.   Correct. The entry of Third World nations into the bipolar contest between the United States and the Soviet Union both diffused power and challenged the bipolar nature of the Cold War. See pages 953–954.

6a.   No. Although some Republicans favored ratification of the Equal Rights Amendment (ERA), the party itself stood against ratification. For that reason, most advocates of the ERA did not support Republican presidential candidates during the 1970s and 1980s. See page 957.

6b.   No. The Republican party and Republican presidential candidates tend to take stands against government regulatory agencies and regulatory legislation such as the Clean Air Act. Therefore, one who advocated strict enforcement of the Clean Air Act would most likely not vote for Republican presidential candidates. See page 957.

6c.   No. The Republican party, especially in the 1980s, has stood against abortion rights. Therefore, an advocate of abortion would most likely not vote for Republican presidential candidates. See page 957.

6d.   Correct. Cultural conservatives who advocate "family values" are a major element in the Republican coalition. Therefore, especially during the 1970s and 1980, an advocate of family values would most likely vote for Republican presidential candidates. See page 957.

7a.   Correct. It seemed to most Americans that members of the House of Representatives had unwarranted privileges when it was revealed that many representatives overdrew their accounts and were not penalized. See page 957.

7b.   No. The House banking scandal did not involve the misuse of funds on the part of the manager of the House bank. See page 957.

7c.   No. Vice-President Quayle did not write checks against the House bank. See page 957.

7d.   No. Money in the House bank was not used to finance CIA operations. See page 957.

8a.   No. Although ordinances of this type did cause protest in some American cities, such an ordinance was not the cause of the Los Angeles riots of 1992. See pages 958–959.

8b.   No. Such an incident did not cause the Los Angeles riots of 1992. See pages 958–959.

8c.   No. The city of Los Angeles did not close a recreational center in Watts and such a closing was not the cause of the Los Angeles riots of 1992. See pages 958–959.

8d.   Correct. The spark that was the immediate cause of the Los Angeles riots of 1992 was the acquittal by an all-white jury of four Los Angeles police officers in the beating of Rodney King. See pages 958–959.

9a.   No. The Democrats retained control of both the Senate and the House as a result of the 1992 election. See page 959.

9b.   Correct. Women gained four seats in the Senate and 19 seats in the House as a result of the 1992 election. See page 959.

9c.   No. Bill Clinton, a Democrat, was elected to the presidency over Republican candidate George Bush in the 1992 election. See page 959.

9d.   No. Nonwhites gained representation in Congress as a result of the 1992 election. See page 959.

10a.   No. Polling did not indicate that 75 percent of the American public supported Clinton's original plan to lift the ban on homosexuals in the military. See page 960.

10b.   No. Vice-President Gore supported President Clinton's original plan to lift the ban on homosexuals in the military. See page 960.

10c.   No. Leaders of the Republican party were strongly opposed to Clinton's original plan to lift the ban on homosexuals in the military. See page 960.

10d.   Correct. Military officials were opposed to and critical of Clinton's original plan to lift the ban on homosexuals in the military. See page 960.

11a.   Correct. Clinton's 1993 economic plan called for an energy tax. See page 960.

11b.   No. While campaigning in the primaries against his rivals for the Democratic nomination, Bill Clinton indicated that he would reduce the tax burden on the middle class. However, Clinton was not making that pledge by the time of the Democratic Convention, did not make that pledge during the general campaign, and did not make that part of the economic plan he sent to Congress in 1993. See page 960.

11c.   No. Clinton was very consistent in the primaries and the general campaign in calling for higher taxes on the wealthiest Americans. His 1993 economic plan did not call for tax breaks for the wealthy. See page 960.

11d.   No. Clinton's 1993 economic plan called for higher corporate taxes. See page 960.

12a.   No. The Brady bill did not deal with the issue of discrimination in hiring on the basis of sexual orientation. See page 960.

12b.   Correct. One of the provisions of the Brady bill was a required waiting period for persons wanting to buy a handgun. See page 960.

12c.   No. The Brady bill did not ban the sale of assault weapons in the United States. See page 960.

12d.   No. The Brady bill did not deal with the use of Medicaid funds for abortions. See page 960.

13a.   No. As stated in the text, "the public was inconvenienced and angry" over the government shutdowns of 1995 and 1996. See page 964.

13b.   No. The public generally saw President Clinton as moderate and reasonable and did not blame him for the government shutdowns of 1995 and 1996. See page 964.